Taste of Home's
Light&Tasty
Annual Recipes 2002

PICTURED ABOVE AND ON FRONT COVER: Tangy Pork Loin Roast
(page 240) and Strawberry Rhubarb Tart (page 242).

Taste of Home's
Light&Tasty
Annual Recipes 2002

Editor: Julie Schnittka
Art Director: Linda Dzik
Food Editor: Janaan Cunningham
Associate Editors: Heidi Reuter Lloyd, Jean Steiner
Art Associate: Maribeth Greinke
Production: Ellen Lloyd, Catherine Fletcher
Cover Photography: Rob Hagen
Food Photography Artist: Stephanie Marchese

Taste of Home's
Light&Tasty

Executive Editor: Kathy Pohl
Food Editor: Janaan Cunningham
Associate Food Editors: Diane Werner RD, Coleen Martin
Managing Editor: Julie Kastello
Associate Editors: Mark Hagen, Sharon Selz, Barbara Schuetz,
Faithann Stoner, Ann Kaiser, Kristine Krueger
Recipe Editor: Janet Briggs
Test Kitchen Director: Karen Johnson RD
Test Kitchen Home Economists: Mark Morgan RD, Wendy Stenman,
Sue Draheim, Peggy Fleming RD, Julie Herzfeldt, Joylyn Jans,
Kristin Koepnick, Pat Schmeling, Karen Wright
Test Kitchen Assistants: Suzanne Hampton, Megan Taylor
Editorial Assistants: Ursula Maurer, Joanne Wied,
Barb Czysz, Mary Ann Koebernik
Design Director: Jim Sibilski
Art Director: Julie Wagner
Food Photography: Dan Roberts, Rob Hagen
Food Photography Artists: Stephanie Marchese, Vicky Marie Moseley
Photo Studio Manager: Anne Schimmel
Production: Ellen Lloyd, Catherine Fletcher
Publisher: Roy Reiman

Taste of Home Books
© 2002 Reiman Publications, LLC
5400 S. 60th St., Greendale WI 53129

International Standard Book Number: 0-89821-326-6
International Standard Serial Number: 1537-3134

Contents

502 Low-in-Fat, Full-Flavored Favorites!

AS A wife, mother, home economist and registered dietitian, I know how challenging it can be to find light recipes that are lean on fat and calories but that are also full of enough flavor to please and satisfy a family.

That's why I was thrilled when we launched *Light & Tasty* magazine in 2001.

Unlike most other light food magazines, *Light & Tasty* takes a common-sense approach to calorie-wise eating by using fresh and delicious ingredients. It doesn't lecture or urge diet and exercise but instead suggests simple options with lighter ingredient choices. Best of all, *Light & Tasty* features good-for-you recipes packed with down-home flavor.

Our determination to offer great-tasting lighter fare paid off, and soon we had *1 million subscribers*! It wasn't long before they started asking us to put all of the mouth-watering recipes published during the first year of *Light & Tasty* into a single source.

We pride ourselves on listening to readers, and this cookbook is proof of that. *2002 Light & Tasty Annual Recipes* features every light-done-right recipe published in the magazine during 2001. That's 502 in all!

Many of the dishes are family-favorites of our readers, so they're guaranteed to offer great, home-style flavor. The taste is still there…these recipes have just been lightened up a bit with less fat, calories, cholesterol, etc.

Yet, these dishes won't send you away hungry. You'll find lots of tried-and-true foods, like Simmered Sirloin Over Noodles, Chicken Parmigiana, Barbecued Pork Potpie, Apple Cobbler, Chocolate Meringue Torte and much more. Each of these mouth-watering dishes is leaner on fat, calories or sodium…but not leaner on flavor.

Most important, every recipe in this book has been reviewed by a registered dietitian and includes Nutritional Analysis, plus Diabetic Exchanges where appropriate.

With *2002 Light & Tasty Annual Recipes*, healthy eating the whole year through has never been easier…or more enjoyable!

Diane Werner, R.D.

Associate Food Editor, *Light & Tasty*

What's Inside These Recipe-Packed Pages?

AS IF 502 great-tasting, good-for-you recipes aren't enough reasons to love *2002 Light & Tasty Annual Recipes*, the following helpful features will certainly make this big book a valued reference in your kitchen for years to come!

User-Friendly Chapters. We've compiled all 502 recipes from the first year of *Light & Tasty* magazine into 15 convenient chapters, such as Light Bites & Beverages, Beefed-Up Main Dishes, Chicken & Turkey Entrees and Dazzling Desserts. There's even a Trimmed-Down Dishes for Two chapter, which offers foods sized just right for one or two people. (For a complete listing of chapters, turn to page 3.)

Mouth-Watering Meals. You'll find 16 complete menus (including pictures!), which are perfect for either weekend entertaining (page 237) or weekday family dining (page 250).

De-Light-Ful Dinner Planner. It's a challenge to come up with satisfying well-balanced meals throughout the year. So in addition to the meal chapters mentioned above, we've created 27 menu plans that include a main dish and side dish or dessert. (See the De-Light-Ful Dinner Planner on page 7.) Each meal features at least two recipes found inside this book, as well as suggestions for "appealing partners" (side dishes, desserts or beverages) and meal-preparation pointers.

Hundreds of Color Photos. *More than half* of the 502 recipes in this timeless collection are shown in full color. So you can be sure these full-flavored foods not only taste terrific, but are eye-appealing as well.

Easy-to-Use Indexes. Finding all 502 recipes in this cookbook is a snap with two simple-to-use indexes. The general index lists every recipe by food category, major ingredient and/or cooking technique. The alphabetical recipe listing is perfect for folks looking for a specific family-favorite.

There's also a reference index that refers you to the many helpful kitchen tips and healthy-eating hints throughout the book. (The indexes begin on page 272.)

Nutritional Analysis Nuggets

EVERY RECIPE in *2002 Light & Tasty Annual Recipes* has been reviewed by a registered dietitian and includes Nutritional Analysis, plus Diabetic Exchanges where appropriate.

The Nutritional Analysis gives you the breakdown for calories, fat, saturated fat, cholesterol, sodium, carbohydrate, fiber and protein.

How we calculated the Nutritional Analysis.

- Whenever a choice of ingredients is given in a recipe (such as 1/3 cup of sour cream or plain yogurt), the first ingredient listed is the one calculated in the Nutritional Analysis.
- When a range is given for an ingredient (such as 2 to 3 teaspoons), we calculate the first amount given.
- Only the amount of marinade absorbed during preparation is calculated.
- Garnishes listed in recipes are generally included in our calculations.

Key ingredients used in our recipe testing.

The following are the standard ingredients we use in recipe testing and in Nutritional Analysis unless otherwise indicated in a recipe:

- Large eggs
- Regular canned chicken broth
- 90% lean ground beef
- Regular long grain white rice
- Stick margarine containing 80% vegetable oil
- Nonstick cooking spray (used on cookware)
- Refrigerated butter-flavored spray (used to enhance flavor in certain dishes). Our Test Kitchen uses I Can't Believe It's Not Butter Spray.
- Baking fat replacement. Our Test Kitchen sometimes uses Smucker's Baking Healthy or Sunsweet's Lighter Bake to replace some of the fat in baked goods.

Daily Nutrition Guide

	Women 25-50	Women over 50	Men over 24
Calories	2,200	1,900 or less	2,900
Fat	73 g or less	63 g or less	96 g or less
Saturated Fat	24 g or less	21 g or less	32 g or less
Cholesterol	300 mg or less	300 mg or less	300 mg or less
Sodium	2,400 mg or less	2,400 mg or less	2,400 mg or less
Carbohydrates	335 g	283 g	446 g
Fiber	20-30 g	20-30 g	20-30 g
Protein	50 g	50 g or less	63 g

This chart is only a general guide. Calorie requirements vary, depending on size, weight and amount of activity. Children's calorie and protein needs vary as they grow.

Food Guide Pyramid Serving Sizes

Bread, cereal, rice and pasta group
(6 to 11 servings a day)
- One slice of bread
- Half of an average bagel (the size of a hockey puck)
- 1 ounce dry cereal (about 2 handfuls)
- 1/2 cup cooked cereal, rice or pasta

Vegetable group
(3 to 5 servings a day)
- 1 cup raw leafy greens
- 1/2 cup of any chopped vegetable, raw or cooked
- 6-ounce glass of vegetable juice

Fruit group
(2 to 3 servings a day)
- 1 medium banana
- One medium apple or orange
- 6-ounce glass of orange juice or any 100% fruit juice

Milk, yogurt and cheese group
(2 to 3 servings a day)
- 8-ounce container of yogurt
- 1 cup cottage cheese
- 1-1/2-ounce chunk of hard cheese (size of two dominoes)
- 8-ounce glass of milk

Meat, poultry, fish and other proteins group
(2 to 3 servings a day)
- 3 ounces cooked lean meat or poultry (size of a deck of cards)
- 3 ounces lean cooked fish (size of a cassette tape)
- Eggs, dry beans, peanut butter, nuts or seeds are also good sources of protein, although they are not always eaten in the quantity required to equal a full serving. These foods are a good way to add a variety of additional protein to your diet.

De-Light-ful Dinner Planner

To make meal planning easy,
turn to these 27 tasty menu suggestions
featuring recipes from this book, "appealing
partners" to round out the dinners and
meal-preparation pointers.

Hearty Ham Dinner (page 9)

Seafood Fare

You'll make your week a little more special when you serve **Basil Shrimp Fettuccine** (p. 163) from Cathy Carroll of Bossier City, Louisiana. This seafood and pasta combo is lightly coated with a basil-seasoned sauce and quick to fix on the stovetop after a full day.

To complement this effortless entree, we paired it with a snappy vegetable side dish sent in by Estelle Hardin of Santa Ana, California. **Broccoli with Orange Sauce** (p. 85) is packed with citrus flavor and sure to please even those family members who aren't fond of that robust green veggie.

Appealing Partners

♦ Iced tea
♦ Light chocolate cake

Practical Tips

🍎 Most any kind of pasta you have on hand can be used in place of fettuccine. Just be sure to use 8 ounces and cook it according to package directions.

🍎 Grate the peel of one orange and use some in the side dish. Freeze the rest for future use.

Pork Chop Supper

Spending a couple minutes in the kitchen the night before will be time well spent when you serve **Honey-Lime Pork Chops** (p. 156) from Janice Mitchell of Aurora, Colorado. An overnight marinade gives the chops a pleasant lime taste that's echoed by a tangy sauce.

A comforting counterpart to the hearty pork is **Garlic Mashed Red Potatoes** (p. 83) from Val Mitchell of Hudson, Ohio. With just six ingredients, you can have this super spud side dish on the table in no time.

Appealing Partners

♦ Steamed baby carrots
♦ Emerald Fruit Salad (p. 49)

Practical Tips

🍎 Dovetail some of the recipe steps. For example, fix the sauce for the entree while the chops are cooking on the grill or under the broiler.

🍎 Cut down on prep time when making the marinade. Instead of mincing fresh garlic cloves, take advantage of convenient minced garlic available in jars. A half teaspoon is equal to one clove of minced garlic.

Meaty Main Dish

Deluxe Meat Loaf (p. 121) from Patricia Zwerk, Tucson, Arizona adds a comforting tone to your table. The moist nicely seasoned slices are the perfect start to a hearty homemade meal.

For a light and lovely accompaniment to your entree, toss together **Spiced Fruit Salad** (p. 78) from Lavonne Hartel. The Williston, North Dakota cook drizzles a cool combination of fruits with a cinnamony dressing.

Appealing Partners

♦ Mashed potatoes
♦ Steamed brussels sprouts

Practical Tips

🍎 To further reduce fat and calories in the meat loaf, use lean ground turkey instead of lean ground beef.

🍎 Patricia says she refrigerates leftover meat loaf and slices it when it's cold to make delicious sandwiches.

🍎 When Lavonne makes her fruit salad, she pulls the apples and grapes out of the fridge right before assembling and serving. "Then the yogurt dressing will chill the bananas to the perfect serving temperature," she explains.

Enchilada Entree

Hearty Ham Dinner

Easy Oven Favorite

Even if you have a family that's used to meat-and-potato meals, they'll love **Black Bean Enchiladas** (p. 176) developed by our Test Kitchen home economists. These hearty wraps have plenty of protein and so much zippy flavor that folks will never miss the meat!

Serve these enchiladas with Edna Coons' refreshing **Mandarin Tossed Salad** (p. 55). The Sherman, Connecticut cook says the colorful blend also makes an attractive addition to a potluck dinner.

Appealing Partners

♦ Fresh lemonade
♦ A scoop of low-fat frozen vanilla yogurt or pineapple sherbet

Practical Tips

🍎 If your family is fond of corn tortillas, warm them and use instead of flour tortillas when assembling the enchiladas. They add fiber and a nice change of pace to the dish.

🍎 To enhance the flavor of the sunflower kernels in the salad, toast them in a dry skillet over low heat just until golden. (But watch them carefully, so they don't burn.)

You'll have most of your meal taken care of when you put **Asparagus Ham Dinner** (p. 157) on your menu. This meal-in-one dish from Rhonda Zavodny, David City, Nebraska is fun and fresh tasting.

End the evening on a sweet note with **Fudgy Peanut Butter Brownies** (p. 228) from Martha Domeny of Overland Park, Kansas. Her recipe makes a big panful, so you'll have plenty to share with friends.

Appealing Partners

♦ Spinach salad with low-fat ranch dressing
♦ Crusty Italian bread

Practical Tips

🍎 If fresh asparagus isn't available or you don't have any on hand, you can substitute a 10-ounce package of frozen cut asparagus. Just thaw it before sauteing with the yellow pepper.

🍎 Make the brownies the night before; cool and cut into squares. Set aside enough for the next day's dessert, then freeze the rest in a freezer container for up to 3 months. Thaw them to pack into bag lunches or to serve when you need a sweet treat for company.

Chili Mac Casserole (p. 124) is filling fare from Marlene Wilson of Rolla, North Dakota. It's simple to assemble yet loaded with hearty ground beef and beans.

Cool off from its slightly spicy flavor by sipping **Frosty Chocolate Malted Shakes** (p. 21). Dora Dean of Hollywood, Florida uses her blender to whip up these mellow malts in a jiffy.

Appealing Partners

♦ Tossed salad with vinaigrette
♦ Cinnamon-sugared peach slices

Practical Tips

🍎 Marlene says her husband and children don't like dishes that are very spicy, so she usually omits the green chilies when making the Chili Mac Casserole. But if your family enjoys lots of spice, add a chopped and seeded jalapeno pepper to the mixture.

🍎 To give this main dish a different look, use 1 cup uncooked small pasta such as shells, ziti or wagon wheels in place of 1 cup uncooked elbow macaroni called for in the recipe.

Anytime Egg Wraps

Don't limit breakfast foods to the first meal of the day. Serve **Suppertime Egg Burritos** (p.107) from Scott Jones of Tulsa, Oklahoma for a delicious main course anytime. Scrambled eggs are jazzed up with vegetables and folded into flour tortillas, while salsa wakes up their flavor.

A refreshing accompaniment is **Minty Fruit Salad** (p. 52) shared by Becky Murdock of Hernando, Mississippi. The colorful medley can be assembled early in the day—or the night before. It showcases a simple assortment of fruits lightly dressed with a coating of citrus juices and mint.

Appealing Partners

♦ Mini blueberry muffins
♦ Fruit-flavored iced tea

Practical Tips

👌 When preparing the burritos, use an electric hand or stand mixer to beat the eggs and cream cheese. But don't worry if small lumps of cream cheese remain—they'll melt during cooking.

👌 Use whatever fruits your family enjoys when assembling the salad.

Sandwich Supper

Planning and preparing dinner is a picnic when you put **Pepper-Topped Beef Sandwiches** (p. 120) on the menu. Leota Recknor from Ash Grove, Missouri sautes sweet red and green peppers with onions. Then she uses the warm mixture to dress up rolls filled with convenient deli roast beef.

We paired these special sandwiches with crunchy **Two-Cabbage Slaw** (p. 58) from Carol Gaus of Itasca, Illinois. The crisp combination has a confetti-like look and gets tangy flavor from the sour cream dressing.

Appealing Partners

♦ Frozen yogurt with fresh berries
♦ Steamed carrots sprinkled with lemon juice and your favorite herb

Practical Tips

👌 Instead of roast beef from the deli, make roast beef for Sunday dinner and use the leftovers to assemble the sandwiches.

👌 Buy coleslaw mix equivalent to 5 cups shredded cabbage from your supermarket's produce department rather than shredding the green and red cabbage yourself.

Twist on Tradition

Mary Louise Chubb of Perkasie, Pennsylvania jazzes up a classic combination to create her **Chicken Rice Casserole** (p. 140). Tender chicken breasts and fluffy rice get added color from vegetables and a satisfying crunch from almonds sprinkled over the top.

Round out the meal with a tossed green salad dressed with **Dill Vinaigrette** (p. 79). Joyce Clifford of Mansfield, Ohio says the easy-to-assemble dressing is a family favorite.

Appealing Partners

♦ Banana bread
♦ Herbed peas

Practical Tips

👌 When assembling the dish for company, Mary Louise sometimes substitutes portobello mushrooms for the regular mushrooms and pine nuts for the almonds to give it special flavor.

👌 You can use ready-to-serve salad greens with Dill Vinaigrette, but you may also want to add other fixings (cucumbers, tomatoes, carrots, etc.).

Mexican Meal

A traditional Italian specialty gets Mexican flair in this convenient casserole from Sheree Swistun of Selkink, Manitoba. The recipe for **Mexican Lasagna** (p. 121) calls for salsa instead of tomato sauce and uncooked noodles so there's no need to boil them ahead of time.

Although the flavorful entree is filling, save room for one or two **Chocolate Chip Cookies** (p. 209) from Linda Todd. The Coldwater, Michigan cook stirs plenty of chocolate chips into the batter that makes a big batch of crowd-pleasing cookies.

Appealing Partners

- Tossed salad with low-fat vinaigrette
- Baked tortilla chips with salsa

Practical Tips

🍎 For a meatless entree, eliminate the ground beef and add a can of rinsed and drained black beans to the refried beans. This switch boosts fiber content.

🍎 If you don't have time to bake all of the cookies, Linda suggests freezing some of the dough. "Then just thaw and bake fresh cookies whenever you want them," she advises.

Comforting Classic

Enjoy the taste of a traditional Sunday supper without all the effort when you serve **Crunchy Baked Chicken** (p. 129). This tender chicken from Essie Malatt, Converse, Indiana has a crisp cornflake coating and is served with a tangy dipping sauce.

To complement the main dish, try **Hash Brown Casserole** (p. 92) from Sue Ann O'Buck of Sinking Spring, Pennsylvania. Canned soup and frozen hash browns hurry along the preparation.

Appealing Partners

- Strawberry Spinach Salad (p. 56)
- Angel food cake with a drizzle of fat-free chocolate ice cream topping

Practical Tips

🍎 When making the crumb mixture for the chicken, replace the cornflakes with crushed crisp rice cereal or corn or wheat Chex for a change of pace.

🍎 Experiment with the salad dressing that's used to coat the chicken and create the dipping sauce. Try ranch dressing or another favorite flavor.

Spaghetti Standby

Nothing satisfies like a family-pleasing pasta dish. **Turkey Spaghetti Pie** (p. 127) from Anita Cunningham of Blaine, Washington features a moist tasty noodle layer covered with creamy cottage cheese and a hearty ground turkey mixture.

For dessert, bite into **Mock Ice Cream Sandwiches** (p. 203) from Tony Kern of Milwaukee, Wisconsin. The sweet squares are simple to fix ahead of time and freeze. There's no need to thaw—just pull out the number you need to cap off the meal or enjoy as a snack.

Appealing Partners

- Crusty French bread
- Steamed garlic green beans

Practical Tips

🍎 For more authentic Italian flavor, use 3/4 pound of turkey Italian sausage (with the casings removed) in place of the ground turkey. Or, for a zippier taste, try hot turkey Italian sausage.

🍎 Instead of using chocolate graham crackers in the dessert, sandwich the creamy filling between regular or cinnamon graham crackers.

Pleasing Pork

It's easy to get a head start on dinner when you serve **Grilled Pork with Hot Mustard** (p. 152) from Kyle Spencer of Havre, Montana. The pork can be marinated overnight, then grilled in minutes for flavorful results.

Enhance the Oriental flair of that main dish by pairing it with **Almond Broccoli Stir-Fry** (p. 95) sent in by Margery Bryan of Royal City, Washington. Ginger and soy sauce add spark to this stovetop side dish, making it a nice change of pace from the usual veggies.

Appealing Partners

♦ Herbed breadsticks
♦ Hot tea

Practical Tips

🍴 Kyle says the grilled pork is equally delicious when served cold for a light summer supper. You can also serve the slices on a bun as an easy sandwich for lunch.

🍴 Before making the side dish, grate the peel from a lemon and freeze it for future use. Then squeeze 2 teaspoons of juice from the lemon to use in the broccoli recipe.

Filling Family Fare

Your crew is sure to appreciate the garden-fresh goodness of **Beefy Tomatoes** (p. 118) shared by Liz Gallagher of Gilbertsville, Pennsylvania. The oven-warmed tomatoes make a pretty presentation when heaped with a ground beef and rice filling.

Accompany this memorable main dish with **Spinach-Stuffed Bread** (p. 197) from Terry Byrne, Warwick, New York. Served warm, the slices are terrific with a meal, as a snack or as an appetizer.

Appealing Partners

♦ Carrot sticks
♦ Fresh fruit with yogurt dip

Practical Tips

🍴 Tomato pulp not used in the Beefy Tomatoes can be frozen up to 3 months. Use it to perk up tomato soup, spaghetti sauce or other tomato-based dishes.

🍴 The golden bread takes advantage of convenient frozen bread dough, so it's easy to assemble. But plan ahead—you'll need to thaw it first. Wrap it in plastic wrap and place in the fridge for 6-12 hours or on the counter for 2-3 hours until thawed but still cold.

Italian Favorites

Prepare **Turkey Manicotti** (p. 138) for your family and then prepare to collect the compliments. Mary Gunderson of Conrad, Iowa tucks good-for-you grain into the filling for nutrition and taste. Best of all, this appealing entree is a snap to put together because you don't have to precook the manicotti shells.

For a new way to serve broccoli, try **Broccoli Italiano** (p. 100) shared by Melanie Habener of Lompoc, California. Fresh garlic and lemon boost the taste of this swift side dish.

Appealing Partners

♦ Breadsticks
♦ Rainbow sherbet

Practical Tips

🍴 Give the manicotti a taste twist by using shredded reduced-fat Mexican cheese blend instead of mozzarella.

🍴 Melanie says she often makes this side dish with baby broccoli, a cross between regular broccoli and Chinese kale. Baby broccoli has long tender stems topped with florets, and a milder, sweeter taste. It's available in the produce section of some supermarkets.

Beef Is Best!

The wonderful aroma of **Simmered Sirloin with Noodles** (p. 115) from Jack Harrigan of Interlochen, Michigan will draw your family to the table. Once they taste it, the mouth-watering flavor will have them requesting this dish often.

Cap off the meal with **Mixed Berry Pizza** (p. 220) from Gretchen Widner of Sun City West, Arizona. These fruit-topped squares make a refreshing dessert, but they also can be served as appetizers at parties and picnics.

Appealing Partners

◆ Steamed asparagus spears
◆ Sparkling water

Practical Tips

🍎 You'll need to buy two cans of condensed beef consomme for the entree. Refrigerate the leftovers for up to 2 days, then use to add flavor to gravies, sauces or soups.

🍎 Instead of apricot preserves, try other types of fruit preserves when assembling the fruit pizza. You can also experiment with a combination of sliced fruit, such as peaches, bananas and kiwifruit, in place of the berries.

Summer Specialty

Cut down on cleanup when you use your grill to prepare **Herbed Lime Chicken** (p. 139). This moist and juicy entree shared by Kay Alliman of Biggsville, Illinois gets its tangy citrus flavor from an easy-to-stir-up lime marinade.

For a refreshing dessert, present pretty individual servings of **Watermelon Ice** (p. 203) sent in by Kaaren Jurack of Virginia Beach, Virginia. The yummy melon flavor of this light and frosty treat is simply irresistible.

Appealing Partners

◆ Garlic Green and Wax Beans (p. 60)
◆ Iced tea

Practical Tips

🍎 If the weather isn't conducive to grilling, simply broil the chicken 4-6 inches from the heat for the same amount of time directed in the recipe.

🍎 For a sensational slushy beverage, place a few scoops of Watermelon Ice in a tall glass and add club soda.

🍎 You can use cantaloupe or honeydew instead of watermelon in the dessert recipe for a tantalizing twist.

Stovetop Supper

Treat yourself to a simple skillet sensation with **Turkey Quesadillas** (p. 138) from Wendy Greinke of Round Rock, Texas. The tasty wedges are chock-full of seasoned ground turkey, zucchini, corn, red pepper and just enough melted cheese.

Cooked rice hurries along preparation of **Lemon Fried Rice** (p. 89) from Janice Mitchell of Aurora, Colorado. With its pleasant lemon flavor, this side dish will complement most entrees.

Appealing Partners

◆ Chopped tomatoes and cucumbers in a fat-free vinaigrette
◆ Low-fat chocolate muffins

Practical Tips

🍎 Feel free to use fresh corn for the frozen corn called for in the quesadillas recipe. Cut the kernels from 2 medium ears of corn to equal 1 cup.

🍎 Be sure to start with cold rice when making the fried rice. Chilling the rice helps keep the grains separate and prevents it from sticking to the skillet. Simply break up the clumps of rice before adding to the skillet.

Slow-Cooked Supper

A few minutes spent one night will reap big rewards the next day when you come home to the aroma of **Marinated Pot Roast** (p. 120) simmering in your slow cooker. This homespun supper from Marijane Rea of Milwaukie, Oregon features tender beef served with a family-pleasing gravy.

Zippy Green Beans (p. 99) shared by Suzanne McKinley from Lyons, Georgia make a colorful side dish. A tangy glaze prepared with crumbled bacon and onion jazzes it up.

Appealing Partners

♦ Red potato wedges
♦ Butternut Squash Rolls (p. 197)

Practical Tips

🖐 The pot roast recipe makes quite a bit, so use up the leftovers to make sandwiches for the next day's lunch. Simply reheat the extra meat and gravy and serve in multigrain rolls.

🖐 Don't have the green beans called for in the side dish recipe? Try the zippy treatment with cooked broccoli florets instead.

Flavorful Fare

Your family's sure to greet you with smiles when you put **Turkey Tomato Pizza** (p. 142) on the table. Michelle Beall of Westminster, Maryland uses a lemony spread in place of traditional tomato sauce on the golden pizza crust, then tops it with deli turkey, bacon, tomato slices and two kinds of cheese.

Bowls of **Basil Tortellini Soup** (p. 40) from Jayne Dwyer-Reff of Fort Wayne, Indiana are a tasty accompaniment to the pizza. Balsamic vinegar perks up the flavor of this hearty soup that stars cheese tortellini and beans.

Appealing Partners

♦ Sparkling water
♦ Low-fat banana pudding

Practical Tips

🖐 Grate 1/4 teaspoon of peel from a lemon for the pizza. Then refrigerate the lemon so you can squeeze a bit of juice from it over cooked vegetables at a different meal.

🖐 The tortellini soup is nicely seasoned with fresh basil, but if you don't have any on hand, you can use 1 teaspoon dried basil instead.

Spiced-Up Supper

For a meal that sticks to your ribs and not your waistline, ladle up bowls of **Flavorful White Chili** (p. 45) from Wilda Bensenhaver of Deland, Florida. With a little prep work done ahead of time, you can put the mixture into the slow cooker to simmer in the morning and have dinner ready when you come home.

Accompany it with squares of golden **Southwestern Corn Bread** (p. 198) from Tena Edyvean of Rapid City, South Dakota. It's delicious served warm.

Appealing Partner

♦ Spinach salad with low-fat French dressing

Practical Tips

🖐 If the weather isn't conducive to grilling, Wilda says she sometimes broils or poaches the chicken breast when fixing the chili.

🖐 For zestier chili, increase the cayenne pepper, cumin and garlic.

🖐 "If you like your corn bread a little spicier, like our family does, use chopped jalapeno peppers instead of the canned chilies," Tena recommends.

All-In-One Oven Meal

Roasted Pork Tenderloin and Vegetables (p. 148) is often requested at the home of Diane Martin of Brown Deer, Wisconsin. Her clan loves the tender pork slices and vegetables that are roasted in one pan. The fuss-free combination is so special, she serves it to company.

Complete the meal with a tossed salad dolloped with **Buttermilk Salad Dressing** (p. 65). Vicki Floden of Story City, Iowa needs just three ingredients to blend together the thick, creamy dressing.

Appealing Partners

♦ Hot spiced apple cider
♦ Fat-free vanilla ice cream

Practical Tips

🥄 When preparing the pork and veggies, vary the flavor by combining your own blend of herbs in place of the rosemary and sage. Experiment with mint and marjoram or basil and rosemary.

🥄 To save time at dinner, make the Buttermilk Salad Dressing early in the day.

Down-Home Dinner

For a satisfying meal-in-one dish, try Carolyn Wolbers' recipe for **Shepherd's Pie** (p. 116). The Loveland, Ohio cook seasons a ground beef and carrot layer with rosemary, thyme and sage, then tops it with freshly mashed potatoes before popping it in the oven.

Powdered sugar gives a pretty look to **Crinkle-Top Chocolate Cookies** (p. 216) from Maria Groff of Ephrata, Pennsylvania. She says the tender-textured treats are easy to make and have a terrific chocolate flavor.

Appealing Partners

♦ Steamed broccoli
♦ Low-fat milk

Practical Tips

🥄 If you have leftover mashed potatoes, use them instead of cooking the potatoes for Shepherd's Pie. Eliminate the milk and butter, too.

🥄 The batch of cookies makes 3-1/2 dozen. Set aside some for dessert, then store the rest in an airtight container to add to brown-bag lunches. These yummy treats are best eaten within 3-5 days.

Mouth-Watering Menu

From Magnolia, Texas, Rhonda Schiel shares **Chicken Parmigiana** (p. 140). The moist chicken breasts are lightly coated with a mixture of Parmesan and bread crumbs, then topped with spaghetti sauce and cheese.

To complement the Italian entree, toss together refreshing **Apple Pear Salad** (p. 67) from Cathy Seed of Hudson, Ohio. Her beautiful blend of fruit and walnuts is pulled together with a tasty vinaigrette dressing that's a snap to stir up.

Appealing Partners

♦ Garlic bread prepared with reduced-fat margarine
♦ Hot cooked spiral pasta

Practical Tips

🥄 The recipe for Chicken Parmigiana calls for plenty of spaghetti sauce, so make the most of it by serving pasta alongside this main dish.

🥄 To quickly toast chopped walnuts for the fruity salad, spread them on a baking sheet. Bake at 350° for 6-10 minutes or until they're golden brown, stirring occasionally.

Marvelous Meatballs

Coated in plenty of homemade barbecue sauce and served over hot cooked noodles, these **Zesty Meatballs** (p. 124) from Debbie Segate of Grande Prairie, Alberta make a satisfying supper that the whole family is sure to enjoy.

Complete the meal with a tossed salad dolloped with **Creamy French Dressing** (p. 73). This made-in-minutes mixture was created by our Test Kitchen.

Appealing Partners

♦ Chunky applesauce
♦ Ice water with a lemon wedge

Practical Tips

🍎 Debbie often serves her Zesty Meatballs as an appetizer instead of a main dish. Or, for a change of pace, top the meatballs with the sauce of your choice. Try them covered in brown gravy or along with pineapple and green pepper chunks in a sweet-sour sauce.

🍎 When preparing the noodles to accompany the main dish, remember 2 ounces of dry medium egg noodles equals 1 cup of cooked noodles. So you'll need 12 ounces of uncooked noodles to get 6 cups of cooked noodles.

Simmered Sandwiches

Take advantage of your slow cooker to simmer the moist filling for **Italian Turkey Sandwiches** (p. 136). Carol Riley of Galva, Illinois says the tender turkey tastes just like Italian beef, but without the fat.

Seven-Vegetable Salad (p. 64) from Sara Lindler of Irmo, South Carolina is a delightfully bright addition to this meal. The medley promises a rainbow of color in every crunchy bite.

Appealing Partners

♦ Light strawberry mousse
♦ Lemon iced tea

Practical Tips

🍎 If you'd like the Italian Turkey Sandwiches to have more zip, sprinkle crushed red pepper flakes into the slow cooker when you add the oregano.

🍎 When assembling the salad, swap out seasonal veggies where appropriate. Broccoli, cauliflower and celery are easy options available most any time of year. Also, feel free to use a favorite reduced-fat vinaigrette, such as raspberry or red wine vinaigrette, in place of the Italian salad dressing.

Speedy Skillet

Your stovetop simplifies suppertime when you fix **Ham Mushroom Fettuccine** (p. 153) from Michelle Armistead of Keyport, New Jersey. This pretty pasta toss showcases ham, mushrooms and peas in a creamy sauce.

Kay McMicken of Charlotte, North Carolina dresses up a boxed cake mix to bake the **Ultimate Chocolate Cake** (p. 234). Serve up slices of this moist bundt cake for dessert, and you're sure to satisfy the chocolate lovers in your home.

Appealing Partners

♦ Crusty Italian bread
♦ Sauteed zucchini

Practical Tips

🍎 Dried rosemary seasons this main dish nicely, but you can use the same amount of dried basil instead if your family prefers.

🍎 When fixing the pasta, Michelle frequently uses regular and spinach fettuccine noodles for extra color.

🍎 For a change of taste, add some ground cinnamon to the powdered sugar before sprinkling over the chocolate cake.

Light Bites & Beverages

The next time you're in the mood for a satisfying snack or a thirst-quenching beverage, try one of the tempting treats or refreshing drinks on the following pages. They're anything but lightweight in taste!

Mozzarella Pepperoni Bread (page 18)

Mozzarella Pepperoni Bread

(Pictured on page 17)

My family enjoys this tempting bread as an appetizer when we have company...and as a quick meal on hectic evenings. With five children at home, and all involved in sports, we have this hot snack sandwich often.
—Terri Toti, Eureka, Missouri

1 loaf (1 pound) unsliced French bread
3 tablespoons butter *or* stick margarine, melted
3 ounces sliced turkey pepperoni
1-1/2 cups (6 ounces) shredded part-skim mozzarella cheese
3 tablespoons minced fresh parsley

Cut loaf of bread in half widthwise; cut into 1-in. slices, leaving slices attached at bottom. Brush butter on both sides of each slice. Arrange pepperoni between slices; sprinkle with cheese and parsley. Place on an ungreased baking sheet. Bake at 350° for 12-15 minutes or until cheese is melted. **Yield:** 24 slices.

Nutritional Analysis: One slice equals 91 calories, 4 g fat (2 g saturated fat), 12 mg cholesterol, 229 mg sodium, 10 g carbohydrate, 1 g fiber, 5 g protein.
Diabetic Exchanges: 1 lean meat, 1/2 starch.

Layered Oriental Dip

Guests at gatherings are quick to dig into this delectable dip. With tender chunks of chicken and Oriental seasonings, it's a nice switch from taco dip.
—Bonnie Mazur, Reedsburg, Wisconsin

1 cup chopped cooked chicken breast
1/2 cup shredded carrot
1/4 cup chopped unsalted peanuts
3 tablespoons chopped green onions
3 tablespoons reduced-sodium soy sauce, *divided*
1 tablespoon minced fresh parsley
1 garlic clove, minced
1 teaspoon sesame seeds, toasted
2 tablespoons packed brown sugar
1-1/2 teaspoons cornstarch
1/2 cup water
2 tablespoons ketchup
1-1/2 teaspoons Worcestershire sauce
1/2 teaspoon cider vinegar
2 drops hot pepper sauce
1 package (8 ounces) reduced-fat cream cheese
Baked tortilla chips

In a bowl, combine the chicken, carrot, peanuts, onions, 2 tablespoons soy sauce, parsley, garlic and sesame seeds. Cover and refrigerate for several hours.

In a saucepan, combine the brown sugar and cornstarch; stir in water, ketchup, Worcestershire sauce, vinegar and hot pepper sauce until smooth. Bring to a boil; cook and stir for 1-2 minutes or until thickened. Cool for 5 minutes. Cover and refrigerate.

Just before serving, in a mixing bowl, beat cream cheese and remaining soy sauce until smooth. Spread evenly into a 12-in. serving dish. Cover with chicken mixture; drizzle with sauce. Serve with tortilla chips. **Yield:** 10 servings.

Nutritional Analysis: One serving (2 tablespoons dip with 5 tortilla chips) equals 163 calories, 7 g fat (3 g saturated fat), 25 mg cholesterol, 400 mg sodium, 17 g carbohydrate, 1 g fiber, 9 g protein.
Diabetic Exchanges: 1 starch, 1 lean meat, 1/2 fat.

Lemon Fruit Dip

(Pictured below)

For a party, brunch buffet or healthy snack anytime, fresh fruit with this sweet lemony dip can't be beat. When I worked in a cafeteria, I'd make up small plates of fruit and this dip. They sold very well.
—Regina King, Watertown, Wisconsin

2 cups (16 ounces) reduced-fat sour cream
1 package (1 ounce) sugar-free instant vanilla pudding mix
1/4 cup fat-free milk
4 teaspoons lemon juice
1 teaspoon grated lemon peel
Assorted fresh fruit

In a bowl, whisk the sour cream, pudding mix, milk, lemon juice and peel until blended. Serve with fruit. **Yield:** 2 cups.

Nutritional Analysis: One serving (1/3 cup dip) equals 127 calories, 7 g fat (5 g saturated fat), 27 mg cholesterol, 255 mg sodium, 10 g carbohydrate, trace fiber, 6 g protein.
Diabetic Exchanges: 1 starch, 1 fat.

Cheesy Zucchini Bites

(Pictured above)

Garden-fresh zucchini and cherry tomatoes are tastefully combined in these colorful appetizers. Folks tend to hang around the appetizer tray whenever I serve these party bites. These make for a pretty presentation on a buffet table.
—Amy Frombach, Bradford, Pennsylvania

    5 medium zucchini (about 6 inches long)
    4 ounces blue cheese, crumbled
    3 tablespoons grated Parmesan cheese
    1 teaspoon dried basil
 1/8 teaspoon pepper
    1 pint cherry tomatoes, thinly sliced

Cut zucchini into 3/4-in. slices. Using a melon baller or small spoon, scoop out the insides and discard, leaving the bottom intact. Place zucchini on an ungreased baking sheet; spoon 1/2 teaspoon crumbled blue cheese into each.

Combine the Parmesan cheese, basil and pepper; sprinkle half over blue cheese. Top each with a tomato slice; sprinkle with the remaining Parmesan mixture. Bake at 400° for 5-7 minutes or until cheese is melted. Serve warm. **Yield:** 35 appetizers.

Nutritional Analysis: One appetizer equals 19 calories, 1 g fat (1 g saturated fat), 3 mg cholesterol, 58 mg sodium, 1 g carbohydrate, trace fiber, 1 g protein.
Diabetic Exchange: Free food.

Four-Berry Smoothies

This smoothie tastes even more scrumptious when I think of how much money I save by whipping up my own at home. As a breakfast, it keeps me satisfied and full of energy all morning.
—Krista Johnson, Crosslake, Minnesota

 1-1/2 cups fat-free milk
    1/2 cup frozen blackberries
    1/2 cup frozen blueberries
    1/2 cup frozen unsweetened raspberries
    1/2 cup frozen unsweetened strawberries
       2 tablespoons lemonade concentrate
       1 tablespoon sugar
    1/2 teaspoon vanilla extract

In a blender or food processor, combine all ingredients. Cover and process until smooth. Pour into glasses; serve immediately. **Yield:** 2 servings.

Nutritional Analysis: One serving (1-1/2 cups) equals 172 calories, 1 g fat (trace saturated fat), 4 mg cholesterol, 100 mg sodium, 36 g carbohydrate, 4 g fiber, 8 g protein.
Diabetic Exchanges: 1-1/2 fruit, 1 fat-free milk.

 Celery Stick Snack

For a quick crunchy snack, I spread fat-free cream cheese on celery sticks, then sprinkle them with garlic salt for a little zip.   *—Kathy Vanderbilt*
Goodyear, Arizona

Nutritional Analysis: One serving (6 tostadas) equals 141 calories, 3 g fat (trace saturated fat), 3 mg cholesterol, 347 mg sodium, 25 g carbohydrate, 1 g fiber, 5 g protein.
Diabetic Exchanges: 1-1/2 starch, 1 vegetable.

Ginger-Cranberry Chutney Spread

I first became acquainted with chutney while I was serving overseas. I prefer a tart, rather than a sweet, taste—and that's just what the ginger, apple juice and lemon juice bring to this ruby-red spread. I usually serve it with cream cheese and crackers, but it's wonderful with turkey slices and pork chops, too.
—LaVonne Wettering, Clermont, Florida

1/2 cup water
  2 tablespoons minced fresh gingerroot*
  1 package (12 ounces) cranberries
  1 large tart apple, peeled, cored and diced
3/4 cup sugar
2/3 cup unsweetened apple juice concentrate
1/2 cup raisins
1/4 cup lemon juice
  2 tablespoons grated orange peel
  1 teaspoon ground cinnamon
1/2 teaspoon ground allspice
1/8 to 1/4 teaspoon ground cloves
1/8 to 1/4 teaspoon cayenne pepper
  3 packages (8 ounces *each*) reduced-fat cream cheese, softened
Crackers

In a saucepan, heat water and ginger until the water is evaporated. Stir in the cranberries, apple, sugar, apple juice concentrate, raisins, lemon juice, orange peel and seasonings. Bring to a boil. Reduce heat; simmer, uncovered, for 25 minutes or until thickened. Cool. Cover and store in the refrigerator. Serve 1 cup of chutney over each package of cream cheese. Spread on crackers. **Yield:** 24 servings.
  *Editor's Note: 1-1/2 teaspoons of ground ginger may be substituted for the fresh gingerroot; omit the 1/2 cup of water and the first step of recipe.

Nutritional Analysis: One serving (2 tablespoons chutney and 1 ounce of cream cheese with 4 crackers) equals 178 calories, 6 g fat (2 g saturated fat), 17 mg cholesterol, 215 mg sodium, 28 g carbohydrate, 2 g fiber, 5 g protein.
Diabetic Exchanges: 1 starch, 1 fat, 1/2 lean meat, 1/2 fruit.

Corn Salsa Tostadas

(Pictured above)

I make these "South-of-the-Border" treats when I have a craving for something a little spicy. These bite-size morsels are as tasty as they are attractive. They make fun appetizers for a party, too.
—Laurie Todd, Columbus, Mississippi

  3 flour tortillas (8 inches)
3/4 cup fat-free sour cream
  2 green onions, finely chopped
  3 teaspoons minced fresh cilantro *or* parsley, divided
1/4 teaspoon garlic powder
3/4 cup fresh *or* frozen corn, thawed
  1 plum tomato, diced
  1 tablespoon chopped jalapeno pepper*
  2 tablespoons orange juice
  1 teaspoon canola oil
1/2 teaspoon salt

Using a 2-in. round cookie cutter, cut 12 circles from each tortilla. Coat both sides of circles with nonstick cooking spray. Place in a single layer on a baking sheet. Bake at 400° for 4-5 minutes or until crisp. Cool. In a small bowl, combine the sour cream, onions, 1 teaspoon cilantro and garlic powder; cover and refrigerate. In another bowl, combine the corn, tomato, jalapeno, orange juice, oil, salt and remaining cilantro; cover and refrigerate. Just before serving, spread 1 teaspoon sour cream mixture over each tostada. Using a slotted spoon, top each with a teaspoonful of corn salsa. **Yield:** 3 dozen.
  *Editor's Note: When cutting or seeding hot peppers, use rubber or plastic gloves to protect your hands. Avoid touching your face.

Asparagus Guacamole

(Pictured below)

To trim down traditional guacamole, I experimented with asparagus instead. My husband and our three hungry sons say this chunky low-fat version is as tasty as the original. I love the guilt-free dipping.
—*Judi Hummer, Lititz, Pennsylvania*

1 pound fresh asparagus, trimmed and cut into
  1-inch pieces
1/3 cup chopped onion
1 garlic clove
1/3 cup chopped seeded tomato
2 tablespoons reduced-fat mayonnaise
1 tablespoon lemon juice
1/2 teaspoon salt
3/4 teaspoon minced fresh cilantro *or* parsley
1/4 teaspoon chili powder
6 drops hot pepper sauce
Assorted raw vegetables and baked tortilla chips

Place 1/2 in. of water and asparagus in a saucepan; bring to a boil. Reduce heat; cover and simmer for 5 minutes or until tender. Drain; place asparagus in a blender or food processor. Add onion and garlic; cover and process until smooth.

In a bowl, combine tomato, mayonnaise, lemon juice, salt, cilantro, chili powder and hot pepper sauce. Stir in the asparagus mixture until blended. Serve with vegetables and chips. Refrigerate leftovers; stir before serving. **Yield:** 2 cups.

Nutritional Analysis: *One serving (1/3 cup guacamole) equals 42 calories, 2 g fat (trace saturated fat), 2 mg cholesterol, 240 mg sodium, 5 g carbohydrate, 1 g fiber, 3 g protein.*
Diabetic Exchange: *1-1/2 vegetable.*

Frosty Chocolate Malted Shakes

(Pictured above)

I played around with our favorite milk shake recipe to come up with this lighter version. I serve it all the time, and no one misses the extra fat or calories.
—*Dora Dean, Hollywood, Florida*

6 cups reduced-fat frozen vanilla yogurt
3-1/2 cups fat-free milk
1/4 cup sugar-free instant chocolate drink mix
1/4 cup malted milk powder
1-1/2 teaspoons vanilla extract

In batches, process all ingredients in a blender until smooth. Pour into tall glasses. **Yield:** 10 servings.

Nutritional Analysis: *One serving (1 cup) equals 193 calories, 1 g fat (trace saturated fat), 2 mg cholesterol, 172 mg sodium, 37 g carbohydrate, trace fiber, 9 g protein.*
Diabetic Exchanges: *1-1/2 fat-free milk, 1/2 starch.*

🍎 Calcium-Filled Treat

Here's a creative way to encourage kids to get plenty of calcium. Keep a quart jar filled with 2 cups fat-free milk in the refrigerator. When they want a snack, have them select their favorite instant pudding mix, add it to the jar, cover it tightly and shake until it turns into pudding.
—*Lynda Atteberry Hoskins, Mathis, Texas*

Fresh Veggie Pizza

(Pictured below)

There's no need to bring confetti to your next snack-time gathering. Just carry in this colorful pizza that's topped with a rainbow of crunchy vegetables!
—Brooke Wiley, Halifax, Virginia

1 tube (8 ounces) reduced-fat crescent rolls
1 package (8 ounces) reduced-fat cream cheese
1 envelope ranch salad dressing mix
2 tablespoons fat-free milk
1/2 cup *each* chopped fresh broccoli, cauliflower, carrots, green pepper, sweet red pepper and mushrooms

Unroll crescent roll dough into one long rectangle. Press onto the bottom of a 13-in. x 9-in. x 2-in. baking pan coated with nonstick cooking spray; seal seams and perforations. Bake at 375° for 11-13 minutes or until golden brown. Cool completely.

In a mixing bowl, beat cream cheese, salad dressing mix and milk until smooth. Spread over crust. Sprinkle with vegetables. Cover and refrigerate for at least 1 hour before serving. Cut into 16 pieces. **Yield:** 8 servings.

Nutritional Analysis: One serving (2 pieces) equals 164 calories, 7 g fat (3 g saturated fat), 10 mg cholesterol, 623 mg sodium, 18 g carbohydrate, 1 g fiber, 6 g protein.
Diabetic Exchanges: 1 starch, 1 lean meat, 1 vegetable.

Soy Good Snack Mix

This medley stirred up by our Test Kitchen blends nutritious roasted soybeans with crunchy cereal. Worcestershire sauce, vinegar and garlic powder combine for the zesty coating.

5 cups Cheerios
5 cups Bran Chex
1/2 cup dry roasted soybeans
1/4 cup butter *or* stick margarine, melted
3 tablespoons Worcestershire sauce

1 tablespoon red wine vinegar *or* cider vinegar
1/2 teaspoon garlic powder

In a large bowl, combine the cereals and soybeans. Combine the butter, Worcestershire sauce, vinegar and garlic powder; drizzle over cereal mixture and mix well. Transfer to two ungreased 15-in. x 10-in. x 1-in. baking pans. Bake at 250° for 40-50 minutes, stirring every 15 minutes. Store in airtight containers. **Yield:** 8 servings.

Nutritional Analysis: One serving (1 cup) equals 255 calories, 10 g fat (4 g saturated fat), 16 mg cholesterol, 513 mg sodium, 39 g carbohydrate, 5 g fiber, 9 g protein.
Diabetic Exchanges: 2 starch, 1 lean meat, 1 fat.

Chocolate Cereal Bars

A little bit of chocolate and cocoa goes a long way to give Rice Krispies treats a scrumptious new twist. I especially like these bars because they are crisp, not sticky. They disappear in a flash whenever I serve them.
—Gretchen Hickman, Galva, Illinois

2 tablespoons butter *or* stick margarine
1 square (1 ounce) unsweetened chocolate
1 jar (7 ounces) marshmallow creme
2 tablespoons baking cocoa
1 teaspoon vanilla extract
6 cups crisp rice cereal

In a heavy saucepan over low heat, melt butter and chocolate; stir until smooth. Stir in the marshmallow creme and cocoa; cook and stir until smooth. Remove from the heat; stir in vanilla and cereal. Pat into a 13-in. x 9-in. x 2-in. pan coated with nonstick cooking spray. Cool before cutting. **Yield:** 2 dozen.

Nutritional Analysis: One bar equals 69 calories, 2 g fat (1 g saturated fat), 3 mg cholesterol, 87 mg sodium, 13 g carbohydrate, trace fiber, 1 g protein.
Diabetic Exchange: 1 starch.

Banana Cocoa Smoothies

With its chocolaty twist, this frothy concoction appeals to folks of all ages. The zippy sipper is a great way to ensure youngsters get plenty of calcium-packed yogurt and milk, too.
—Anne Yaeger, Houston, Texas

1 cup (8 ounces) fat-free vanilla yogurt
3/4 cup fat-free milk
1 medium ripe banana, frozen and cut into chunks
3 tablespoons sugar-free chocolate drink mix
1/4 teaspoon vanilla extract

In a blender or food processor, combine all ingredients. Cover and process until smooth. Pour into glasses; serve immediately. **Yield:** 3 servings.

Nutritional Analysis: One serving (1 cup) equals 155 calories, 1 g fat (trace saturated fat), 3 mg cholesterol, 100 mg sodium, 30 g carbohydrate, 2 g fiber, 7 g protein.
Diabetic Exchanges: 1-1/2 starch, 1/2 fruit.

Favorite Dip Recipe Made Lighter

FOLKS always seem to flock to the snack table when the lineup includes a warm cheesy dip. "When my brother-in-law brought Cheesy Bean Dip to our house for a get-together, everyone asked for the recipe," says Katrina Turner of West Chester, Ohio. "He first tasted this delectable dip at a football party. We've made it many times—it's so popular."

If you'd like to add a new appetizer to your buffet table for an upcoming gathering, be sure to try Katrina's recipe. Or, if you would prefer a lighter version, why not sample the Makeover Cheesy Bean Dip created by our Test Kitchen home economists?

They modified Katrina's recipe by substituting reduced-fat for regular cheese and using a cup less of it. They also substituted reduced-fat sour cream and cream cheese plus fat-free refried beans. To make up for less fat (which adds moisture), they stirred in a can of diced tomatoes and green chilies.

This lightened-up version has a third fewer calories than the original, less than half the fat (and saturated fat) and about half the cholesterol—but it's still delicious and delightfully fun to dip!

Cheesy Bean Dip

- **2 cups (8 ounces) shredded Monterey Jack cheese**
- **2 cups (8 ounces) shredded cheddar cheese**
- **1 can (16 ounces) refried beans**
- **1 cup (8 ounces) sour cream**
- **1 package (8 ounces) cream cheese, softened**
- **2 tablespoons taco seasoning**
Tortilla chips

In a bowl, combine the cheeses; set aside 2 cups for topping. Add the beans, sour cream, cream cheese and taco seasoning to the remaining cheese. Transfer to a greased 2-qt. baking dish; sprinkle with the reserved cheese. Bake, uncovered, at 350° for 20-30 minutes or until bubbly around the edges. Serve warm with tortilla chips. **Yield:** about 5 cups.

Nutritional Analysis: One serving (2 tablespoons dip) equals 88 calories, 7 g fat (4 g saturated fat), 22 mg cholesterol, 134 mg sodium, 3 g carbohydrate, 1 g fiber, 4 g protein.

Makeover Cheesy Bean Dip

(Pictured at right)

- **1-1/2 cups (6 ounces) shredded reduced-fat Mexican cheese blend**
- **1-1/2 cups (6 ounces) shredded reduced-fat cheddar cheese**
- **1 can (16 ounces) fat-free refried beans**
- **1 can (10 ounces) diced tomatoes and green chilies**
- **1 package (8 ounces) reduced-fat cream cheese, cubed**
- **1/2 cup reduced-fat sour cream**
- **1 tablespoon taco seasoning**
Baked tortilla chips and assorted fresh vegetables

In a bowl, combine the cheeses; set aside 1 cup for topping. Add beans, tomatoes, cream cheese, sour cream and taco seasoning to the remaining cheese; mix well. Transfer to a 2-qt. baking dish coated with nonstick cooking spray; sprinkle with reserved cheese. Bake, uncovered, at 350° for 20-25 minutes or until bubbly around the edges. Serve warm with tortilla chips and vegetables. **Yield:** 4 cups.

Nutritional Analysis: One serving (2 tablespoons dip) equals 61 calories, 3 g fat (2 g saturated fat), 10 mg cholesterol, 177 mg sodium, 4 g carbohydrate, 1 g fiber, 5 g protein.
Diabetic Exchanges: 1/2 starch, 1/2 lean meat.

Tomato Black Bean Salsa

(Pictured below)

This fresh-tasting medley bursts with homegrown garden goodness, including tomatoes, red pepper and crunchy corn. Serve this salsa in the traditional way with baked tortilla chips and veggies, or as a condiment for fish.
—Chris Schnittka, Charlottesville, Virginia

3 medium tomatoes, seeded and chopped
1 can (15 ounces) black beans, rinsed and drained
3/4 cup fresh *or* frozen corn
1/2 cup finely chopped red onion
1/2 cup chopped roasted red pepper
1 jalapeno pepper, finely chopped*
2 tablespoons minced fresh cilantro *or* parsley
1/4 cup lime juice
1 garlic clove, minced
1 teaspoon dried oregano
1 teaspoon ground cumin
1/2 teaspoon salt
1/2 teaspoon ground coriander
Baked tortilla chips

In a large bowl, combine the first 13 ingredients. Cover and refrigerate for at least 2 hours before serving. Serve with tortilla chips. **Yield:** 4 cups.

*Editor's Note: When cutting or seeding hot peppers, use rubber or plastic gloves to protect your hands. Avoid touching your face.

Nutritional Analysis: One serving (1/2 cup salsa) equals 80 calories, 1 g fat (trace saturated fat), 0 cholesterol, 318 mg sodium, 15 g carbohydrate, 4 g fiber, 4 g protein.
Diabetic Exchanges: 1 vegetable, 1/2 starch.

Asparagus in Puff Pastry

(Pictured above)

Fast and easy, these golden bites are always a huge hit. I make and freeze batches of them during asparagus season for dinner parties throughout the year.
—Dianne Werdegar, Naperville, Illinois

2 cups water
24 fresh asparagus spears (about 1 pound), trimmed
1 package (8 ounces) reduced-fat cream cheese
1/2 teaspoon salt
1 package (17-1/4 ounces) frozen puff pastry dough, thawed
1/4 cup egg substitute

In a large nonstick skillet, bring water to a boil. Add asparagus; cover and cook for 3 minutes. Drain asparagus and immediately place in ice water; drain and pat dry. In a mixing bowl, beat cream cheese and salt until smooth; set aside.

Unfold the dough on a lightly floured surface. Cut each sheet in half widthwise. For each rectangle, spread cream cheese mixture lengthwise over half of the dough to within 1/2 in. of edges. Arrange two rows of three asparagus spears lengthwise in a single layer over cream cheese.

Brush edges of dough with some of the egg substitute; fold dough over filling and press edges together to seal. Cover and refrigerate for 1 hour.

Cut widthwise into 1-1/4-in. pieces. Place 1 in. apart on a baking sheet coated with nonstick cooking spray. Brush with remaining egg substitute. Bake at 425° for 8-12 minutes or until golden. Serve warm. **Yield:** 28 servings.

Nutritional Analysis: One serving (2 pieces) equals 87 calories, 6 g fat (3 g saturated fat), 9 mg cholesterol, 156 mg sodium, 6 g carbohydrate, 1 g fiber, 3 g protein.
Diabetic Exchanges: 1 vegetable, 1/2 starch, 1/2 fat.

Roasted Garlic Appetizers

These are my favorite appetizers. Whenever I host a get-together, the tiny toast cups with creamy filling go quickly.
—Lee Campbell, Bartow, Florida

24 very thin slices white bread
Refrigerated butter-flavored spray*
6 to 8 unpeeled garlic cloves
1 tablespoon olive *or* canola oil
1 package (8 ounces) reduced-fat cream cheese
2 tablespoons butter *or* stick margarine, softened
2 teaspoons minced chives
1/4 teaspoon salt
Fresh parsley sprigs

Cut each slice of bread with a 2-in. round cookie cutter. Spritz one side of each bread round with butter-flavored spray; press spritzed side up into miniature muffin cups coated with nonstick cooking spray. Bake at 350° for 10-15 minutes or until golden.

Place garlic cloves on a piece of aluminum foil. Pour oil over garlic; fold foil around garlic and seal tightly. Bake at 350° for 25-30 minutes or until garlic is very soft. When garlic is cool, remove from skins and mash.

In a mixing bowl, beat cream cheese, butter, chives and salt until smooth. Add garlic; beat until combined. Mound rounded teaspoonfuls of cream cheese mixture into each bread cup. Garnish with parsley. **Yield:** 12 servings.

***Editor's Note:** This recipe was tested with I Can't Believe It's Not Butter Spray.

Nutritional Analysis: One serving (2 appetizers) equals 154 calories, 7 g fat (4 g saturated fat), 16 mg cholesterol, 286 mg sodium, 17 g carbohydrate, 1 g fiber, 5 g protein.
Diabetic Exchanges: 1-1/2 fat, 1 starch.

Frosty Strawberry Slims

I once won first place with this recipe in the low-calorie division of a state strawberry contest.
—Patricia Schroedl, Jefferson, Wisconsin

1 package (16 ounces) frozen unsweetened whole strawberries
1 pint fat-free frozen vanilla yogurt, softened
1 package (.3 ounce) sugar-free strawberry gelatin
1/2 cup boiling water
2 teaspoons lemon juice
9 cups (72 ounces) diet lemon-lime soda

In a large bowl, mash strawberries with a fork. Stir in yogurt. In a small bowl, dissolve gelatin in boiling water; add lemon juice. Stir into strawberry mixture. Transfer to a freezer-proof container. Cover and freeze for 4 hours or until firm. Remove from the freezer 15 minutes before serving. To serve, scoop 1/2 cup frozen mixture into a glass; fill with 1 cup soda. **Yield:** 9 servings.

Nutritional Analysis: One serving equals 63 calories, 1 g fat (trace saturated fat), 4 mg cholesterol, 77 mg sodium, 12 g carbohydrate, 1 g fiber, 3 g protein.
Diabetic Exchange: 1 fruit.

Olive Pepper Pinwheels

(Pictured below)

These zippy pinwheels are surprisingly simple to prepare ahead of time and have on hand whenever hunger hits. They're also attractive to serve as appetizers for guests.
—Kristin Manley, Montesano, Washington

1 package (8 ounces) reduced-fat cream cheese
1 teaspoon fat-free milk
1/3 cup *each* finely chopped sweet red, green and yellow peppers
1 can (2-1/4 ounces) chopped ripe olives, drained
2 tablespoons ranch salad dressing mix
6 flour tortillas (6 inches)

In a mixing bowl, beat cream cheese and milk until smooth; stir in the peppers, olives and dressing mix. Spread over tortillas. Roll up jelly-roll style; wrap tightly in plastic wrap. Refrigerate for 2 hours or until firm. Just before serving, cut into 1-in. pieces. **Yield:** 3 dozen.

Nutritional Analysis: One serving (2 pieces) equals 68 calories, 4 g fat (1 g saturated fat), 7 mg cholesterol, 226 mg sodium, 6 g carbohydrate, trace fiber, 2 g protein.
Diabetic Exchanges: 1 vegetable, 1/2 starch.

🍎 Reach for Rice Cakes

Rice cakes make a healthy snack, but I like to dress them up a little to add extra flavor. I just sweeten reduced-fat cream cheese with a teaspoon of confectioners' sugar and spread it over the rice cake. Then I top it off with sliced fruits. —*Larry Miller Muncie, Indiana*

Berry Yogurt Shakes

We have a few raspberry bushes in our backyard. If my grandchildren don't get the berries first, I use them in recipes like this one. Of course, the kids love the mellow flavor of these shakes. So either way, they win!
—Jacquie Adams, Coquitlam, British Columbia

2 cartons (8 ounces *each*) reduced-fat lemon
    yogurt
1-1/2 cups fat-free milk
1 cup unsweetened raspberries
Sugar substitute equivalent to 2 tablespoons sugar

In a blender or food processor, combine all ingredients. Cover and process until smooth. Pour into glasses; serve immediately. **Yield:** 4 servings.

Nutritional Analysis: One serving (1 cup) equals 152 calories, 2 g fat (1 g saturated fat), 7 mg cholesterol, 161 mg sodium, 25 g carbohydrate, 2 g fiber, 9 g protein.
Diabetic Exchanges: 1-1/2 fruit, 1 lean meat.

Raspberry Tomato Salsa

(Pictured below)

Inspired by a gift of gourmet salsa, I created my own delightful version that pairs fresh tomatoes and raspberries. My husband and son especially enjoy this salsa with crunchy tortilla chips.
—Dianne Koskinen, Baraga, Michigan

2 cups diced peeled fresh tomatoes
1 cup unsweetened raspberries, mashed
3 tablespoons chopped green chilies
2 tablespoons brown sugar
2 tablespoons finely chopped onion
2 tablespoons grated carrot
2 tablespoons water
1 tablespoon lemon juice
1 teaspoon minced jalapeno pepper*
1 garlic clove, minced
1/2 teaspoon salt

1/4 teaspoon chili powder
Baked tortilla chips

In a bowl, combine the first 12 ingredients. Cover and refrigerate for 2 hours. Serve with chips. **Yield:** 2-1/2 cups.
*Editor's Note: When cutting or seeding hot peppers, use rubber or plastic gloves to protect your hands. Avoid touching your face.

Nutritional Analysis: One serving (2 tablespoons salsa) equals 16 calories, trace fat (trace saturated fat), 0 cholesterol, 71 mg sodium, 4 g carbohydrate, 1 g fiber, trace protein.
Diabetic Exchange: Free food.

Eggplant Snack Sticks

My kids love this unusual snack—and I like that it's healthy. Coated with Italian seasoning, Parmesan cheese and garlic salt, the veggie sticks are broiled so there's no guilt when you crunch into them.
—Mary Murphy, Atwater, California

1 medium eggplant (1-1/4 pounds)
1/2 cup toasted wheat germ
1/2 cup grated Parmesan cheese
1 teaspoon Italian seasoning
3/4 teaspoon garlic salt
1/2 cup egg substitute
1 cup meatless spaghetti sauce, warmed

Cut eggplant lengthwise into 1/2-in.-thick slices, then cut each slice lengthwise into 1/2-in. strips. In a shallow dish, combine the wheat germ, Parmesan cheese, Italian seasoning and garlic salt. Dip eggplant sticks in egg substitute, then coat with wheat germ mixture. Arrange in a single layer on a baking sheet coated with nonstick cooking spray.

Spritz eggplant with cooking spray. Broil 4 in. from the heat for 3 minutes. Remove from the oven. Turn sticks and spritz with cooking spray. Broil 2 minutes longer or until golden brown. Serve immediately with spaghetti sauce. **Yield:** 8 servings.

Nutritional Analysis: One serving (4 sticks with 2 tablespoons sauce) equals 85 calories, 3 g fat (1 g saturated fat), 5 mg cholesterol, 440 mg sodium, 10 g carbohydrate, 3 g fiber, 7 g protein.
Diabetic Exchange: 1 starch.

Spinach Cheese Mushrooms

(Pictured above right)

These stuffed tidbits pack a surprising crunch, thanks to chopped pecans in the cheesy spinach filling. They're fun to serve for a special occasion.
—Debbie Hert, Columbus, Indiana

1/2 pound torn fresh spinach
2 tablespoons water
3/4 cup reduced-fat ricotta cheese
3 tablespoons butter *or* stick margarine, softened
1 egg
2/3 cup grated Parmesan cheese
1/2 cup water chestnuts, chopped
1/3 cup finely chopped pecans, *divided*

56 large fresh mushrooms (about 3-1/2 pounds)
Refrigerated butter-flavored spray*

In a saucepan, bring spinach and water to a boil. Reduce heat; cover and cook for 3 minutes. Drain; squeeze dry and finely chop. In a mixing bowl, beat ricotta and butter until smooth. Beat in egg. Stir in Parmesan cheese, water chestnuts, 3 tablespoons pecans and chopped spinach.

Remove stems from mushrooms (discard or save for another use). Spray inside of mushroom caps with butter-flavored spray. Place caps on a baking sheet coated with nonstick cooking spray. Stuff with spinach mixture; sprinkle with remaining pecans. Bake, uncovered, at 400° for 15-20 minutes or until lightly browned. **Yield:** 28 servings.

***Editor's Note:** This recipe was tested with I Can't Believe It's Not Butter Spray.

Nutritional Analysis: One serving (2 stuffed mushrooms) equals 59 calories, 4 g fat (2 g saturated fat), 15 mg cholesterol, 82 mg sodium, 3 g carbohydrate, 1 g fiber, 4 g protein.
Diabetic Exchange: 2 vegetable.

Frosty Fruit Slush

(Pictured above)

This yummy fruit-filled slush sports a tangy citrus flavor. It's especially refreshing on a warm day, but I make it year-round as an after-school snack. I've found that a soup ladle works well for scooping the mixture into glasses or plastic cups.
—Debra Cornelius, Grant, Nebraska

2 cans (8 ounces *each*) crushed pineapple, drained
1 can (11 ounces) mandarin oranges, drained
5 large ripe bananas, sliced
2 cups sliced fresh strawberries
2 cups water
1 can (12 ounces) frozen lemonade concentrate, thawed
1 can (12 ounces) frozen orange juice concentrate, thawed
1 cup diet lemon-lime soda

In a blender or food processor, place half of the pineapple, oranges, bananas and strawberries; cover and process until smooth. Pour into a large bowl. Repeat. Stir in the remaining ingredients; mix well. Pour or spoon 1/2 cup each into 24 glass or plastic cups. Cover and freeze for at least 2 hours. Remove from the freezer 15 minutes before serving. May be frozen for up to 1 month. **Yield:** 24 servings.

Nutritional Analysis: One serving equals 95 calories, trace fat (0 saturated fat), 0 cholesterol, 4 mg sodium, 24 g carbohydrate, 1 g fiber, 1 g protein.
Diabetic Exchange: 1-1/2 fruit.

Lemon Orange Refresher

This cool thirst-quenching beverage is in hot demand around our home. The tangy flavor of lemon and orange comes through sip after sip in this frosty drink.
—Jodi Tuell, Raymond, California

1 carton (8 ounces) reduced-fat lemon yogurt
1 cup fat-free milk
1 can (6 ounces) frozen unsweetened orange
   juice concentrate
1 tablespoon honey
1 teaspoon vanilla extract
1/4 teaspoon orange extract
15 ice cubes
5 long strips orange *or* lemon peel, twisted into
   spirals

In a blender or food processor, combine the first seven ingredients; cover and blend until slushy. Pour into chilled glasses. Garnish with orange or lemon spirals. Serve immediately. **Yield:** 5 servings.

Nutritional Analysis: One serving (1 cup) equals 124 calories, 1 g fat (trace saturated fat), 3 mg cholesterol, 57 mg sodium, 25 g carbohydrate, trace fiber, 5 g protein.
Diabetic Exchanges: 1-1/2 fruit, 1/2 fat-free milk.

Maple Fruit Dip

Cinnamon pairs nicely with maple syrup in this delicious dip. It makes a wonderful coating for strawberries, bananas and apples...and it's a great way to get people to eat fresh fruit.
—Cathy Liebert, Hartland, Wisconsin

1/2 cup fat-free vanilla yogurt
1/2 cup reduced-fat whipped topping
  4 teaspoons reduced-calorie pancake syrup
Dash ground cinnamon
Assorted berries and fruit chunks

In a bowl, combine the first four ingredients. Cover and refrigerate until serving. Serve with fruit. **Yield:** 1 cup.

Nutritional Analysis: One serving (2 tablespoons of dip) equals 22 calories, 1 g fat (1 g saturated fat), trace cholesterol, 16 mg sodium, 3 g carbohydrate, 0 fiber, trace protein.
Diabetic Exchange: Free food.

Asparagus Ham Rolls

(Pictured at right)

Chock-full of fresh flavor, these scrumptious snacks are perfect to pack for a picnic or ball game. When I'm pressed for time, I prepare the dough for the flaky golden rolls in my bread machine.
—Amy Davis, Folsom, New Mexico

3 to 4 cups all-purpose flour
2 tablespoons sugar
1 package (1/4 ounce) active dry yeast
1 teaspoon salt

1/2 cup fat-free milk
1/2 cup water
  2 tablespoons canola oil
  2 egg whites, *divided*
  1 egg
  1 pound fresh asparagus, trimmed and cut into
    1/2-inch pieces
  1 block (4 ounces) reduced-fat cheddar cheese,
    cut into 1-inch cubes
  2 cups diced fully cooked lean ham

In a large mixing bowl, combine 2-1/2 cups flour, sugar, yeast and salt. In a saucepan, heat milk, water and oil to 120°-130°. Add to dry ingredients; beat just until moistened. Add one egg white and egg; beat until smooth. Stir in enough remaining flour to form a soft dough.

Turn onto a floured surface; knead until smooth and elastic, about 6-8 minutes. Place in a greased bowl, turning once to grease top. Cover and let rise in a warm place until doubled, about 1 hour. Punch dough down. Turn onto a lightly floured surface. Cover and let stand for 15 minutes.

Meanwhile, place 1/2 in. of water and asparagus in a saucepan; bring to a boil. Reduce heat; cover and simmer for 3-5 minutes. Drain. Divide dough into 24 pieces; roll each piece into a 5-in. circle. Place a few pieces of asparagus, a cheese cube and a tablespoon of ham in the center of each circle. Wrap dough around filling, pinching seams to seal.

Place rolls, seam side down, 2 in. apart on baking sheets coated with nonstick cooking spray. Cover and let rise in a warm place until doubled, about 30 minutes. Beat remaining egg white; brush over rolls. Bake at 350° for 18-20 minutes or until golden brown. Remove to wire racks. Refrigerate leftovers. **Yield:** 2 dozen.

Nutritional Analysis: One roll equals 129 calories, 3 g fat (1 g saturated fat), 17 mg cholesterol, 237 mg sodium, 18 g carbohydrate, 1 g fiber, 7 g protein.
Diabetic Exchanges: 1 starch, 1/2 lean meat.

Apricot Peach Smoothies

(Pictured at right)

The mellow mingling of peach, banana and apricot flavors makes this refreshing smoothie so soothing. A spark of tart lemon adds a little tang, but honey keeps the drink on the lightly sweet side.
—DeAnn Alleva, Hudson, Wisconsin

- 1 can (5-1/2 ounces) apricot nectar
- 1 medium ripe banana, frozen and cut into chunks
- 1 cup (8 ounces) fat-free vanilla yogurt
- 2 cups sliced fresh *or* frozen unsweetened peaches
- 1 tablespoon lemon juice
- 1 tablespoon honey
- 1 teaspoon grated lemon peel
- 6 ice cubes

In a blender or food processor, combine all ingredients. Cover and process until smooth. Pour into glasses; serve immediately. **Yield:** 4 servings.

Nutritional Analysis: One serving (1 cup) equals 160 calories, trace fat (0 saturated fat), 2 mg cholesterol, 35 mg sodium, 37 g carbohydrate, 3 g fiber, 4 g protein.
Diabetic Exchanges: *2 fruit, 1/2 starch.*

Strawberry Smoothies

(Pictured above right)

Sun-ripened strawberries are all the fruit you'll want in this basic-but-tasty beverage. If you use fresh berries, set aside a few to garnish glassfuls of the pretty pink drink.
—Diana Leskauskas, Chatham, New Jersey

- 3 cups sliced unsweetened strawberries
- 1 cup (8 ounces) fat-free vanilla yogurt
- 1 cup fat-free milk
- 2 tablespoons nonfat dry milk powder
- 2 tablespoons sugar
- 2 tablespoons reduced-sugar strawberry fruit spread

In a blender or food processor, combine all ingredients. Cover and process until smooth. Pour into glasses; serve immediately. **Yield:** 4 servings.

Nutritional Analysis: One serving (1 cup) equals 153 calories, trace fat (trace saturated fat), 3 mg cholesterol, 79 mg sodium, 32 g carbohydrate, 3 g fiber, 6 g protein.
Diabetic Exchanges: *1 starch, 1/2 fruit.*

Vegetable Spiral Sticks

I love to serve these savory wrapped vegetable sticks for parties or special occasions. They're an easy and impressive appetizer.
—Teri Albrecht, Mt. Airy, Maryland

- 3 medium carrots
- 12 fresh asparagus spears, trimmed
- 1 tube (11 ounces) refrigerated breadsticks
- 1 egg white, beaten
- 1/4 cup grated Parmesan cheese
- 1/2 teaspoon dried oregano

Cut carrots lengthwise into quarters. In a large skillet, bring 2 in. of water to a boil. Add carrots; cook for 3 minutes. Add asparagus; cook 2-3 minutes longer. Drain and rinse with cold water; pat dry.

Cut each piece of breadstick dough in half. Roll each piece into a 7-in. rope. Wrap one rope in a spiral around each vegetable. Place on a baking sheet coated with nonstick cooking spray; tuck ends of dough under vegetables to secure. Brush with egg white. Combine Parmesan cheese and oregano; sprinkle over sticks. Bake at 375° for 12-14 minutes or until golden brown. Serve warm. **Yield:** 2 dozen.

Nutritional Analysis: One serving (2 sticks) equals 97 calories, 2 g fat (trace saturated fat), 2 mg cholesterol, 247 mg sodium, 15 g carbohydrate, 1 g fiber, 4 g protein.
Diabetic Exchanges: *1 starch, 1 vegetable.*

Savory Swiss Cheesecake

(Pictured above)

Big on Swiss cheese flavor, this creamy appetizer is irresistible at a festive buffet table! I served this savory cheesecake before a holiday meal several years ago, and it was the hit of the evening.
—Marjorie Turner, Poquoson, Virginia

1 cup finely crushed thin wheat crackers
3 tablespoons butter *or* stick margarine, melted
12 ounces reduced-fat cream cheese
2 cartons (8 ounces *each*) reduced-fat plain yogurt
1 egg
1 egg yolk
1/4 teaspoon dried basil
1/8 teaspoon dried rosemary, crushed
2 cups (8 ounces) shredded reduced-fat Swiss cheese
Assorted crackers

In a bowl, combine cracker crumbs and butter. Press onto the bottom of a 9-in. springform pan; set aside. In a mixing bowl, beat cream cheese until smooth. Add the yogurt, egg, egg yolk, basil and rosemary; beat on low speed just until blended. Stir in Swiss cheese.

Pour into prepared crust. Place pan on a baking sheet. Bake at 350° for 40-50 minutes or until center is almost set. Cool on a wire rack for 10 minutes. Carefully run a knife around edge of pan to loosen; cool 1 hour longer. Refrigerate overnight. Remove sides of pan. Cut into wedges; serve with crackers. **Yield:** 16 servings.

Nutritional Analysis: One serving (calculated without crackers) equals 169 calories, 11 g fat (7 g saturated fat), 57 mg cho- lesterol, 170 mg sodium, 7 g carbohydrate, trace fiber, 9 g protein.
***Diabetic Exchanges:** 1-1/2 fat, 1 lean meat, 1/2 starch.*

Herbed Cheese Dip

(Pictured above)

A variety of herbs sparks the flavor of this creamy mixture, which is great for dipping fresh veggies.
—Tracy Morgan, Louisville, Tennessee

2/3 cup 1% cottage cheese
1 package (8 ounces) reduced-fat cream cheese, cubed
1 teaspoon red wine vinegar *or* cider vinegar
1/2 teaspoon Worcestershire sauce
1 garlic clove, minced
1/4 teaspoon garlic salt
1/8 teaspoon *each* dried basil, marjoram, savory and thyme
1 tablespoon minced fresh parsley
Green and sweet red pepper strips *or* raw vegetables of your choice

Place cottage cheese in a blender or food processor; cover and process until smooth. Add the cream cheese, vinegar, Worcestershire sauce, garlic and seasonings; cover and process until smooth. Transfer to a bowl. Cover and refrigerate for at least 1 hour. Sprinkle with parsley. Serve with vegetables. **Yield:** 1-1/2 cups dip.

Nutritional Analysis: One serving (2 tablespoons dip) equals 53 calories, 3 g fat (2 g saturated fat), 11 mg cholesterol, 147 mg sodium, 2 g carbohydrate, trace fiber, 4 g protein.
***Diabetic Exchanges:** 1/2 lean meat, 1/2 fat.*

Favorite Eggnog Recipe Made Lighter

CELEBRATING the holidays with eggnog is an American tradition that dates back to Colonial days. Pat Waymire of Yellow Springs, Ohio toasts the season with a smooth and creamy concoction that keeps family and friends coming back for more.

If Pat's classic version is too rich for your taste, try serving your gang a lightened-up alternative from our Test Kitchen. Our home economists fine-tuned the recipe so it calls for 2% milk, fat-free half-and-half cream and just half the number of eggs.

Remarkably, Makeover Eggnog has almost a third fewer calories, just a quarter of the fat and less than half the cholesterol—yet it's still a frothy blend that's thick and satisfying…and is sure to spice up your holidays quite nicely!

Old-Fashioned Eggnog

12 eggs
1-1/2 cups sugar
1/2 teaspoon salt
2 quarts milk, *divided*
2 tablespoons vanilla extract
1 teaspoon ground nutmeg
2 cups whipping cream
Whipped cream and additional nutmeg, optional

In a heavy saucepan, whisk together the eggs, sugar and salt. Gradually add 1 qt. of milk. Cook and stir over low heat until a thermometer reads 160°, about 25 minutes. Pour into a large bowl; stir in vanilla, nutmeg and remaining milk. Place bowl in an ice-water bath; stir frequently until cool. If mixture separates, process in a blender until smooth. Cover and refrigerate for at least 3 hours.

When ready to serve, beat cream in a mixing bowl on high until soft peaks form; whisk gently into cooled mixture. Pour into a chilled 5-qt. punch bowl. If desired, top with dollops of whipped cream and sprinkle with nutmeg. **Yield:** 18 servings (about 3 quarts).

Nutritional Analysis: One serving (3/4 cup) equals 268 calories, 15 g fat (9 g saturated fat), 186 mg cholesterol, 182 mg sodium, 24 g carbohydrate, trace fiber, 9 g protein.

Makeover Eggnog

(Pictured at right)

1-3/4 cups sugar
1/4 cup all-purpose flour
1/2 teaspoon salt
2 quarts 2% milk

6 eggs, lightly beaten
3 teaspoons vanilla extract
2 teaspoons rum extract
4 cups fat-free half-and-half cream
1/2 teaspoon ground nutmeg

In a large heavy saucepan, combine the sugar, flour and salt. Gradually whisk in milk and eggs until smooth. Cook and stir over low heat until a thermometer reads 160°, about 20 minutes. Remove from the heat; stir in extracts. Cover and refrigerate until well chilled, about 2 hours.

Just before serving, strain eggnog mixture; stir in the cream and nutmeg. Pour into glasses. **Yield:** 18 servings (about 3 quarts).

Nutritional Analysis: One serving (3/4 cup) equals 197 calories, 4 g fat (2 g saturated fat), 79 mg cholesterol, 194 mg sodium, 32 g carbohydrate, trace fiber, 8 g protein.
Diabetic Exchanges: 1 starch, 1 reduced-fat milk.

Chocolate Pudding Sandwiches

(Pictured above)

These cookies are a favorite after-school snack for my kids...and even my diabetic husband enjoys one now and then.
—Jan Thomas, Richmond, Virginia

1-1/2 cups cold fat-free milk
  1 package (1.4 ounces) sugar-free instant chocolate pudding mix
  1 carton (8 ounces) frozen reduced-fat whipped topping, thawed
  1 cup miniature marshmallows
  2 packages (9 ounces *each*) chocolate wafers

In a bowl, whisk milk and pudding mix for 2 minutes or until slightly thickened. Fold in whipped topping and marshmallows. For each sandwich, spread about 2 tablespoons of pudding mixture on a chocolate wafer; top with another wafer. Stack sandwiches in an airtight container. Freeze until firm, about 3 hours. Remove from the freezer 5 minutes before serving. **Yield:** 43 sandwiches.

Nutritional Analysis: One sandwich equals 73 calories, 2 g fat (1 g saturated fat), 1 mg cholesterol, 114 mg sodium, 12 g carbohydrate, trace fiber, 1 g protein.
Diabetic Exchange: 1 starch.

Chicken Salad Wonton Stars

This recipe packs a bite-size punch of creamy chicken salad wrapped in a crispy shell. These yummy wonton cups make a great appetizer for a ladies' luncheon or a fun snack anytime.
—Starr Tharp, Parchment, Michigan

  1 package (8 ounces) reduced-fat cream cheese
  3 tablespoons fat-free milk
1/2 teaspoon garlic salt

1/4 teaspoon pepper
  2 cups cubed cooked chicken breast
  2 tablespoons chopped green onion
 36 wonton wrappers
Refrigerated butter-flavored spray*
Paprika

In a mixing bowl, beat the cream cheese, milk, garlic salt and pepper until smooth. Stir in chicken and green onion; set aside. Spritz one side of each wonton wrapper with butter spray; press into mini muffin cups, buttered side down. Bake at 350° for 4-5 minutes or until golden brown. Fill each cup with about 1 tablespoon chicken salad. Bake 5 minutes longer. Sprinkle with paprika. **Yield:** 3 dozen.

Editor's Note: This recipe was tested with I Can't Believe It's Not Butter Spray.

Nutritional Analysis: One serving (1 filled wonton cup) equals 46 calories, 1 g fat (trace saturated fat), 10 mg cholesterol, 101 mg sodium, 5 g carbohydrate, trace fiber, 4 g protein.
Diabetic Exchange: 1 meat.

Salmon-Stuffed Snow Peas

These colorful pea pods are a welcome treat at luncheons and family gatherings. They're simple to make—I just fill a plastic bag with the smoked salmon filling, snip off a corner and pipe it into the pods.
—Leona Schmidt, Madras, Oregon

1/2 pound fresh snow peas (about 75)
  1 package (8 ounces) reduced-fat cream cheese
  1 package (3 ounces) fully cooked smoked salmon, finely chopped
1/4 teaspoon garlic salt
1/8 teaspoon pepper

Place 1 in. of water in a saucepan; add peas. Bring to a boil. Reduce heat; cover and simmer for 1-2 minutes or until crisp-tender. Drain and immediately place peas in ice water. Drain and pat dry; refrigerate.
In a mixing bowl, beat cream cheese until smooth. Stir in salmon, garlic salt and pepper. Transfer to a pastry bag or heavy-duty resealable plastic bag; cut a corner off of bag. Using a sharp knife, make a slit in the top of each pea pod. Pipe in about 1 teaspoon salmon mixture. Cover and refrigerate for at least 1 hour before serving. **Yield:** 25 servings.

Nutritional Analysis: One serving (3 filled snow peas) equals 29 calories, 2 g fat (1 g saturated fat), 6 mg cholesterol, 72 mg sodium, 1 g carbohydrate, trace fiber, 2 g protein.
Diabetic Exchange: 1 vegetable.

🍎 Snack on Frozen Grapes

Frozen seedless red grapes are a delicious and healthy treat. (We like the small dark ones because they're the sweetest.) I just rinse and pat them dry with a paper towel, then put bunches of them in small freezer bags. They make a great anytime snack...and kids love them, too.   *—Loni Milz*
Chippewa Falls, Wisconsin

Simmer Up a Souper Bowl!

Soups are naturally nutritious, oh-so flavorful and sure to please in any season. Whether it's a cool soup in summer or a steaming pot of hearty chili on a winter's day, soup is good for the body—and the spirit!

White Bean Turkey Chili (page 37)

Chicken Dumpling Soup

(Pictured below)

My husband was fooled with this low-fat recipe and I'm sure your family will be, too! A savory broth, hearty chunks of chicken and thick chewy dumplings provide plenty of comforting flavor.
—*Brenda White, Morrison, Illinois*

    1 pound boneless skinless chicken breasts, cut
      into 1-1/2-inch cubes
    3 cans (14-1/2 ounces *each*) reduced-sodium
      chicken broth
    3 cups water
    4 medium carrots, chopped
    1 medium onion, chopped
    1 celery rib, chopped
    1 teaspoon minced fresh parsley
  1/2 teaspoon salt
  1/4 teaspoon garlic powder
  1/4 teaspoon poultry seasoning
  1/4 teaspoon pepper
DUMPLINGS:
    3 egg whites
  1/2 cup 1% cottage cheese
    2 tablespoons water
  1/4 teaspoon salt
    1 cup all-purpose flour

In a large nonstick skillet coated with nonstick cooking spray, brown chicken. Add the broth, water, vegetables and seasonings. Bring to a boil. Reduce heat; simmer, uncovered, for 30 minutes.

Meanwhile, for dumplings, beat the egg whites and cottage cheese in a mixing bowl. Add water and salt. Stir in the flour; mix well.

Bring soup to a boil. Drop dumplings by tablespoonfuls onto the boiling soup. Reduce heat; cover and simmer for 15 minutes or until a toothpick inserted in dumplings comes out clean (do not lift cover while simmering). Serve immediately. **Yield:** 4 servings.

Nutritional Analysis: *One serving (1-1/2 cups) equals 363 calories, 4 g fat (2 g saturated fat), 73 mg cholesterol, 900 mg sodium, 39 g carbohydrate, 4 g fiber, 42 g protein.*
Diabetic Exchanges: *4 lean meat, 1-1/2 starch.*

Canadian Bacon Potato Soup

Canadian bacon adds a hint of smoky flavor to this hearty soup that my husband loves. It doesn't have the typical butter and heavy cream you'll find in many potato soups, but it's still rich and satisfying.
—*Cheryl Morgan, Dover, Minnesota*

    2 medium onions, chopped
    4 medium potatoes, peeled and quartered
    2 cups chicken broth
    1 can (12 ounces) fat-free evaporated milk
    5 slices (3 ounces) Canadian bacon, chopped
    1 packet butter-flavored granules*
  1/4 teaspoon salt
  1/8 teaspoon pepper
    7 tablespoons fat-free sour cream
  1/3 cup minced chives

In a large saucepan or Dutch oven coated with nonstick cooking spray, saute onions until tender. Add potatoes and broth; bring to a boil. Reduce heat; cover and simmer for 20-25 minutes or until potatoes are very tender. Set aside 1 cup potato mixture.

Puree remaining mixture in batches in a blender or food processor; return to the pan. Stir in the milk, Canadian bacon, butter-flavored granules, salt, pepper and reserved potato mixture. Heat through (do not boil). Garnish each serving with 1 tablespoon sour cream; sprinkle with chives. **Yield:** 7 servings.

*Editor's Note: This recipe was tested with Butter Buds mix.

Nutritional Analysis: *One serving (1 cup) equals 156 calories, 2 g fat (trace saturated fat), 9 mg cholesterol, 609 mg sodium, 28 g carbohydrate, 3 g fiber, 11 g protein.*
Diabetic Exchanges: *1 starch, 1 lean meat, 1 vegetable.*

Turkey Tomato Soup

(Pictured above right)

Turkey and tomatoes are high on my list of favorite foods. My husband grows the best tomatoes ever… and I made up this recipe to complement both ingredients. It's wonderful anytime of year.
—*Carol Brunelle, Ascutney, Vermont*

    4 pounds tomatoes, seeded and chopped (about
      8 large tomatoes)
    3 medium green peppers, chopped
    2 cans (14-1/2 ounces *each*) reduced-sodium
      chicken broth
    1 can (14-1/2 ounces) vegetable broth

1-1/2 cups water
1-1/2 teaspoons beef bouillon granules
2 garlic cloves, minced
1 teaspoon dried oregano
1 teaspoon dried basil
1/2 teaspoon pepper
3 cups cubed cooked turkey
3 cups cooked elbow macaroni
Minced fresh basil, optional

In a large saucepan or Dutch oven, combine the first 10 ingredients. Bring to a boil. Reduce heat; cover and simmer for 2 hours. Stir in turkey and macaroni; heat through. Garnish with fresh basil if desired. **Yield:** 12 servings (3 quarts).

Nutritional Analysis: One serving (1 cup) equals 150 calories, 3 g fat (1 g saturated fat), 28 mg cholesterol, 221 mg sodium, 17 g carbohydrate, 2 g fiber, 14 g protein.
Diabetic Exchanges: 1 starch, 1 lean meat, 1/2 vegetable.

Zippy Vegetable Chili

Pinto beans lend protein while vegetables provide home-grown goodness and pretty color to this chunky chili recipe. Green chilies and salsa add a spicy kick.
—Patricia Gibson, Ferguson, North Carolina

1-1/2 cups chopped onions
3/4 cup chopped sweet red pepper
3/4 cup chopped green pepper
1 can (14-1/2 ounces) vegetable broth
2 cans (10 ounces *each*) diced tomatoes and green chilies
1/2 cup salsa
1 tablespoon chili powder
1 teaspoon ground cumin
3/4 teaspoon garlic powder
1 can (15 ounces) pinto beans, rinsed and drained
1 cup fresh *or* frozen corn
1 cup (4 ounces) shredded reduced-fat cheddar cheese

In a large saucepan, bring onions, peppers and broth to a boil. Reduce heat; cover and simmer for 5 minutes. Add tomatoes, salsa and seasonings; return to a boil. Reduce heat; simmer, uncovered, for 12-15 minutes. Add beans and corn; simmer 5 minutes longer or until heated through, stirring occasionally. Garnish each serving with cheese. **Yield:** 7 servings.

Nutritional Analysis: One serving (1 cup) equals 157 calories, 3 g fat (1 g saturated fat), 3 mg cholesterol, 946 mg sodium, 27 g carbohydrate, 6 g fiber, 10 g protein.
Diabetic Exchanges: 2 vegetable, 1 starch, 1 very lean meat.

Sweet Pepper Chowder

Ladle out this hearty soup at your next church potluck and you're sure to win praise! Packed with potatoes, carrots and sweet peppers, this soup is nicely seasoned but not too spicy. My friend's mother made this soup for years. When I decided to open a cafe on the Alaska Highway, I put this chowder on the menu as my house special.
—*Beverly Leveque, Fireside, British Columbia*

6 cups chicken broth
6 medium potatoes, peeled and shredded
4 medium carrots, shredded
4 celery ribs, diced
1 large onion, chopped
1 large green pepper, diced
1 large sweet red pepper, diced
1 small sweet yellow pepper, diced
1/2 cup all-purpose flour
1-1/2 teaspoons salt
1 teaspoon Italian seasoning
1/4 to 1/2 teaspoon pepper
1 cup water
4 cups 2% milk

In a Dutch oven or soup kettle, combine the broth, potatoes, carrots, celery and onion; bring to a boil. Reduce heat; cover and simmer for 20 minutes. Add the peppers; return to a boil. Reduce heat; cover and simmer for 10-15 minutes or until vegetables are tender.

In a bowl, combine the flour, salt, Italian seasoning, pepper and water until blended. Stir into the vegetable mixture. Bring to a boil; cook and stir for 2 minutes until thickened. Reduce heat. Stir in milk; heat through (do not boil). **Yield:** 20 servings.

Nutritional Analysis: One serving (1 cup) equals 92 calories, 1 g fat (1 g saturated fat), 4 mg cholesterol, 500 mg sodium, 18 g carbohydrate, 2 g fiber, 5 g protein.
Diabetic Exchanges: 2 vegetable, 1/2 starch.

Cream of Cauliflower Soup

(Pictured above)

This mildly cheesy cauliflower soup is one of my favorites. I first served it for a bridge luncheon, but it's not just appealing to women. Guys, including my two sons and husband, enjoy it, too.
—*Karen Brown, West Lafayette, Ohio*

1/3 cup green onions (tops only)
2 tablespoons butter *or* stick margarine
2 tablespoons all-purpose flour
1/2 teaspoon salt
2 cups chicken broth
1 package (10 ounces) frozen cauliflower, thawed and chopped
2 cups 1% milk
1-1/2 cups (6 ounces) shredded reduced-fat cheddar cheese
2 tablespoons dry sherry, optional
1 tablespoon minced chives

In a saucepan, saute onions in butter until tender. Stir in flour and salt until blended. Gradually add broth. Bring to a boil; cook and stir for 2 minutes or until thickened. Reduce heat. Add cauliflower; simmer for 2 minutes. Add the milk and cheese; cook and stir until cheese is melted. Stir in sherry if desired. Garnish with chives. **Yield:** 6 servings.

Nutritional Analysis: One serving (1 cup) equals 190 calories, 10 g fat (6 g saturated fat), 32 mg cholesterol, 706 mg sodium, 10 g carbohydrate, 1 g fiber, 15 g protein.
Diabetic Exchanges: 2 lean meat, 1 fat, 1 vegetable.

Flavorful Vegetable Stocks

- When I prepare vegetables, I throw the carrot and potato peels, bean tips, asparagus and broccoli stems, etc. into a small plastic bag in the refrigerator. When the bag is full after a few days, I put these vegetable peelings into a pot of water, boil it for an hour or two, then strain the liquid. It makes a wonderful base for almost any soup.
—*Len Weiss, Poughkeepsie, New York*
- I save the cooking liquid used for boiling vegetables and store it in a container in my freezer. It makes perfect stock for a very tasty and nutritious batch of vegetable soup. —*Barb Schutz, Pandora, Ohio*

Sixteen-Bean Soup

Count on this pleasingly seasoned, hearty soup to satisfy the whole family. My husband and kids say brimming bowls of it are flavorful and filling. I also love the fact that I can make a big pot from a handy bean mix.
—*Laura Prokash, Algoma, Wisconsin*

   1 package (12 ounces) 16-bean soup mix
   1 large onion, chopped
   2 garlic cloves, minced
   1 teaspoon salt
   1 teaspoon chili powder
1/4 teaspoon pepper
1/8 teaspoon hot pepper sauce
   1 bay leaf
   2 quarts water
   1 can (14-1/2 ounces) stewed tomatoes
   1 tablespoon lemon juice

Set seasoning packet from beans aside. Place beans in a Dutch oven or soup kettle; add water to cover by 2 in. Bring to a boil; boil for 2 minutes. Remove from the heat; cover and let stand for 1 hour. Drain and rinse beans, discarding liquid.

Return beans to the pan. Add contents of bean seasoning packet, onion, garlic, salt, chili powder, pepper, hot pepper sauce, bay leaf and water. Bring to a boil. Reduce heat; cover and simmer for 2-1/2 to 3 hours or until beans are tender. Add tomatoes and lemon juice. Simmer, uncovered, until heated through. Discard bay leaf before serving. **Yield:** 10 servings (2-1/2 quarts).

Nutritional Analysis: *One serving (1 cup) equals 79 calories, trace fat (trace saturated fat), 0 cholesterol, 746 mg sodium, 22 g carbohydrate, 11 g fiber, 7 g protein.*
Diabetic Exchange: *1 starch.*

White Bean Turkey Chili

(Pictured at right and on page 33)

Looking for a hearty but healthy chili for your crew? Well, look no further. I serve this robust meal to my gang and they keep coming back for more. Chock-full of ground turkey, white kidney beans and diced tomatoes, it's so full of flavor, your family won't even miss the ground beef!
—*Dorothy Muenzer, Perry, New York*

1-1/2 pounds lean ground turkey
   2 medium onions, chopped
1-1/2 teaspoons dried oregano
1-1/2 teaspoons ground cumin
   1 can (28 ounces) diced tomatoes, undrained
   3 cups beef broth
   1 can (8 ounces) tomato sauce
   1 tablespoon chili powder
   1 tablespoon baking cocoa
   2 bay leaves
   1 teaspoon salt
1/4 teaspoon ground cinnamon
   3 cans (15 ounces *each*) white kidney *or* cannellini beans, rinsed and drained

In a Dutch oven or soup kettle, cook the turkey and onions over medium heat until meat is no longer pink; drain. Add oregano and cumin; cook and stir 1 minute longer. Stir in the tomatoes, broth, tomato sauce, chili powder, cocoa, bay leaves, salt and cinnamon. Bring to a boil. Reduce heat; cover and simmer for 45 minutes. Add beans; heat through. Discard bay leaves before serving. **Yield:** 12 servings.

Nutritional Analysis: *One serving (1 cup) equals 276 calories, 6 g fat (1 g saturated fat), 45 mg cholesterol, 948 mg sodium, 34 g carbohydrate, 13 g fiber, 22 g protein.*
Diabetic Exchanges: *2 starch, 2 lean meat.*

Pasta Sausage Soup

Our family looks forward to a pot of soup every Saturday. This one ranks high at our house because the flavor is so good! The wonderful aroma of Italian seasonings simmering always brings folks to the table. The soup's nicely spiced, and the turkey sausage makes it a little lighter.
—Janet Eggers, Pound, Wisconsin

1-1/2 pounds turkey Italian sausage links
   1 medium green pepper, cut into 1-inch strips
1/2 cup chopped onion
   1 garlic clove, minced
   6 cups water
   1 can (28 ounces) diced tomatoes, undrained
   1 tablespoon sugar
   1 tablespoon Worcestershire sauce
   2 teaspoons chicken bouillon granules
   1 teaspoon salt
   1 teaspoon dried basil
   1 teaspoon dried thyme
2-1/2 cups uncooked bow tie pasta

Remove casings from sausage; cut links into 1/2-in. pieces. In a Dutch oven or soup kettle, cook sausage over medium heat for 5-7 minutes or until no longer pink. Remove with a slotted spoon; drain, reserving 2 tablespoons drippings. In the drippings, saute green pepper, onion and garlic for 4-5 minutes or until tender.

Add the water, tomatoes, sugar, Worcestershire sauce, bouillon, salt, basil, thyme and sausage. Bring to a boil; add pasta. Reduce heat; simmer, uncovered, for 18-22 minutes or until pasta is tender. **Yield:** 10 servings (2-1/2 quarts).

Nutritional Analysis: *One serving (1 cup) equals 222 calories, 12 g fat (4 g saturated fat), 109 mg cholesterol, 761 mg sodium, 15 g carbohydrate, 2 g fiber, 15 g protein.*
Diabetic Exchanges: *2-1/2 lean meat, 2 vegetable, 1/2 starch.*

🍎 Freezing Vegetables for Soups

• When tomatoes are tasty and abundant, wash them and freeze whole in resealable plastic freezer bags. Take them out of the freezer all year as needed. The skins will come right off… and you'll have tomatoes that are ideal in cooked dishes such as soups, chili or spaghetti sauce.
—*Shirley Keiter, Hellertown, Pennsylvania*

• I like to use okra in soups, so I try to keep some on hand in my freezer. I wash fresh okra, blanch it, cool it quickly, then drain it well on a paper towel. I slice it, arrange the slices on a baking sheet and freeze.

Once frozen, the okra can easily be transferred to heavy-duty resealable plastic bags in the amounts called for in my recipes. I stash the bags in the freezer and use as needed.
—*Maxine Ball, La Quinta, California*

Chilled Bean Soup

(Pictured above)

Crunchy fresh veggies combined with black beans and a splash of hot pepper sauce create this spicy chilled soup. I often serve this during the warm summer months, when tomatoes are in season. It tastes best when you let it mellow overnight in the refrigerator.
—Betty Nickels, Tampa, Florida

   4 cups chopped seeded tomatoes
   2 cups picante V8 juice
   1 can (15 ounces) black beans, rinsed and drained
   1 cup chopped cucumber
   1 cup chopped sweet red *or* yellow pepper
1/2 cup chopped red onion
   2 tablespoons balsamic vinegar
   1 teaspoon sugar
1/4 to 1/2 teaspoon hot pepper sauce
1/4 teaspoon ground cumin
1/4 teaspoon salt
1/4 teaspoon pepper
   7 tablespoons reduced-fat sour cream
Sliced cucumber, optional

In a blender or food processor, combine tomatoes and V8 juice; cover and process just until blended. Transfer to a large bowl. Stir in the beans, chopped cucumber, sweet pepper, onion, vinegar, sugar and seasonings. Cover and refrigerate for at least 4 hours or overnight. Serve with sour cream. Garnish with sliced cucumber if desired. **Yield:** 7 servings.

Nutritional Analysis: One serving (1 cup with 1 tablespoon sour cream) equals 122 calories, 2 g fat (1 g saturated fat), 4 mg cholesterol, 485 mg sodium, 21 g carbohydrate, 5 g fiber, 6 g protein.
Diabetic Exchanges: 1 starch, 1 vegetable.

Tomato Green Bean Soup

(Pictured below)

This colorful soup is delicious anytime of year. When I can't get homegrown tomatoes and green beans, I've found that frozen beans and canned tomatoes (or even stewed tomatoes) work just fine. Served with warm breadsticks, this soup is a complete meal. My husband and I enjoy it as a meatless dish, but you could also add diced chicken or ham.
—Bernice Nolan, Granite City, Illinois

1 cup chopped onion
1 cup chopped carrots
2 teaspoons butter *or* stick margarine
6 cups chicken broth
1 pound fresh green beans, cut into 1-inch pieces
1 garlic clove, minced
3 cups diced fresh tomatoes
1/4 cup minced fresh basil *or* 1 tablespoon dried basil
1/2 teaspoon salt
1/4 teaspoon pepper

In a large saucepan, saute onion and carrots in butter for 5 minutes. Stir in the broth, beans and garlic; bring to a boil. Reduce heat; cover and simmer for 20 minutes or until vegetables are tender. Stir in the tomatoes, basil, salt and pepper. Cover and simmer 5 minutes longer. **Yield:** 9 servings.

Nutritional Analysis: One serving (1 cup) equals 71 calories, 1 g fat (1 g saturated fat), 2 mg cholesterol, 779 mg sodium, 12 g carbohydrate, 4 g fiber, 3 g protein.
Diabetic Exchanges: 2 vegetable, 1/2 fat.

Mediterranean Seafood Chowder

My family is not overly fond of seafood. But they really enjoy this rich-tasting soup that combines shrimp and cod. Toss in a green salad and you have a satisfying meal.
—Erin Nicole Morris, St. Peters, Missouri

1-1/2 cups chopped sweet yellow *or* red peppers
1 large onion, quartered and thinly sliced
3 garlic cloves, minced
2 tablespoons olive *or* canola oil
1 can (28 ounces) crushed tomatoes
2-1/4 cups water
1 can (14-1/2 ounces) chicken broth
1 cup uncooked long grain rice
1/2 cup white wine *or* additional chicken broth
1/2 to 1 teaspoon dried thyme
1/2 to 1 teaspoon dried basil
1/2 teaspoon salt
1/8 teaspoon crushed red pepper flakes
8 ounces uncooked medium shrimp, peeled and deveined
8 ounces cod fillets, cut into pieces

In a large saucepan or Dutch oven, saute the peppers, onion and garlic in oil until tender. Add the next nine ingredients; bring to a boil. Cover and simmer for 15-20 minutes or until rice is tender. Add shrimp and cod; cover and simmer for 2-4 minutes or until shrimp turn pink and fish flakes easily with a fork. **Yield:** 10 servings.

Nutritional Analysis: One serving (1 cup) equals 187 calories, 4 g fat (1 g saturated fat), 44 mg cholesterol, 433 mg sodium, 25 g carbohydrate, 3 g fiber, 12 g protein.
Diabetic Exchanges: 2 lean meat, 1 starch.

Chilled Cream of Cucumber Soup

This is a good make-ahead summer soup that is so cool and refreshing. If people like cucumbers, they will enjoy this.
—Doris Heath, Franklin, North Carolina

    1 medium onion, chopped
    2 tablespoons butter *or* stick margarine
    2 pounds cucumbers, peeled
    5 cups chicken broth
1/4 cup minced fresh dill *or* 1 tablespoon dill weed
    1 tablespoon balsamic vinegar *or* white vinegar
1/4 teaspoon salt
1/4 cup quick-cooking farina
    1 cup (8 ounces) reduced-fat sour cream, *divided*

In a large saucepan, saute onion in butter until tender. Slice 1/3 cup cucumbers; refrigerate. Chop the remaining cucumbers and add to onion mixture. Add the broth, dill, vinegar and salt; bring to a boil. Gradually add farina, stirring constantly. Reduce heat; simmer, uncovered, for 20 minutes, stirring occasionally. Cool slightly.

In a blender or food processor, process soup in batches until pureed. Pour into a container; refrigerate until chilled. Just before serving, whisk in 1/2 cup sour cream. Garnish each serving with reserved cucumber slices and 1 tablespoon sour cream. **Yield:** 8 servings.

Nutritional Analysis: *One serving (1 cup) equals 116 calories, 6 g fat (4 g saturated fat), 18 mg cholesterol, 707 mg sodium, 11 g carbohydrate, 1 g fiber, 5 g protein.*
Diabetic Exchanges: *1 vegetable, 1 lean meat, 1/2 starch.*

Herbed Vegetable Soup

You'll get garden-fresh flavor in every spoonful of this satisfying soup. Basil and rosemary accent the veggies nicely.
—Carol Jean Lopez, Westwood, Massachusetts

    3 cups finely shredded cabbage
    1 package (16 ounces) frozen cut green beans
    2 celery ribs, thinly sliced
    2 medium carrots, thinly sliced
    2 small zucchini, chopped
    1 small onion, chopped
    3 cups tomato juice
    2 teaspoons chicken bouillon granules
    1 teaspoon salt-free seasoning blend
1/2 teaspoon dried basil
1/4 teaspoon dried rosemary, crushed

In a large saucepan, combine the first seven ingredients; bring to a boil. Reduce heat; cover and cook for 15 minutes or until vegetables are tender. Add the remaining ingredients; bring to a boil. Reduce heat; cover and simmer for 10 minutes. **Yield:** 8 servings.

Nutritional Analysis: *One serving (1 cup) equals 66 calories, trace fat (trace saturated fat), trace cholesterol, 493 mg sodium, 13 g carbohydrate, 5 g fiber, 3 g protein.*
Diabetic Exchanges: *1 vegetable, 1/2 starch.*

Basil Tortellini Soup

(Pictured above)

This soup is delicious and colorful. I keep the ingredients on hand for a fast meal with a loaf of crusty bread. It's also good warmed up the next day—if there's any left! Making homemade soup couldn't be easier.
—Jayne Dwyer-Reff, Fort Wayne, Indiana

4-1/2 cups chicken broth
    1 package (9 ounces) refrigerated cheese tortellini
    1 can (15 ounces) white kidney *or* cannellini beans, rinsed and drained
    1 cup chopped fresh tomato
1/3 to 1/2 cup shredded fresh basil
    1 to 2 tablespoons balsamic vinegar
1/4 teaspoon salt
1/8 to 1/4 teaspoon pepper
1/3 cup shredded Parmesan cheese

In a large saucepan, bring broth to a boil. Add tortellini; cook until tender, about 6 minutes. Stir in the beans, tomato and basil. Reduce heat; simmer, uncovered, for 5 minutes. Add the vinegar, salt and pepper. Serve with cheese. **Yield:** 6 servings.

Nutritional Analysis: *One serving (1 cup) equals 238 calories, 6 g fat (3 g saturated fat), 20 mg cholesterol, 1,170 mg sodium, 33 g carbohydrate, 4 g fiber, 13 g protein.*
Diabetic Exchanges: *2 starch, 1 lean meat, 1/2 fat.*

Making Homemade Stock

HAVING homemade stock on hand allows you to add a tasty boost to recipes calling for broth, such as soups, gravies and sauces.

To make stock, put the meat/bones, vegetables and seasonings in a stockpot or soup kettle and add cold water. Bring to a boil slowly, then reduce heat to a simmer. As the stock cooks, skim the foam off the top with a slotted spoon to prevent the liquid from clouding.

When it's done, strain the stock; quickly cool it by ladling into smaller containers. Refrigerate. The next day, use a spoon to remove any remaining fat from the surface of the stock. Store in the refrigerator for 1 to 2 days or in the freezer for up to 6 months.

Homemade Chicken Stock

Peppercorns and a handful of herbs add the perfect seasoning to this low-sodium stock developed in our Test Kitchen. To give it even more flavor, we first browned the chicken and sauteed the veggies.

  1 whole chicken (3 pounds)
  1 teaspoon canola oil
  2 medium carrots, cut into chunks
  1 medium onion, cut into chunks
  3 sprigs fresh parsley
  1 bay leaf
1/2 teaspoon dried thyme
1/4 teaspoon dried rosemary
1/4 teaspoon whole peppercorns
2-1/2 quarts cold water
  1 celery rib with leaves, cut into chunks

Cut chicken into parts, reserving back and neck. In a soup kettle, cook chicken breast halves in oil over medium heat until browned, about 5 minutes; remove and set aside. Cook remaining chicken pieces, including back and neck, in two batches until browned; set aside. In the same pan, saute the carrots and onion until onion is tender.

Place seasonings on a double thickness of cheesecloth; bring up corners of cloth and tie with kitchen string to form a bag.

Return chicken to the pan. Add cold water, celery and spice bag. Slowly bring to a boil over medium-low heat. Reduce heat; simmer, uncovered, for 30 minutes. Skim foam. Remove chicken breast halves from pan. Remove meat from bones; return bones to pan. Refrigerate chicken breast meat for another use.

Simmer stock, uncovered, 3-4 hours longer. Strain; discard chicken, bones, vegetables and spice bag. Refrigerate for 8 hours or overnight. Remove fat from surface. **Yield:** about 2 quarts.

Nutritional Analysis: One cup equals 33 calories, trace fat (trace saturated fat), 1 mg cholesterol, 89 mg sodium, 6 g carbohydrate, 1 g fiber, 2 g protein.
Diabetic Exchange: 1 vegetable.

Italian Chicken Soup

(Pictured below)

This satisfying soup from our Test Kitchen gets its Italian flair from fennel, thyme, basil and orzo pasta. If you don't start with a low-sodium or sodium-free stock, you might want to decrease the amount of salt called for in the recipe.

  1 fennel bulb, chopped
1/2 cup chopped onion
  2 teaspoons olive *or* canola oil
  4 cups Homemade Chicken Stock (recipe at left)
    or reduced-sodium broth
  2 cups water
1-1/2 cups chopped carrots
  1 teaspoon salt
1/4 teaspoon dried thyme
1/4 teaspoon dried basil
1/4 teaspoon pepper
  2 cups cubed cooked chicken breast
1/2 cup uncooked orzo pasta
  2 tablespoons finely chopped fennel fronds

In a Dutch oven or soup kettle, saute fennel bulb and onion in oil until fennel is softened. Add the next seven ingredients. Bring to a boil. Reduce heat; cover and simmer for 15 minutes. Stir in chicken and orzo. Cover and cook for 20 minutes or until orzo is tender. Stir in fennel fronds. **Yield:** 4 servings.

Nutritional Analysis: One serving (1-1/2 cups) equals 282 calories, 5 g fat (1 g saturated fat), 55 mg cholesterol, 769 mg sodium, 33 g carbohydrate, 5 g fiber, 26 g protein.
Diabetic Exchanges: 2-1/2 very lean meat, 1-1/2 starch, 1 vegetable.

Peppery Sweet Potato Soup

Roasted jalapeno and red peppers plus garlic accent the delicate sweet potato flavor in this golden soup. The recipe is from my grandmother, who loved making soups that were fast, easy and great-tasting. My family always asks for seconds.
—*Suzan Wiener, Spring Hill, Florida*

    1 jalapeno pepper*
    2 medium sweet red peppers
    5 garlic cloves
    1 teaspoon olive *or* canola oil
    5 cups reduced-sodium chicken broth
    4 cups cold mashed sweet potatoes (prepared
        without milk *or* butter)
1/2 teaspoon salt
    1 cup fat-free milk

Broil whole jalapeno and red peppers 4 in. from the heat until the skins blister, about 7 minutes. With tongs, rotate peppers a quarter turn. Broil and rotate until all sides are blistered and blackened. Immediately place peppers in a bowl; cover with plastic wrap. Let stand for 15-20 minutes. Peel off and discard charred skin; remove stems and seeds. Finely chop peppers.

Place garlic on a double thickness of heavy-duty foil; drizzle with oil. Wrap foil around garlic. Bake at 425° for 15-20 minutes. Cool for 10-15 minutes. Squeeze softened garlic from skins into a small bowl and mash.

In a large saucepan or soup kettle, combine the peppers, garlic, broth, sweet potatoes and salt. Bring to a boil. Reduce heat; simmer, uncovered, for 25 minutes, stirring occasionally. Stir in milk; heat through. Cool slightly. Process soup in batches in a blender or food processor until smooth; return all to the pan and heat through. **Yield:** 10 servings (2-1/2 quarts).

***Editor's Note:** When cutting or seeding hot peppers, use rubber or plastic gloves to protect your hands. Avoid touching your face.

Nutritional Analysis: *One serving (1 cup) equals 166 calories, 1 g fat (trace saturated fat), 1 mg cholesterol, 613 mg sodium, 36 g carbohydrate, 3 g fiber, 4 g protein.*
Diabetic Exchange: *2 starch.*

Fresh Pumpkin Soup

(Pictured below)

This appealing soup harvests the fall flavors of just-picked pumpkins and tart apples...and is sure to warm you up on a crisp autumn day. For an extra festive look, top the creamy puree with a sprinkling of toasted pumpkin seeds.
—*Jane Shapton, Tustin, California*

    8 cups chopped fresh pumpkin (about 3 pounds)
    4 cups chicken broth
    3 small tart apples, peeled and chopped
    1 medium onion, chopped
    2 tablespoons lemon juice
1/2 teaspoon ground ginger *or* 2 tablespoons
        minced fresh gingerroot
    2 garlic cloves, minced
1/2 teaspoon salt
TOASTED PUMPKIN SEEDS:
1/2 cup pumpkin seeds
    1 teaspoon canola oil
1/8 teaspoon salt

In a slow cooker, combine the first eight ingredients; mix well. Cover and cook on low for 8-10 hours or until pumpkin and apples are tender. Meanwhile, toss pumpkin seeds with oil and salt. Spread in an ungreased 15-in. x 10-in. x 1-in. baking pan. Bake at 250° for 50-60 minutes or until golden brown. Set aside.

Cool pumpkin mixture slightly; process in batches in a

blender or food processor. Transfer to a large saucepan; heat through. Garnish with toasted pumpkin seeds. **Yield:** 9 servings.

Nutritional Analysis: One serving (1 cup) equals 102 calories, 2 g fat (trace saturated fat), 0 cholesterol, 567 mg sodium, 22 g carbohydrate, 3 g fiber, 3 g protein.
Diabetic Exchanges: 1 starch, 1/2 fruit.

Broccoli Cheddar Soup

Healthy chunks of broccoli are paired with the tangy taste of cheddar cheese in this hearty soup. A dash of nutmeg and a splash of sherry add pizzazz to a kitchen classic. Using fat-free milk instead of cream reduces the fat but not the flavor.
—Jean Komlos, Plymouth, Michigan

- 1 medium bunch broccoli, coarsely chopped (4 cups)
- 5 teaspoons cornstarch
- 1-1/2 cups fat-free milk
- 1 cup chicken broth
- 1 tablespoon butter *or* stick margarine
- 1 tablespoon sherry, optional
- 1/4 teaspoon salt
- 1/8 teaspoon pepper
- 1/8 teaspoon ground nutmeg
- 1 cup (4 ounces) shredded reduced-fat cheddar cheese

Dash paprika

In a saucepan, bring 1 in. of water to a boil. Place broccoli in a steamer basket over water. Cover and steam for 5-8 minutes or until crisp-tender. Meanwhile, in another saucepan, combine the cornstarch, milk and broth until smooth. Bring to a boil; cook and stir for 2 minutes or until thickened.

Stir in the butter, sherry if desired, salt, pepper and nutmeg. Reduce heat. Add cheese and broccoli; heat just until cheese is melted. Sprinkle with paprika. **Yield:** 3 servings.

Nutritional Analysis: One serving (1 cup) equals 203 calories, 7 g fat (4 g saturated fat), 21 mg cholesterol, 873 mg sodium, 18 g carbohydrate, 1 g fiber, 18 g protein.
Diabetic Exchanges: 2 vegetable, 1 lean meat, 1 fat, 1/2 fat-free milk.

Campfire Bean 'n' Ham Soup

(Pictured above)

These are the best beans and ham you'll ever taste—bar none! Friends rave about this hearty soup that I serve hot off the grill. For easy cleanup, cover the outside of your Dutch oven with heavy-duty foil first.
—Tom Greaves, Carrollton, Illinois

- 1 pound dry navy beans
- 2 small onions
- 8 cups water
- 2 cups chopped celery
- 2 smoked ham hocks
- 4 cups cubed fully cooked lean ham (1-1/2 pounds)
- 1 cup chopped carrots
- 1/2 teaspoon dried basil
- 1/2 teaspoon pepper

Place beans in an ovenproof Dutch oven; add enough water to cover by 2 in. Bring to a boil; boil for 2 minutes. Remove from the heat; cover and let stand for 1 hour. Chop one onion; slice the second onion and separate into rings.

Drain and rinse beans, discarding liquid. Return beans to the pan. Add onions and remaining ingredients. Cover pan and place on the grill rack over indirect medium heat. Cover grill; cook for 1 hour or until beans are almost tender. Uncover grill and pan; cook 30 minutes longer or until beans are tender. Discard ham hocks. **Yield:** 12 servings (3 quarts).

Nutritional Analysis: One serving (1 cup) equals 293 calories, 9 g fat (3 g saturated fat), 43 mg cholesterol, 692 mg sodium, 26 g carbohydrate, 7 g fiber, 27 g protein.
Diabetic Exchanges: 3 lean meat, 1-1/2 starch, 1 vegetable.

3 cups cooked wild rice
1 cup cubed cooked chicken breast
1/4 teaspoon salt
1/4 teaspoon pepper
1 cup fat-free evaporated milk
1/4 cup snipped chives

In a large saucepan, saute the onion, carrot and celery in butter until tender. Stir in flour until blended. Gradually add broth. Stir in the rice, chicken, salt and pepper. Bring to a boil over medium heat; cook and stir for 2 minutes or until thickened. Stir in milk; cook 3-5 minutes longer. Garnish with chives. **Yield:** 10 servings (2-1/2 quarts).

Nutritional Analysis: *One serving (1 cup) equals 180 calories, 6 g fat (3 g saturated fat), 25 mg cholesterol, 899 mg sodium, 22 g carbohydrate, 2 g fiber, 11 g protein.*
Diabetic Exchanges: *1 starch, 1 very lean meat, 1 vegetable, 1 fat.*

Cream of Wild Rice Soup

(Pictured below)

Tender cubes of chicken, fresh vegetables and wild rice make this soup hearty enough for a meal. You can't beat the down-home comfort of a warm bowlful. I like to serve it with whole wheat rolls.
—*J. Beatrice Hintz, Neenah, Wisconsin*

1 large onion, chopped
1 large carrot, shredded
1 celery rib, chopped
1/4 cup butter *or* stick margarine
1/2 cup all-purpose flour
8 cups chicken broth

Bulgur Whets Appetites

DESPITE its exotic-sounding name, bulgur is simply whole grain wheat that has been steamed, dried, then cracked or crushed.

A staple in the Near and Middle East, it comes in coarse, medium and fine grinds. Its chewy texture is similar to oatmeal and it is often found in the cereal or rice aisle in grocery stores.

Bulgur is easy to prepare. Simply place a cup of bulgur in 2 cups of boiling water and cook about 15 minutes. Or bring water to a boil, add bulgur, cover pan and remove from stovetop. Let stand until water is absorbed, 30 to 45 minutes.

It's even easier to serve, warm or cold. Once it's been reconstituted, mix bulgur in salads and side or main dishes for a whole grain boost.

For a different hot breakfast cereal, add a little more water or milk to the reconstituted bulgur in a pan over low heat and simmer until creamy.

Bulgur Chili

(Pictured above right)

This vegetarian chili is zesty, but it also offers a slight hint of sweetness. It doesn't have to simmer for hours like other chili recipes.
—*Jeraldine Hall, Ravenden Springs, Arkansas*

3/4 cup bulgur*
2 cups boiling water
1-1/2 cups finely chopped green peppers
1 large onion, chopped
2 teaspoons canola oil
2 cups reduced-sodium tomato juice
1 can (16 ounces) kidney beans, rinsed and drained
1 can (15 ounces) ranch-style beans, undrained
1 can (14-1/2 ounces) diced tomatoes, undrained

1 can (8 ounces) tomato sauce
1 cup water
2 to 3 tablespoons chili powder
2 garlic cloves, minced
1/2 teaspoon ground cumin
1/8 to 1/4 teaspoon cayenne pepper
3/4 cup shredded reduced-fat cheddar cheese

Place bulgur in a bowl; stir in boiling water. Cover and let stand for 30 minutes or until most of the liquid is absorbed. Drain and squeeze dry. In a large saucepan, saute green peppers and onion in oil until tender. Stir in the bulgur, tomato juice, beans, tomatoes, tomato sauce, water, chili powder, garlic, cumin and cayenne. Bring to a boil. Reduce heat; cover and simmer for 20-25 minutes or until heated through. Garnish with cheese. **Yield:** 9 servings.

*Editor's Note: Bulgur may be found in the cereal, rice or organic food aisle of most grocery stores.

Nutritional Analysis: One serving (1 cup) equals 195 calories, 3 g fat (1 g saturated fat), 5 mg cholesterol, 657 mg sodium, 33 g carbohydrate, 7 g fiber, 11 g protein.
Diabetic Exchanges: 2 vegetable, 1-1/2 starch, 1 very lean meat.

Flavorful White Chili

(Pictured at right)

For a tasty twist on conventional chili, try this low-fat version. It's packed with plenty of beans, tender grilled chicken and a zippy blend of spices.
—Wilda Bensenhaver, Deland, Florida

1 pound dry great northern beans, rinsed and sorted
4 cups chicken broth
2 cups chopped onions
3 garlic cloves, minced
2 teaspoons ground cumin
1-1/2 teaspoons dried oregano
1 teaspoon ground coriander
1/8 teaspoon ground cloves
1/8 teaspoon cayenne pepper
1 can (4 ounces) chopped green chilies
1/2 pound boneless skinless chicken breast, grilled and cubed
1 teaspoon salt
3/4 cup shredded reduced-fat Mexican-blend cheese

Place beans in a soup kettle or Dutch oven; add water to cover by 2 in. Bring to a boil; boil for 2 minutes. Remove from the heat; cover and let stand for 1 hour. Drain and rinse beans, discarding liquid.

Place beans in a slow cooker. Add the broth, onions, garlic and seasonings. Cover and cook on low for 7-8 hours or until beans are almost tender. Add the chilies, chicken and salt; cover and cook for 1 hour or until the beans are tender. Serve with cheese. **Yield:** 6 servings.

Nutritional Analysis: One serving (1-1/3 cups chili with 2 tablespoons cheese) equals 384 calories, 5 g fat (2 g saturated fat), 37 mg cholesterol, 1,224 mg sodium, 53 g carbohydrate, 16 g fiber, 34 g protein.
Diabetic Exchanges: 4 very lean meat, 3 starch.

1/4 teaspoon chili powder
1/4 teaspoon pepper
   1 can (16 ounces) kidney beans, rinsed and
      drained

In a large saucepan or soup kettle, cook the sausage and onion until meat is no longer pink; drain. Add the next 12 ingredients. Bring to a boil. Reduce heat; cover and simmer for 45 minutes, stirring occasionally. Add beans; heat through. **Yield:** 8 servings (2 quarts).

Nutritional Analysis: One serving (1 cup) equals 232 calories, 8 g fat (2 g saturated fat), 47 mg cholesterol, 1,132 mg sodium, 29 g carbohydrate, 5 g fiber, 14 g protein.
Diabetic Exchanges: 2 lean meat, 1 vegetable, 1 fruit, 1/2 starch.

Vegetable Beef Chili

Folks who like their chili hot really get a kick out of this zippy recipe. I serve steaming bowls of it with oven-fresh corn bread. It's so full of garden goodness— with two kinds of squash, tomatoes, green chilies, black beans, etc.—that you can leave out the meat altogether and not miss it a bit.
—Amy Baxter, Bishop, California

   1 pound lean ground beef
   1 large onion, chopped
   1 medium zucchini, diced
   1 medium yellow summer squash, diced
   1 medium sweet red pepper, chopped
   1 can (15-1/2 ounces) hominy, drained
   1 can (15 ounces) black beans, rinsed and
      drained
   1 can (14-1/2 ounces) diced tomatoes with green
      peppers and onions, undrained
   1 cup light beer *or* beef broth
   1 can (4 ounces) chopped green chilies
   1 tablespoon minced fresh parsley
   2 garlic cloves, minced
   2 teaspoons ground cumin
   2 teaspoons dried coriander
   1 teaspoon minced fresh cilantro *or* additional
      parsley
   1 teaspoon chili powder
1/4 teaspoon cayenne pepper

In a large saucepan, cook beef and onion over medium heat until meat is no longer pink; drain. Add the zucchini, yellow squash and red pepper; cook and stir until crisp-tender. Stir in the remaining ingredients. Bring to a boil. Reduce heat; cover and simmer for 20 minutes or until the vegetables are tender. **Yield:** 8 servings (2 quarts).

Nutritional Analysis: One serving (1 cup) equals 223 calories, 6 g fat (2 g saturated fat), 21 mg cholesterol, 439 mg sodium, 23 g carbohydrate, 7 g fiber, 17 g protein.
Diabetic Exchanges: 2 lean meat, 1 starch, 1 vegetable.

Red Bean 'n' Sausage Soup

(Pictured above)

We have many cold months here, and hearty soups served with hot rolls help warm us up. My mom got the recipe for this delicious soup—chock-full of kidney beans, apples and turkey sausage— at a country restaurant in Lima, Montana.
—Tami Christman, Soda Springs, Idaho

   1 pound turkey Italian sausage links, casings
      removed
   1 medium onion, diced
   3 cups chicken broth
   3 medium tart apples, peeled and chopped
   1 can (14-1/2 ounces) crushed tomatoes,
      undrained
   2 tablespoons cider vinegar
   2 tablespoons chopped green pepper
   2 tablespoons chopped sweet red pepper
   2 tablespoons brown sugar
1/2 teaspoon seasoned salt
1/2 teaspoon ground mustard
1/4 teaspoon rubbed sage

Step Up to The Salad Bar

Whether you're looking for a standout side dish to accompany a main course, a tangy take-along for the neighborhood barbecue or an appealing addition to your lunchtime lineup, nothing beats garden-fresh salads!

Antipasto Tossed Salad (page 48)

Antipasto Tossed Salad

(Pictured on page 47)

This is one of the few lettuce salads my husband will eat! Adding lemon juice to bottled dressing is an easy way to give it homemade flair.
—Amy Bauman, Modesto, California

1-3/4 cups thinly sliced halved zucchini
1-1/2 cups cauliflowerets
1/4 cup thinly sliced green onions
1 cup reduced-fat Italian salad dressing
1 tablespoon lemon juice
12 cups torn romaine
2 medium tomatoes, cut into wedges
4 large fresh mushrooms, thinly sliced
4 ounces sliced turkey salami, julienned
4 ounces reduced-fat provolone cheese, julienned
1 can (2-1/4 ounces) sliced ripe olives, drained
1 cup fat-free Italian croutons
1/4 cup shredded Parmesan cheese

In a bowl, combine the zucchini, cauliflower and onions. Combine the salad dressing and lemon juice; pour over vegetables and toss to coat. Cover and refrigerate for at least 4 hours.

Just before serving, combine the romaine, tomatoes, mushrooms, salami, provolone and olives in a serving bowl. Add marinated vegetables; toss to coat. Top with the croutons and Parmesan cheese. **Yield:** 16 servings.

Nutritional Analysis: One serving (1 cup) equals 86 calories, 5 g fat (2 g saturated fat), 12 mg cholesterol, 329 mg sodium, 7 g carbohydrate, 1 g fiber, 6 g protein.
Diabetic Exchanges: 1/2 lean meat, 1/2 starch, 1/2 fat.

🍎 Don't Know Beans About Beans?

ACCORDING to the Michigan Bean Commission, here's what nutrient-rich legumes offer:

- A cholesterol-free, low-fat food by nature, beans are high in fiber. When cooked alone, beans are also very low in sodium.
- Beans supply more calcium and iron per cup than 3 ounces of cooked meat. What's more, beans have fewer calories.
- Think biting into a banana is the best way to get your potassium? One cup of cooked beans will actually give you more.
- Beans are also packed with protein. One cup provides one-fourth of the U.S. recommended daily allowance of protein for adults.
- The protein power of beans is enhanced when you serve them with small amounts of meat, poultry, cheese, eggs or milk.

Confetti Bean Salad

(Pictured above)

This medley of beans won the enthusiastic approval of my husband, who says he'll eat low-fat, low-cholesterol food only if it tastes really good. The peas and corn add crunch and color.
—Bonnie McKinsey, Greenville, South Carolina

1 can (16 ounces) kidney beans, rinsed and drained
1 can (15 ounces) garbanzo beans *or* chickpeas, rinsed and drained
1 can (14-1/2 ounces) Italian diced tomatoes, drained
1-1/2 cups frozen peas
1-1/2 cups frozen corn
1/2 cup chopped onion
1/2 cup chopped green pepper
3 tablespoons red wine vinegar *or* cider vinegar
2 tablespoons olive *or* canola oil
1 garlic clove, minced
1/2 teaspoon salt
1/4 teaspoon pepper

In a large bowl, combine the first seven ingredients. In a small bowl, combine the vinegar, oil, garlic, salt and pepper until blended. Pour over bean mixture; toss gently to coat. Cover and refrigerate for at least 4 hours. **Yield:** 10 servings.

Nutritional Analysis: One serving (3/4 cup) equals 176 calories, 4 g fat (trace saturated fat), 0 cholesterol, 358 mg sodium, 30 g carbohydrate, 8 g fiber, 7 g protein.
Diabetic Exchanges: 1-1/2 starch, 1 vegetable, 1 fat.

Emerald Fruit Salad

This recipe coats an appealing assortment of green fruits with a tangy citrus dressing to create a refreshing salad. It's great for picnics and family gatherings because it's simple yet crowd-pleasing.
—Beth Scholke, Barrington, Illinois

   3 medium tart green apples, cubed
   2 cups cubed honeydew
   2 cups halved green grapes
   3 kiwifruit, peeled, sliced and quartered
   1 cup (8 ounces) reduced-fat plain yogurt
   3 tablespoons confectioners' sugar
   3 tablespoons orange juice
1/2 teaspoon grated orange peel

In a large bowl, combine the fruit. In a small bowl, combine the yogurt, sugar, orange juice and peel. Spoon over fruit; serve immediately. **Yield:** 7 servings.

Nutritional Analysis: One serving (1 cup) equals 136 calories, 1 g fat (trace saturated fat), 2 mg cholesterol, 31 mg sodium, 32 g carbohydrate, 3 g fiber, 3 g protein.
Diabetic Exchange: 2 fruit.

Snow Peas and Beef Salad

(Pictured below)

In this delicious main-dish salad, savory strips of broiled steak are lightly dressed along with water chestnuts, mushrooms and onions, then tossed with crisp snow peas. Ketchup and ginger add a bit of zip to the sweet dressing.
—Janeen Kilpatrick, Fairbury, Illinois

   1 beef flank steak (1 pound)
1/4 cup ketchup
   2 tablespoons canola oil
   2 tablespoons lemon juice
   1 tablespoon brown sugar
1/4 teaspoon *each* garlic powder, garlic salt, ground ginger and pepper
1/2 pound fresh mushrooms, sliced
   1 can (8 ounces) sliced water chestnuts, drained
   1 medium onion, sliced and separated into rings
   1 cup fresh *or* frozen snow peas
  12 lettuce leaves
   2 medium tomatoes, cut into wedges

Broil steak 4-6 in. from the heat for 8-10 minutes on each side or until a meat thermometer reads 170°. Cool completely. Thinly slice meat across the grain; place in a large resealable plastic bag. In a jar with tight-fitting lid, combine the ketchup, oil, lemon juice, brown sugar and seasonings; shake well. Pour over meat; seal bag and turn to coat.

Add the mushrooms, water chestnuts and onion. Refrigerate for 8 hours or overnight, turning occasionally. Just before serving, add snow peas. Serve on lettuce; garnish with tomatoes. **Yield:** 6 servings.

Nutritional Analysis: One serving (about 1 cup salad with 2 lettuce leaves and 1/3 of a tomato) equals 304 calories, 15 g fat (5 g saturated fat), 54 mg cholesterol, 263 mg sodium, 19 g carbohydrate, 4 g fiber, 25 g protein.
Diabetic Exchanges: 3 lean meat, 2 vegetable, 1 starch.

Colorful Tossed Salad

I give fun crunch to a combination of fruit and mixed greens by sprinkling it with macadamia nuts. The vinaigrette enhances the taste of the salad without adding lots of extra calories.
—Lee Bremson, Kansas City, Missouri

1/4 cup white grape juice concentrate
   3 tablespoons white wine vinegar *or* cider vinegar
   2 teaspoons canola oil
1/2 teaspoon salt
1/4 teaspoon onion powder
  10 cups torn mixed salad greens
   8 large fresh strawberries, quartered
   1 kiwifruit, peeled and sliced
   2 tablespoons sliced green onion
   2 tablespoons chopped macadamia nuts, toasted

In a jar with a tight-fitting lid, combine the first five ingredients; shake well. Refrigerate until serving. Set aside 2 tablespoons of dressing. Place the greens in a salad bowl and drizzle with remaining dressing. Top with strawberries, kiwi and onion; drizzle with reserved dressing. Sprinkle with nuts. **Yield:** 8 servings.

Nutritional Analysis: One serving (1-1/4 cups) equals 67 calories, 3 g fat (trace saturated fat), 0 cholesterol, 165 mg sodium, 10 g carbohydrate, 2 g fiber, 2 g protein.
Diabetic Exchanges: 1/2 fruit, 1/2 fat.

Zesty Veggie Salad

This colorful blend of vegetables has been a family favorite for years. I like to pair the salad with seafood.
—Gloria Wall, Buxton, North Carolina

> 2 medium cucumbers, peeled, seeded and chopped
> 2 medium carrots, finely chopped
> 1 cup fresh *or* frozen corn
> 1 cup chopped sweet onion
> 3/4 cup chopped green pepper
> 3/4 cup chopped sweet red pepper
> 3/4 cup fat-free Italian salad dressing
> 2 tablespoons white wine vinegar *or* cider vinegar
> 1 tablespoon lemon juice
> 2 teaspoons sugar
> 1 to 2 teaspoons grated lemon peel
> 1/8 teaspoon pepper

In a large bowl, combine the first six ingredients. In a jar with a tight-fitting lid, combine the salad dressing, vinegar, lemon juice, sugar, lemon peel and pepper; shake well. Pour over vegetables. Cover and refrigerate for at least 2 hours. **Yield:** 6 servings.

Nutritional Analysis: One serving (3/4 cup) equals 85 calories, trace fat (trace saturated fat), 0 cholesterol, 277 mg sodium, 20 g carbohydrate, 3 g fiber, 2 g protein.
Diabetic Exchanges: 2 vegetable, 1/2 starch.

Tossed Greek Salad

(Pictured at right)

Topped with a lemony dressing, this combination of greens, cucumber, olives and feta cheese is typical of a Greek salad. I love the flavors.
—Lisa Hooker, Eugene, Oregon

> 12 cups torn romaine
> 2 medium tomatoes, cut into wedges
> 1 medium cucumber, peeled, halved and sliced
> 1/2 medium green pepper, thinly sliced
> 1/2 medium red onion, cut into rings
> 1/2 cup sliced ripe olives
> 1/2 cup crumbled feta cheese
> **LEMON DRESSING:**
> 1/4 cup olive *or* canola oil
> 2 tablespoons lemon juice
> 2 teaspoons Dijon mustard
> 2 garlic cloves, minced
> 1/2 teaspoon sugar
> 1/2 teaspoon dried oregano
> 1/4 teaspoon salt
> 1/4 teaspoon dried thyme
> 1/8 teaspoon pepper

In a salad bowl, combine the first seven ingredients. In a jar with a tight-fitting lid, combine the dressing ingredients; shake well. Pour over salad and toss to coat. Serve immediately. **Yield:** 12 servings.

Nutritional Analysis: One serving (1-1/4 cups) equals 87 calories, 7 g fat (2 g saturated fat), 6 mg cholesterol, 196 mg sodium, 6 g carbohydrate, 2 g fiber, 2 g protein.
Diabetic Exchanges: 1-1/2 fat, 1 vegetable.

Turkey Salad Sundaes

(Pictured at right)

Here's a fancy way to serve turkey salad. The cute toast cups are easy to assemble, and everyone raves about how well their hearty whole wheat flavor complements the turkey salad.
—Sandra Preuss, Monticello, Mississippi

> 12 slices whole wheat bread, crusts removed
> Refrigerated butter-flavored spray*
> 2 tablespoons grated Parmesan cheese
> 1/8 teaspoon onion powder
> **SALAD:**
> 3 cups cubed cooked turkey
> 1/4 cup finely chopped celery
> 1/4 cup finely chopped onion
> 1/2 cup fat-free mayonnaise
> 1/2 teaspoon seasoned salt
> 1 cup shredded lettuce
> 6 tablespoons salsa
> 1 cup fat-free cottage cheese
> 2 tablespoons crumbled blue cheese
> 3 tablespoons minced fresh parsley
> 6 pitted ripe olives

For each toast cup, place one slice of bread halfway over another; roll flat. Press into jumbo muffin cups coated with nonstick cooking spray. Spritz bread cups with butter spray. Combine Parmesan cheese and onion powder; sprinkle over cups. Bake at 350° for 13-15 minutes or until the bread is toasted. Cool for 5 minutes before removing from pan to a wire rack to cool completely.

For salad, combine the turkey, celery and onion in a bowl. Stir in mayonnaise and salt; spoon into toast cups. Top with lettuce and salsa. Combine cheeses; dollop over each serving. Garnish with parsley and olives. **Yield:** 6 servings.

Editor's Note: This recipe was tested with I Can't Believe It's Not Butter Spray.

Nutritional Analysis: One serving (1 filled toast cup) equals 317 calories, 7 g fat (2 g saturated fat), 68 mg cholesterol, 896 mg sodium, 30 g carbohydrate, 2 g fiber, 34 g protein.
Diabetic Exchanges: 3-1/2 lean meat, 1-1/2 starch.

Minty Fruit Salad

(Pictured below)

Refreshing mint gives this gorgeous salad an unusual twist. It's a "must" on my brunch buffet. Even people who aren't big fruit eaters devour this colorful combination...then ask for the recipe.
—Becky Murdock, Hernando, Mississippi

2 cups cubed honeydew
2 cups halved unsweetened strawberries
1 cup sliced banana
1 cup grapefruit segments
1 cup sliced halved peeled kiwifruit
1 cup mandarin oranges
1/2 cup sugar
1/3 cup orange juice
1/3 cup lemon juice
1/8 teaspoon peppermint extract

In a large bowl, combine the fruit. In a small bowl, combine the remaining ingredients. Pour over fruit and gently stir to coat. Cover and refrigerate for at least 3 hours. **Yield:** 8 servings.

Nutritional Analysis: One serving (1 cup) equals 134 calories, trace fat (trace saturated fat), 0 cholesterol, 6 mg sodium, 34 g carbohydrate, 3 g fiber, 1 g protein.
Diabetic Exchange: 2 fruit.

True-Blue Potato Salad

Blue cheese makes this a deliciously different potato salad. It disappears fast at family gatherings or potluck dinners.
—Wilma Bailey, Sedona, Arizona

2-1/2 pounds small red potatoes, cooked and cubed
3/4 cup chopped green onions

3/4 cup chopped celery
3/4 cup fat-free sour cream
1/4 cup reduced-fat mayonnaise
2 tablespoons minced fresh parsley
1 tablespoon white wine vinegar *or* cider vinegar
1-1/2 teaspoons salt
1/4 teaspoon pepper
1/4 teaspoon celery seed
1/2 cup (2 ounces) crumbled blue cheese

In a large bowl, toss the potatoes, onions and celery. In a small bowl, combine the sour cream, mayonnaise, parsley, vinegar, salt, pepper and celery seed. Pour over potato mixture; toss to coat. Sprinkle with blue cheese. Cover and refrigerate for several hours before serving. **Yield:** 8 servings.

Nutritional Analysis: One serving (1 cup) equals 175 calories, 4 g fat (2 g saturated fat), 12 mg cholesterol, 622 mg sodium, 31 g carbohydrate, 3 g fiber, 7 g protein.
Diabetic Exchanges: 2 starch, 1/2 fat.

Nine-Fruit Medley

I developed this recipe to try to get more fruit into my family's diet. I make it with whatever fruits are in season.
—Barbara Garity, New Windsor, New York

4 cups cubed apples
3 cups cubed honeydew
2 cups cubed cantaloupe
2 cups green grapes
2 medium firm bananas, sliced
1 cup quartered strawberries
1 medium red grapefruit, peeled and sectioned
1 medium navel orange, peeled and sectioned
1/2 cup fresh *or* frozen blueberries
1 cup (8 ounces) reduced-fat vanilla yogurt
1-1/2 cups reduced-fat granola

In a large bowl, combine the fruits; fold in yogurt. Just before serving, sprinkle with granola. **Yield:** 12 servings.

Nutritional Analysis: One serving (1 cup) equals 183 calories, 2 g fat (trace saturated fat), 1 mg cholesterol, 53 mg sodium, 43 g carbohydrate, 5 g fiber, 3 g protein.
Diabetic Exchanges: 1-1/2 starch, 1 fruit.

Kidney Bean and Chickpea Salad

I pick this zesty salad when I need a crowd-pleaser. The dressing blends nicely with the combination of canned beans, tomato and onion. This salad tastes just as good when it's made a day ahead. I've never seen a bowl empty so quickly!
—Terri Webber, Miami, Florida

1 can (16 ounces) kidney beans, rinsed and drained
1 can (15 ounces) chickpeas *or* garbanzo beans, rinsed and drained
1 cup chopped tomatoes
1/2 cup julienned green pepper

1/4 cup thinly sliced onion
1/2 cup reduced-fat ranch salad dressing

In a large bowl, combine the beans, chickpeas, tomatoes, green pepper and onion. Cover and refrigerate. Toss with dressing just before serving. **Yield:** 6 servings.

Nutritional Analysis: One serving (2/3 cup) equals 218 calories, 6 g fat (trace saturated fat), 6 mg cholesterol, 358 mg sodium, 32 g carbohydrate, 10 g fiber, 9 g protein.
Diabetic Exchanges: 2 starch, 1 fat.

Shrimp Salad with Vinaigrette

This is a wonderful light main dish to serve when you aren't in the mood for a heavy meal. I love the fresh seafood flavor and hint of citrus in the dressing.
—*Lisa Casey, Roanoke, Virginia*

3 tablespoons white wine vinegar *or* cider vinegar
1 garlic clove, minced
1 teaspoon sugar
1 teaspoon grated orange peel
3 tablespoons olive *or* canola oil
2 medium navel oranges, peeled
1 pound cooked medium shrimp, peeled and deveined
1 tablespoon diced pimientos
5 cups torn Bibb *or* Boston lettuce
5 cups torn leaf lettuce
1/4 cup sliced green onions

In a large bowl, combine the first four ingredients. Whisk in oil; set aside. Cut oranges into 1/2-in. slices; cut slices into quarters. Add shrimp, pimientos and oranges to dressing; toss to coat. Cover and chill for at least 1 hour. Just before serving, toss shrimp mixture with lettuce and onions. **Yield:** 6 servings.

Nutritional Analysis: One serving (2 cups) equals 174 calories, 8 g fat (1 g saturated fat), 115 mg cholesterol, 130 mg sodium, 9 g carbohydrate, 2 g fiber, 17 g protein.
Diabetic Exchanges: 2 lean meat, 1 fat, 1/2 fruit.

Bacon-Mustard Salad Dressing

The tangy-sweet blend of flavors in this creamy dressing complements lettuce so nicely.
—*Fran Scott, Birmingham, Michigan*

1 bacon strip, diced
6 tablespoons orange juice
1/2 cup fat-free sour cream
3 tablespoons finely chopped green onions (white portion only)
1 tablespoon Dijon mustard
1 garlic clove, minced
2 teaspoons brown sugar
1/4 teaspoon salt
1/8 teaspoon pepper

In a nonstick skillet, cook bacon over medium heat until crisp. Remove with a slotted spoon to drain on paper towels. Add orange juice to the drippings; stir to loosen browned

bits from pan. Place the remaining ingredients in a blender or food processor; add orange juice mixture and bacon. Cover and process until smooth. Store in the refrigerator. **Yield:** 3/4 cup.

Nutritional Analysis: One serving (2 tablespoons) equals 62 calories, 2 g fat (1 g saturated fat), 4 mg cholesterol, 206 mg sodium, 8 g carbohydrate, trace fiber, 2 g protein.
Diabetic Exchanges: 1/2 starch, 1/2 fat.

Colorful Pepper Salad

(Pictured above)

Honey adds a sweet touch to this combination of colorful peppers. I've made it a number of times for small dinner parties.
—*Christa Boylston, Shelby, North Carolina*

3 *each* large green, sweet red and yellow peppers, thinly sliced
18 cherry tomatoes, halved
DRESSING:
1/4 cup finely chopped red onion
3 tablespoons cider vinegar
3 tablespoons olive *or* canola oil
3 tablespoons honey
1 tablespoon Dijon mustard
1/4 teaspoon salt
1/4 teaspoon garlic powder
1/4 teaspoon celery seed
1/4 teaspoon pepper
1/8 teaspoon crushed red pepper flakes, optional

In a large bowl, combine peppers and tomatoes. In a jar with tight-fitting lid, combine the dressing ingredients; shake well. Pour over vegetables and toss to coat. **Yield:** 16 servings.

Nutritional Analysis: One serving (3/4 cup) equals 71 calories, 3 g fat (0 saturated fat), 0 cholesterol, 54 mg sodium, 11 g carbohydrate, 2 g fiber, 1 g protein.
Diabetic Exchanges: 2 vegetable, 1/2 fat.

Curried Walnut Rice Salad

As a busy wife and mother of eight, I'm always on the lookout for tasty and nutritious recipes. With its mild curry flavor, nutty crunch and veggie garnish, this one easily passed my test!
—*Rhoda Wenger, Pilot Mountain, North Carolina*

1-3/4 cups brown rice, cooked and cooled
1 medium cucumber, diced
1/2 cup chopped onion
1 large carrot, shredded
1 tablespoon minced fresh parsley
3 tablespoons fat-free mayonnaise
2 tablespoons canola oil
1 tablespoon lemon juice
2 teaspoons honey
1 teaspoon curry powder
2 garlic cloves, minced
1 teaspoon salt
1/4 teaspoon pepper
1/2 cup chopped walnuts, toasted
4 medium tomatoes, cut into wedges

In a large bowl, combine the first five ingredients. In another bowl, whisk mayonnaise, oil, lemon juice, honey, curry powder, garlic, salt and pepper; stir into rice mixture. Just before serving, stir in nuts. Garnish with tomatoes. **Yield:** 10 servings.

Nutritional Analysis: One serving (3/4 cup) equals 198 calories, 7 g fat (1 g saturated fat), 0 cholesterol, 276 mg sodium, 31 g carbohydrate, 3 g fiber, 4 g protein.
Diabetic Exchanges: 2 starch, 1 vegetable, 1 fat.

2 tablespoons orange marmalade
1 tablespoon lime juice
1/2 teaspoon salt
Dash ground ginger *or* 1/2 teaspoon minced fresh gingerroot
7 cups torn mixed salad greens
3 tablespoons sunflower kernels, toasted

Place asparagus in a 13-in. x 9-in. x 2-in. baking dish. Drizzle with oil. Bake, uncovered, at 400° for 10 minutes or until crisp-tender. Cool.

For dressing, combine the orange juice, oil, marmalade, lime juice, salt and ginger in a jar with tight-fitting lid; shake well. Refrigerate.

To serve, place the greens in a salad bowl or on individual plates; top with asparagus. Drizzle with dressing and sprinkle with sunflower kernels. **Yield:** 6 servings.

Nutritional Analysis: One serving (1-1/4 cups salad with about 2 tablespoons dressing) equals 124 calories, 7 g fat (1 g saturated fat), 0 cholesterol, 224 mg sodium, 14 g carbohydrate, 4 g fiber, 4 g protein.
Diabetic Exchanges: 1 vegetable, 1/2 starch, 1/2 fat.

Roasted Asparagus Salad

(Pictured above right)

Our grandchildren love roasted asparagus—especially in this refreshing salad. The orange dressing gives it "zing", and sunflower kernels add crunch. I like to make it with my homegrown asparagus.
—*Virginia Anthony, Jacksonville, Florida*

1 pound fresh asparagus, trimmed and cut into 1-inch pieces
1/2 teaspoon olive *or* canola oil
DRESSING:
1/2 cup orange juice
2 tablespoons olive *or* canola oil

Summer Spiral Salad

(Pictured below)

Celebrate the freshest tastes of the season by tossing together an herb-enhanced salad. It's a simple and delicious way to perk up picnics and potlucks. Be creative and add sliced zucchini, yellow summer squash or any vegetables your family fancies.
—Evelyn Billingsley, San Antonio, Texas

- **4 cups cooked spiral pasta**
- **1 can (15 ounces) garbanzo beans *or* chickpeas, rinsed and drained**
- **1 cup cherry tomatoes, halved**
- **4 ounces part-skim mozzarella cheese, cut into thin strips**
- **2 ounces turkey salami, cut into thin strips**
- **1/2 cup pitted ripe olives**
- **3 tablespoons canola oil**
- **1/3 cup tarragon vinegar *or* cider vinegar**
- **1-1/2 teaspoons salt**
- **4-1/2 teaspoons minced fresh oregano *or* 1-1/2 teaspoons dried oregano**
- **4-1/2 teaspoons minced fresh basil *or* 1-1/2 teaspoons dried basil**
- **1/8 teaspoon pepper**

In a large bowl, combine the first six ingredients. In a jar with a tight-fitting lid, combine the oil, vinegar and seasonings; shake well. Pour over pasta mixture and toss to coat. Cover and refrigerate for several hours or overnight. **Yield:** 8 servings.

Nutritional Analysis: *One serving (1 cup) equals 269 calories, 10 g fat (2 g saturated fat), 13 mg cholesterol, 801 mg sodium, 34 g carbohydrate, 4 g fiber, 11 g protein.*
Diabetic Exchanges: *2 fat, 1-1/2 starch, 1 lean meat.*

Mandarin Tossed Salad

(Pictured above)

This unique medley with its light dressing is probably my most requested recipe. I often double it and serve it at fancy parties in a clear glass bowl...it's beautiful.
—Edna Coons, Sherman, Connecticut

- **9 cups torn mixed salad greens**
- **1 can (11 ounces) mandarin oranges, drained**
- **1/3 cup thinly sliced green onions**
- **2 teaspoons unsalted sunflower kernels**
- **DRESSING:**
- **3 tablespoons canola oil**
- **2 tablespoons sugar**
- **2 tablespoons cider vinegar**
- **1 tablespoon orange juice concentrate**
- **1-1/2 teaspoons red wine vinegar *or* additional cider vinegar**
- **1-1/2 teaspoons chopped green onion**
- **1/2 teaspoon ground mustard**
- **1/4 teaspoon salt**

In a large salad bowl, gently toss greens, oranges, onions and sunflower kernels. In a measuring cup, combine the dressing ingredients. Add water to measure 1 cup. Pour into a jar with a tight-fitting lid; shake well. Pour over salad and toss to coat. Serve immediately. **Yield:** 6 servings.

Nutritional Analysis: *One serving (1-1/2 cups) equals 140 calories, 9 g fat (1 g saturated fat), 0 cholesterol, 130 mg sodium, 16 g carbohydrate, 4 g fiber, 2 g protein.*
Diabetic Exchanges: *1-1/2 fat, 1 vegetable, 1/2 starch.*

Greek Orzo Salad

Tart and refreshing, this side salad is a big hit at home. With all the tasty toppings—including red onion, tomatoes, olives, feta cheese and a zesty dressing—you'd never know it has just 7 grams of fat. Tiny pasta called orzo gives it extra interest.
—*Judy Roberts, Las Vegas, Nevada*

  1 cup uncooked orzo pasta
  6 teaspoons olive *or* canola oil, *divided*
  1 medium red onion, finely chopped
1/2 cup minced fresh parsley
1/3 cup red wine vinegar *or* cider vinegar
1-1/2 teaspoons dried oregano
  1 teaspoon salt
1/2 teaspoon sugar
1/8 teaspoon pepper
  2 large tomatoes, seeded and chopped
  1 medium cucumber, peeled, seeded and chopped
12 pitted ripe *or* Greek olives, halved
1/2 cup crumbled feta cheese

Cook orzo according to package directions; drain. In a serving bowl, toss orzo with 2 teaspoons oil. In another bowl, combine the onion, parsley, vinegar, oregano, salt, sugar, pepper and remaining oil; pour over orzo and toss to coat. Cover and refrigerate for 2-24 hours. Just before serving, gently stir in tomatoes, cucumber, olives and cheese. **Yield:** 8 servings.

Nutritional Analysis: One serving (3/4 cup) equals 120 calories, 7 g fat (2 g saturated fat), 8 mg cholesterol, 498 mg sodium, 11 g carbohydrate, 1 g fiber, 3 g protein.
Diabetic Exchanges: 1 vegetable, 1 fat, 1/2 starch.

Sesame Chicken Over Greens

(Pictured at right)

My teenage sons can't get enough of this dish. I like it, too. The grilled chicken strips make the salad hearty enough for a meal...but the assorted fresh veggies keep it nice and light.
—*Diana Mullins, Lexington, Kentucky*

1/4 cup reduced-sodium teriyaki sauce
  2 tablespoons red wine vinegar *or* cider vinegar
  2 tablespoons canola oil
  2 tablespoons honey
  2 teaspoons crushed red pepper flakes
  1 garlic clove, minced
  4 boneless skinless chicken breast halves (1 pound)
  5 cups torn mixed salad greens
1/2 cup sliced sweet red pepper
1/2 cup shredded carrot
  4 green onions, sliced
  1 can (2-1/4 ounces) sliced ripe olives, drained
1/2 cup reduced-fat ranch salad dressing
  1 tablespoon sesame seeds, toasted

In a large resealable plastic bag, combine the first six ingredients; mix well. Add chicken; seal bag and turn to coat. Refrigerate for several hours or overnight. Drain and discard marinade. Grill chicken, uncovered, over medium heat for 5-7 minutes on each side or until juices run clear.

On four serving plates, divide the greens, red pepper, carrot, onions and olives. Thinly slice chicken and arrange over salad. Drizzle with ranch dressing; sprinkle with sesame seeds. **Yield:** 4 servings.

Nutritional Analysis: One serving (1 chicken breast half with about 1-1/2 cups salad and 2 tablespoons dressing) equals 347 calories, 16 g fat (2 g saturated fat), 71 mg cholesterol, 788 mg sodium, 21 g carbohydrate, 2 g fiber, 30 g protein.
Diabetic Exchanges: 3-1/2 lean meat, 2 fat, 2 vegetable.

Strawberry Spinach Salad

(Pictured at right)

Not only is this salad a treat to eat, it's a delight to the eyes, thanks to the vibrant green and red ingredients. I made it by combining several recipes, then added a few extra touches. It's great to serve at a ladies' luncheon.
—*Cathy Linzbach, East Grand Forks, Minnesota*

  8 cups torn fresh spinach
  2 cups sliced fresh strawberries
  2 tablespoons finely chopped onion
  1 tablespoon sunflower kernels
1/2 teaspoon sesame seeds, toasted
  2 tablespoons canola oil
  2 tablespoons red wine vinegar *or* cider vinegar
4-1/2 teaspoons sugar
1-1/2 teaspoons snipped fresh dill *or* 1/2 teaspoon dill weed
1/8 teaspoon salt
1/8 teaspoon garlic powder
1/8 teaspoon ground mustard

In a salad bowl, combine the spinach, strawberries, onion, sunflower kernels and sesame seeds. In a jar with a tight-fitting lid, combine the remaining ingredients; shake well. Pour over salad and gently toss to coat. Serve immediately. **Yield:** 8 servings.

Nutritional Analysis: One serving (1 cup) equals 68 calories, 4 g fat (trace saturated fat), 0 cholesterol, 61 mg sodium, 7 g carbohydrate, 2 g fiber, 1 g protein.
Diabetic Exchanges: 1 vegetable, 1/2 fruit, 1/2 fat.

Two-Cabbage Slaw

(Pictured below)

If you'd like to make a summer barbecue festive, bring out this eye-catching side dish with a zesty dressing. It's a great way to use up homegrown produce.
—Carol Gaus, Itasca, Illinois

    4 cups shredded green cabbage
    1 cup shredded red cabbage
    1 medium green pepper, chopped
    1 medium sweet red pepper, chopped
    4 green onions, finely chopped
DRESSING:
    1 cup (8 ounces) reduced-fat sour cream
    3 tablespoons tarragon vinegar *or* cider vinegar
    1 tablespoon sugar
    1 teaspoon salt
    3/4 teaspoon celery seed
    1/4 teaspoon white pepper

In a large bowl, combine the first five ingredients. In a small bowl, combine the dressing ingredients. Pour over cabbage mixture and stir to coat. Serve immediately. **Yield:** 6 servings.

Nutritional Analysis: One serving (1 cup) equals 140 calories, 4 g fat (3 g saturated fat), 13 mg cholesterol, 465 mg sodium, 21 g carbohydrate, 6 g fiber, 6 g protein.
Diabetic Exchanges: 2 vegetable, 1 fat, 1/2 starch.

Vegetable Barley Salad

I serve this salad to family, friends and even people who don't like barley—and they end up asking for the recipe. I sometimes turn it into a main dish by adding leftover meat.
—Marge Chapko, Eau Claire, Wisconsin

    1 can (14-1/2 ounces) chicken broth
    1/2 cup medium pearl barley
    1 cup chopped fresh mushrooms
    3/4 cup chopped celery
    1/2 cup chopped water chestnuts
    1/2 cup chopped green pepper
    1/3 cup shredded carrot
    1/4 cup chopped green onions
    1 garlic clove, minced
 1-1/2 teaspoons dill weed
    1/2 teaspoon dried basil
    1/2 teaspoon salt
    1/3 cup red wine vinaigrette salad dressing

In a saucepan, bring broth to a boil. Stir in barley. Reduce heat; cover and simmer for 40-45 minutes or until tender. Meanwhile, in a salad bowl, combine mushrooms, celery, water chestnuts, green pepper, carrot, onions, garlic, dill, basil and salt; mix well. Add the barley and salad dressing; stir to coat. Serve warm or cold. **Yield:** 4 servings.

Nutritional Analysis: One serving (1 cup) equals 191 calories, 8 g fat (1 g saturated fat), 0 cholesterol, 1,067 mg sodium, 26 g carbohydrate, 6 g fiber, 5 g protein.
Diabetic Exchanges: 1-1/2 starch, 1 fat, 1/2 lean meat.

Grilled Corn Pasta Salad

This colorful dish from our Test Kitchen is especially tasty when sweet corn, tomatoes and zucchini are in season. The garden-fresh ingredients are lightly dressed with basil vinegar and oil.

    4 large ears sweet corn in husks
    2 cups cooked medium tube pasta
    2 cups cherry tomatoes
    1 medium zucchini, thinly sliced
    1/2 cup sliced ripe olives
    1/3 cup basil vinegar (recipe on page 84)
    2 tablespoons olive *or* canola oil
    1 tablespoon chopped fresh basil *or* 1 teaspoon dried basil
    1 teaspoon sugar
    1 teaspoon salt
    1/2 teaspoon ground mustard
    1/4 teaspoon garlic powder
    1/4 teaspoon pepper

Grill corn in husks, covered, over medium heat for 10-15 minutes or until tender, turning often. Cool. Cut corn off the cob; place in a large bowl. Add pasta, tomatoes, zucchini and olives. In a small bowl, combine the remaining ingredients; mix well. Pour over salad and stir gently. Cover and refrigerate until serving. **Yield:** 8 servings.

Nutritional Analysis: One serving (1 cup) equals 164 calories, 6 g fat (1 g saturated fat), 0 cholesterol, 382 mg sodium, 27 g carbohydrate, 3 g fiber, 5 g protein.
Diabetic Exchanges: 1-1/2 starch, 1 fat.

Ham and Turkey Pasta Salad

When a potluck's coming up, people always ask me to bring what they call "that noodle salad you make". Based on the raves it's received at past gatherings, I know folks are referring to this delicious meaty dish.
—*Lori Cole, Broken Arrow, Oklahoma*

3-3/4 cups uncooked bow tie pasta
    1 cup chopped fully cooked lean ham
    1 cup chopped cooked turkey breast
    1 cup (4 ounces) shredded reduced-fat cheddar cheese
  1/4 cup chopped onion
  1/4 cup chopped celery
    1 hard-cooked egg, chopped
    1 cup fat-free mayonnaise
  1/4 cup picante sauce
    1 teaspoon salt
  1/4 teaspoon pepper
  1/4 teaspoon sugar

Cook pasta according to package directions; drain and rinse with cold water. In a large bowl, combine the pasta, ham, turkey, cheese, onion, celery and egg. In a small bowl, combine the remaining ingredients. Pour over salad and gently toss to coat. Cover and refrigerate for 2 hours before serving. **Yield:** 10 servings.

Nutritional Analysis: One serving (about 3/4 cup) equals 203 calories, 4 g fat (1 g saturated fat), 50 mg cholesterol, 734 mg sodium, 26 g carbohydrate, 2 g fiber, 16 g protein.
Diabetic Exchanges: 1-1/2 starch, 1-1/2 lean meat.

Grapefruit Pork Salad

(Pictured above)

I found the recipe for this salad starring stir-fried pork tenderloin years ago and adapted it a bit.
—*Sarah Hickman, Cardington, Ohio*

  1/4 cup unsweetened grapefruit juice
    2 tablespoons red wine vinegar *or* cider vinegar
    1 tablespoon canola oil
    2 teaspoons honey
    1 teaspoon prepared mustard
    1 teaspoon poppy seeds
  1/8 plus 1/4 teaspoon salt, *divided*
    1 pound pork tenderloin, julienned
    1 bunch leaf lettuce, torn
    1 medium pink grapefruit, peeled and sectioned
    1 medium white grapefruit, peeled and sectioned
1-1/2 cups halved green grapes
    1 cup quartered fresh strawberries

In a jar with a tight-fitting lid, combine the grapefruit juice, vinegar, oil, honey, mustard, poppy seeds and 1/8 teaspoon salt; shake well and set aside.

In a nonstick skillet coated with nonstick cooking spray, stir-fry pork with remaining salt until no longer pink. Place lettuce on a platter; top with warm pork. Arrange grapefruit, grapes and strawberries around pork. Shake dressing; drizzle over salad. **Yield:** 4 servings.

Nutritional Analysis: One serving equals 311 calories, 10 g fat (2 g saturated fat), 62 mg cholesterol, 354 mg sodium, 30 g carbohydrate, 6 g fiber, 28 g protein.
Diabetic Exchanges: 3 lean meat, 1-1/2 fruit, 1 fat.

Brown and Wild Rice Salad

This side dish, developed by our Test Kitchen, is twice as nice since it stars both brown and wild rice! Tangy raspberry vinegar complements the nutty flavor of the rice, while dried cranberries provide sweetness.

    1 cup brown rice, cooked
    1 cup wild rice, cooked
    6 green onions, chopped
  3/4 cup dried cranberries
  1/3 cup coarsely chopped pecans, toasted
    2 tablespoons chopped fresh parsley
  1/4 cup olive *or* canola oil
    6 tablespoons raspberry vinegar (recipe on page 84)
    2 tablespoons honey
1-1/2 teaspoons salt
  1/2 teaspoon pepper

In a large bowl, combine the first six ingredients. In a small bowl, combine the oil, vinegar, honey, salt and pepper. Pour over salad and toss to coat. **Yield:** 8 servings.

Nutritional Analysis: One serving (1 cup) equals 343 calories, 12 g fat (1 g saturated fat), 0 cholesterol, 450 mg sodium, 55 g carbohydrate, 5 g fiber, 6 g protein.
Diabetic Exchanges: 2-1/2 starch, 2 fat, 1 fruit.

Black Bean Pasta Salad

Cooking healthy doesn't mean you have to spend hours in a hot kitchen. I serve a low-fat, fuss-free fiesta at my home by simply combining and refrigerating a few tasty ingredients.
—*Debbie Jones, California, Maryland*

8 ounces rigatoni *or* penne pasta
1 jar (16 ounces) salsa
1 can (15 ounces) black beans, rinsed and drained
2 cups (8 ounces) shredded reduced-fat Mexican-blend cheese
1/2 cup chopped green pepper
1 small onion, chopped
1/2 teaspoon salt
1/8 teaspoon pepper

Cook pasta according to package directions; drain and rinse in cold water. Place in a bowl; stir in the remaining ingredients. Cover and refrigerate for 30 minutes before serving. **Yield:** 9 servings.

Nutritional Analysis: One serving (1 cup) equals 203 calories, 5 g fat (3 g saturated fat), 9 mg cholesterol, 538 mg sodium, 28 g carbohydrate, 4 g fiber, 13 g protein.
Diabetic Exchanges: 1-1/2 starch, 1-1/2 lean meat.

Garlic Green and Wax Beans

(Pictured above)

This fresh-tasting salad often appears on my summer menus. Even non-garlic lovers can't get enough of it.
—*Marilou Robinson, Portland, Oregon*

1-1/2 pounds fresh green beans
1-1/2 pounds fresh wax beans
7 garlic cloves, minced, *divided*
1/4 cup reduced-fat sour cream
1/4 cup fat-free milk
1 teaspoon white wine vinegar *or* cider vinegar
1 teaspoon olive *or* canola oil
1/2 teaspoon salt
1/8 teaspoon pepper
1 cup shredded part-skim mozzarella cheese
Minced fresh parsley

In a large saucepan, place beans and six garlic cloves in a steamer basket over 1 in. of boiling water. Cover and steam for 8-10 minutes or until beans are crisp-tender. Transfer to a large bowl; set aside. In a small bowl, combine sour cream, milk and vinegar; let stand for 1 minute. Whisk in the oil, salt, pepper and remaining garlic. Pour over beans and toss. Cover and chill for at least 2 hours. Just before serving, sprinkle with cheese and parsley. **Yield:** 12 servings.

Nutritional Analysis: One serving (3/4 cup) equals 76 calories, 2 g fat (1 g saturated fat), 7 mg cholesterol, 157 mg sodium, 9 g carbohydrate, 4 g fiber, 5 g protein.
Diabetic Exchanges: 2 vegetable, 1/2 fat.

Tangy Vegetable Pasta Salad

The variety of ingredients in this delicious pasta salad will take your taste buds in different directions. It's surprising how well the zippy citrus and raw vegetable flavors blend.
—*Wilma Jones, Mobile, Alabama*

2-1/4 cups uncooked spiral pasta
2 tablespoons lemon juice
3 plum tomatoes, sliced
1/2 cup chopped green pepper
1/2 cup sliced radishes
1/2 cup chopped peeled cucumber

Steaming Secrets

- Don't overload your steamer. Food should be spread in a shallow layer so that each piece cooks evenly.
- Add subtle flavor by putting fresh herbs, spices, seasoning mixes or flavored vinegar in the water before cooking.
- Leave the lid on and restrain yourself from peeking repeatedly. The temperature and pressure inside the pan need to rise sufficiently to steam the food.
- Timing is important to avoid under- or over-cooking. When food is put in the steamer, the water temperature drops slightly. Begin timing as soon as the water begins boiling again.

DRESSING:
- 1/3 cup picante V8 juice
- 1/4 cup orange juice
- 2 tablespoons lemon juice
- 2 tablespoons chopped green onion
- 1 tablespoon canola oil
- 1-1/2 teaspoons sugar
- 1 teaspoon grated lemon peel
- 1 teaspoon grated orange peel
- 1/2 teaspoon salt
- 1/2 teaspoon dill weed

Cook pasta according to package directions, adding the lemon juice to the water. Drain and cool. In a large bowl, combine the pasta, tomatoes, green pepper, radishes and cucumber. In a jar with a tight-fitting lid, combine the dressing ingredients; shake well. Pour over salad and toss to coat. Cover and refrigerate until serving. **Yield:** 6 servings.

Nutritional Analysis: One serving (1 cup) equals 184 calories, 3 g fat (trace saturated fat), 0 cholesterol, 254 mg sodium, 31 g carbohydrate, 2 g fiber, 8 g protein.
Diabetic Exchanges: 1-1/2 starch, 1 vegetable, 1/2 fat.

Tortellini Bean Salad

(Pictured below)

Beans will bring bravos when you present this pleasant pasta and veggie salad. I first made it for friends who are very good cooks. When it was gone, they asked where the second bowl was. Among my make-ahead favorites, it's a hit every time I serve it.
—Lenore Adams, Dayton, Ohio

- 1 package (10 ounces) refrigerated spinach tortellini
- 2 cups broccoli florets
- 1/2 large red onion, thinly sliced
- 1 cup canned garbanzo beans *or* chickpeas, rinsed and drained
- 1 cup canned red kidney beans, rinsed and drained
- 1 cup canned white kidney *or* cannellini beans, rinsed and drained
- 1 can (6 ounces) pitted ripe olives, drained
- 1 bottle (8 ounces) fat-free creamy Italian salad dressing
- 1/4 cup shredded Parmesan cheese, *divided*
- 1 teaspoon dried oregano
- 24 cherry tomatoes, halved

Prepare tortellini according to package directions; drain and place in a serving bowl. Add broccoli, onion, beans and olives. Combine the salad dressing, 2 tablespoons Parmesan cheese and oregano; pour over salad and toss gently. Cover and refrigerate for at least 8 hours. Just before serving, stir in tomatoes and sprinkle with remaining Parmesan. **Yield:** 9 servings.

Nutritional Analysis: One serving (1 cup) equals 218 calories, 6 g fat (2 g saturated fat), 44 mg cholesterol, 758 mg sodium, 31 g carbohydrate, 7 g fiber, 10 g protein.
Diabetic Exchanges: 2 starch, 1 lean meat.

Layered Fruit Salad

To dress up a fresh fruit salad, top it with a sweet creamy concoction. The original recipe called for heavy whipping cream, but I lightened it up a little. Served in a cut-glass bowl, this salad looks elegant on any table. It's quick and easy to make but looks like you fussed.
—Linda Cowan, Fayette, Alabama

- 2 cups sliced fresh peaches
- 2 cups fresh blueberries
- 2 cups sliced fresh strawberries
- 2 cups halved green grapes
- 1 package (8 ounces) reduced-fat cream cheese
- 1/2 cup confectioners' sugar
- 1 carton (8 ounces) reduced-fat frozen whipped topping, thawed
- 1/4 cup chopped pecans

In a 2-1/2-qt. glass bowl, layer the fruits in the order listed. In a mixing bowl, beat the cream cheese and confectioners' sugar until smooth; fold in whipped topping. Spoon over fruit. Refrigerate until serving. Sprinkle with pecans. **Yield:** 10 servings.

Nutritional Analysis: One serving (3/4 cup) equals 206 calories, 9 g fat (6 g saturated fat), 13 mg cholesterol, 69 mg sodium, 27 g carbohydrate, 3 g fiber, 3 g protein.
Diabetic Exchanges: 1-1/2 fat, 1 starch, 1 fruit.

Red Pepper Salad with Parsley Dressing

(Pictured at right)

A tangy sour cream dressing tops this colorful combination of veggies. I get rave reviews whenever I serve this crunchy salad.
—Mary-Lynne Mason, Janesville, Wisconsin

1/3 cup finely chopped onion
1/3 cup olive *or* canola oil
1/4 cup minced fresh parsley
  2 tablespoons red wine vinegar *or* cider vinegar
  2 tablespoons reduced-fat sour cream
  1 teaspoon salt
  1 teaspoon sugar
1/4 to 1/2 teaspoon pepper
  6 cups torn Boston lettuce
  2 cups watercress, stems removed
3-1/2 cups sliced fresh mushrooms
  1 teaspoon lemon juice
  2 large sweet red peppers, cut into 1-inch pieces

In a jar with a tight-fitting lid, combine the first eight ingredients; shake well. Refrigerate until serving. In a salad bowl, combine the lettuce and watercress. Toss the mushrooms with lemon juice; add to greens. Top with red peppers. Add dressing and toss to coat. **Yield:** 8 servings.

Nutritional Analysis: One serving (1 cup) equals 116 calories, 10 g fat (2 g saturated fat), 1 mg cholesterol, 305 mg sodium, 7 g carbohydrate, 2 g fiber, 2 g protein.
Diabetic Exchanges: 2 fat, 1 vegetable.

Corn Relish Salad

(Pictured at right)

My family enjoys hiking in the mountains. This salad is great with chicken or trout grilled over a campfire. It's also perfect for backyard picnics.
—Claudia Poynter, Augusta, Kansas

  2 cups fresh *or* frozen corn
  3 medium tomatoes, seeded and chopped
  1 medium green pepper, diced
1/2 cup chopped red onion
1/2 cup sliced celery
  1 can (2-1/4 ounces) sliced ripe olives, drained
  1 jar (6-1/2 ounces) marinated artichoke hearts, undrained
1/4 cup reduced-fat Italian salad dressing
  5 fresh basil leaves, finely chopped *or* 1 teaspoon dried basil
1/2 teaspoon garlic powder
1/2 teaspoon dried oregano
1/4 teaspoon lemon-pepper seasoning

In a large bowl, combine the first six ingredients. In another bowl, combine the artichokes, salad dressing, basil, garlic powder, oregano and lemon-pepper. Add to corn mixture and toss gently. Cover and refrigerate for at least 6 hours before serving. **Yield:** 10 servings.

Nutritional Analysis: One serving (3/4 cup) equals 68 calories, 2 g fat (trace saturated fat), trace cholesterol, 193 mg sodium, 13 g carbohydrate, 2 g fiber, 2 g protein.
Diabetic Exchange: 1 starch.

Veggies in Vinaigrette

This garden-fresh veggie side dish is so good, even people who don't like turnips ask for the recipe. Try substituting a different flavored vinegar to put a personal touch on this colorful crowd-pleaser.
—Wendy Oler, Winnipeg, Manitoba

  1 cup broccoli florets
  1 cup thinly sliced carrots
  1 cup cauliflowerets
  1 small turnip, peeled and cut into 2-inch julienne strips
  1 small onion, halved and thinly sliced
1/4 cup cider vinegar
1/4 cup canola oil
  2 tablespoons sugar
  1 tablespoon minced fresh parsley
  1 garlic clove, minced
  1 teaspoon salt
1/4 teaspoon dried basil
1/4 teaspoon dried tarragon

Place the broccoli, carrots, cauliflower and turnip in a large saucepan; cover with water. Bring to a boil. Reduce heat; cover and simmer for 3-5 minutes or until vegetables are crisp-tender. Drain and rinse in cold water. Place vegetables in a large bowl; add onion. In a jar with a tight-fitting lid, combine the remaining ingredients; shake well. Pour over vegetables and toss to coat. Cover and refrigerate for at least 2 hours, stirring occasionally. **Yield:** 6 servings.

Nutritional Analysis: One serving (2/3 cup) equals 126 calories, 9 g fat (1 g saturated fat), 0 cholesterol, 420 mg sodium, 11 g carbohydrate, 1 g fiber, 1 g protein.
Diabetic Exchanges: 2 vegetable, 1-1/2 fat.

Cannellini Spinach Pasta Salad

To put a hearty spin on spinach salad, I added white beans and pasta shells. It makes a pretty side dish with any meal.
—*Virgie Praglowski, Torrance, California*

8 cups fresh spinach, coarsely chopped
3 cups small shell pasta, cooked and drained
1 can (15 ounces) cannellini *or* white kidney beans
3 tablespoons balsamic vinegar
2 tablespoons olive *or* canola oil
2 teaspoons sugar
2 garlic cloves, minced
1/2 teaspoon salt
1/4 teaspoon pepper
1/2 cup shredded Parmesan cheese

In a large bowl, combine the spinach, pasta and beans. In a jar with a tight-fitting lid, combine the vinegar, oil, sugar, garlic, salt and pepper; shake well. Pour over salad; toss to coat. Sprinkle with cheese. Serve immediately. **Yield:** 10 servings.

Nutritional Analysis: *One serving (1 cup) equals 157 calories, 5 g fat (2 g saturated fat), 3 mg cholesterol, 243 mg sodium, 21 g carbohydrate, 3 g fiber, 7 g protein.*
Diabetic Exchanges: *1 starch, 1 vegetable, 1 fat.*

Seven-Vegetable Salad

Italian dressing jazzed up with basil and chives sparks the flavor of this eye-catching salad. The blanched veggies in this colorful combination retain their crispness quite nicely.
—*Sara Lindler, Irmo, South Carolina*

1 cup cut fresh green beans
1 cup fresh sugar snap peas
1 cup sliced yellow summer squash
1 cup sliced zucchini
1/2 cup julienned onion
2 small tomatoes, seeded and chopped
1 cup coarsely grated carrots
2/3 cup reduced-fat Italian salad dressing
4 teaspoons minced chives
2 teaspoons dried basil

In a saucepan, bring 2 in. of water to a boil. Add beans, peas, yellow squash, zucchini and onion. Reduce heat; cover and simmer for 2-3 minutes or until vegetables are crisp-tender. Drain; rinse with cold water and pat dry.
Place vegetables in a bowl; add the remaining ingredi-

ents. Gently stir to coat. Refrigerate until serving. **Yield:** 12 servings.

Nutritional Analysis: *One serving (1/2 cup) equals 47 calories, 2 g fat (trace saturated fat), 0 cholesterol, 132 mg sodium, 6 g carbohydrate, 2 g fiber, 1 g protein.*
Diabetic Exchange: *2 vegetable.*

Fruity Chicken Salad

(Pictured below)

When served with hot rolls or muffins, this tangy salad is a terrific alternative to the usual lunchtime fare. It is also a great way to use leftover chicken or turkey.
—*Diane Bradley, Sparta, Michigan*

2 cups cubed cooked chicken breast
2 cups cubed cantaloupe
2 cups cubed honeydew
1 can (11 ounces) mandarin oranges, drained
1 cup green grapes
1 cup halved fresh strawberries
1/2 cup thinly sliced celery
2 tablespoons finely chopped green onion
1/4 cup reduced-fat sour cream
3 tablespoons reduced-fat mayonnaise
1 tablespoon orange juice concentrate
1 tablespoon sugar
1/4 teaspoon celery salt
4 to 5 teaspoons water
Leaf lettuce
1/4 cup sliced almonds, toasted

In a large bowl, combine the chicken, fruit, celery and onion. In a small bowl, combine the sour cream, mayonnaise, orange juice concentrate, sugar and celery salt. Add enough water to achieve drizzling consistency. Place lettuce on

plates; top with chicken mixture. Drizzle with dressing; sprinkle with almonds. Serve immediately. **Yield:** 6 servings.

Nutritional Analysis: One serving (1-1/3 cups) equals 236 calories, 7 g fat (2 g saturated fat), 46 mg cholesterol, 184 mg sodium, 26 g carbohydrate, 2 g fiber, 18 g protein.
Diabetic Exchanges: 2 lean meat, 1-1/2 fat, 1 fruit.

Sausage Potato Salad

(Pictured above)

One night I added turkey Italian sausage to plain potato salad, and my family raved about it. I've refined the recipe since then to create this hearty, comforting dish.
—Lorraine Caland, Thunder Bay, Ontario

    6 medium red potatoes, cubed
    3 turkey Italian sausage links, casings removed
1/2 cup reduced-fat mayonnaise
1/2 cup reduced-fat sour cream
    1 tablespoon red wine vinegar *or* cider vinegar
    1 tablespoon Dijon mustard
    1 teaspoon dried oregano
3/4 teaspoon salt
1/8 teaspoon white pepper
    6 green onions, sliced
Leaf lettuce, optional

Place potatoes in a saucepan and cover with water; bring to a boil. Reduce heat; cover and simmer for 15 minutes or just until tender. Drain; rinse with cold water and set aside.

Cut sausage into bite-size pieces; cook in a nonstick skillet over medium heat until no longer pink. Drain and cool.

In a small bowl, combine the mayonnaise, sour cream, vinegar, mustard, oregano, salt and pepper. In a large bowl, combine the potatoes, sausage and onions; add dressing and toss to coat. Cover and refrigerate for at least 2 hours. Serve in a lettuce-lined bowl if desired. **Yield:** 7 servings.

Nutritional Analysis: One serving (1 cup) equals 233 calories, 11 g fat (3 g saturated fat), 31 mg cholesterol, 682 mg sodium, 27 g carbohydrate, 3 g fiber, 11 g protein.
Diabetic Exchanges: 1-1/2 starch, 1 lean meat, 1 fat.

Buttermilk Salad Dressing

(Pictured below)

This thick creamy mixture has the flavor of ranch dressing and is a breeze to blend together. Use it to top mixed greens or as a dip for raw vegetables.
—Vicki Floden, Story City, Iowa

3/4 cup 1% buttermilk
    2 cups (16 ounces) 2% cottage cheese
    1 envelope ranch salad dressing mix
Salad greens and vegetables of your choice

In a blender or food processor, combine the buttermilk, cottage cheese and salad dressing mix; cover and process for 20 seconds or until smooth. Pour into a small pitcher or bowl. Cover and refrigerate for 1 hour. Stir before serving with salad. **Yield:** 2-3/4 cups.

Nutritional Analysis: One serving (2 tablespoons dressing) equals 23 calories, 1 g fat (trace saturated fat), 3 mg cholesterol, 177 mg sodium, 2 g carbohydrate, 0 fiber, 3 g protein.
Diabetic Exchange: 1/2 fat-free milk.

Shrimp and Crab Salad

For an impressive salad, try this tasty mixture of hearty shrimp and crabmeat with a creamy dressing.
—Melissa Stroupe, Stanley, North Carolina

> 2 pounds cooked medium shrimp, peeled and deveined
> 2 packages (8 ounces *each*) imitation crabmeat, flaked
> 4 celery ribs, finely chopped
> 1 medium onion, finely chopped
> 1/2 cup sliced ripe olives
> 1/2 cup reduced-fat mayonnaise
> 2 tablespoons prepared horseradish
> 1 teaspoon seasoned salt

Leaf lettuce

In a large bowl, combine the first five ingredients. In a small bowl, combine the mayonnaise, horseradish and seasoned salt; mix well. Add to the shrimp mixture and stir well. Cover and refrigerate. Serve on a lettuce-lined plate. **Yield:** 9 servings.

Nutritional Analysis: One serving (1 cup) equals 223 calories, 8 g fat (1 g saturated fat), 168 mg cholesterol, 964 mg sodium, 11 g carbohydrate, 1 g fiber, 27 g protein.
Diabetic Exchanges: 3 lean meat, 1/2 starch.

Sweet-Sour Citrus Salad

The combination of vegetables and fruits tossed with a honey and poppy seed dressing makes this salad versatile enough to accompany any entree.
—Dorothy Swanson, St. Louis, Missouri

> 1 large pink grapefruit, peeled and sectioned
> 1 large navel orange, peeled and sectioned
> 1 tablespoon sugar
> 1 large sweet red pepper, julienned
> 1 small red onion, sliced and separated into rings
> 1/3 cup honey
> 1/4 cup cider vinegar
> 2 tablespoons poppy seeds
> 2 teaspoons grated onion
> 2 teaspoons lemon juice
> 1 teaspoon salt
> 1 teaspoon ground mustard
> 1/2 teaspoon grated lemon peel
> 4 cups torn salad greens
> 2 cups sliced fresh mushrooms

In a bowl, combine the grapefruit and orange sections; sprinkle with sugar. Add red pepper and red onion.

In a blender, combine the honey, vinegar, poppy seeds, grated onion, lemon juice, salt, mustard and lemon peel; cover and process until blended. Pour over fruit mixture and toss to coat. In a serving bowl, toss greens, mushrooms and fruit mixture. Serve immediately. **Yield:** 6 servings.

Nutritional Analysis: One serving (1 cup) equals 132 calories, 2 g fat (trace saturated fat), 0 cholesterol, 404 mg sodium, 30 g carbohydrate, 3 g fiber, 3 g protein.
Diabetic Exchanges: 1-1/2 fruit, 1-1/2 vegetable.

Southwestern Rice Salad

(Pictured above)

This meatless salad makes a robust side dish, filling lunch or satisfying snack. Try spooning some into low-fat tortillas for a main course. If you're counting fat grams, it's also tasty without the olives.
—Rita Zagrzebski, Eagle River, Wisconsin

> 2 cups cooked long grain rice, cooled
> 1 cup cooked wild rice, cooled
> 1 can (16 ounces) kidney beans, rinsed and drained
> 1-1/2 cups frozen corn, thawed
> 1/2 cup diced red onion
> 1/2 cup diced green pepper
> 1 can (2-1/4 ounces) sliced ripe olives, drained
> 1-1/2 cups chunky salsa
> 1/2 cup reduced-fat Italian salad dressing
> 1 teaspoon ground cumin
> 1/4 teaspoon salt

In a large bowl, combine the first seven ingredients. In a jar with a tight-fitting lid, combine salsa, salad dressing, cumin and salt; shake well. Pour over rice mixture and stir to coat. Cover and refrigerate for at least 2 hours. **Yield:** 7 servings.

Nutritional Analysis: One serving (1 cup) equals 257 calories, 4 g fat (trace saturated fat), trace cholesterol, 537 mg sodium, 48 g carbohydrate, 12 g fiber, 12 g protein.
Diabetic Exchanges: 2 starch, 1 lean meat, 1 fat.

Cashew Snow Pea Salad

(Pictured below)

I like to serve this cool and refreshing dish on hot summer days. My guests enjoy the crunchy snow peas, cauliflower and cashews tossed with a light ranch dressing.
—Beth Gambro, Yorkville, Illinois

3 cups fresh snow peas, halved
2 cups chopped cauliflower
1 cup chopped celery
1/4 cup chopped green onions
1/2 cup reduced-fat sour cream
1/2 cup reduced-fat ranch salad dressing
Leaf lettuce, optional
3 bacon strips, cooked and crumbled
1/3 cup chopped cashews

In a bowl, combine the peas, cauliflower, celery and onions. Combine the sour cream and salad dressing; pour over the vegetables and toss to coat. Serve in a lettuce-lined bowl if desired. Sprinkle with the bacon and cashews before serving. **Yield:** 5 servings.

Nutritional Analysis: *One serving (1 cup) equals 159 calories, 10 g fat (3 g saturated fat), 12 mg cholesterol, 297 mg sodium, 12 g carbohydrate, 3 g fiber, 7 g protein.*
Diabetic Exchanges: *2 vegetable, 1-1/2 fat, 1/2 lean meat.*

Apple Pear Salad

(Pictured above)

When very good friends drove a long way to visit me after I moved, I served them this wonderful salad with fruit and nuts. Needless to say, we had a great visit and lots of good food.
—Cathy Seed, Hudson, Ohio

2 medium tart apples, cut into chunks
2 medium firm pears, cut into chunks
1 tablespoon lemon juice
3/4 cup seedless red grapes
2 tablespoons water
2 tablespoons balsamic vinegar
2 tablespoons olive *or* canola oil
1 tablespoon prepared mustard
1 teaspoon sugar
1/8 teaspoon salt
1/8 teaspoon coarsely ground pepper
1 head Boston *or* Bibb lettuce
1/3 cup chopped walnuts, toasted

In a bowl, toss apples and pears with lemon juice. Add grapes; toss gently. In another bowl, combine the water, vinegar, oil, mustard, sugar, salt and pepper. Pour over fruit and toss to coat. Serve in lettuce-lined bowls; sprinkle with walnuts. **Yield:** 8 servings.

Nutritional Analysis: *One serving (3/4 cup) equals 117 calories, 7 g fat (1 g saturated fat), 0 cholesterol, 86 mg sodium, 16 g carbohydrate, 3 g fiber, 1 g protein.*
Diabetic Exchanges: *1 fruit, 1 fat.*

Zucchini Slaw

A friend gave me the recipe for this best-of-the-season slaw. If you like the light taste of zucchini in a simple salad, you're sure to ask for a second helping of this one.
—Nadeen Shrewsberry, Hickory, North Carolina

2 medium zucchini, coarsely shredded and
    squeezed dry
1/4 cup finely chopped onion
1 cup coarsely shredded carrots
3 tablespoons reduced-fat mayonnaise
1 tablespoon cider vinegar
1/2 teaspoon sugar
1/4 teaspoon salt
Dash pepper

In a bowl, combine all ingredients; mix well. Cover and refrigerate for at least 1 hour before serving. **Yield:** 4 servings.

Nutritional Analysis: One serving (3/4 cup) equals 71 calories, 4 g fat (1 g saturated fat), 4 mg cholesterol, 249 mg sodium, 9 g carbohydrate, 2 g fiber, 2 g protein.
Diabetic Exchanges: 2 vegetable, 1/2 fat.

Orange Lime Gelatin Ring

(Pictured at right)

Red grapes tucked into the center of a molded gelatin ring accent the tangy taste of lime, orange and pineapple in this colorful salad. It's festive enough to serve guests and goes perfectly with ham or pork roast. Plus, it's cool, tasty and easy to prepare.
—Janice Pardue, Naples, Florida

1 can (11 ounces) mandarin oranges, drained
1 can (20 ounces) crushed pineapple, undrained
2 tablespoons lemon juice

🍎 Gelatin Gems

DO YOU want your Jell-O to gel just right? Follow these simple tips to achieve success.

- For layered perfection, chill the first layer of a gelatin salad or dessert until set but not firm. For additional layers, the gelatin mixture should be cool and slightly thickened before pouring onto the layer beneath it.
- Make unmolding easier by first spraying the mold with nonstick cooking spray.
- To center the mold on a plate, rinse plate with cold water before unmolding the gelatin—it'll slip into place.
- Here's a low-cal treat with extra flavor and vitamin C: Prepare sugar-free gelatin with 1 cup of a vitamin C-packed fruit juice instead of cold water. Try orange juice with strawberry gelatin, or pineapple juice with cranberry gelatin.

1 package (3 ounces) lime gelatin
1 package (8 ounces) reduced-fat cream cheese,
    cubed
Lettuce leaves
2 cups seedless red grapes

Arrange oranges in the bottom of a 9-in. ring mold coated with nonstick cooking spray. Cover and freeze for 30 minutes. Meanwhile, drain pineapple, reserving 1 cup juice (discard any remaining juice or save for another use); set pineapple aside.

In a saucepan, bring lemon juice and reserved pineapple juice to a boil. Remove from the heat; cool for 10 minutes. Pour into a blender or food processor. Add gelatin powder; cover and process for 30 seconds or until gelatin is dissolved. Add cream cheese; cover and process for 1 minute or until smooth.

Stir in pineapple. Pour into ring mold. Cover and refrigerate for 8 hours or until firm. Unmold onto a lettuce-lined serving platter. Fill center with grapes. **Yield:** 10 servings.

Nutritional Analysis: One serving equals 158 calories, 5 g fat (3 g saturated fat), 16 mg cholesterol, 126 mg sodium, 25 g carbohydrate, 1 g fiber, 4 g protein.
Diabetic Exchanges: 1 fruit, 1 fat, 1/2 starch.

Melon Turkey Salad

(Pictured at right)

With its combination of tender chunks of turkey, sweet melon balls and juicy grapes, this salad is a winner at our ladies' club.
—Carolyn Zimmerman, Fairbury, Illinois

4 medium cantaloupes, halved and seeded
4 cups cubed cooked turkey breast
1-1/2 cups seedless red grapes, halved
1 cup chopped celery
1/2 cup fat-free plain yogurt
1/4 cup reduced-fat mayonnaise
1 teaspoon lemon juice
1/2 teaspoon ground ginger
1/8 teaspoon salt
1/2 cup chopped unsalted dry roasted cashews

Make melon balls from one cantaloupe half; refrigerate remaining cantaloupe halves. In a large bowl, combine the turkey, grapes, celery and cantaloupe balls. In a small bowl, combine the yogurt, mayonnaise, lemon juice, ginger and salt. Pour over turkey mixture and stir gently to coat. Cover and refrigerate for 1 hour. Stir in cashews just before serving. Spoon 1 cup salad into each cantaloupe half. **Yield:** 7 servings.

Nutritional Analysis: One serving equals 327 calories, 9 g fat (2 g saturated fat), 71 mg cholesterol, 207 mg sodium, 36 g carbohydrate, 3 g fiber, 30 g protein.
Diabetic Exchanges: 3 very lean meat, 2-1/2 fruit, 1-1/2 fat.

Step Up to the Salad Bar

Rainbow Fruit Salad

(Pictured below)

This fresh fruit medley makes a wonderful addition to the breakfast table. A few pinches of ground ginger and nutmeg put a flavorful twist on familiar tastes.
—Barbara Smithberger, Pickerington, Ohio

1/2 cup honey
1/3 cup orange juice
2 tablespoons lemon juice
1/4 teaspoon ground ginger
1/8 teaspoon ground nutmeg
5 cups cubed cantaloupe
1 cup fresh blueberries
2 large firm bananas, sliced
2 medium nectarines, peeled and sliced
2 cups sliced fresh strawberries
2 cups halved seedless grapes

In a small bowl, combine the first five ingredients; mix well. In a large bowl, combine the fruit. Add dressing and toss to coat. Serve immediately with a slotted spoon. **Yield:** 12 servings.

Nutritional Analysis: One serving (1 cup) equals 126 calories, 1 g fat (trace saturated fat), 0 cholesterol, 8 mg sodium, 32 g carbohydrate, 3 g fiber, 1 g protein.
Diabetic Exchange: *2 fruit.*

Stewed Holiday Fruit

Dried apricots, prunes and fresh bananas are drizzled with a sweet cider and marmalade sauce in this fruity concoction from our Test Kitchen. Hints of cinnamon and citrus lend a festive zest to each cool spoonful. Serve a bowlful of this fun fruit for breakfast, snacktime or dessert.

12 dried apricots
12 dried prunes
1-1/2 cups apple cider *or* unsweetened apple juice
2 cinnamon sticks (3 inches)
8 whole cloves
2 whole allspice
1/4 cup orange marmalade
2 teaspoons lemon juice
1 teaspoon butter *or* stick margarine
2 medium firm bananas, sliced
2 tablespoons sliced almonds, toasted

In a small saucepan, combine the apricots, prunes, cider, cinnamon, cloves and allspice. Bring to a boil. Remove from the heat; refrigerate overnight.

Strain cider, reserving liquid; set apricots and prunes aside. Discard spices. In a small saucepan, combine the marmalade, lemon juice, butter and reserved cider. Bring to a boil, stirring occasionally. Cool. Divide apricots, prunes and bananas among serving dishes; drizzle with cooled sauce. Sprinkle with almonds. **Yield:** 4 servings.

Nutritional Analysis: One serving (3/4 cup fruit with 1/4 cup sauce) equals 259 calories, 3 g fat (1 g saturated fat), 3 mg cholesterol, 26 mg sodium, 61 g carbohydrate, 5 g fiber, 2 g protein.

Shrimp Linguine Salad

A variation of this recipe was originally served as a side dish at a popular French restaurant. I added a few more ingredients to make it a cool and hearty meal. The recipe is very adaptable— it's also delicious with chicken and snow peas.
—Eileen Herr, Indianapolis, Indiana

8 ounces uncooked linguine, broken in half
1 pound cooked medium shrimp, peeled and deveined
3 cups fresh broccoli florets
1 can (14 ounces) water-packed artichoke hearts, drained and chopped
1/2 pound fresh mushrooms, sliced
12 cherry tomatoes, halved
3/4 cup shredded carrots
1/2 cup sliced green onions
1/3 cup olive *or* canola oil
1/3 cup reduced-sodium soy sauce
1 tablespoon lemon juice
1 garlic clove, minced
1/2 teaspoon hot pepper sauce
2 tablespoons sesame seeds, toasted

Cook linguine according to package directions; drain and rinse in cold water. Place in a bowl; add the shrimp, broccoli, artichokes, mushrooms, tomatoes, carrots and onions.

In a jar with a tight-fitting lid, combine the oil, soy sauce, lemon juice, garlic and hot pepper sauce; shake well. Pour over salad and toss to coat. Cover and refrigerate for at least 1 hour. Just before serving, sprinkle with sesame seeds. **Yield:** 9 servings.

Nutritional Analysis: One serving (1-1/3 cups) equals 286 calories, 10 g fat (1 g saturated fat), 77 mg cholesterol, 721 mg sodium, 31 g carbohydrate, 5 g fiber, 18 g protein.
Diabetic Exchanges: *2 vegetable, 1-1/2 starch, 1-1/2 fat, 1 lean meat.*

Nutritional Analysis: *One serving (3/4 cup) equals 141 calories, 1 g fat (trace saturated fat), 1 mg cholesterol, 392 mg sodium, 26 g carbohydrate, 7 g fiber, 8 g protein.*
Diabetic Exchanges: *2 vegetable, 1 starch.*

Peachy Rice Salad

(Pictured below)

We especially love this refreshing rice salad in summer, when fresh peaches are available. Yogurt and honey make a light dressing while celery and walnuts add crunch.
—*Linda Goshorn, Bedford, Virginia*

1/3 cup plain yogurt
  2 tablespoons honey
  4 teaspoons lemon juice
1/2 teaspoon salt
  2 cups cold cooked rice
  2 medium peaches, peeled and diced *or* 1-1/2 cups frozen unsweetened peach slices, thawed and diced
1/2 cup sliced celery
1/4 cup coarsely chopped walnuts, toasted

In a bowl, combine the yogurt, honey, lemon juice and salt. Stir in the rice, peaches and celery. Cover and refrigerate. Just before serving, stir in the walnuts. **Yield:** 4 servings.

Nutritional Analysis: *One serving (3/4 cup) equals 226 calories, 6 g fat (1 g saturated fat), 3 mg cholesterol, 313 mg sodium, 41 g carbohydrate, 2 g fiber, 4 g protein.*
Diabetic Exchanges: *2 starch, 1/2 fruit, 1/2 fat.*

Black-Eyed Pea Salad

(Pictured above)

Whenever I get asked to potluck parties, this salad usually gets an invitation, too. Since it takes a little time for the flavors to meld, I sometimes toss it together a day ahead, then add the fresh peppers just before serving.
—*Joy Polito Young, Chocowinity, North Carolina*

  1 pound dry black-eyed peas
  1 cup fat-free Italian salad dressing
1/2 cup chopped onion
  2 cups chopped green pepper
  1 cup chopped sweet red pepper
3/4 cup finely chopped green onions
1/2 cup finely chopped seeded jalapeno peppers*
1/4 cup minced fresh parsley
  3 garlic cloves, minced
1/2 teaspoon salt
1/8 teaspoon hot pepper sauce

Place peas in a Dutch oven or soup kettle; add water to cover by 2 in. Bring to a boil; boil for 2 minutes. Remove from the heat; cover and let stand for 1 hour. Drain and rinse peas, discarding liquid. Return peas to pan; cover with water. Bring to a boil. Reduce heat; cover and simmer for 1 hour or until tender.

Drain peas and place in a large bowl. Add salad dressing and onion; toss to coat. Cover and refrigerate until cool. Add the remaining ingredients; toss gently. **Yield:** 12 servings.

Brown Rice Salad with Grilled Chicken

(Pictured below)

This delightful dish is nutritious, simple to fix and brightens up any buffet table. It's a terrific way to use up leftover chicken, and you can add veggies according to your family's liking.
—Glenda Harper, Cable, Ohio

3 cups cooked brown rice
2 cups cubed grilled chicken breast
2 medium tart apples, diced
1 medium sweet red pepper, diced
2 celery ribs, finely chopped
2/3 cup chopped green onions
1/2 cup chopped pecans
3 tablespoons minced fresh parsley
1/4 cup cider vinegar
3 tablespoons olive *or* canola oil
1 tablespoon lemon juice
1 teaspoon salt
1/4 teaspoon pepper
Lettuce leaves, optional

In a large bowl, combine the first eight ingredients. In a jar with a tight-fitting lid, combine the vinegar, oil, lemon juice, salt and pepper; shake well. Pour over the rice mixture and toss to coat. Serve immediately or refrigerate. Serve in a lettuce-lined bowl if desired. **Yield:** 9 servings.

Nutritional Analysis: One serving (1 cup) equals 236 calories, 11 g fat (1 g saturated fat), 26 mg cholesterol, 295 mg sodium, 23 g carbohydrate, 3 g fiber, 12 g protein.
Diabetic Exchanges: 1-1/2 fat, 1 starch, 1 lean meat, 1/2 fruit.

Southwestern Chicken Salad

(Pictured above)

We have five children who love Mexican food, salads and chicken. So I combined all three to make this crunchy main dish. There's no groaning from anyone when I set it on the table!
—Margaret Yost, Casstown, Ohio

1/3 cup fat-free Thousand Island salad dressing
1/3 cup salsa
1/4 cup reduced-fat sour cream
1 teaspoon seasoned salt
1 teaspoon garlic powder
1/2 teaspoon salt-free lemon-pepper seasoning
1/4 teaspoon cayenne pepper
1 pound boneless skinless chicken breasts, cut into 1/4-inch strips
1 tablespoon olive *or* canola oil
1 *each* medium sweet red and green pepper, cut into 1/4-inch strips
2 teaspoons lime juice
12 cups torn romaine
1-1/2 cups (6 ounces) shredded reduced-fat cheddar cheese
1 cup shredded red cabbage
1 medium tomato, chopped
1 medium carrot, grated
Baked tortilla chips

In a small bowl, combine the salad dressing, salsa and sour cream. Cover and refrigerate until serving.

Combine the seasonings; sprinkle over chicken. In a nonstick skillet, saute chicken in oil for 6 minutes. Add pep-

pers; saute 2-3 minutes longer or until chicken is no longer pink. Drizzle with lime juice; keep warm.

In a large bowl, toss the romaine, cheese, cabbage, tomato and carrot. Add chicken mixture. Serve over chips; drizzle with dressing. **Yield:** 8 servings.

Nutritional Analysis: One serving (1-1/2 cups salad with 20 tortilla chips) equals 360 calories, 8 g fat (3 g saturated fat), 47 mg cholesterol, 813 mg sodium, 49 g carbohydrate, 6 g fiber, 25 g protein.
Diabetic Exchanges: 3 starch, 2 lean meat, 1 vegetable.

Tuscan Bean Salad

I love to cook for my family and friends and to try new recipes. This delicious marinated bean salad is a favorite folks request often. We think it's especially good alongside a pork entree.
—*Dixie Cannafax, Onoville, California*

    1 cup dry navy beans
    4 cups cold water
 1/2 cup diced red onion
 1/2 cup thinly sliced celery
 1/4 cup chopped fresh parsley
    3 tablespoons chicken broth
    2 tablespoons balsamic vinegar
    1 tablespoon olive *or* canola oil
    1 teaspoon Dijon mustard
 1/2 teaspoon minced garlic
    1 teaspoon salt
 1/4 teaspoon ground oregano
 1/4 teaspoon ground thyme

Place beans in a Dutch oven or kettle; add water to cover by 2 in. Bring to a boil; boil for 2 minutes. Remove from the heat; cover and let stand for 1 hour. Drain and rinse beans, discarding liquid. Return beans to the pan; add cold water. Bring to a boil. Reduce heat; cover and simmer for 50-60 minutes or until beans are tender.

Drain beans; place in a bowl. Add onion, celery and parsley. In a jar with a tight-fitting lid, combine the remaining ingredients; shake well. Pour over bean mixture and stir to coat. Cover and refrigerate for at least 2 hours. **Yield:** 4 servings.

Nutritional Analysis: One serving (3/4 cup) equals 224 calories, 4 g fat (1 g saturated fat), 0 cholesterol, 682 mg sodium, 36 g carbohydrate, 14 g fiber, 12 g protein.
Diabetic Exchanges: 2 starch, 1 lean meat, 1 vegetable.

Creamy French Dressing

(Pictured below)

You'll need just a few ingredients from your pantry to blend together this mild homemade dressing from our Test Kitchen. It's very thick, creamy and perfect on tossed salad greens.

    1 cup ketchup
 1/2 cup reduced-fat mayonnaise
    3 tablespoons cider vinegar
    3 tablespoons honey
    2 tablespoons water
    1 tablespoon olive *or* canola oil
    1 teaspoon lemon juice
 1/2 teaspoon ground mustard
 1/4 teaspoon salt
Salad greens and vegetables of your choice

In a blender or food processor, combine the first nine ingredients; cover and process until blended. Serve over salad. Refrigerate leftovers. **Yield:** 1-3/4 cups.

Nutritional Analysis: One serving (2 tablespoons dressing) equals 70 calories, 4 g fat (1 g saturated fat), 3 mg cholesterol, 318 mg sodium, 10 g carbohydrate, trace fiber, trace protein.
Diabetic Exchanges: 1/2 starch, 1/2 fat.

Barley Corn Salad

A great alternative to pasta salads, this colorful side dish adds refreshing herb flavor to corn, barley, and red and green peppers. Bring it to your next get-together and see how fast it disappears!
—Mary Ann Kieffer, Lawrence, Kansas

2 cups cooked medium pearl barley
2 cups frozen corn, thawed
1/2 cup chopped sweet red pepper
1/2 cup chopped green pepper
3 green onions, chopped
1 tablespoon minced fresh cilantro *or* parsley
2 tablespoons lemon juice
2 tablespoons canola oil
1/2 teaspoon salt
1/2 teaspoon dried thyme
1/8 teaspoon pepper

In a large bowl, combine the first six ingredients. In a jar with a tight-fitting lid, combine the lemon juice, oil, salt, thyme and pepper; shake well. Pour over salad and toss to coat. Cover and refrigerate for at least 2 hours before serving. **Yield:** 6 servings.

Nutritional Analysis: One serving (2/3 cup) equals 163 calories, 5 g fat (trace saturated fat), 0 cholesterol, 201 mg sodium, 29 g carbohydrate, 4 g fiber, 3 g protein.
Diabetic Exchanges: 1-1/2 starch, 1 vegetable, 1 fat.

Crab Coleslaw Medley

This salad gets its pleasant crunch from ramen noodles, almonds and sesame seeds. It's my most asked-for recipe. An adaptable main dish, it works well with chicken or turkey, too.
—Edith Frost, Mountain View, California

1 package (16 ounces) coleslaw mix
6 cups torn romaine
3/4 cup finely chopped onion
1 package (8 ounces) imitation crabmeat, chopped
1/3 cup canola oil
3 tablespoons cider vinegar
2 tablespoons sugar
1 teaspoon salt
1/2 teaspoon pepper
1 package (3 ounces) chicken ramen noodles
2 tablespoons slivered almonds, toasted
2 tablespoons sesame seeds, toasted

In a large bowl, combine the coleslaw mix, romaine, onion and crab. In a jar with a tight-fitting lid, combine the oil, vinegar, sugar, salt, pepper and contents of seasoning packet from noodles; shake well. Break noodles into small pieces. Sprinkle noodles, almonds and sesame seeds over salad; mix well. Drizzle with dressing and toss to coat. Serve immediately. **Yield:** 12 servings.

Nutritional Analysis: One serving (1 cup) equals 149 calories, 8 g fat (1 g saturated fat), 4 mg cholesterol, 527 mg sodium, 15 g carbohydrate, 3 g fiber, 5 g protein.
Diabetic Exchanges: 1 starch, 1 vegetable, 1 fat.

Cranberry Gelatin Salad

(Pictured below)

We don't miss the sugar in this cool, tart and tangy gelatin salad. It's my family's favorite, especially at the holidays because of its festive color. Walnuts and celery add a delightful crunch.
—Janet Davis, Atkinson, Nebraska

1 package (12 ounces) fresh *or* frozen cranberries, thawed
1 can (12 ounces) frozen apple juice concentrate, thawed
2 packages (.3 ounce *each*) sugar-free raspberry gelatin
1 can (8 ounces) crushed pineapple, undrained
1 cup chopped celery
1 medium navel orange, peeled, sectioned and chopped
1/2 cup chopped walnuts

In a 3-qt. microwave-safe dish, combine cranberries and apple juice concentrate; cover with waxed paper. Microwave on high for 8-10 minutes or until most of the berries have popped. Immediately stir in gelatin powder until dissolved. Cool for 10-15 minutes. Add remaining ingredients; mix well. Pour into a 2-qt. ring mold coated with nonstick cooking spray. Refrigerate until firm, about 3 hours. Unmold onto a serving plate just before serving. **Yield:** 12 servings.

Editor's Note: This recipe was tested in an 850-watt microwave.

Nutritional Analysis: One serving (1/2 cup) equals 115 calories, 3 g fat (trace saturated fat), 0 cholesterol, 49 mg sodium, 20 g carbohydrate, 2 g fiber, 2 g protein.
Diabetic Exchanges: 1 fruit, 1/2 fat.

Fresh Fruit with Balsamic Vinaigrette

(Pictured above)

This colorful fruit platter always looks beautiful on our Christmas dinner table. The light dressing is a nice complement to the fun assortment of winter fruits.
—Marie Day, Suamico, Wisconsin

1/4 cup orange juice
  3 tablespoons balsamic vinegar
  3 tablespoons olive *or* canola oil
  2 tablespoons water
  1 tablespoon honey
1/2 teaspoon coarsely ground pepper
1/4 teaspoon salt
Red leaf lettuce
  2 medium grapefruit, peeled and sectioned
  1 medium navel orange, peeled and sectioned
  2 medium pears, sliced
  1 can (11 ounces) mandarin oranges, drained
  1 cup seedless grapes

In a jar with a tight-fitting lid, combine the first seven ingredients; shake well. Refrigerate for 1 hour. Line a platter with lettuce. Arrange fruit over lettuce; drizzle with dressing. Serve immediately. **Yield:** 6 servings.

Nutritional Analysis: One serving (3/4 cup) equals 191 calories, 7 g fat (1 g saturated fat), 0 cholesterol, 102 mg sodium, 34 g carbohydrate, 7 g fiber, 2 g protein.
Diabetic Exchanges: 2 fruit, 1-1/2 fat.

🍎 Making an Orange Rose Bloom

ADD an eye-catching touch to any serving plate by crafting an easy yet impressive orange rose garnish (shown in photo above on fruit platter). Follow these simple steps:

- Cut a very thin slice from the bottom of an orange and discard. Starting at the top of the orange, with a vegetable peeler, cut a continuous narrow strip of peel in a spiral fashion around the entire orange.
- Working with the end of the strip where you started, wrap the strip around itself to form a coil.
- Insert one or two toothpicks horizontally into the base of the "rose" to hold it secure.

Sweet Potato Salad

Skip the traditional sweet potato casserole and try this salad sensation instead. I really like this different treatment for sweet potatoes—I first tasted something similar at a friend's house years ago. This was a favorite of our children during the holidays. Now it's our grandson's favorite, too.
—Roberta Freedman, Mesilla Park, New Mexico

    2 pounds sweet potatoes (about 3 medium),
       peeled and cubed
    4 tablespoons lemon juice, *divided*
    2 celery ribs, thinly sliced
    1 can (11 ounces) mandarin oranges, drained
    1 cup fat-free mayonnaise
    2 tablespoons orange juice
    1 tablespoon honey
  1/2 teaspoon salt
  1/4 teaspoon ground ginger
  1/8 teaspoon ground nutmeg
  1/4 cup chopped pecans

Place sweet potatoes in a large saucepan and cover with water; bring to a boil. Reduce heat. Cover and cook for 9-10 minutes or until tender; drain and place in a bowl. Add 2 tablespoons lemon juice and toss. Add the celery and oranges.

In a small bowl, combine the mayonnaise, orange juice, honey, salt, ginger, nutmeg and remaining lemon juice. Pour over potato mixture and toss to coat. Cover and refrigerate for at least 2 hours. Just before serving, stir in pecans. **Yield:** 8 servings.

Nutritional Analysis: *One serving (3/4 cup) equals 200 calories, 4 g fat (trace saturated fat), 3 mg cholesterol, 415 mg sodium, 41 g carbohydrate, 4 g fiber, 3 g protein.*
Diabetic Exchanges: *2 starch, 1/2 fat, 1/2 fruit.*

Santa Fe Rice Salad

(Pictured at right)

This warm rice and bean salad served with crunchy tortilla chips is sure to make any mealtime a fiesta! My whole family enjoys this snappy salad. Occasionally I add other ingredients, depending on what I have on hand, but this combination is most popular at our house.
—Marilyn Sherwood, Fremont, Nebraska

    1 medium green pepper, julienned
    1 medium sweet red pepper, julienned
    1 small onion, thinly sliced
    2 teaspoons canola oil
    2 cups cooked rice
    1 can (16 ounces) kidney beans, rinsed and
       drained
    1 can (11 ounces) Mexicorn, drained
    1 jar (8 ounces) picante sauce
    6 cups shredded lettuce
  3/4 cup shredded reduced-fat cheddar cheese
    6 tablespoons reduced-fat sour cream
Baked tortilla chips

In a nonstick skillet, saute peppers and onion in oil for 6-7 minutes or until tender. Stir in the rice, beans, corn and picante sauce; heat through.

For each serving, place 1 cup of lettuce on a plate. Top with 1 cup of the rice mixture, 2 tablespoons of cheese and 1 tablespoon of sour cream. Serve with tortilla chips. **Yield:** 6 servings.

Nutritional Analysis: *One serving (1 cup salad with 10 tortilla chips) equals 353 calories, 7 g fat (3 g saturated fat), 15 mg cholesterol, 800 mg sodium, 59 g carbohydrate, 9 g fiber, 15 g protein.*
Diabetic Exchanges: *3 starch, 2 vegetable, 1 lean meat.*

Green Bean and Tomato Salad

(Pictured at right)

Crisp-tender green beans are paired with cherry tomatoes and seasoned with onion, celery and lemon in this refreshing side dish. There's nothing quite like a colorful salad to perk up a gray winter day.
—Diane Hixon, Niceville, Florida

    1 pound fresh green beans, trimmed
  1/2 cup thinly sliced red onion
    1 pint grape *or* **cherry tomatoes, halved**
    2 tablespoons lemon juice
    1 tablespoon olive *or* **canola oil**
    1 tablespoon water
  3/4 teaspoon salt
  1/4 teaspoon pepper
    1 cup chopped celery

Place beans in a saucepan and cover with water; bring to a boil. Cook, uncovered, for 8-10 minutes or until crisp-tender. Drain and rinse with cold water. Place in a large bowl; add onion. Place tomatoes in another bowl. In a small bowl, whisk together the lemon juice, oil, water, salt and pepper. Pour over the vegetables in each bowl; toss to coat. Cover and refrigerate for at least 1 hour.

Stir celery into bean mixture; transfer to a serving platter. Surround with tomatoes. **Yield:** 8 servings.

Nutritional Analysis: *One serving (3/4 cup) equals 48 calories, 2 g fat (trace saturated fat), 0 cholesterol, 239 mg sodium, 7 g carbohydrate, 3 g fiber, 2 g protein.*
Diabetic Exchanges: *1 vegetable, 1/2 fat.*

Spiced Fruit Salad

(Pictured at right)

This is a fresh-tasting salad that's easy to double for a crowd. The cinnamon and nutmeg in the yogurt dressing provide just the right amount of spice to this cool fruit medley.
—Lavonne Hartel, Williston, North Dakota

1-1/2 cups fat-free plain yogurt
1/4 cup packed brown sugar
1/4 teaspoon ground cinnamon
1/8 teaspoon ground nutmeg
2 pounds ripe bananas (about 3 medium), sliced
1 pound apples (about 2 medium), cubed
1 tablespoon lemon juice
1 pound red *and/or* green seedless grapes

In a small bowl, combine the yogurt, brown sugar, cinnamon and nutmeg. Gently toss bananas and apples with lemon juice; add grapes. Divide among individual bowls. Drizzle with the yogurt mixture. Serve immediately. **Yield:** 12 servings.

Nutritional Analysis: One serving (3/4 cup) equals 136 calories, 1 g fat (trace saturated fat), 1 mg cholesterol, 26 mg sodium, 34 g carbohydrate, 2 g fiber, 3 g protein.
Diabetic Exchange: 2 fruit.

mayonnaise, lemon juice and salt; fold into macaroni mixture. Sprinkle with paprika. Cover and refrigerate for at least 2 hours before serving. **Yield:** 9 servings.

Nutritional Analysis: One serving (3/4 cup) equals 176 calories, 1 g fat (trace saturated fat), 9 mg cholesterol, 453 mg sodium, 27 g carbohydrate, 1 g fiber, 13 g protein.
Diabetic Exchanges: 1-1/2 starch, 1 lean meat.

Mandarin Tuna Salad

Crisp apple pieces and tangy mandarin oranges give tuna salad a twist. Every summer I get requests from my husband and daughters to make this dish. There's never any left over.
—Elizabeth Kennedy, Dover, Delaware

1 package (8 ounces) elbow macaroni
1 can (11 ounces) mandarin oranges, drained
1 can (9 ounces) water-packed tuna, drained
1 cup chopped apple
1 cup diced celery
1 cup fat-free mayonnaise *or* salad dressing
1 teaspoon lemon juice
1/2 teaspoon salt
1/8 teaspoon paprika

Prepare macaroni according to package directions; drain and rinse in cold water. Place in a large bowl; add the oranges, tuna, apple and celery. In a small bowl, combine the

Orange Yogurt Dressing

Honey brings a hint of sweetness to this creamy citrus salad dressing. The orange flavor in this dressing is a wonderful complement to fresh spinach. It's also terrific served over lettuce or fruit.
—Beverly Florence, Midwest City, Oklahoma

1/4 cup reduced-fat mayonnaise
1/4 cup fat-free plain yogurt
2 tablespoons orange juice
2 teaspoons honey
1 teaspoon grated orange peel
1/4 teaspoon salt
Dash white pepper

In a small bowl, whisk together all ingredients; cover and refrigerate for at least 1 hour. **Yield:** 2/3 cup.

Nutritional Analysis: One serving (2 tablespoons) equals 57 calories, 4 g fat (1 g saturated fat), 4 mg cholesterol, 220 mg sodium, 5 g carbohydrate, trace fiber, 1 g protein.
Diabetic Exchanges: 1/2 fruit, 1/2 fat.

Tasty Salad Toppings

- If you want to sprinkle cheese over a salad, pick feta instead of shredded cheddar—it has considerably less fat. Another good choice is low-fat or nonfat cottage cheese.
- For creamy dressings, puree cottage cheese with buttermilk and use it instead of sour cream. Fat-free yogurt will also add body and flavor to a salad dressing.
- Want to cut back on the oil in homemade vinaigrette dressings? No problem! Simply combine equal amounts of vinegar, oil and strong brewed tea, along with seasonings of your choice, and you'll whisk together a tasty concoction in no time at all.

Lime Fruit Medley

Lime adds refreshing zest to this luscious fruit medley. The light dressing lets the fruits' natural flavors shine through.
—Renee Gastineau, Seattle, Washington

2 cups cubed cantaloupe
2 cups cubed peeled fresh peaches
2 cups halved fresh strawberries *or* raspberries
1/2 cup reduced-fat sour cream
1 tablespoon honey
1 tablespoon lime juice
1/4 teaspoon grated lime peel

In a large bowl, combine the fruit. In a small bowl, combine the sour cream, honey, lime juice and peel. Drizzle over fruit; serve immediately. **Yield:** 6 servings.

Nutritional Analysis: One serving (1 cup) equals 96 calories, 2 g fat (1 g saturated fat), 7 mg cholesterol, 19 mg sodium, 19 g carbohydrate, 3 g fiber, 3 g protein.
Diabetic Exchange: 1-1/2 fruit.

Curried Brown Rice Salad

Whenever I need a potluck salad, I turn to this tried-and-true favorite. It's among my most requested recipes—everyone raves about it. Folks love the crunch from the chopped apple and toasted almonds. And I love that I can cook the rice ahead ...then it's just a few simple steps to complete it later.
—Carol Dodds, Aurora, Ontario

4 cups cooked brown rice, cooled
1 cup chopped unpeeled tart apple
1/2 cup raisins
1/2 cup chopped onion
1/2 cup slivered almonds, toasted
1/4 cup reduced-fat mayonnaise
1/4 cup fat-free plain yogurt
3 teaspoons curry powder
1/2 teaspoon salt

In a large bowl, combine the rice, apple, raisins, onion and almonds. In another bowl, combine the remaining ingredi-

ents. Pour over rice mixture and stir to combine. Refrigerate for at least 1 hour before serving. **Yield:** 6 cups.

Nutritional Analysis: One serving (2/3 cup) equals 205 calories, 7 g fat (1 g saturated fat), 2 mg cholesterol, 194 mg sodium, 32 g carbohydrate, 4 g fiber, 5 g protein.
Diabetic Exchanges: 1-1/2 starch, 1 fat, 1/2 fruit.

Dill Vinaigrette

(Pictured below)

This quick-to-fix combination is my favorite salad dressing. It gets its pleasant herb flavor from dill weed, celery seed and a handful of other seasonings. My family often reaches for this dressing.
—Joyce Clifford, Mansfield, Ohio

1/4 cup cider vinegar
2 tablespoons water
2 tablespoons olive *or* canola oil
2 tablespoons honey
1/2 teaspoon garlic powder
1/2 teaspoon dill weed
1/2 teaspoon dried parsley flakes
1/4 teaspoon salt
1/8 teaspoon pepper
1/8 teaspoon celery seed
Salad greens and vegetables of your choice

In a jar with a tight-fitting lid, combine the first 10 ingredients; shake well. Serve with salad. Refrigerate leftovers; shake well before serving. **Yield:** 2/3 cup.

Nutritional Analysis: One serving (2 tablespoons dressing) equals 48 calories, 3 g fat (trace saturated fat), 0 cholesterol, 74 mg sodium, 5 g carbohydrate, trace fiber, trace protein.
Diabetic Exchanges: 1/2 fruit, 1/2 fat.

Salad with Raspberry Vinaigrette

(Pictured above)

Our Test Kitchen suggests you try combining raspberry vinegar with oil and herbs or other seasonings for a lovely rosy vinaigrette you can serve over mixed greens and fruit.

1/2 cup raspberry vinegar (recipe on page 84)
1/3 cup canola oil
  1 envelope Italian salad dressing mix
  2 teaspoons sugar
Salad greens, fresh raspberries and chopped
  hazelnuts

In a jar with tight-fitting lid, combine the vinegar, oil, salad dressing mix and sugar; shake well. Serve over greens with raspberries and hazelnuts. **Yield:** 1 cup.

Nutritional Analysis: 2 tablespoons dressing equals 98 calories, 10 g fat (1 g saturated fat), 0 cholesterol, 27 mg sodium, 2 g carbohydrate, 0 fiber, 0 protein.
Diabetic Exchange: 2 fat.

New Waldorf Salad

A nice blend of colorful fruits and nuts gives this refreshing salad a great flavor and tempting texture. The citrusy topping dresses it up perfectly. It's hard to believe something so easy to fix can be this tasty and attractive.
—Marie Engwall, Willmar, Minnesota

1 medium unpeeled red apple, chopped
1 medium unpeeled green apple, chopped
1 medium unpeeled pear, chopped
1/2 cup green grapes
1/4 cup raisins
1/4 cup slivered almonds, toasted
  1 carton (6 ounces) reduced-fat lemon yogurt
  2 teaspoons lemon juice
  2 teaspoons orange juice
  2 teaspoons honey
  1 teaspoon grated orange peel
Lettuce leaves, optional

In a large bowl, combine the first six ingredients. In a small bowl, combine the yogurt, lemon and orange juices, honey and orange peel; pour over fruit mixture and stir to coat. Serve immediately in lettuce-lined bowls if desired. **Yield:** 4 servings.

Nutritional Analysis: One serving (1 cup) equals 193 calories, 5 g fat (1 g saturated fat), 2 mg cholesterol, 33 mg sodium, 35 g carbohydrate, 4 g fiber, 5 g protein.
Diabetic Exchanges: 2 fruit, 1/2 fat-free milk, 1/2 fat.

A Serving of Salad Savvy

- With so many kinds of lettuce available, you have a virtual garden of good eating at your fingertips! Just remember dark green leaves are packed with more nutrients than lighter ones.
- When buying lettuce, look for crisp blemish-free heads. Stem ends should appear freshly cut, not dried-out or discolored. Store it in the produce compartment of your refrigerator.
- After washing lettuce, dry it well—wet leaves will dilute salad dressings, especially those that are low in fat.
- Tear greens by hand. Chopping with a knife will cause the edges of the leaves to turn brown.
- To cut down on cutting time, slice carrots, celery, radishes and the like ahead for use over a couple of days. Wrap a damp paper towel around the veggies, place in an airtight plastic bag and refrigerate.

Side Dishes & Condiments

In this chapter, you'll find just the right accompaniment for your meals...from fresh vegetables, pleasing pasta and hearty potatoes to satisfying rice, mouth-watering relishes and perfectly seasoned spices.

Makeover Twice-Baked Potatoes (page 87)

Creamy Macaroni 'n' Cheese

(Pictured below)

I prepare this cheesy recipe when I'm craving "comfort food" but trying to eat a little lighter. The hint of mustard adds zip to this creamy side dish—and it makes a pleasing meatless entree, too.
—Dawn Royer, Albany, Oregon

1/3 cup finely chopped onion
3-1/2 cups cooked elbow macaroni
1-3/4 cups shredded reduced-fat cheddar cheese
2 tablespoons minced fresh parsley
1/2 cup fat-free evaporated milk
1-3/4 cups 2% cottage cheese
1 teaspoon Dijon mustard
1/2 teaspoon salt
1/4 teaspoon pepper

In a microwave-safe bowl, cover and microwave onion on high for 2 minutes or until tender; drain. Add the macaroni, cheddar cheese and parsley. In a blender or food processor, combine the milk, cottage cheese, mustard, salt and pepper; cover and process until smooth. Stir into macaroni mixture. Pour into a 1-1/2-qt. baking dish coated with non-stick cooking spray. Bake, uncovered, at 350° for 20-25 minutes or until lightly browned. **Yield:** 8 servings.

Nutritional Analysis: *One serving (2/3 cup) equals 229 calories, 6 g fat (4 g saturated fat), 19 mg cholesterol, 491 mg sodium, 24 g carbohydrate, 1 g fiber, 20 g protein.*
Diabetic Exchanges: *2 starch, 1/2 lean meat.*

Chinese Five Spice

I regularly mix up my own spice blends. My favorite is this Chinese version with its strong anise flavor. It's so convenient to make this mix from pantry staples I have on hand.
—Lydia Scott, Englehart, Ontario

2 tablespoons aniseed
2 tablespoons fennel seed
2 tablespoons ground cinnamon
2 tablespoons whole cloves
2 tablespoons whole peppercorns

In a spice grinder or with a mortar and pestle, combine all ingredients (in batches if necessary); grind until mixture becomes a fine powder. Store in an airtight container for up to 6 months. **Yield:** about 1/2 cup.

Nutritional Analysis: *1 teaspoon equals 8 calories, trace fat (trace saturated fat), 0 cholesterol, 2 mg sodium, 2 g carbohydrate, 1 g fiber, trace protein.*
Diabetic Exchange: *Free food.*

Creamy Pasta with Florets

Cottage cheese is the surprising base for the wonderfully creamy sauce that coats the pasta and veggies in this side dish. My husband, who doesn't like to compromise good taste for low-fat foods, didn't even realize this dish was lower in fat.
—Barbara Tober, Lexington, Kentucky

1 cup 1% cottage cheese
1/2 cup 1% milk
1/4 cup reduced-fat sour cream
1/4 cup grated Parmesan cheese
1/2 teaspoon salt
1/8 teaspoon cayenne pepper
5 cups broccoli florets
4 cups cauliflowerets
4 ounces uncooked angel hair pasta
3 garlic cloves, minced
2 teaspoons olive *or* canola oil
2-1/2 cups sliced fresh mushrooms

In a blender or food processor, combine the cottage cheese, milk, sour cream, Parmesan cheese, salt and cayenne; cover and process until smooth. Set aside.

In a saucepan, bring 1 in. of water to a boil; place broccoli and cauliflower in a steamer basket over water. Cover and steam for 3-4 minutes or until crisp-tender. Meanwhile, cook pasta according to package directions; drain.

In a large nonstick skillet, saute garlic in oil for 2 minutes. Add mushrooms; saute 5 minutes longer. Stir in the broccoli, cauliflower, pasta and cottage cheese mixture; heat through. **Yield:** 8 servings.

Nutritional Analysis: *One serving (1 cup) equals 151 calories, 4 g fat (2 g saturated fat), 7 mg cholesterol, 357 mg sodium, 20 g carbohydrate, 2 g fiber, 11 g protein.*
Diabetic Exchanges: *1 starch, 1 meat, 1 vegetable.*

Broiled Zucchini with Rosemary Butter

I spread garden-fresh zucchini with a buttery herb topping for a succulent side dish.
—Sandra Hart, Central Point, Oregon

3 tablespoons butter (no substitutes), softened
1/4 cup finely chopped green onions
1 to 2 tablespoons minced fresh rosemary
  ***or* 1 to 2 teaspoons dried rosemary, crushed**
1 teaspoon lemon juice
1/2 teaspoon grated lemon peel
1/4 teaspoon pepper
1/8 teaspoon cayenne pepper
4 medium zucchini

In a bowl, combine the first seven ingredients; set aside. Cut zucchini lengthwise into 1/2-in. slices. Place on a broiler pan coated with nonstick cooking spray. Broil 4 in. from the heat for 10-12 minutes, turning occasionally, or until crisp-tender. Spread with rosemary butter; serve immediately. **Yield:** 4 servings.

Nutritional Analysis: One serving (3 zucchini slices with 4 teaspoons rosemary butter) equals 101 calories, 9 g fat (5 g saturated fat), 23 mg cholesterol, 94 mg sodium, 5 g carbohydrate, 3 g fiber, 2 g protein.
Diabetic Exchanges: 1-1/2 fat, 1 vegetable.

Garlic Mashed Red Potatoes

(Pictured above)

These creamy garlic mashed potatoes are so good, you can serve them plain—no butter or gravy is needed. Now, this is the only way we prepare mashed potatoes.
—Val Mitchell, Hudson, Ohio

8 medium red potatoes, quartered
3 garlic cloves, peeled
2 tablespoons butter *or* stick margarine
1/2 cup fat-free milk, warmed
1/2 teaspoon salt
1/4 cup grated Parmesan cheese

Place potatoes and garlic in a large saucepan; cover with water. Bring to a boil. Reduce heat; cover and simmer for 20-25 minutes or until the potatoes are very tender. Drain well. Add the butter, milk and salt; mash. Stir in Parmesan cheese. **Yield:** 6 servings.

Nutritional Analysis: One serving (1/2 cup) equals 190 calories, 5 g fat (3 g saturated fat), 14 mg cholesterol, 275 mg sodium, 36 gm carbohydrate, 4 g fiber, 8 g protein.
Diabetic Exchanges: 2 starch, 1/2 fat.

🍎 Low-Fat Mashed Potatoes

Here's my trick from making mashed potatoes without adding butter and milk. I simply boil four to five medium potatoes and mash them. Then I stir in one undiluted can of 98% fat-free condensed soup (any cream variety is fine). I add a little salt and pepper to taste for creamy potatoes without all the fat.
—Linda Hollenbeck, Beloit, Wisconsin

Triple-Grain Pilaf

Looking for a side dish with a pleasant nutty flavor? Our Test Kitchen came up with this easy pilaf recipe that's a perfect mild accompaniment to poultry, beef or fish. The combination of rice, bulgur and barley gives it a nice blend of textures.

1/2 cup sliced green onions
1 tablespoon butter *or* stick margarine
1 cup uncooked long grain rice
1/2 cup bulgur*
1/2 cup quick-cooking barley
3-1/2 cups beef broth
1/2 teaspoon salt
1/4 teaspoon pepper
1/4 cup chopped fresh parsley

In a nonstick saucepan, saute onions in butter for 2 minutes. Stir in the rice, bulgur and barley; saute for 3 minutes. Add broth, salt and pepper. Bring to a boil. Reduce heat; cover and simmer for 20-25 minutes or until the rice is tender. Stir in parsley. **Yield:** 7 servings.

***Editor's Note:** Look for bulgur in the cereal, rice or organic food aisle of your grocery store.

Nutritional Analysis: One serving (3/4 cup) equals 208 calories, 3 g fat (1 g saturated fat), 4 mg cholesterol, 600 mg sodium, 41 g carbohydrate, 5 g fiber, 6 g protein.
Diabetic Exchange: 2-1/2 starch.

Raspberry Vinegar

(Pictured at right)

We have an abundance of raspberries at our house every year. After making lots of freezer jam, I use the remainder of the berries in this recipe.
—Claudia Kane, Bar Harbor, Maine

1 quart fresh raspberries
2 cups cider vinegar
2 tablespoons sugar

In a saucepan over medium heat, bring raspberries just to a boil, stirring constantly. Remove from the heat. Strain through a double layer of cheesecloth (do not press fruit). Let juice stand for 1 hour. Add vinegar and sugar. Store in a sterilized jar or decorative bottle in a cool dark place. **Yield:** 2-3/4 cups.

Nutritional Analysis: 1 tablespoon equals 6 calories, 0 fat (0 saturated fat), 0 cholesterol, trace sodium, 2 g carbohydrate, 0 fiber, 0 protein.
Diabetic Exchange: Free food.

Basil Vinegar

(Pictured above right)

Never made an herb vinegar? It's easy! Our Test Kitchen came up with a super simple recipe with just three ingredients. If your family prefers tarragon instead of basil, just substitute it in the same amount called for in the recipe.

1 cup fresh basil leaves, crushed
2 cups white wine vinegar
Basil sprigs, optional

Place crushed basil leaves in a sterilized pint jar. Heat vinegar just until simmering; pour over basil. Cool to room temperature. Cover and let stand in a cool dark place for 24 hours; strain and discard basil. Pour into a sterilized jar or decorative bottle. Add a basil sprig if desired. Store in a cool dark place. **Yield:** 2 cups.

Nutritional Analysis: 1 tablespoon equals 0 calories, 0 fat (0 saturated fat), 0 cholesterol, 1 mg sodium, 0 carbohydrate, 0 fiber, 0 protein.
Diabetic Exchange: Free food.

Fruit 'n' Nut Spread

I adapted this spread from a higher-calorie version without losing its fruity flavor. It's excellent on bagels, whole wheat toast and muffins.
—Caralyn Berigan, Golden, Colorado

1 cup fat-free cottage cheese
1 to 2 teaspoons lemon juice
1/8 teaspoon ground allspice
1/2 cup mixed dried fruit, chopped
1/4 cup chopped pecans, toasted

In a blender or food processor, combine the cottage cheese, lemon juice and allspice; cover and process until smooth. Stir in fruit and nuts. **Yield:** 1 cup.

Nutritional Analysis: One serving (2 tablespoons) equals 67 calories, 3 g fat (trace saturated fat), 3 mg cholesterol, 94 mg sodium, 7 g carbohydrate, 1 g fiber, 4 g protein.
Diabetic Exchanges: 1/2 fruit, 1/2 lean meat, 1/2 fat.

Grilled Greek-Style Zucchini

I made this side dish for my Women's Health Initiative Group at our local university, and everyone just loved it. The grilled vegetables pick up a pleasantly mild flavor from the lemon juice and herb seasonings.
—Betty Washburn, Reno, Nevada

4 small zucchini, thinly sliced
1 medium tomato, seeded and chopped
1/4 cup pitted ripe olives, halved
2 tablespoons chopped green onion
4 teaspoons olive *or* canola oil
2 teaspoons lemon juice
1/2 teaspoon dried oregano
1/2 teaspoon garlic salt
1/4 teaspoon pepper
2 tablespoons grated Parmesan cheese

In a bowl, combine the zucchini, tomato, olives and onion. Combine oil, lemon juice, oregano, garlic salt and pepper; pour over vegetables and toss to coat. Place on a double thickness of heavy-duty foil (about 23 in. x 18 in.). Fold foil around vegetables and seal tightly. Grill, covered, over medium heat for 10-15 minutes or until vegetables are tender. Sprinkle with Parmesan cheese. **Yield:** 6 servings.

Nutritional Analysis: One serving (1/2 cup) equals 51 calories, 4 g fat (1 g saturated fat), 2 mg cholesterol, 241 mg sodium, 2 g carbohydrate, 1 g fiber, 1 g protein.
Diabetic Exchanges: 1 vegetable, 1/2 fat.

Barley Casserole

Growing up on a farm, I was used to eating good wholesome food, including a variety of barley dishes. This casserole was my first attempt at cooking with barley. The results were as yummy and comforting as I'd remembered.
—Alice Kaluzy, Saskatoon, Saskatchewan

2 celery ribs, chopped
2 medium carrots, finely chopped
7 green onions, chopped
4 garlic cloves, minced
1 tablespoon butter *or* stick margarine
1-1/2 cups uncooked medium pearl barley
1/2 teaspoon salt
1/8 teaspoon pepper
4-1/2 cups chicken broth, *divided*
2 tablespoons minced fresh parsley
1/2 cup slivered almonds

In a large ovenproof skillet, saute the celery, carrots, onions and garlic in butter until tender. Stir in the barley, salt and pepper. Stir in 2-1/2 cups broth. Cover and bake at 350° for 30 minutes.

Stir in parsley and remaining broth; sprinkle with almonds. Bake, uncovered, 30-40 minutes longer or until liquid is absorbed and barley is tender. **Yield:** 8 servings.

Nutritional Analysis: *One serving (3/4 cup) equals 222 calories, 7 g fat (1 g saturated fat), 4 mg cholesterol, 711 mg sodium, 35 g carbohydrate, 8 g fiber, 7 g protein.*
Diabetic Exchanges: *2 starch, 1 lean meat.*

Saucy Mushrooms

Fresh mushrooms take center stage in this flavorful recipe. Serve the mouth-watering morsels over noodles or rice, or alongside beef.
—Ellen Benninger, Greenville, Pennsylvania

1 pound fresh mushrooms, halved
2 tablespoons olive *or* canola oil
1/2 cup water, *divided*
1 tablespoon soy sauce
1/4 teaspoon sugar
2 teaspoons cornstarch

In a nonstick skillet, stir-fry mushrooms in oil for 2 minutes. Combine 1/4 cup water, soy sauce and sugar; pour over mushrooms and toss to coat. Cook and stir for 1-2 minutes. Combine cornstarch and remaining water until smooth; gradually stir into mushrooms. Bring to a boil; cook and stir for 2 minutes or until thickened. **Yield:** 4 servings.

Nutritional Analysis: *One serving (1/4 cup) equals 97 calories, 7 g fat (1 g saturated fat), 0 cholesterol, 156 mg sodium, 6 g carbohydrate, 1 g fiber, 4 g protein.*
Diabetic Exchanges: *2 vegetable, 1 fat.*

Broccoli with Orange Sauce

(Pictured below)

If you like oranges, you'll enjoy this citrusy sauce I adapted when looking for a more interesting way to serve broccoli. It's also nice as a dipping sauce for pork chops and chicken.
—Estelle Hardin, Santa Ana, California

1 pound fresh *or* frozen broccoli spears
4-1/2 teaspoons sugar
2 teaspoons cornstarch
1/2 teaspoon chicken bouillon granules
1/4 cup water
1/4 cup orange juice
1 teaspoon grated orange peel
1 medium navel orange, thinly sliced

Place broccoli and a small amount of water in a saucepan; bring to a boil. Reduce heat; cover and cook for 5-8 minutes or until crisp-tender. Meanwhile, in a small saucepan, combine the sugar, cornstarch and bouillon. Stir in water, orange juice and peel until blended. Bring to a boil; cook and stir for 2 minutes until thickened.

Drain broccoli and place in a serving bowl. Garnish with orange slices and drizzle with sauce. **Yield:** 6 servings.

Nutritional Analysis: *One serving equals 54 calories, trace fat (trace saturated fat), trace cholesterol, 108 mg sodium, 13 g carbohydrate, 3 g fiber, 3 g protein.*
Diabetic Exchanges: *1 vegetable, 1/2 fruit.*

Ziti with Vegetables

Basil, marjoram and thyme flavor this rich pasta side dish. This recipe is my older son's favorite. I came up with it when we were staying with friends and I was asked to prepare dinner one evening without making a trip to the store. You can easily vary it, using vegetables and herbs to suit your family's tastes.
—*Scott Eighme, Barrington, Rhode Island*

   12 ounces uncooked ziti *or* other medium pasta
    1 package (16 ounces) frozen broccoli, carrots and water chestnuts
    2 tablespoons olive *or* canola oil
    2 tablespoons butter *or* stick margarine
    2 teaspoons dried basil
    2 teaspoons dried marjoram
    1 teaspoon dried thyme
  3/4 teaspoon salt
    4 teaspoons cornstarch
    1 cup chicken broth
  1/2 cup dry white wine *or* additional chicken broth
  1/2 cup grated Parmesan cheese

Cook pasta according to package directions. Meanwhile, in a saucepan, bring 1 in. of water to a boil; place vegetables in a steamer basket over water. Cover and steam for 5-7 minutes or until tender.

In a Dutch oven or large saucepan, combine the oil, butter, basil, marjoram, thyme and salt. Cook and stir over medium heat for 1 minute. Combine cornstarch, broth and wine or additional broth until smooth; stir into the pan. Bring to a boil; cook and stir for 2 minutes or until thickened.

Drain pasta. Add pasta and vegetables to the sauce; toss to combine. Sprinkle with Parmesan cheese. **Yield:** 8 servings.

Nutritional Analysis: One serving (1 cup) equals 181 calories, 9 g fat (3 g saturated fat), 13 mg cholesterol, 500 mg sodium, 18 g carbohydrate, 3 g fiber, 6 g protein.
***Diabetic Exchanges:** 1 starch, 1 lean meat, 1 fat.*

Potatoes with Beans 'n' Pasta

(Pictured above)

Starring both pasta and potatoes, this is a hearty choice to round out almost any menu.
—*Dorothy Smith, El Dorado, Arkansas*

  3/4 pound small red potatoes, cut into 1-inch pieces
  3/4 pound fresh green beans, cut into 2-inch pieces
  1/2 cup chopped sweet red pepper
  1/2 cup chopped sweet yellow pepper
    3 garlic cloves, minced
    2 tablespoons olive *or* canola oil
  1/2 cup reduced-sodium chicken broth
    1 tablespoon lemon juice
  1/4 cup minced fresh basil *or* 4 teaspoons dried basil
  1/4 cup minced fresh parsley
    1 teaspoon finely grated lemon peel
  3/4 teaspoon salt
  1/4 teaspoon pepper
    2 cups cooked tube pasta
  1/4 cup grated Parmesan cheese

Add 1 in. of water to a large saucepan; add the potatoes and beans. Bring to a boil. Reduce heat; cover and simmer for 10 minutes or until potatoes are tender. Meanwhile, in a large nonstick skillet, saute peppers and garlic in oil for 3 minutes. Stir in the broth, lemon juice, basil, parsley, lemon peel, salt and pepper. Cook over low heat for 2 minutes. Drain potatoes and beans. Add potatoes, beans and pasta to pepper mixture; heat through. Sprinkle with Parmesan cheese. **Yield:** 8 servings.

Nutritional Analysis: One serving (1/2 cup) equals 154 calories, 5 g fat (1 g saturated fat), 3 mg cholesterol, 371 mg sodium, 24 g carbohydrate, 3 g fiber, 5 g protein.
***Diabetic Exchanges:** 1 starch, 1 vegetable, 1 fat.*

Favorite Potato Recipe Made Lighter

RICH, CREAMY Twice-Baked Potatoes can make any meal seem like a special occasion.

Debbie Jones from California, Maryland shares her tempting traditional version below. "I like these potatoes because they're so versatile," she says. "They can be served alongside a fancy entree when company comes...or they can stand as the main course with a salad for an easy supper. Either way, they're wonderful. My family loves them.

"The recipe is quite high in fat, though, and I was wondering if there is a way your Test Kitchen could lighten it," she says.

Our home economists took a look at Debbie's recipe and came up with a slimmed-down version by substituting 1% milk, turkey bacon and reduced-fat cheddar cheese.

The end result? Our Makeover Twice-Baked Potatoes have 38 fewer grams of fat than the original recipe...but are still wonderfully tasty and comforting.

Why not try this lighter version on your family soon—and see if they can tell the difference?

Twice-Baked Potatoes

      6 large baking potatoes
  1/2 cup butter *or* stick margarine, softened
      1 cup milk *or* whipping cream
  1/2 pound sliced bacon, cooked and crumbled
1-1/2 cups (6 ounces) shredded cheddar cheese, *divided*
      1 tablespoon minced chives
  1/2 teaspoon salt
Dash pepper
Paprika

Bake the potatoes at 375° for 1 hour or until tender. Cool. Cut a thin slice off the top of each potato and discard. Scoop out pulp, leaving a thin shell. In a bowl, mash the pulp with butter. Stir in milk, bacon, 1 cup of cheese, chives, salt and pepper. Spoon into the potato shells.

Place on an ungreased baking sheet. Bake at 375° for 25-30 minutes or until heated through. Sprinkle with remaining cheese. Bake 2 minutes longer or until cheese is melted. Garnish with paprika. **Yield:** 6 servings.

Nutritional Analysis: One potato equals 630 calories, 48 g fat (24 g saturated fat), 102 mg cholesterol, 834 mg sodium, 35 g carbohydrate, 3 g fiber, 16 g protein.

Makeover Twice-Baked Potatoes

(Pictured below and on page 81)

      6 large baking potatoes
      2 tablespoons butter *or* stick margarine, softened
      1 cup 1% milk
  1/4 pound turkey bacon (about 9 slices), diced and cooked
1-1/2 cups (6 ounces) shredded reduced-fat cheddar cheese, *divided*
      2 tablespoons minced chives
  1/2 teaspoon salt
Dash pepper

Bake the potatoes at 375° for 1 hour or until tender. Cool. Cut a thin slice off the top of each potato and discard. Scoop out pulp, leaving a thin shell. In a bowl, mash the pulp with butter. Stir in milk, bacon, 1 cup of cheese, chives, salt and pepper. Spoon into the potato shells.

Place on an ungreased baking sheet. Bake at 375° for 25-30 minutes or until heated through. Sprinkle with remaining cheese. Bake 2 minutes longer or until cheese is melted. **Yield:** 6 servings.

Nutritional Analysis: One potato equals 298 calories, 10 g fat (5 g saturated fat), 37 mg cholesterol, 717 mg sodium, 36 g carbohydrate, 3 g fiber, 15 g protein.
Diabetic Exchanges: 2 starch, 2 fat, 1 lean meat.

Asparagus Mushroom Casserole

(Pictured below)

This colorful casserole is a palate-pleaser. Asparagus, mushrooms, onions and pimientos make a mouth-watering medley. Lemon and nutmeg give this dish a slightly tangy taste.
—*M. Kay Lacey, Apache Junction, Arizona*

       4 cups sliced fresh mushrooms
       1 cup chopped onion
       4 tablespoons butter *or* stick margarine, *divided*
       2 tablespoons all-purpose flour
       1 teaspoon chicken bouillon granules
    1/2 teaspoon salt
    1/8 teaspoon ground nutmeg
    1/8 teaspoon pepper
       1 cup 2% milk
       1 package (12 ounces) frozen cut asparagus,
          thawed and drained
    1/4 cup diced pimientos
 1-1/2 teaspoons lemon juice
    3/4 cup soft bread crumbs

In a nonstick skillet, cook mushrooms and onion in 3 table-spoons butter until tender. Remove vegetables with a slotted spoon and set aside. Stir the flour, bouillon, salt, nutmeg and pepper into drippings until smooth. Gradually add milk. Bring to a boil; cook and stir for 2 minutes or until thickened. Stir in asparagus, pimientos, lemon juice and the mushroom mixture.

Pour into a 1-1/2-qt. baking dish coated with nonstick cooking spray. Melt remaining butter; toss with bread crumbs. Sprinkle over top. Bake, uncovered, at 350° for 35-40 minutes or until heated through. **Yield:** 6 servings.

Nutritional Analysis: *One serving (1 cup) equals 162 calories, 9 g fat (5 g saturated fat), 24 mg cholesterol, 532 mg sodium, 16 g carbohydrate, 2 g fiber, 6 g protein.*
Diabetic Exchanges: *1 starch, 1 fat, 1/2 lean meat.*

Spinach Rice Casserole

This nicely seasoned casserole combines popular rice and the goodness of fresh spinach. Topped with Parmesan cheese, it's a savory side dish with any meat.
—*Mathilda Navias, Tiffin, Ohio*

       1 cup chopped onion
       1 teaspoon olive *or* canola oil
 1-1/2 cups uncooked long grain rice
       2 cups chicken broth
       2 cups water
       1 package (10 ounces) fresh spinach, torn
    1/2 teaspoon salt
    1/8 teaspoon pepper
    1/4 cup shredded Parmesan cheese

In a large saucepan, saute onion in oil until tender. Add rice; cook and stir for 2 minutes. Add broth and water; bring to a boil. Reduce heat; cover and simmer for 15 minutes. Stir in the spinach, salt and pepper; cook until spinach is wilted.

Transfer to a 2-qt. baking dish coated with nonstick cooking spray. Sprinkle with Parmesan cheese. Cover and bake at 375° for 20-25 minutes or until rice is tender. **Yield:** 8 servings.

Nutritional Analysis: *One serving (3/4 cup) equals 174 calories, 2 g fat (1 g saturated fat), 2 mg cholesterol, 386 mg sodium, 33 g carbohydrate, 1 g fiber, 6 g protein.*
Diabetic Exchange: *2 starch.*

Scalloped Corn

This is my family's all-time favorite corn dish. The buttery cornflake topping and chopped green peppers inside give it a different twist. It is always a success at potluck dinners. Plus, it's special enough to plan into a holiday meal or buffet.
—*Nancy McDonald, Burns, Wyoming*

    1/2 cup chopped green pepper
    1/4 cup chopped onion
       2 teaspoons canola oil
       1 tablespoon all-purpose flour
       1 teaspoon salt
    1/2 teaspoon paprika
    1/4 teaspoon ground mustard
Dash white pepper
       1 cup fat-free evaporated milk
       1 package (16 ounces) frozen corn, thawed
    1/4 cup egg substitute
    1/3 cup crushed cornflakes
       2 teaspoons butter *or* margarine, melted

In a nonstick skillet, saute green pepper and onion in oil until tender. In a small bowl, combine the flour, salt, paprika, mustard and pepper. Stir in milk until smooth; add to skillet. Bring to a boil; cook and stir for 2 minutes or until thickened. Stir in corn and egg substitute.

Pour into a 1-qt. baking dish coated with nonstick cooking spray. Toss cornflakes and butter; sprinkle over the top. Bake, uncovered, at 350° for 30 minutes or until center is partially set. Let stand for 10 minutes before serving. **Yield:** 6 servings.

Nutritional Analysis: One serving (2/3 cup) equals 157 calories, 4 g fat (1 g saturated fat), 5 mg cholesterol, 529 mg sodium, 26 g carbohydrate, 2 g fiber, 7 g protein.
Diabetic Exchange: 2 starch.

Citrus Cranberry Relish

(Pictured below)

This spiced relish is a wonderful side dish for turkey or ham. I especially appreciate it during the hectic holiday season because it can be made ahead of time and refrigerated until serving.
—Julie Wesson, Hainesville, Illinois

1-1/2 cups fresh *or* frozen cranberries
  1 medium navel orange, peeled, chopped and seeded
  1 medium tangerine, peeled, chopped and seeded
1/2 cup raisins
1/2 cup reduced-calorie pancake syrup
1/2 cup orange marmalade
1/2 cup orange juice
  2 teaspoons ground allspice

In a saucepan, combine all of the ingredients. Bring to a boil over medium heat. Reduce heat; cook, uncovered, for 15 minutes, stirring occasionally. Cover and refrigerate for 4 hours or overnight. Store in the refrigerator. **Yield:** 3 cups.

Nutritional Analysis: One serving (1/4 cup) equals 96 calories, trace fat (trace saturated fat), 0 cholesterol, 35 mg sodium, 25 g carbohydrate, 2 g fiber, 1 g protein.
Diabetic Exchange: 1-1/2 fruit.

Lemon Fried Rice

(Pictured above)

This appealing combination of rice and veggies complements most meats. The lemon peel and hot sauce transform regular fried rice into a distinctive side dish.
—Janice Mitchell, Aurora, Colorado

1/2 cup sliced green onions
1/4 cup minced fresh parsley
1/4 cup butter *or* stick margarine
  4 cups cold cooked rice
  1 package (10 ounces) frozen peas, thawed
  2 tablespoons reduced-sodium soy sauce
  2 teaspoons grated lemon peel
1/2 teaspoon salt
1/8 teaspoon hot pepper sauce

In a large nonstick skillet or wok, stir-fry onions and parsley in butter for 1 minute. Add the remaining ingredients; stir-fry for 4-6 minutes or until peas are tender and rice is heated through. **Yield:** 8 servings.

Nutritional Analysis: One serving (2/3 cup) equals 186 calories, 6 g fat (4 g saturated fat), 16 mg cholesterol, 391 mg sodium, 28 g carbohydrate, 2 g fiber, 4 g protein.
Diabetic Exchanges: 2 starch, 1/2 fat.

Red Beans 'n' Brown Rice

This side dish takes a flavorful twist on traditional red beans and rice. The sweetness of the molasses and ketchup contrasts nicely with the garlic and onion...and reminds some people of barbecued beans. This dish never fails to spark compliments.
—Rita Farmer, Houston, Texas

1/2 cup chopped onion
2 garlic cloves, minced
2 teaspoons canola oil
2 cans (15-1/2 ounces *each*) red beans, rinsed and drained
1 can (4 ounces) chopped green chilies
1/2 cup light beer *or* beef broth
1/4 cup ketchup *or* seafood sauce
1/4 cup molasses
1 tablespoon chili powder
1 tablespoon cider vinegar
2 teaspoons reduced-sodium soy sauce
3 cups hot cooked brown *or* white rice

In a large saucepan, saute onion and garlic in oil until tender. Add the beans, chilies, beer or broth, ketchup, molasses, chili powder, vinegar and soy sauce. Bring to a boil. Reduce heat; simmer, uncovered, for 20-30 minutes. Serve over rice. **Yield:** 4 servings.

Nutritional Analysis: One serving (3/4 cup bean mixture with 3/4 cup rice) equals 476 calories, 5 g fat (1 g saturated fat), 0 cholesterol, 1,172 mg sodium, 92 g carbohydrate, 19 g fiber, 16 g protein.

Spaghetti Squash with Sweet Peppers

For a dish with harvesttime appeal, you can't go wrong with this veggie medley I created. Served with breadsticks, it makes a satisfying side or main dish. I grow so much spaghetti squash, I often prepare this through February.
—Julie Backes, Box Elder, South Dakota

1 medium spaghetti squash (2 pounds)
1/2 medium green pepper, sliced
1/2 medium sweet red pepper, sliced
4 medium fresh mushrooms, sliced
1 small onion, chopped
1 tablespoon olive *or* canola oil
2 medium tomatoes, quartered
1 garlic clove, minced
1/2 cup chicken broth
1/4 teaspoon salt
3 tablespoons shredded Parmesan cheese

Cut squash in half lengthwise; discard seeds. Place squash cut side down on a paper towel. Microwave, uncovered, on high for 15 minutes or until tender. Cool.

In a large nonstick skillet, saute the peppers, mushrooms and onion in oil until tender. Add tomatoes and garlic; saute 4-5 minutes longer. Add the broth and salt; simmer, uncovered, for 3-4 minutes.

When squash is cool enough to handle, use a fork to separate strands. Place squash on a serving platter or individual plates; top with the pepper mixture. Sprinkle with Parmesan cheese. **Yield:** 4 servings.
Editor's Note: This recipe was tested in an 850-watt microwave.

Nutritional Analysis: One serving (1/2 cup spaghetti squash with 1/2 cup pepper mixture) equals 110 calories, 5 g fat (1 g saturated fat), 4 mg cholesterol, 372 mg sodium, 13 g carbohydrate, 3 g fiber, 4 g protein.
Diabetic Exchanges: 3 vegetable, 1 fat.

Vegetable Medley

(Pictured at right)

With its red pepper slices and green broccoli florets, this merry medley will brighten any holiday table. Use mild seasonings to let the variety of veggie flavors shine through.
—Sara Lindler, Irmo, South Carolina

1 teaspoon chicken bouillon granules
1/4 cup water
1 teaspoon salt
1/4 teaspoon garlic powder
1/4 teaspoon pepper
1 teaspoon plus 1 tablespoon olive *or* canola oil, *divided*
2 cups broccoli florets
2 medium carrots, thinly sliced
1 large onion, sliced and quartered
1 cup sliced celery
2 medium zucchini, halved lengthwise and thinly sliced
1 medium sweet red pepper, thinly sliced
1 cup sliced fresh mushrooms
2 cups thinly sliced cabbage

In a small saucepan, heat bouillon and water for 1 minute; stir well. Stir in the salt, garlic powder, pepper and 1 teaspoon oil.

In a large nonstick skillet or wok, stir-fry the broccoli, carrots, onion and celery in remaining oil for 2-3 minutes. Add the bouillon mixture; cook and stir for 3 minutes. Add zucchini and red pepper; stir-fry for 3 minutes. Add mushrooms and cabbage; stir-fry 1-2 minutes longer or until crisp-tender. Serve immediately. **Yield:** 8 servings.

Nutritional Analysis: One serving (1 cup) equals 67 calories, 3 g fat (trace saturated fat), trace cholesterol, 473 mg sodium, 10 g carbohydrate, 3 g fiber, 3 g protein.
Diabetic Exchanges: 2 vegetable, 1/2 fat.

Raisin Vegetable Stuffing

When a bowlful of this special stuffing starts circulating, the table will be ringed with smiles in no time. I like to surprise guests with this interesting mix of textures and tastes. They have fun trying to identify the ingredients—everything from allspice and caraway seeds to molasses and soy sauce.
—Sheryl McDonnell Rak, Chicago, Illinois

4 cups day-old white bread cubes
4 cups day-old whole wheat bread cubes
1/2 cup unsweetened pineapple *or* apple juice
1/2 cup golden raisins
1/2 teaspoon ground allspice *or* pumpkin pie spice
1/2 teaspoon molasses
2 cups chopped celery
1 cup chopped carrots
1 medium onion, chopped
3 garlic cloves, minced
2 tablespoons minced chives
2 tablespoons minced fresh parsley
2 tablespoons olive *or* canola oil
2 tablespoons reduced-sodium soy sauce
1-1/4 cups chopped apple
1/4 cup unsalted sunflower kernels
1 teaspoon caraway seeds
1 egg
1/4 cup egg substitute
2 cups chicken broth
1 teaspoon dried marjoram

Place bread cubes in a single layer on two ungreased baking sheets. Bake at 275° for 25-30 minutes or until partially dried, stirring occasionally. Meanwhile, in a saucepan, combine the juice, raisins, allspice and molasses; bring to a boil. Remove from the heat; let stand for 15 minutes.

In a large nonstick skillet, saute the celery, carrots, onion, garlic, chives and parsley in oil and soy sauce for 10 minutes or until vegetables are tender. Remove from the heat. Stir in the apple, sunflower kernels and caraway seeds. In a small bowl, beat egg, egg substitute, broth and marjoram; add to vegetable mixture. Add bread cubes and raisin mixture. Transfer to a 3-qt. baking dish coated with nonstick cooking spray. Bake, uncovered, at 325° for 40-45 minutes or until lightly browned. **Yield:** 12 servings.

Nutritional Analysis: One serving (2/3 cup) equals 179 calories, 6 g fat (1 g saturated fat), 18 mg cholesterol, 452 mg sodium, 28 g carbohydrate, 4 g fiber, 6 g protein.
Diabetic Exchanges: *1 starch, 1 fruit, 1 fat.*

🍎 Rely on Rice

- Substitute the white rice called for in recipes with brown rice. Not only will your family be eating healthier, but your favorite dishes will be enhanced with a slightly nutty flavor.
- Forget the mashed potatoes and bring a side dish of wild rice to the table. Or try something new such as couscous (tiny pasta granules), available in your grocer's rice aisle.

Hash Brown Casserole

(Pictured above)

Be prepared to make this pleasing potato dish again and again. Creamy and cheesy, it's hard to believe this is a reduced-fat casserole. No potluck buffet should be without it!
—Sue Ann O'Buck, Sinking Spring, Pennsylvania

1 can (15 ounces) reduced-fat creamy potato soup*
1 cup (8 ounces) reduced-fat sour cream
1 tablespoon all-purpose flour
1/2 teaspoon garlic salt
1 package (24 ounces) frozen hash brown potatoes
2 cups (8 ounces) shredded reduced-fat cheddar cheese
1/3 cup grated Parmesan cheese
Paprika

In a bowl, combine the soup, sour cream, flour and garlic salt. Stir in potatoes and cheddar cheese. Pour into a 13-in. x 9-in. x 2-in. baking dish coated with nonstick cooking spray. Sprinkle with Parmesan cheese and paprika. Bake, uncovered, at 350° for 50-60 minutes or until potatoes are tender. **Yield:** 8 servings.

***Editor's Note:** This recipe was tested with Healthy Choice ready-to-serve Baked Potato-Style soup.*

Nutritional Analysis: One serving (1 cup) equals 246 calories, 9 g fat (6 g saturated fat), 30 mg cholesterol, 437 mg sodium, 25 g carbohydrate, 2 g fiber, 16 g protein.
Diabetic Exchanges: *1-1/2 starch, 1-1/2 fat, 1 lean meat.*

Armenian Pilaf

My grandfather was born in Armenia in the mid-1800s. This pilaf recipe is adapted from one he brought to this country. At our house, it's a standard with shish kabobs and chicken dishes.
—Susan Lederer, Fallon, Nevada

1 medium onion, chopped
1/2 cup bulgur*
1/2 cup uncooked long grain rice
1/2 cup uncooked broken vermicelli (1-inch pieces)
2 tablespoons butter *or* stick margarine
1 can (14-1/2 ounces) beef broth
1/3 cup water
1/4 teaspoon dried oregano

In a large nonstick skillet, saute the onion, bulgur, rice and vermicelli in butter for 6-7 minutes or until golden brown. Add the broth, water and oregano; bring to a boil. Reduce heat; cover and simmer for 20-25 minutes or until rice is tender. Remove from the heat; let stand for 5 minutes. Fluff with a fork. **Yield:** 6 servings.

*Editor's Note: Look for bulgur in the cereal, rice or organic food aisle of your grocery store.

Nutritional Analysis: One serving (3/4 cup) equals 183 calories, 5 g fat (3 g saturated fat), 10 mg cholesterol, 282 mg sodium, 31 g carbohydrate, 3 g fiber, 5 g protein.
Diabetic Exchanges: 2 starch, 1/2 fat.

Salt Substitute

I find filling a salt shaker with this mixture of spices reduces the automatic reach for salt. I sprinkle the fragrant fusion of flavors on meat, fish, poultry and vegetables.
—Joy Beck, Cincinnati, Ohio

3 bay leaves, broken into pieces
3 teaspoons dried minced onion
2 teaspoons dried rosemary, crushed
1 teaspoon garlic powder
1 teaspoon dried marjoram
1 teaspoon rubbed sage
1 teaspoon dried thyme
1/2 teaspoon lemon-pepper seasoning
1/2 teaspoon pepper

Place all ingredients in a food processor or blender; cover and process until finely ground. Transfer to a salt shaker; use in place of salt. **Yield:** 8 teaspoons.

Nutritional Analysis: One serving (1/4 teaspoon) equals 2 calories, trace fat (trace saturated fat), 0 cholesterol, 9 mg sodium, trace carbohydrate, trace fiber, trace protein.
Diabetic Exchange: Free food.

Roasted Corn and Garlic Rice

(Pictured below)

I usually roast quite a few ears of corn when they are on sale and freeze what I don't use at that time. This is a wonderful side dish to go with a fish fry, barbecue or almost any summer meal. It's a constant at my house.
—Marilyn Rodriguez, Fairbanks, Alaska

4 ears sweet corn in husks
2 to 3 garlic cloves, peeled
2-1/4 teaspoons olive *or* canola oil, *divided*
1 cup uncooked long grain rice
2 cups chicken broth
1 bay leaf
1/4 teaspoon salt
1/8 to 1/4 teaspoon pepper

Carefully peel back husks from corn to within 1 in. of bottom; remove silk. Rewrap corn in husks. Place garlic cloves on a piece of heavy-duty foil; drizzle with 1/4 teaspoon oil. Fold foil around garlic and seal tightly. Place corn and garlic directly on oven rack. Bake at 400° for 30 minutes. Remove corn; bake garlic 5-10 minutes longer or until softened.

Remove garlic from foil and place in a small bowl; cool. Mash with a fork. When corn is cool enough to handle, remove corn from cobs with a sharp knife.

In a saucepan over medium heat, heat remaining oil. Add rice; cook and stir for 2 minutes. Gradually add broth, bay leaf, salt, pepper and roasted garlic. Bring to a boil. Reduce heat; cover and cook for 13 minutes. Stir in roasted corn; cover and cook 7-10 minutes longer or until rice is tender. Discard bay leaf. **Yield:** 4 servings.

Nutritional Analysis: One serving (1 cup) equals 291 calories, 4 g fat (1 g saturated fat), 0 cholesterol, 628 mg sodium, 59 g carbohydrate, 3 g fiber, 7 g protein.
Diabetic Exchange: 3-1/2 starch.

In a bowl, beat the egg; add spinach, bread crumbs, tomato sauce, Parmesan cheese, onion, garlic, salt, pepper and zucchini pulp. Spoon into zucchini shells.

Place in an ungreased 13-in. x 9-in. x 2-in. baking dish. Bake, uncovered, at 350° for 20 minutes. Top each with tomatoes and Swiss cheese. Bake 5-10 minutes longer or until cheese is melted. **Yield:** 8 servings.

Nutritional Analysis: One serving (1 zucchini boat) equals 148 calories, 6 g fat (3 g saturated fat), 40 mg cholesterol, 429 mg sodium, 15 g carbohydrate, 3 g fiber, 10 g protein.
Diabetic Exchanges: 2 vegetable, 1-1/2 lean meat, 1/2 fat.

Carrot Zucchini Saute

I concocted this eye-pleasing recipe as a quick-and-easy side dish, and it's fast become a family favorite. It's a wonderful way to use up an abundance of veggies from your garden.
—Mildred Ricket, Magnolia, Texas

1 pound carrots, cut into 2-inch julienne strips
1 tablespoon olive *or* canola oil
3/4 pound zucchini, cut into 2-inch julienne strips
1 tablespoon balsamic vinegar
1/2 teaspoon Italian seasoning
1/2 teaspoon salt

In a large nonstick skillet, saute carrots in oil for 10 minutes. Add zucchini; saute 10 minutes longer or until vegetables

Stuffed Zucchini Boats

(Pictured above)

This savory side dish is reason enough to give zucchini extra space in your garden. These veggie-stuffed boats are wonderful paired with any meat. Or serve them alongside a loaf of homemade bread and slices of melon and avocado nestled on crisp lettuce leaves.
—Billie Moss, El Sobrante, California

4 medium zucchini
1 egg
1 cup chopped fresh spinach
3/4 cup dry bread crumbs
1/2 cup tomato sauce
1/3 cup grated Parmesan cheese
1/3 cup finely chopped onion
1 garlic clove, minced
1/4 teaspoon salt
1/8 teaspoon pepper
1 can (14-1/2 ounces) diced tomatoes, drained and finely chopped
1 cup (4 ounces) shredded reduced-fat Swiss cheese

Trim ends of zucchini; place in a steamer basket. In a saucepan, bring 1 in. of water to a boil; add basket. Cover and steam for 5 minutes. When zucchini is cool enough to handle, cut in half lengthwise; scoop out pulp, leaving a 1/4-in. shell. Set pulp aside.

🍎 Zucchini, A to Z

- Handle zucchini carefully—they are thin-skinned and easily damaged.
- To pick the freshest zucchini, look for a firm heavy squash with a moist stem end and a shiny skin.
- Smaller squash are generally sweeter and more tender than larger ones.
- One medium (1/3 pound) zucchini yields about 2 cups sliced or 1-1/2 cups shredded zucchini.
- Store zucchini in a plastic bag in the refrigerator crisper for 4 to 5 days. Do not wash until ready to use.
- When grating zucchini, leave the stem on to give you a grip as you work.
- Zucchini is wonderful steamed, sauteed, grilled or stuffed and baked. You can also cut uncooked zucchini into strips and serve it as an appetizer...or dice or grate it into a salad.
- Overcooked zucchini will end up as mush. To salvage it, make soup!
- 1/2 cup cooked sliced zucchini has about 15 calories. It provides some beta-carotene, B vitamins, folic acid, vitamin C and calcium, plus a healthy amount of potassium.

are crisp-tender. Sprinkle with vinegar, Italian seasoning and salt; toss. **Yield:** 6 servings.

Nutritional Analysis: *One serving (1/2 cup) equals 64 calories, 2 g fat (trace saturated fat), 0 cholesterol, 237 mg sodium, 10 g carbohydrate, 3 g fiber, 2 g protein.*
Diabetic Exchange: *2 vegetable.*

Almond Broccoli Stir-Fry

(Pictured above)

The broccoli retains its lovely green color when stir-fried, so this dish is not only easy to make but pretty to serve. The almonds add a nutty crunch.
—*Margery Bryan, Royal City, Washington*

10 cups broccoli florets
2 tablespoons canola oil
2 to 3 garlic cloves, minced
1/4 cup reduced-sodium soy sauce
2 tablespoons sugar
1/2 teaspoon ground ginger
2 teaspoons lemon juice
1/2 cup chopped almonds, toasted

In a nonstick skillet or wok, stir-fry broccoli in oil for 2 minutes or until crisp-tender. Add garlic; stir-fry for 1 minute. Stir in the soy sauce, sugar and ginger; cook for 1-2 minutes or until sugar is dissolved. Sprinkle with lemon juice and almonds. **Yield:** 8 servings.

Nutritional Analysis: *One serving (3/4 cup) equals 132 calories, 8 g fat (1 g saturated fat), 0 cholesterol, 333 mg sodium, 12 g carbohydrate, 2 g fiber, 6 g protein.*
Diabetic Exchanges: *2 vegetable, 2 fat.*

Tex-Mex Corn on the Cob

(Pictured below)

It's a snap to add zippy flavor to fresh corn on the cob. The tender ears get a summery treatment when seasoned with chili powder, cilantro and lime.
—*Helen Jacobs, Euless, Texas*

12 small ears fresh corn on the cob (about 6 inches)
3 tablespoons minced fresh cilantro *or* parsley
1-1/2 teaspoons chili powder
1-1/2 teaspoons grated lime peel
3/4 teaspoon salt
3/4 teaspoon ground cumin
1/4 teaspoon garlic powder
Refrigerated butter-flavored spray*

Place corn in a Dutch oven or kettle; cover with water. Bring to a boil; cook for 3-5 minutes or until tender. Meanwhile, in a small bowl, combine the cilantro, chili powder, lime peel, salt, cumin and garlic powder. Drain the corn. Spritz with butter-flavored spray; brush or pat seasonings over corn. **Yield:** 12 servings.

***Editor's Note:** This recipe was tested with I Can't Believe It's Not Butter Spray.

Nutritional Analysis: *One serving (1 ear) equals 85 calories, 1 g fat (trace saturated fat), 0 cholesterol, 164 mg sodium, 20 g carbohydrate, 2 g fiber, 3 g protein.*
Diabetic Exchange: *1 starch.*

Roasted Brussels Sprouts

Although the brussels sprouts are very simply seasoned, roasting them caramelizes their natural sugars, giving them a subtle sweetness.
—Tina Repak, Johnstown, Pennsylvania

- **2 pounds fresh *or* frozen brussels sprouts, thawed**
- **1 tablespoon butter *or* stick margarine**
- **1 tablespoon olive *or* canola oil**
- **1/2 teaspoon salt**
- **1/4 teaspoon pepper**

Cut an "X" in the core end of each brussels sprout with a sharp knife. Place 1 in. of water in a saucepan; add sprouts. Bring to a boil. Reduce heat; cover and simmer for 5-6 minutes or until crisp-tender. Drain. Add the remaining ingredients; toss to coat.

Arrange sprouts in a single layer in a 15-in. x 10-in. x 1-in. baking pan coated with nonstick cooking spray. Bake, uncovered, at 425° for 15-20 minutes, stirring occasionally. Serve immediately. **Yield:** 6 servings.

Nutritional Analysis: One serving (2/3 cup) equals 101 calories, 5 g fat (2 g saturated fat), 5 mg cholesterol, 244 mg sodium, 14 g carbohydrate, 4 g fiber, 4 g protein.
Diabetic Exchanges: 2 vegetable, 1 fat.

East Indian Split Pea Pilaf

Yellow split peas, chicken broth and savory spices turn long grain rice into a piquant pilaf. This recipe was given to me by a friend from India.
—Marilyn Rodriguez, Fairbanks, Alaska

- **2/3 cup dry yellow split peas**
- **4-3/4 cups water, *divided***
- **1 bay leaf**
- **3 tablespoons canola oil**
- **1 large onion, chopped**
- **1/2 to 1 teaspoon ground cinnamon**
- **3/4 teaspoon ground cumin**
- **1/2 teaspoon salt**
- **1/4 teaspoon ground cloves**
- **1/4 teaspoon ground turmeric**
- **1-1/2 cups uncooked long grain rice**
- **2-1/2 cups chicken broth**

In a saucepan, combine peas and 4 cups water. Bring to a boil; reduce heat and simmer, uncovered, for 30-35 minutes or until tender. Drain and keep warm.

In a large nonstick skillet, cook the bay leaf in oil until golden, about 3 minutes. Add onion; saute until tender. Stir in the seasonings; saute for 30 seconds. Add the rice; cook and stir for 3 minutes. Stir in broth and remaining water. Bring to a boil. Reduce heat; cover and simmer for 20-25 minutes or until rice is tender. Add peas; heat through. Discard bay leaf before serving. **Yield:** 6 servings.

Nutritional Analysis: One serving (1 cup) equals 214 calories, 7 g fat (1 g saturated fat), 0 cholesterol, 572 mg sodium, 30 g carbohydrate, 1 g fiber, 8 g protein.
Diabetic Exchanges: 2 starch, 1 fat.

Twice-Baked Acorn Squash

(Pictured above)

Once you taste this scrumptious side dish, you'll want to double your garden space for squash! Acorn is my favorite kind of winter squash. It's so versatile—I use it in all kinds of recipes. And the hollowed-out shells make such pretty serving bowls.
—Holly Ogilvie, Lino Lakes, Minnesota

- **2 medium acorn squash (about 1-1/2 pounds each)**
- **1 package (10 ounces) frozen chopped spinach, thawed and squeezed dry**
- **2 bacon strips, cooked and crumbled**
- **10 tablespoons shredded Parmesan cheese, divided**
- **2 tablespoons thinly sliced green onion**
- **1 tablespoon butter *or* stick margarine, softened**
- **1/4 teaspoon salt**
- **Dash to 1/8 teaspoon cayenne pepper**

Cut squash in half; discard seeds. Place squash upside down on a baking sheet coated with nonstick cooking spray. Bake at 350° for 50-55 minutes or until tender. Scoop out squash, leaving a 1/4-in. shell.

In a bowl, combine the squash pulp, spinach, bacon, 6 tablespoons Parmesan cheese, green onion, butter, salt and cayenne; spoon into shells. Sprinkle with remaining Parmesan cheese. Bake for 25-30 minutes or until heated through and top is golden brown. **Yield:** 4 servings.

Nutritional Analysis: One serving (1 filled squash half) equals 248 calories, 10 g fat (5 g saturated fat), 23 mg cholesterol, 579 mg sodium, 34 g carbohydrate, 11 g fiber, 12 g protein.
Diabetic Exchanges: 2 starch, 1 lean meat, 1 fat.

Favorite Casserole Recipe Made Lighter

GREEN BEAN CASSEROLE conjures up memories of Mom's traditional Christmas dinner with all the trimmings. "Everyone loves green beans when they're dressed up in a creamy sauce and topped with golden french-fried onions," says Christy Hinrichs of Parkville, Missouri.

Your family is likely expecting this classic side dish to be served at your holiday table, too. If you want to offer them a slimmed-down version instead, try our Test Kitchen's Makeover Green Bean Casserole. The recipe calls for frozen green beans instead of canned, a from-scratch sauce in place of a can of soup and a home-made onion topping.

The result? A creamy casserole with wonderful flavor—yet each serving has almost a third fewer calories, nearly two-thirds less sodium and about 90% less fat than the original!

Green Bean Casserole

  1 can (10-3/4 ounces) condensed cream of mushroom soup, undiluted
1/2 cup milk
  1 teaspoon soy sauce
1/8 teaspoon pepper
  2 cans (14-1/2 ounces *each*) cut green beans, drained
  1 can (2.8 ounces) french-fried onions, *divided*

In a bowl, combine the soup, milk, soy sauce and pepper. Stir in beans and 1/2 cup onions. Transfer to a greased 1-1/2-qt. baking dish. Sprinkle with remaining onions. Bake, uncovered, at 400° for 12-15 minutes or until bubbly. **Yield:** 8 servings.

Nutritional Analysis: *One serving (1/2 cup) equals 125 calories, 8 g fat (3 g saturated fat), 2 mg cholesterol, 565 mg sodium, 11 g carbohydrate, 1 g fiber, 2 g protein.*

Makeover Green Bean Casserole

(Pictured at right)

  1 package (16 ounces) frozen cut green beans
  1 medium onion, chopped
  1 garlic clove, minced
  1 teaspoon butter *or* stick margarine
1/2 pound fresh mushrooms, chopped
  1 can (12 ounces) fat-free evaporated milk
1/4 cup all-purpose flour
1/2 cup fat-free milk
  1 teaspoon reduced-sodium soy sauce

1/2 teaspoon salt
1/4 teaspoon poultry seasoning
1/8 to 1/4 teaspoon pepper
TOPPING:
  2 cups sliced onions
  1 teaspoon butter *or* stick margarine
1/2 cup soft bread crumbs

Place beans in a microwave-safe dish. Cover and cook on high for 7-9 minutes or until tender; drain.

In a nonstick skillet, cook onion and garlic in butter over medium heat until tender, about 4 minutes. Add mushrooms; cook until softened. Reduce heat to medium-low; gradually stir in evaporated milk. Combine flour and milk until smooth; stir into mushroom mixture. Add the soy sauce, salt, poultry seasoning and pepper. Bring to a boil; cook and stir for 2 minutes or until thickened. Stir in beans. Transfer to a 2-qt. baking dish coated with nonstick cooking spray. Bake, uncovered, at 375° for 15 minutes.

For topping, in a large nonstick skillet, cook onions in butter over medium-low heat until golden brown. Add the bread crumbs; cook until dry and golden brown. Sprinkle over casserole. Bake 7-10 minutes longer or until heated through and topping is browned. Let stand for 10 minutes before serving. **Yield:** 12 servings.

Nutritional Analysis: *One serving (1/2 cup) equals 86 calories, 1 g fat (1 g saturated fat), 3 mg cholesterol, 200 mg sodium, 15 g carbohydrate, 2 g fiber, 5 g protein.*
Diabetic Exchanges: *2 vegetable, 1/2 fat-free milk.*

Cheesy Broccoli Rigatoni

(Pictured below)

This cheese- and veggie-packed pasta side dish always brings compliments. Add chicken or shrimp, and you'll have a well-balanced entree. The tasty white sauce can be used on many foods. My husband even likes it spooned over eggs!
—Lisa Csiki, North Windham, Connecticut

12 ounces uncooked rigatoni *or* medium
   tube pasta
3 garlic cloves, minced
1/4 cup butter *or* stick margarine
1/4 cup all-purpose flour
1 teaspoon salt
2-1/2 cups fat-free milk
1 tablespoon olive *or* canola oil
5 cups broccoli florets
2 cups (8 ounces) shredded part-skim mozzarella
   cheese, *divided*

Cook pasta according to package directions. Meanwhile, in a saucepan, saute garlic in butter over medium heat for 2 minutes. Stir in flour and salt until blended. Gradually add milk. Bring to a boil; cook and stir for 2 minutes or until thickened. Remove from the heat; set aside. Drain pasta and toss with oil; set aside.

Add 1 in. of water to a large saucepan; add broccoli. Bring to a boil. Reduce heat; cover and simmer for 4-5 minutes or until crisp-tender. Drain and rinse with cold water.

In a 13-in. x 9-in. x 2-in. baking dish coated with nonstick cooking spray, layer 1 cup white sauce, half of the pasta and broccoli and 1/2 cup cheese. Repeat layers. Top with remaining sauce and cheese. Cover and bake at 350° for 25-30 minutes or until heated through. **Yield:** 10 servings.

Nutritional Analysis: One serving (1 cup) equals 280 calories, 11 g fat (6 g saturated fat), 27 mg cholesterol, 434 mg sodium, 34 g carbohydrate, 2 g fiber, 14 g protein.
Diabetic Exchanges: 2 starch, 1 vegetable, 1 lean meat, 1 fat.

Cranberry Beets

When I'm looking for a different way to put cranberries on the menu, this unique side dish comes immediately to mind. Paired with beets, the berries are tasty and tangy...and their ruby-red color really brightens up my holiday dinner table.
—Donna Smith, Fairport, New York

6 cups sliced peeled fresh beets*
1 can (16 ounces) whole-berry cranberry sauce
2 tablespoons orange juice
1 teaspoon grated orange peel
1/2 teaspoon salt

Place beets in a saucepan and cover with water; bring to a boil. Reduce heat; cover and simmer for 10 minutes or until tender. In another saucepan, heat cranberry sauce over medium heat until melted. Add orange juice, orange peel and salt. Drain beets; gently stir into cranberry mixture. Heat through. **Yield:** 8 servings.

***Editor's Note:** To avoid staining your hands, wear rubber or plastic gloves when peeling and slicing beets.*

Nutritional Analysis: One serving (1/2 cup) equals 127 calories, trace fat (trace saturated fat), 0 cholesterol, 238 mg sodium, 31 g carbohydrate, 4 g fiber, 2 g protein.
Diabetic Exchanges: 2 vegetable, 1-1/2 fruit.

🍎 A Bowlful of Cranberry Facts

RICH in color, tangy in taste, cranberries are an unbeatable winter treat. And they add zing to almost everything—from breads and beverages to salads, sauces, soups and more. Here are some berry tidbits from the Wisconsin State Cranberry Growers Association:

- Cranberries are one of three native North American fruits of commercial value, along with blueberries and Concord grapes.
- This beneficial berry is high in fiber, has just 25 calories per 1/2 cup and is a good source of vitamin C. Cranberries are also low in sodium and contain vitamins A and B, calcium, phosphorus and iron.
- Look for firm, plump cranberries with a lustrous color. You'll find fresh cranberries in the produce section from September through December. They freeze well, so buy extra.
- Fresh cranberries will keep in the refrigerator for up to 4 weeks. Wash berries only when ready to use.

Southern Stir-Fry

A pinch of cayenne pepper lends a little
kick to this veggie blend.
—Lynn Burnett, Raymore, Missouri

1/2 cup chopped celery
1/3 cup chopped onion
  1 tablespoon canola oil
  1 can (15-1/2 ounces) black-eyed peas, rinsed
    and drained
  1 cup frozen whole kernel corn, thawed
1-1/2 teaspoons minced fresh thyme *or* 1/2 teaspoon
    dried thyme
  1 garlic clove, minced
1/2 teaspoon salt
1/8 teaspoon cayenne pepper
  2 tablespoons chicken broth
  1 tablespoon white wine *or* additional chicken
    broth
  2 cups fresh spinach, chopped
  1 cup cooked rice

In a large nonstick skillet or wok, stir-fry celery and onion in oil until tender. Add the peas, corn, thyme, garlic, salt and cayenne; cook and stir over medium heat for 1 minute. Add broth and wine or additional broth; cook and stir for 1 minute. Add spinach and rice; cook and stir 2 minutes more or until spinach is wilted. **Yield:** 4 servings.

   Nutritional Analysis: One serving (3/4 cup) equals 216 calories, 5 g fat (1 g saturated fat), 0 cholesterol, 679 mg sodium, 37 g carbohydrate, 6 g fiber, 8 g protein.
   Diabetic Exchanges: 2 starch, 1 vegetable, 1/2 fat.

Zippy Green Beans

(Pictured above)

A sweet-and-sour sauce makes fresh green beans
a little special. The tangy treatment for this
everyday vegetable dresses them up nicely, so they
complement most any meal.
—Suzanne McKinley, Lyons, Georgia

  4 cups fresh *or* frozen green beans, cut into
    2-inch pieces
  2 bacon strips, diced
  1 medium onion, thinly sliced
1/2 cup white wine *or* apple juice
  3 tablespoons sugar
  3 tablespoons tarragon vinegar *or* cider vinegar
1/4 teaspoon salt
  2 teaspoons cornstarch
  1 tablespoon cold water

Place beans in a saucepan and cover with water; bring to a boil. Cook, uncovered, for 8-10 minutes or until crisp-tender. Meanwhile, in a large nonstick skillet, cook bacon over medium heat until crisp. Remove with a slotted spoon to paper towels. Drain, reserving 1 teaspoon drippings.
   In the drippings, saute onion until tender. Add wine or apple juice, sugar, vinegar and salt. Combine cornstarch and cold water until smooth; add to the skillet. Bring to a boil; cook and stir for 2 minutes or until thickened. Drain beans; top with onion mixture. Sprinkle with bacon; toss to coat. **Yield:** 6 servings.

   Nutritional Analysis: One serving (3/4 cup) equals 98 calories, 2 g fat (1 g saturated fat), 3 mg cholesterol, 140 mg sodium, 16 g carbohydrate, 3 g fiber, 2 g protein.
   Diabetic Exchanges: 2 vegetable, 1/2 fruit, 1/2 fat.

Pasta Shells with Herbs

Red pepper slices and a sprinkling of parsley dress up
pasta shells in a simple yet eye-pleasing way.
—Marilyn Pozzo, Fruitvale, British Columbia

12 ounces uncooked medium pasta shells
  1 medium sweet red pepper, julienned
  2 garlic cloves, minced
  2 tablespoons butter *or* stick margarine
  2 tablespoons olive *or* canola oil
1/2 cup minced fresh parsley
1/2 cup 2% milk
1/3 cup chopped fresh tarragon, basil, thyme *or*
    oregano *or* 1 tablespoon dried tarragon, basil,
    thyme *or* oregano
  1 teaspoon salt
1/8 teaspoon pepper

Cook pasta according to package directions. Meanwhile, in a large nonstick skillet, saute the red pepper and garlic in butter and oil until tender. Drain pasta; add to pepper mixture. Add the remaining ingredients; toss to combine. Serve immediately. **Yield:** 6 servings.

   Nutritional Analysis: One serving (1 cup) equals 308 calories, 10 g fat (3 g saturated fat), 12 mg cholesterol, 448 mg sodium, 46 g carbohydrate, 2 g fiber, 9 g protein.
   Diabetic Exchanges: 3 starch, 1-1/2 fat.

Horseradish Sauce for Veggies

Horseradish adds zing to the warm sour cream sauce I often drape over vegetables. This sauce is incredibly quick to make. And it really perks up cooked broccoli and cauliflower.
—*Dolores Lueken, Ferdinand, Indiana*

1 cup (8 ounces) reduced-fat sour cream
2 teaspoons prepared horseradish
2 teaspoons Dijon mustard
1/4 teaspoon salt

In a small saucepan, combine all ingredients. Cook and stir over medium-low heat until heated through. Serve immediately. **Yield:** 1 cup.

Nutritional Analysis: One serving (2 tablespoons) equals 42 calories, 3 g fat (2 g saturated fat), 10 mg cholesterol, 129 mg sodium, 2 g carbohydrate, trace fiber, 2 g protein.
Diabetic Exchange: 1 fat.

Herb Butter

The only thing better than homemade bread hot from the oven is a slice of it spread with this zesty butter! The fresh herbs make a little of this butter go a long way—you'll find you use less but still get great flavor. It's also a wonderful potato topper.
—*Jill Smith, Irmo, South Carolina*

4 ounces fat-free cream cheese
2 tablespoons butter *or* stick margarine, softened
2 teaspoons minced fresh basil
2 teaspoons minced fresh parsley
1 teaspoon dill weed
1/4 teaspoon minced garlic
Dash pepper
1/8 teaspoon zesty Italian salad dressing mix
1/8 teaspoon lemon juice

In a bowl, combine all ingredients until smooth. Cover and refrigerate until serving. Spread on bread or crackers or use to top baked potatoes. **Yield:** 1/2 cup.

Nutritional Analysis: One serving (1-1/2 teaspoons) equals 20 calories, 2 g fat (1 g saturated fat), 4 mg cholesterol, 54 mg sodium, 1 g carbohydrate, trace fiber, 1 g protein.
Diabetic Exchange: 1/2 fat.

Broccoli Italiano

My husband didn't like broccoli until I gave it some of my special Italian touches. Now I can't serve this delicious side dish often enough.
—*Melanie Habener, Lompoc, California*

5-1/2 cups broccoli florets
1/2 cup thinly sliced green onions
4 teaspoons olive *or* canola oil
4 garlic cloves, minced
2 tablespoons lemon juice
1/2 teaspoon salt
1/4 teaspoon pepper
2 large fresh mushrooms, sliced

In a large saucepan, bring 1 in. of water to a boil. Place broccoli in a steamer basket over water; cover and steam for 4-5 minutes or until crisp-tender.

In a nonstick skillet, cook onions in oil over medium heat for 1 minute. Add garlic; cook 30 seconds longer. Reduce heat. Add the broccoli, lemon juice, salt and pepper; toss to coat. Remove from the heat; let stand for 5 minutes before serving. Add mushrooms. **Yield:** 7 servings.

Nutritional Analysis: One serving (3/4 cup) equals 49 calories, 3 g fat (trace saturated fat), 0 cholesterol, 188 mg sodium, 5 g carbohydrate, 1 g fiber, 2 g protein.
Diabetic Exchanges: 1 vegetable, 1/2 fat.

Breakfast & Brunch

Breakfast boosts your energy level, which is
bound to give you a sunny outlook on the
day and help you perform your best. So
open your family's eyes to good eating
with these day-brightening recipes.

Raspberry Coffee Cake and Sausage Egg Squares (page 104)

Homemade Egg Substitute

Egg substitute can be used to replace whole eggs in many recipes with good results, especially in frittatas, omelets and quiches. Our Test Kitchen came up with this homemade version that you can quickly whip up.

2 large egg whites, lightly beaten
1 tablespoon nonfat dry milk powder
1 teaspoon canola *or* vegetable oil
4 drops yellow food coloring, optional

In a bowl, whisk the egg whites, milk powder and oil until well blended. Add food coloring if desired. **Yield:** 1/4 cup egg substitute equivalent to 1 large egg.

Editor's Note: The cholesterol in 1 large whole fresh egg is 213 mg.

Nutritional Analysis: 1/4 cup equals 100 calories, 5 g fat (trace saturated fat), 1 mg cholesterol, 150 mg sodium, 5 g carbohydrate, 0 fiber, 10 g protein.
Diabetic Exchanges: *1 lean meat, 1 fat.*

Hearty Carrot Muffins

(Pictured at right)

These moist muffins are a wonderful morning treat. My husband and our two daughters also love them as a snack.
—Margriet Neels, Ancaster, Ontario

3/4 cup fat-free milk
1/2 cup maple syrup
2 egg whites
1 tablespoon canola oil
1/2 cup grated tart apple
1/2 cup shredded carrot
3/4 cup whole wheat flour
1/2 cup wheat bran
1/4 cup all-purpose flour
3 tablespoons sugar
1 teaspoon baking powder
1 teaspoon baking soda
1/2 teaspoon salt
1/2 teaspoon ground cinnamon

In a large bowl, beat the milk, syrup, egg whites and oil until smooth. Stir in apple and carrot. Combine the dry ingredients; stir into milk mixture just until moistened. Coat muffin cups with nonstick cooking spray; fill two-thirds full. Bake at 375° for 18-20 minutes or until a toothpick comes out clean. Cool for 5 minutes before removing from pan to a wire rack. **Yield:** 1 dozen.

Nutritional Analysis: One muffin equals 109 calories, 1 g fat (trace saturated fat), trace cholesterol, 242 mg sodium, 23 g carbohydrate, 2 g fiber, 3 g protein.
Diabetic Exchanges: *1 starch, 1/2 fruit.*

Ham and Cheese Strudel

(Pictured at right)

I wrap phyllo dough around a creamy filling of ham, cheese and egg substitute to create pretty golden-brown roll-ups.
—Jo Groth, Plainfield, Iowa

1 tablespoon butter *or* stick margarine
2 tablespoons all-purpose flour
1 cup fat-free milk
1/4 pound fully cooked lean ham, finely chopped
1/3 cup shredded reduced-fat Swiss cheese
4 tablespoons grated Parmesan cheese, *divided*
1-1/4 cups egg substitute
6 phyllo dough sheets (18 inches x 14 inches)
Nonstick cooking spray
Refrigerated butter-flavored spray*
1/4 cup dry bread crumbs
2 tablespoons minced fresh parsley

In a saucepan, melt butter. Stir in flour until smooth. Gradually stir in milk. Bring to a boil; cook and stir for 1-2 minutes or until thickened. Add ham; heat through. Remove from the heat. Stir in Swiss cheese and 2 tablespoons Parmesan cheese until Swiss is melted; set aside. In a nonstick skillet coated with nonstick cooking spray, cook and stir egg substitute over medium heat until completely set. Stir into cheese mixture.

For each strudel, place one sheet of phyllo dough on work surface with a short side facing you (keep remaining dough covered with waxed paper to avoid drying out). Coat dough with nonstick cooking spray; fold in half lengthwise. Coat with nonstick cooking spray; spritz with butter-flavored spray. Sprinkle with 2 teaspoons bread crumbs. Spread some egg mixture over bottom third of dough to within 3/4 in. of bottom and sides. Fold in sides. Roll up dough, starting at end with egg mixture.

Place seam side down on an ungreased baking sheet. Coat with nonstick cooking spray; spritz with butter-flavored spray. Bake at 375° for 15-18 minutes or until golden brown and filling is heated through (filling may expand and come out of dough during baking). Sprinkle each with parsley and remaining Parmesan cheese. **Yield:** 6 servings.

*Editor's Note: This recipe was tested with I Can't Believe It's Not Butter Spray.

Nutritional Analysis: One serving equals 218 calories, 8 g fat (3 g saturated fat), 18 mg cholesterol, 576 mg sodium, 18 g carbohydrate, 1 g fiber, 18 g protein.
Diabetic Exchanges: *2 lean meat, 1 starch, 1/2 fat.*

Apple Carrot Muffins

This recipe was given to me by a parent of one of my students. These fruity muffins are moist, tender and taste almost like carrot cake. They freeze well, too.
—Elaine Cooley, Louisville, Kentucky

1-3/4 cups raisin bran cereal
1-1/4 cups all-purpose flour
3/4 cup sugar
1-1/4 teaspoons baking soda
1 teaspoon ground cinnamon
1/4 teaspoon salt
1 egg
3/4 cup buttermilk
1/4 cup canola oil
3/4 cup finely chopped peeled tart apple
3/4 cup grated carrots
1/4 cup chopped walnuts

In a bowl, combine the first six ingredients. In a small bowl, beat the egg, buttermilk and oil. Stir into dry ingredients just until moistened. Fold in apple, carrots and walnuts. Fill paper-lined muffin cups or cups coated with nonstick cooking spray three-fourths full. Bake at 400° for 20-23 minutes or until a toothpick comes out clean. Cool for 5 minutes before removing from pan to a wire rack. Serve warm. **Yield:** 1 dozen.

Nutritional Analysis: One muffin equals 199 calories, 7 g fat (1 g saturated fat), 18 mg cholesterol, 256 mg sodium, 32 g carbohydrate, 2 g fiber, 4 g protein.
Diabetic Exchanges: *2 starch, 1/2 fruit.*

Raspberry Coffee Cake

(Pictured at right and on page 101)

Who says you can't eat coffee cake when you're watching your weight? This is one of my favorite recipes. It's perfect for a brunch buffet, with bits of raspberry in every moist bite and a drizzle of frosting and toasted almonds on top. Yum!
—Merle Shapter, Delta, British Columbia

1 cup all-purpose flour
1/3 cup sugar
1/2 teaspoon baking powder
1/4 teaspoon baking soda
1/4 teaspoon salt
1 egg
1/2 cup reduced-fat plain yogurt
2 tablespoons butter *or* stick margarine, melted
1 teaspoon vanilla extract
3 tablespoons brown sugar
1 cup unsweetened fresh *or* frozen raspberries*
1 tablespoon sliced almonds
GLAZE:
1/4 cup confectioners' sugar
1 teaspoon fat-free milk
1/4 teaspoon vanilla extract

In a bowl, combine the flour, sugar, baking powder, baking soda and salt. Combine the egg, yogurt, butter and vanilla;

add to dry ingredients just until moistened. Spoon two-thirds of the batter into an 8-in. round baking pan coated with nonstick cooking spray. Combine the brown sugar and raspberries; sprinkle over batter. Spoon remaining batter over the top. Sprinkle with almonds.

Bake at 350° for 35-40 minutes or until cake springs back when lightly touched and is golden brown. Cool for 10 minutes before removing from pan to a wire rack. In a small bowl, combine the glaze ingredients. Drizzle over coffee cake. Serve warm or at room temperature. **Yield:** 8 servings.

*Editor's Note: If using frozen raspberries, do not thaw before using.

Nutritional Analysis: One piece equals 178 calories, 4 g fat (2 g saturated fat), 35 mg cholesterol, 178 mg sodium, 32 g carbohydrate, 2 g fiber, 4 g protein.
Diabetic Exchanges: *1 starch, 1 fruit, 1 fat.*

Sausage Egg Squares

(Pictured at right and on page 101)

Chock-full of sausage and cheesy flavor, this fluffy egg dish is an absolute winner for breakfast, lunch or anytime. Our four children and six grandkids request it whenever they visit.
—Myrna Duke, Chelan, Washington

1 pound turkey Italian sausage links, casings removed
1 medium green pepper, chopped
1 small onion, chopped
2 cups (16 ounces) small-curd 1% cottage cheese
2 cups (8 ounces) shredded reduced-fat cheddar cheese
1-1/2 cups egg substitute
1 cup fat-free milk
1 cup reduced-fat biscuit/baking mix
1 can (4 ounces) chopped green chilies

In a large nonstick skillet, cook sausage, green pepper and onion over medium heat until meat is no longer pink; drain. Stir in the remaining ingredients. Pour into a 13-in. x 9-in. x 2-in. baking dish coated with nonstick cooking spray. Bake at 350° for 35-40 minutes or until a knife inserted near the center comes out clean. Let stand for 10 minutes before cutting. **Yield:** 12 servings.

Nutritional Analysis: One piece equals 202 calories, 8 g fat (3 g saturated fat), 41 mg cholesterol, 688 mg sodium, 12 g carbohydrate, 1 g fiber, 21 g protein.
Diabetic Exchanges: *3 lean meat, 1/2 starch.*

🍎 Tasty Waffle Topping

I've found a tasty replacement for the syrup and butter that used to top my waffles. I mix equal parts of fat-free fruit-flavored yogurt with fat-free whipped topping. This also makes a refreshing fruit dip.
—Elaine Call, Afton, Wyoming

Berry Blintzes

(Pictured above)

Biting into these delicately thin pancake packets sets off an explosion of flavors with every mouthful. The berries bring a burst of fruity sweetness to the creamy cheese filling. Blintzes make a luxurious breakfast or brunch...or a finishing touch to a meal.
—*Kristine Wright, St. Joseph, Michigan*

    4 egg whites
    1 cup fat-free milk
    1 tablespoon sugar
1/8 teaspoon salt
1/2 cup all-purpose flour
    1 cup part-skim ricotta cheese

    4 ounces reduced-fat cream cheese
3/4 cup reduced-fat sour cream, *divided*
    2 tablespoons sugar
    1 tablespoon plus 2 teaspoons toasted wheat germ, *divided*
    1 teaspoon vanilla extract
    1 tablespoon butter *or* stick margarine, melted
    1 cup unsweetened blueberries
1/2 cup unsweetened raspberries
1/2 cup unsweetened sliced strawberries

In a bowl, whisk egg whites, milk, sugar and salt. Add flour; beat until smooth. Let stand for 30 minutes.

Heat an 8-in. nonstick skillet coated with nonstick cooking spray over medium heat. For each blintze, pour 1/4 cup batter into center of skillet; lift and turn pan to cover bottom. Cook until lightly browned; turn and lightly brown the other side. Remove to a wire rack. When cool, stack blintzes with waxed paper or paper towels in between.

For filling, in a mixing bowl, beat the ricotta, cream cheese, 1/2 cup sour cream, sugar, 1 tablespoon wheat germ and vanilla until blended. Spoon about 1/4 cup onto each blintze; fold ends and sides over filling.

Arrange blintzes folded side down in a 13-in. x 9-in. x 2-in. baking dish; brush with melted butter. Cover and bake at 350° for 10-15 minutes or until heated through. To serve, top each blintze with berries and dollop of remaining sour cream. Sprinkle with remaining wheat germ. **Yield:** 8 servings.

Nutritional Analysis: One serving (1 blintze with 2 tablespoons fruit, 1-1/2 teaspoons sour cream and 1/4 teaspoon wheat germ) equals 210 calories, 9 g fat (6 g saturated fat), 30 mg cholesterol, 194 mg sodium, 22 g carbohydrate, 2 g fiber, 11 g protein. ***Diabetic Exchanges:*** *1 fruit, 1 lean meat, 1/2 starch.*

🍎 The Basics of Blintzes

THE WORD "blintze" comes from the Ukrainian word meaning "pancake". A blintze is very similar to a French crepe except that the traditional fillings vary. A blintze can be made with any number of flours and looks a little like an egg roll.

As a main or side dish, a blintze can be filled with sweetened ricotta or cottage cheese, mashed potatoes and onion and even meat mixtures. A fruit or jam filling turns a blintze into a "berry" good breakfast or dessert.

Blintzes are usually lightly sauteed and almost always folded rather than rolled around the filling. Once filled, they are cooked to golden brown and are often served warm with applesauce or sour cream.

Cherry Almond Granola

(Pictured at right)

Skim milk turns this crunchy snack into a healthy breakfast cereal, while a dollop of low-fat yogurt makes it a delicious dessert. Try adding a little baking cocoa to the brown sugar for a flavor twist.
—*Deborah Purdue, Freeland, Michigan*

    1 cup packed brown sugar
1/2 cup nonfat dry milk powder
1/2 cup honey
1/3 cup unsweetened apple juice concentrate
    2 tablespoons canola oil
    3 teaspoons almond extract
    6 cups old-fashioned oats
1-1/2 cups dried cherries *or* cranberries
    1 cup slivered almonds
Fat-free vanilla yogurt, optional

In a saucepan, combine the brown sugar, milk powder, honey, apple juice concentrate and oil. Cook and stir over medium heat until sugar is dissolved; stir in extract. In a large bowl, combine the oats, cherries and almonds. Drizzle with sugar mixture and mix well.

Spread in a thin layer in two 15-in. x 10-in. x 1-in. baking pans coated with nonstick cooking spray. Bake at 375° for 15-20 minutes or until golden brown, stirring occasionally. Cool completely. Serve with yogurt if desired. Store in an airtight container. **Yield:** 3 quarts.

Nutritional Analysis: *One serving (1/2 cup granola) equals 222 calories, 5 g fat (1 g saturated fat), trace cholesterol, 15 mg sodium, 38 g carbohydrate, 3 g fiber, 5 g protein.*
Diabetic Exchanges: *1-1/2 fruit, 1 starch, 1 fat.*

3/4 cup shredded reduced-fat cheddar cheese
1/2 cup salsa

In a nonstick skillet, saute mushrooms, onion and green pepper in oil until tender. Remove and keep warm. In a mixing bowl, beat the eggs, egg substitute, cream cheese, salt and pepper. Pour into the same skillet; cook and stir over medium heat until the eggs are completely set.

Stir in sauteed vegetables. Spoon about 1/2 cup down the center of each tortilla; top with cheddar cheese and salsa. Fold ends and sides over filling. Serve immediately. **Yield:** 6 servings.

Nutritional Analysis: *One serving (1 burrito) equals 296 calories, 11 g fat (3 g saturated fat), 112 mg cholesterol, 678 mg sodium, 31 g carbohydrate, 1 g fiber, 19 g protein.*
Diabetic Exchanges: *2 lean meat, 1-1/2 starch, 1-1/2 fat.*

Suppertime Egg Burritos

(Pictured at right)

Don't let the name fool you. Our kids love these hearty wraps morning, noon and night. My wife and I appreciate how fast and satisfying they are. The dash of salsa adds just the right "zip".
—Scott Jones, Tulsa, Oklahoma

1 cup sliced fresh mushrooms
1 medium onion, chopped
1/2 cup chopped green pepper
2 teaspoons canola oil
3 eggs
1-1/4 cups egg substitute
3 tablespoons reduced-fat cream cheese, cubed
1/4 teaspoon salt
1/8 teaspoon pepper
6 flour tortillas (8 inches), warmed

Warm Fruit Medley

The gently spiced compote our Test Kitchen staff created is comfort food at its healthiest. Spotlighting wonderful fruit like pears, cherries, apricots, pineapple and cranberries, it makes a beautiful dish that's perfect for a brunch or buffet.

2 tablespoons sugar
2 tablespoons cornstarch
1/2 teaspoon ground ginger
1/4 teaspoon ground allspice
1 cup apricot nectar
2 tablespoons butter *or* stick margarine, melted
2 pounds pears, peeled, cored and sliced
1 can (15 ounces) reduced-sugar apricot halves, drained and halved
1 can (14-1/2 ounces) water-packed pitted sweet cherries, drained
1 can (8 ounces) unsweetened pineapple chunks, drained
3/4 cup dried cranberries

In a large bowl, combine the sugar, cornstarch, ginger and allspice. Stir in nectar and butter until smooth. Add fruit; stir to coat. Pour into a 3-qt. baking dish coated with non-stick cooking spray. Cover and bake at 350° for 30 minutes. Uncover; bake 10 minutes longer or until hot and bubbly. Serve warm. **Yield:** 12 servings.

Nutritional Analysis: One serving (3/4 cup) equals 139 calories, 3 g fat (1 g saturated fat), 5 mg cholesterol, 25 mg sodium, 31 g carbohydrate, 3 g fiber, 1 g protein.
Diabetic Exchanges: 2 fruit, 1/2 fat.

Very Veggie Omelet

(Pictured at right)

I enjoy serving this light and fluffy omelet to my husband, who always appreciates a new twist on breakfast. It's chock-full of garden goodness.
—Jane Houberg, Reddick, Illinois

1 small onion, chopped
1/4 cup chopped green pepper
1 tablespoon butter *or* stick margarine
1 small zucchini, chopped
3/4 cup chopped tomato
1/4 teaspoon dried oregano
1/8 teaspoon pepper
4 egg whites
1/4 cup water
1/4 teaspoon cream of tartar
1/4 teaspoon salt
1/4 cup egg substitute
1/2 cup shredded reduced-fat cheddar cheese, *divided*

In a large nonstick skillet, saute onion and green pepper in butter until tender. Add the zucchini, tomato, oregano and pepper. Cook and stir for 5-8 minutes or until vegetables are tender and liquid is nearly evaporated. Set aside and keep warm. In a mixing bowl, beat egg whites, water, cream of tartar and salt until stiff peaks form. Place egg substitute in another bowl; fold in egg white mixture.

Pour into a 10-in. ovenproof skillet coated with nonstick cooking spray. Cook over medium heat for 5 minutes or until bottom is lightly browned. Bake at 350° for 9-10 minutes or until a knife inserted near the center comes out clean. Spoon vegetable mixture over one side; sprinkle with half of the cheese.

To fold, score middle of omelet with a sharp knife; fold omelet over filling. Transfer to a warm platter. Sprinkle with remaining cheese. Cut in half to serve. **Yield:** 2 servings.

Nutritional Analysis: One serving (half an omelet) equals 197 calories, 9 g fat (5 g saturated fat), 21 mg cholesterol, 639 mg sodium, 10 g carbohydrate, 2 g fiber, 19 g protein.
Diabetic Exchanges: 2-1/2 lean meat, 2 vegetable.

Home-Style Country Sausage

(Pictured at right)

My family loves sausage, but I wanted to reduce the fat and calories. This version, which uses ground turkey, is nicely spiced with garlic, sage, allspice, thyme and cayenne pepper.
—Linda Murray, Allenstown, New Hampshire

1 medium tart apple, peeled and shredded
1/2 cup cooked brown rice
2 tablespoons grated onion
2 garlic cloves, minced
1-1/2 teaspoons rubbed sage
1 teaspoon salt
1/2 teaspoon pepper
1/2 teaspoon dried thyme
1/8 teaspoon cayenne pepper
1/8 teaspoon ground allspice
1 pound lean ground turkey

In a bowl, combine the first 10 ingredients; mix well. Crumble turkey over mixture and mix well. Shape into eight 1/2-in.-thick patties. In a large nonstick skillet coated with nonstick cooking spray, cook patties for 4-6 minutes on each side or until juices run clear. **Yield:** 8 patties.

Nutritional Analysis: One patty equals 111 calories, 5 g fat (1 g saturated fat), 45 mg cholesterol, 348 mg sodium, 6 g carbohydrate, 1 g fiber, 10 g protein.
Diabetic Exchange: 2 lean meat.

Morning Milkshake

Here's a tasty way to get a good start on those recommended fruit and milk servings for the day. Pour 2 cups of fat-free milk in a blender. Add 2 cups of any kind of frozen fruit, a packet of sweetener and half a capful of vanilla extract. Blend it until smooth. —*Sue Ann Shaw, Millville, New Jersey*

Apple Breakfast Popover

Light and delicate, this puffed pancake is easy to assemble but special enough to serve guests. Top the fresh-from-the-oven popover with more chopped apples and cinnamon...and you're sure to pick up a bushel of compliments.
—*Barbara Nowakowski, North Tonawanda, New York*

 4 egg whites
 1/2 cup fat-free milk
 1/2 cup all-purpose flour
 1 tablespoon butter *or* stick margarine, melted
 1/8 teaspoon salt
 1-1/2 cups chopped peeled apples
 1/2 cup apple jelly
 2 tablespoons water
 1/8 teaspoon ground cinnamon

In a mixing bowl, beat the egg whites, milk, flour, butter and salt until smooth. Pour into an 8-in. square baking dish coated with nonstick cooking spray. Bake at 400° for 20-25 minutes or until golden and puffed. Meanwhile, in a small saucepan, combine the apples, jelly, water and cinnamon. Heat over low heat until jelly is melted and mixture is heated through. Cut popover into quarters; serve with apple topping. **Yield:** 4 servings.

Nutritional Analysis: One serving (1/4 of popover with 5 tablespoons apple topping) equals 254 calories, 3 g fat (2 g saturated fat), 8 mg cholesterol, 194 mg sodium, 48 g carbohydrate, 1 g fiber, 6 g protein.
Diabetic Exchanges: 2-1/2 starch, 1/2 fruit, 1/2 fat.

Oat Waffles

(Pictured at right)

These family favorites have more fiber and less fat than standard waffles. My toddler daughter loves them topped with fresh berries.
—*Karen Hayes, Danville, Virginia*

 1 cup all-purpose flour
 1 cup oat flour*
 4 teaspoons baking powder
 1 tablespoon sugar
 1/2 teaspoon salt
 2 eggs
 1-3/4 cups fat-free milk
 2 tablespoons canola oil
 1 teaspoon vanilla extract

In a bowl, combine the first five ingredients. Combine the eggs, milk, oil and vanilla; stir into dry ingredients just until combined. Pour batter by 1/2 cupfuls into a preheated waffle iron; bake according to manufacturer's directions until golden brown. **Yield:** 8 waffles (about 6-1/2 inches).
*Editor's Note: 1-1/4 cups quick-cooking oats, processed in a blender or food processor until finely ground, may be substituted for the oat flour.

Nutritional Analysis: One waffle equals 178 calories, 6 g fat (1 g saturated fat), 54 mg cholesterol, 307 mg sodium, 24 g carbohydrate, 2 g fiber, 7 g protein.
Diabetic Exchanges: 1-1/2 starch, 1 lean meat.

Mini Frittatas

(Pictured at right)

For a fun change-of-pace breakfast try these sausage and hash brown frittatas perked up with salsa. To lower the cholesterol even more, use egg substitute for the whole eggs.
—*Kathy Brodin, Wauwatosa, Wisconsin*

 1/4 pound turkey Italian sausage links, casings removed
 1-1/2 cups frozen shredded hash brown potatoes, thawed
 1/2 cup chopped onion
 1 garlic clove, minced
 1 teaspoon canola oil
 1/3 cup water
 1 teaspoon dried oregano
 1 teaspoon dried thyme
 1/2 teaspoon salt
 1/4 teaspoon pepper
 3 eggs
 2 egg whites
 1 cup 1% buttermilk
 2 tablespoons all-purpose flour
 1/4 cup shredded Parmesan cheese
 3/4 cup salsa

In a nonstick skillet, cook sausage over medium heat until no longer pink. Remove with a slotted spoon to paper towels. Discard drippings. In the same pan, saute potatoes, onion and garlic in oil until potatoes are golden brown, about 5 minutes. Add water, seasonings and sausage; cook and stir over medium heat until the water has evaporated, about 1 minute.

In a bowl, combine the eggs, egg whites, buttermilk, flour and Parmesan cheese. Stir in sausage mixture. Fill muffin cups coated with nonstick cooking spray three-fourths full. Bake at 350° for 20-25 minutes or until a knife comes out clean. Carefully run a knife around the edge of cups to loosen frittatas. Serve with salsa. **Yield:** 4 servings.

Nutritional Analysis: One serving (3 frittatas with 3 tablespoons salsa) equals 283 calories, 11 g fat (4 g saturated fat), 183 mg cholesterol, 954 mg sodium, 28 g carbohydrate, 2 g fiber, 19 g protein.
Diabetic Exchanges: 2 lean meat, 1-1/2 starch, 1 fat.

Set plate aside. In a nonstick skillet, saute mushrooms and onion in oil for 12-14 minutes or until all of the liquid has evaporated. Remove from the heat; stir in spinach.

In a bowl, combine the milk, egg substitute, salt and pepper. Stir in the spinach mixture, 1 cup Mexican cheese blend and Parmesan cheese. Pour into prepared pie plate. Bake at 350° for 35-40 minutes or until a knife inserted near the center comes out clean. Sprinkle remaining cheese around edge of tart. Let stand for 5 minutes before slicing. **Yield:** 6 servings.

Nutritional Analysis: One piece equals 218 calories, 12 g fat (5 g saturated fat), 15 mg cholesterol, 459 mg sodium, 10 g carbohydrate, 2 g fiber, 19 g protein.
Diabetic Exchanges: 2 lean meat, 1 vegetable, 1 fat, 1/2 starch.

Peach Scones

Add variety to breakfast by baking a batch of light fluffy scones. Bits of dried peaches make them a slightly sweet addition to the table.
—Molly Mochamer, Fort Wayne, Indiana

        1-1/3 cups all-purpose flour
        1/2 cup plus 2 teaspoons sugar, *divided*
          1 teaspoon baking powder
        1/2 teaspoon baking soda
        1/2 teaspoon salt
          2 tablespoons cold butter *or* stick margarine
        1/2 cup plus 2 tablespoons reduced-fat sour cream
        1/4 cup chopped dried peaches *or* apricots
        1/2 teaspoon vanilla extract
          1 teaspoon fat-free milk

In a bowl, combine the flour, 1/2 cup sugar, baking powder, baking soda and salt. Cut in butter until mixture resembles coarse crumbs. Add sour cream, peaches and vanilla; stir just until moistened. Turn dough onto a floured surface; knead gently 4-5 times (dough will be sticky).

Divide dough in half; gently pat each portion into an 8-in. circle on a baking sheet coated with nonstick cooking spray. Cut each into four wedges; separate wedges slightly. Brush tops with milk; sprinkle with remaining sugar. Bake at 400° for 10-12 minutes or until golden brown. **Yield:** 8 scones.

Nutritional Analysis: One scone equals 181 calories, 4 g fat (3 g saturated fat), 13 mg cholesterol, 295 mg sodium, 32 g carbohydrate, 1 g fiber, 3 g protein.
Diabetic Exchanges: 2 starch, 1/2 fruit.

Crustless Mushroom Spinach Tart

(Pictured above)

No coaxing is necessary to get my husband to eat his spinach when I stir it into this tempting tart. With no crust, this cheesy veggie dish is so easy to prepare. The aroma alone will be enough to bring your family to the table.
—Mary Lopez, Willow Creek, California

          2 tablespoons seasoned bread crumbs
        1/2 pound fresh mushrooms, sliced
        1/2 cup chopped onion
          2 tablespoons olive *or* canola oil
          1 package (10 ounces) frozen chopped spinach,
            thawed and squeezed dry
          1 cup 2% milk
          1 cup egg substitute
        1/4 teaspoon salt
        1/4 teaspoon pepper
        1-1/4 cups shredded reduced-fat Mexican cheese
            blend, *divided*
        1/3 cup grated Parmesan cheese

Coat a 9-in. pie plate with nonstick cooking spray. Sprinkle bottom and sides with bread crumbs; shake out the excess.

🍎 Produce a Better Breakfast

You don't have to change your lifestyle to boost your intake of fruits and vegetables. It can be as easy as topping your cereal with a sliced banana or fresh berries. And instead of guzzling down coffee, sip a tall glass of orange juice.

Beefed-Up Main Dishes

Even folks watching their diets can indulge in a meaty entree. The secret is to select lean beef cuts and to trim down the accompanying sauces. No one will guess you cheated these dishes out of fat and calories!

Grilled Beef Burgers (page 114)

Grilled Beef Burgers

(Pictured on page 113)

I rely on a few common ingredients to put a new twist on a backyard barbecue staple. To make handling the patties even easier, let them firm up in the freezer a bit before grilling.
—Lynda Ferguson, Sarnia, Ontario

    2 egg whites
    2/3 cup fat-free evaporated milk
    1 cup (4 ounces) shredded reduced-fat cheddar
        cheese
    1/2 cup dry bread crumbs
    1/4 cup chopped onion
    1 teaspoon prepared mustard
    1/4 teaspoon salt
    1/8 teaspoon pepper
1-1/2 pounds lean ground beef
    8 multigrain hamburger buns, split
    8 lettuce leaves
    8 tomato slices

In a bowl, combine the first eight ingredients. Crumble beef over mixture and mix well. Shape into eight patties.
    Coat grill rack with nonstick cooking spray before starting the grill. Grill burgers, uncovered, over medium heat for 5-6 minutes on each side or until juices run clear and a meat thermometer reads 160°. Serve on buns with lettuce and tomato. **Yield:** 8 servings.

Nutritional Analysis: *One serving (1 burger) equals 351 calories, 13 g fat (5 g saturated fat), 40 mg cholesterol, 530 mg sodium, 30 g carbohydrate, 2 g fiber, 29 g protein.*
Diabetic Exchanges: *4 lean meat, 2 starch.*

Easy Beef Goulash

(Pictured at right)

I found the recipe for this stovetop goulash several years ago in an old cookbook. It really hits the spot with warm home-baked bread from the bread machine and a dish of cold applesauce.
—Phyllis Pollock, Erie, Pennsylvania

1-1/2 cups uncooked spiral pasta
    1 pound boneless beef sirloin steak, cut into
        1/8-inch-thick strips
    1 tablespoon canola oil
    1 medium onion, chopped
    1 medium green pepper, chopped
    1 can (14-1/2 ounces) diced tomatoes, undrained
1-1/2 cups water
    1 cup reduced-sodium beef broth
1-1/2 teaspoons red wine vinegar *or* cider vinegar
    1 to 2 teaspoons paprika
    1 teaspoon sugar
    1/2 teaspoon salt
    1/4 teaspoon caraway seeds
    1/4 teaspoon pepper
    2 tablespoons all-purpose flour
    1/4 cup cold water

Cook pasta according to package directions. Meanwhile, in a large nonstick skillet, stir-fry beef in oil for 4-5 minutes or until browned. Add onion and green pepper; cook and stir for 2 minutes. Stir in tomatoes, water, broth, vinegar and seasonings. Bring to a boil. Reduce heat; cover and simmer for 15 minutes. In a small bowl, combine flour and cold water until smooth. Add to skillet. Bring to a boil; cook and stir for 2 minutes or until thickened. Drain pasta; stir into beef mixture. **Yield:** 6 servings.

Nutritional Analysis: *One serving (1 cup) equals 272 calories, 7 g fat (2 g saturated fat), 45 mg cholesterol, 371 mg sodium, 29 g carbohydrate, 2 g fiber, 22 g protein.*
Diabetic Exchanges: *2 starch, 2 lean meat.*

Peppered Beef in Garlic Sauce

Onion, garlic and red wine mingle with beef broth in a pleasant sauce that's similar to au jus in this recipe developed in our Test Kitchen.

Coarsely ground pepper
    1/4 teaspoon salt
    2 boneless beef sirloin steaks (5 ounces *each*)
    3/4 cup beef broth
    3/4 cup dry red wine *or* additional beef broth
    1 small red onion, quartered and thinly sliced
    2 garlic cloves, minced
    1/2 teaspoon sugar
    1/4 teaspoon dried marjoram
Dash hot pepper sauce

Sprinkle pepper and salt over steaks and press into both sides. In a nonstick skillet coated with nonstick cooking spray, brown steaks on both sides over medium-high heat. Remove and keep warm.

In the same skillet, combine the remaining ingredients. Bring to a boil; cover and cook for 2 minutes. Uncover; cook 5-6 minutes longer or until onion is tender and liquid is reduced by a third. Reduce heat. Return steaks to pan; cook for 12-15 minutes or until meat is cooked to desired doneness (for rare, a meat thermometer should read 140°; medium, 160°; well-done, 170°). **Yield:** 2 servings.

Nutritional Analysis: One serving (1 steak with 1/4 cup sauce) equals 304 calories, 9 g fat (3 g saturated fat), 85 mg cholesterol, 1,109 mg sodium, 7 g carbohydrate, trace fiber, 34 g protein.
Diabetic Exchanges: *4-1/2 lean meat, 1 fat.*

Taco Stir-Fry

Spice up dinnertime just right by serving this meaty Mexican stir-fry, a fun variation on a taco salad. It's nice and light, a perfect meal for a summer day. And it's quick to fix, too, making it ideal for an on-the-go family.
—Nila Towler, Baird, Texas

  1 pound lean ground beef
1/4 cup chopped onion
  1 can (14-1/2 ounces) stewed tomatoes
  1 cup frozen corn
  2 tablespoons chili powder
  1 teaspoon sugar
1/2 teaspoon dried oregano
1/4 teaspoon salt
1/8 teaspoon pepper
  1 cup (4 ounces) shredded reduced-fat cheddar cheese
  1 head iceberg lettuce, shredded
Baked tortilla chips
  1 cup salsa

In a nonstick skillet, cook beef and onion over medium heat until meat is no longer pink; drain. Stir in the tomatoes, corn, chili powder, sugar, oregano, salt and pepper. Bring to a boil. Reduce heat; cover and simmer for 10 minutes, stirring occasionally. Stir in cheese. Place shredded lettuce and 10 tortilla chips on each plate; top with taco mixture and 2 tablespoons salsa. **Yield:** 8 servings.

Nutritional Analysis: One serving equals 278 calories, 9 g fat (4 g saturated fat), 29 mg cholesterol, 546 mg sodium, 31 g carbohydrate, 4 g fiber, 20 g protein.
Diabetic Exchanges: *2 starch, 2 lean meat.*

🍎 Savory Spaghetti Sauce

I add shredded zucchini and carrots to my homemade spaghetti sauce to add extra nutrition while disguising those good-for-you vegetables from my husband. —*Brandy Uhlmeyer, Leonard, Missouri*

Simmered Sirloin with Noodles

(Pictured below)

We always have noodles in the pantry and wanted something simple to serve over them for a fuss-free meal. This creation, perfected over the years, is now a family favorite.
—Jack Harrigan, Interlochen, Michigan

1-1/4 pounds boneless beef sirloin steak, cut into thin strips
  2 medium onions, chopped
  1 jar (4-1/2 ounces) sliced mushrooms, drained
  1 garlic clove, minced
  1 tablespoon butter *or* stick margarine
  2 cups condensed beef consomme
4-1/2 teaspoons Worcestershire sauce
  1 teaspoon dried basil
  3 tablespoons all-purpose flour
1/4 cup cold water
  6 cups hot cooked yolk-free noodles

In a large nonstick skillet, cook beef, onions, mushrooms and garlic in butter over medium heat for 5-7 minutes or until the meat is no longer pink. Add the consomme, Worcestershire sauce and basil; bring to a boil. Reduce heat; cover and simmer for 50-60 minutes.

Combine flour and water until smooth; add to beef mixture. Bring to a boil; cook and stir for 2 minutes or until thickened. Serve over noodles. **Yield:** 6 servings.

Nutritional Analysis: One serving (1/2 cup meat mixture with 1 cup noodles) equals 451 calories, 13 g fat (5 g saturated fat), 79 mg cholesterol, 798 mg sodium, 44 g carbohydrate, 4 g fiber, 37 g protein.
Diabetic Exchanges: *3 lean meat, 2-1/2 starch, 2 fat.*

Sweet-and-Sour Meatballs

(Pictured below)

Looking for a savory recipe that combines a hint of pineapple and a dash of soy sauce? These meatballs contrast those flavors in a delightful way. My husband and two young sons request them often.
—Joyce Penney, St. Mary's, Ontario

1 can (20 ounces) unsweetened pineapple chunks
1 egg
1 cup soft bread crumbs
1 garlic clove, minced
1 teaspoon salt
1/4 teaspoon pepper
1-1/2 pounds lean ground beef
2 teaspoons canola oil
2 large green peppers
1 cup chicken broth
1/2 cup sugar
3 tablespoons cornstarch
1/2 cup cider vinegar
3 tablespoons reduced-sodium soy sauce
6 cups hot cooked rice

Drain pineapple, reserving 1/2 cup juice (discard remaining juice or save for another use). Set the juice and pineapple aside. In a bowl, combine the egg, bread crumbs, garlic, salt and pepper. Crumble beef over mixture and mix well. Shape into 40 meatballs.

In a nonstick skillet, brown meatballs in oil; drain. Cut green peppers into chunks. Add broth, peppers and reserved pineapple to meatballs. Bring to a boil. Reduce heat; simmer, uncovered, for 5-7 minutes.

Meanwhile, combine sugar and cornstarch in a bowl. Stir in the vinegar, soy sauce and reserved pineapple juice until smooth. Add to meatball mixture. Bring to a boil; cook and stir for 2 minutes or until thickened. Serve over rice. **Yield:** 8 servings.

Nutritional Analysis: One serving (3/4 cup meatball mixture with 3/4 cup rice) equals 456 calories, 10 g fat (3 g saturated fat), 58 mg cholesterol, 755 mg sodium, 66 g carbohydrate, 2 g fiber, 23 g protein.
Diabetic Exchanges: 3 lean meat, 2-1/2 starch, 1-1/2 vegetable, 1 fat.

Cooking Ground Beef

To help eliminate fat from ground beef, cook it in a microwave-safe strainer or colander in a microwave-safe bowl. Break up the ground beef with a fork and stir it frequently as it's cooking until it's no longer pink. The fat will collect at the bottom of the bowl...and the beef is ready to be used.
—*Patricia Getz, Meeker, Colorado*

Shepherd's Pie

For a real meat-and-potatoes meal, try this satisfying layered casserole. It's easy to assemble with lean ground beef and fresh or leftover mashed potatoes.
—Carolyn Wolbers, Loveland, Ohio

6 medium potatoes
1 pound carrots, cut into 1/4-inch slices
1-1/2 pounds lean ground beef
1 large onion, chopped
1 jar (12 ounces) fat-free beef gravy
1 teaspoon salt, *divided*
1/2 teaspoon rubbed sage
1/2 teaspoon dried thyme
1/4 teaspoon dried rosemary, crushed
1/4 teaspoon pepper
1/3 cup fat-free milk
1 tablespoon butter *or* **stick margarine**
2 tablespoons shredded Parmesan cheese

Peel and cube the potatoes; place in a large saucepan and cover with water. Bring to a boil over medium-high heat; cover and cook for 20 minutes or until tender. Add 1 in. of water to another saucepan; add carrots. Bring to a boil. Reduce heat; cover and simmer until crisp-tender, about 7-9 minutes. Drain.

In a large skillet, cook beef and onion over medium heat until meat is no longer pink; drain. Stir in the carrots, gravy, 1/2 teaspoon salt, sage, thyme, rosemary and pepper. Transfer to a shallow 3-qt. baking dish coated with nonstick cooking spray.

Drain the potatoes; mash with milk, butter and remaining salt. Spread over meat mixture. Sprinkle with Parmesan cheese. Bake, uncovered, at 375° for 40-45 minutes or until heated through. **Yield:** 6 servings.

Nutritional Analysis: One serving equals 390 calories, 13 g fat (6 g saturated fat), 53 mg cholesterol, 859 mg sodium, 43 g carbohydrate, 6 g fiber, 30 g protein.
Diabetic Exchanges: 3 lean meat, 2 vegetable, 2 starch, 1/2 fat.

Zippy Ground Beef Skillet

This zesty combination of ingredients creates
a fun fiesta of flavor no one can resist.
—Vicki Herron, Portland, Maine

8 ounces uncooked small tube pasta
1 pound lean ground beef
3/4 cup diced onion
3/4 cup diced green pepper
1 can (28 ounces) diced tomatoes, undrained
2 jalapeno peppers, seeded and minced*
1 tablespoon honey
2 to 3 teaspoons chili powder
3/4 teaspoon salt
1-1/2 cups reduced-fat sour cream

Cook pasta according to package directions. Meanwhile, in a large nonstick skillet, cook the beef, onion and green pepper over medium heat until meat is no longer pink; drain. Add the tomatoes, jalapenos, honey, chili powder and salt. Reduce heat to low; cook, uncovered, for 10 minutes, stirring occasionally. Drain pasta; add to beef mixture. Add sour cream; cook and stir until heated through (do not boil). **Yield:** 8 servings.

*Editor's Note: When cutting or seeding hot peppers, use rubber or plastic gloves to protect your hands. Avoid touching your face.

Nutritional Analysis: One serving (1 cup) equals 307 calories, 10 g fat (5 g saturated fat), 36 mg cholesterol, 451 mg sodium, 33 g carbohydrate, 3 g fiber, 22 g protein.
Diabetic Exchanges: 2 starch, 2 lean meat, 1 fat.

South-of-the-Border Pizza

(Pictured above right)

When we moved from California to Alaska years
ago, my friends gave me copies of their
Mexican recipes. This remains a favorite.
—Eileen Becker, Homer, Alaska

1 tablespoon cornmeal
1 loaf (1 pound) frozen bread dough, thawed
1/2 pound lean ground beef
1 medium onion, chopped
1 sweet yellow pepper, chopped
1 garlic clove, minced

1 can (16 ounces) fat-free refried beans
1 cup salsa
1 can (4 ounces) chopped green chilies
1 to 2 teaspoons chili powder
2 cups (8 ounces) shredded reduced-fat
  Mexican-blend cheese
2 medium tomatoes, chopped
2 cups shredded lettuce

Coat two 12-in. pizza pans with nonstick cooking spray; sprinkle with cornmeal. Divide the bread dough in half; roll each portion into a 12-in. circle. Transfer to prepared pans. Build up edges slightly; prick dough thoroughly with a fork. Bake at 425° for 12 minutes or until lightly browned.

Meanwhile, in a skillet, cook the beef, onion, yellow pepper and garlic over medium heat until meat is no longer pink; drain. Stir in refried beans, salsa, chilies and chili powder; heat through. Spread over the crusts; sprinkle with cheese.

Bake 6-7 minutes longer or until cheese is melted. Top with tomatoes and lettuce; serve immediately. **Yield:** 2 pizzas (6 slices each).

Nutritional Analysis: One slice equals 250 calories, 7 g fat (3 g saturated fat), 20 mg cholesterol, 706 mg sodium, 31 g carbohydrate, 5 g fiber, 17 g protein.
Diabetic Exchanges: 2 lean meat, 1-1/2 starch, 1 vegetable.

Steak on a Stick

I combine molasses, mustard and soy sauce to make these the most robust kabobs you've ever tasted. You'll never miss the oil in this hearty marinade. Molasses gives each bite wonderful flavor.
—Jennifer Schwerin, Rockford, Illinois

1 beef flank steak (1-1/2 pounds)
1/2 cup reduced-sodium soy sauce
1/4 cup water
2 tablespoons molasses
2 teaspoons ground mustard
1 teaspoon ground ginger
1/2 teaspoon garlic powder

Freeze steak for 1-1/2 hours. Cut diagonally into 1/4-in. slices. In a bowl, combine the remaining ingredients. Pour 1/4 cup into a small bowl for basting; cover and refrigerate. Pour remaining marinade into a large resealable plastic bag; add the beef. Seal bag and turn to coat; refrigerate for at least 4 hours.

Drain and discard marinade. Coat grill rack with nonstick cooking spray before starting the grill. Thread beef ribbon-style on 12 metal or soaked wooden skewers. Grill, uncovered, over medium heat for 3-4 minutes on each side or until meat reaches desired doneness, basting frequently with reserved marinade. **Yield:** 6 servings.

Nutritional Analysis: One serving (2 kabobs) equals 201 calories, 9 g fat (4 g saturated fat), 57 mg cholesterol, 617 mg sodium, 5 g carbohydrate, trace fiber, 24 g protein.
Diabetic Exchange: 3 lean meat.

Deep-Dish Taco Squares

This hearty, comforting dish has plenty of south-of-the-border appeal. I make a quick crust from biscuit mix and top it with a thick layer of ground beef and cheddar cheese.
—Barb Tropansky, Bella Vista, Arkansas

1 pound lean ground beef
1 cup (4 ounces) shredded reduced-fat cheddar cheese
1/3 cup reduced-fat mayonnaise
1/3 cup reduced-fat sour cream
1 tablespoon finely chopped onion
1 cup reduced-fat biscuit/baking mix
1/4 cup cold water
1 small tomato, sliced

In a nonstick skillet, cook beef over medium heat until no longer pink; drain. Remove from the heat; stir in the cheese, mayonnaise, sour cream and onion. In a bowl, combine biscuit mix and water. Spread into an 8-in. square baking dish coated with nonstick cooking spray. Top with beef mixture and tomato.

Bake, uncovered, at 375° for 20 minutes or until the bottom crust is golden brown. **Yield:** 6 servings.

Nutritional Analysis: One serving equals 310 calories, 15 g fat (6 g saturated fat), 46 mg cholesterol, 530 mg sodium, 20 g carbohydrate, 1 g fiber, 24 g protein.
Diabetic Exchanges: 3 lean meat, 1 starch, 1 fat.

Beefy Tomatoes

(Pictured above)

Since my husband loves to garden, I often fix this entree using tomatoes right out of our backyard.
—Liz Gallagher, Gilbertsville, Pennsylvania

6 medium tomatoes
1 pound lean ground beef
1 medium onion, chopped
2 teaspoons dried basil
1 teaspoon salt
1/4 teaspoon pepper
1/2 cup cooked rice
1/2 cup shredded reduced-fat cheddar cheese
1 egg, lightly beaten

Cut a thin slice off the top of each tomato and discard; remove core. Carefully scoop out pulp, leaving a 1/2-in. shell. Reserve 1 cup pulp (discard remaining pulp or save for another use). Invert tomatoes onto paper towels to drain. In a nonstick skillet, cook beef and onion over medium heat until meat is no longer pink; drain. Stir in the basil, salt, pepper and reserved tomato pulp; bring to a boil. Reduce heat; simmer, uncovered, for 10-12 minutes or until the liquid has evaporated.

Stir in the rice, cheese and egg; heat through. Spoon into tomato shells. Place in a shallow 2-qt. baking dish coated with nonstick cooking spray. Bake, uncovered, at 350° for 20-25 minutes or until heated through. **Yield:** 6 servings.

Nutritional Analysis: One serving (1 stuffed tomato) equals 215 calories, 10 g fat (4 g saturated fat), 68 mg cholesterol, 525 mg sodium, 12 g carbohydrate, 2 g fiber, 21 g protein.
Diabetic Exchanges: 2 lean meat, 1-1/2 fat, 1/2 starch.

Favorite Pizza Recipe Made Lighter

SAYS Celia Rossignolo from Athens, Alabama, "Loaded Pizza is one of my husband Louie's specialties." Our Test Kitchen lightened the load by using leaner ingredients.

Loaded Pizza

1 can (8 ounces) mushroom stems and pieces, drained
1/4 cup *each* chopped green pepper, sweet red pepper, ripe olives, white onion and red onion
2 garlic cloves, minced
3 tablespoons olive *or* vegetable oil, *divided*
1/2 pound ground beef
1/4 pound bulk pork sausage
2 teaspoons cornmeal
1 loaf (1 pound) frozen bread dough, thawed
1/2 teaspoon garlic powder
1 can (8 ounces) tomato sauce
2 tablespoons minced fresh parsley
4 teaspoons Italian seasoning
1/4 teaspoon pepper
27 pepperoni slices (1-3/4 ounces)
2 cups (8 ounces) shredded Italian cheese blend *or* mozzarella cheese
1/4 cup shredded cheddar cheese

In a skillet, saute vegetables and garlic in 1 tablespoon oil until tender. Remove; set aside. In the same skillet, cook beef and sausage over medium heat until no longer pink; drain. Grease a 14-in. pizza pan; sprinkle with cornmeal. On a floured surface, roll dough into a 15-in. circle. Transfer to prepared pan. Build up edges slightly; prick dough thoroughly with a fork. Brush with remaining oil; sprinkle with garlic powder. Bake at 400° for 8-10 minutes or until edges are lightly browned.

In a bowl, combine the tomato sauce, parsley, Italian seasoning and pepper; spread over crust. Top with the vegetables, meat mixture and pepperoni. Sprinkle with cheeses. Bake for 17-20 minutes or until crust is golden and cheese is melted. **Yield:** 8 servings.

Nutritional Analysis: One slice equals 543 calories, 34 g fat (12 g saturated fat), 70 mg cholesterol, 1,145 mg sodium, 36 g carbohydrate, 3 g fiber, 25 g protein.

Makeover Loaded Pizza

(Pictured at right)

1-1/2 cups sliced fresh mushrooms
1/4 cup *each* chopped green pepper, sweet red pepper, white onion and red onion
2 garlic cloves, minced
1 tablespoon canola oil

1/4 pound lean ground beef
1 turkey Italian sausage link (4 ounces), casing removed
2 teaspoons cornmeal
1 loaf (1 pound) frozen bread dough, thawed
1 can (8 ounces) tomato sauce
2 tablespoons minced fresh parsley
2 teaspoons Italian seasoning
1/4 teaspoon garlic powder
1/8 teaspoon pepper
15 turkey pepperoni slices (1 ounce)
2 tablespoons sliced ripe olives
1 cup (4 ounces) shredded part-skim mozzarella cheese
1/4 cup shredded reduced-fat cheddar cheese

In a nonstick skillet, saute vegetables and garlic in oil until tender. Remove; set aside. In the same skillet, cook beef and sausage over medium heat until no longer pink; drain. Coat a 14-in. pizza pan with nonstick cooking spray; sprinkle with cornmeal. On a lightly floured surface, roll dough into a 15-in. circle. Transfer to prepared pan. Build up edges slightly; prick dough thoroughly with a fork. Bake at 400° for 8-10 minutes or until lightly browned.

In a bowl, combine tomato sauce, parsley, Italian seasoning, garlic powder and pepper; spread over crust. Top with vegetables, meat mixture, pepperoni and olives. Sprinkle with cheeses. Bake for 8-10 minutes or until crust is golden and cheese is melted. **Yield:** 8 servings.

Nutritional Analysis: One slice equals 300 calories, 11 g fat (3 g saturated fat), 27 mg cholesterol, 758 mg sodium, 36 g carbohydrate, 3 g fiber, 18 g protein.
Diabetic Exchanges: 2 starch, 1 fat, 1 lean meat, 1 vegetable.

Layered Macaroni Casserole

I concocted this quick-and-easy recipe over 40 years ago as a new bride. It's still one of my favorites.
—*Virginia Cherry, Salinas, California*

 1 pound lean ground beef
 1/2 cup chopped onion
 1 garlic clove, minced
 1 can (28 ounces) crushed tomatoes
 1 can (6 ounces) tomato paste
 2 teaspoons sugar
 1 teaspoon salt
 1 teaspoon chili powder
 1/2 teaspoon dried basil
 1/2 teaspoon dried oregano
 1/8 teaspoon pepper
 8 ounces uncooked elbow macaroni
 2 cups (16 ounces) fat-free cottage cheese
 1-1/2 cups (6 ounces) shredded reduced-fat cheddar cheese
TOPPING:
 1/4 cup dry bread crumbs
 1/4 cup grated Parmesan cheese
 1 tablespoon butter *or* stick margarine, melted

In a nonstick skillet, cook ground beef, onion and garlic over medium heat until meat is no longer pink; drain. Add the tomatoes, tomato paste and seasonings. Bring to a boil. Reduce heat; cover and simmer for 1 hour. Meanwhile, cook macaroni according to package directions; drain. Add cottage cheese. In a 13-in. x 9-in. x 2-in. baking dish coated with nonstick cooking spray, layer 1 cup meat sauce, a third of the macaroni mixture and a third of the cheddar cheese. Repeat layers twice. Top with remaining meat sauce. Combine topping ingredients; sprinkle over sauce. Bake, uncovered, at 325° for 40-45 minutes. Let stand for 10 minutes before serving. **Yield:** 8 servings.

Nutritional Analysis: One serving equals 379 calories, 10 g fat (5 g saturated fat), 34 mg cholesterol, 1,087 mg sodium, 40 g carbohydrate, 4 g fiber, 31 g protein.
Diabetic Exchanges: 3 lean meat, 2 starch, 2 vegetable.

Pepper-Topped Beef Sandwiches

(Pictured above)

Peppers provide a perfect way to perk up a plain roast beef sandwich. I make a platterful of these family favorites for gatherings with our five children and grandkids at our country home in the Ozark hills.
—*Leota Recknor, Ash Grove, Missouri*

 1 medium onion, chopped
 2 garlic cloves, minced
 1 tablespoon olive *or* canola oil
 1 medium sweet red pepper, julienned
 1 medium green pepper, julienned
 1 bay leaf
 1/2 teaspoon salt
 1/8 teaspoon pepper
 1 tablespoon sugar
 12 ounces thinly sliced deli roast beef
 6 sandwich rolls, split

In a nonstick skillet, saute onion and garlic in oil until tender. Add the red and green peppers, bay leaf, salt and pepper. Cook and stir until peppers are tender, about 10 minutes. Add sugar; cover and simmer for 10-15 minutes or until flavors are blended. Discard bay leaf. Place beef on rolls; top with pepper mixture. **Yield:** 6 servings.

Nutritional Analysis: One sandwich equals 325 calories, 8 g fat (2 g saturated fat), 46 mg cholesterol, 546 mg sodium, 39 g carbohydrate, 3 g fiber, 23 g protein.
Diabetic Exchanges: 2 starch, 2 lean meat, 1 vegetable, 1/2 fat.

Save Pan Juices from Roasted Meats

Leftover pan juices from roast beef or chicken add great flavor to soups and potpies. Here's an easy way to remove the fat: After the meat is cooked, pour the pan juices into a bowl. Set it in the refrigerator overnight. The next morning, the fat will have hardened on the surface and can be lifted right off with a spoon. —*Shirley Veleba, York, Nebraska*

Marinated Pot Roast

I've long used whole or ground cloves as my secret ingredient in cooking and baking. Added to an overnight marinade, they provide the gravy in this meaty main dish with great flavor.
—*Marijane Rea, Milwaukie, Oregon*

1 cup dry white wine *or* beef broth
1/3 cup reduced-sodium soy sauce
1 tablespoon olive *or* canola oil
4 garlic cloves, minced
2 green onions, thinly sliced
1-1/2 teaspoons ground ginger
1/4 teaspoon pepper
4 whole cloves
1 boneless beef top round roast (4 pounds)
5 teaspoons cornstarch
5 teaspoons cold water

In a gallon-size resealable plastic bag, combine the first eight ingredients. Cut roast in half; add to marinade. Seal bag and turn to coat; refrigerate overnight.

Place roast and marinade in a 5-qt. slow cooker. Cover and cook on low for 8-10 hours or until meat is tender. Remove roast to a serving platter and keep warm. Pour cooking juices into a 2-cup measuring cup; discard whole cloves.

In a saucepan, combine cornstarch and cold water until smooth; stir in 1-1/2 cups cooking juices. Bring to a boil; cook and stir for 2 minutes or until thickened. Serve with the roast. **Yield:** 12 servings.

Nutritional Analysis: *One serving (3 ounces cooked beef with 2 tablespoons gravy) equals 174 calories, 6 g fat (2 g saturated fat), 59 mg cholesterol, 255 mg sodium, 3 g carbohydrate, trace fiber, 25 g protein.*
Diabetic Exchange: *3 lean meat.*

Deluxe Meat Loaf

When I make meat loaf, I usually just mix together whatever I have on hand. One time I added leftover kidney beans I had in the fridge, and my family loved the meat loaf's soft texture. Now it's our favorite.
—*Patricia Zwerk, Tucson, Arizona*

2 eggs, lightly beaten
1-1/2 cups ketchup, *divided*
1 can (16 ounces) kidney beans, rinsed, drained and mashed
1 cup seasoned bread crumbs
1 large onion, chopped
1 celery rib, chopped
2 teaspoons Worcestershire sauce
1 teaspoon salt-free lemon-pepper seasoning
1/2 teaspoon seasoned salt
2-1/2 pounds lean ground beef
1/2 cup water

In a large bowl, combine the eggs, 1 cup ketchup, beans, bread crumbs, onion, celery, Worcestershire sauce, lemon-pepper and seasoned salt; crumble beef over mixture and mix well. Shape into two loaves. Place in a 13-in. x 9-in. x 2-in. baking dish coated with nonstick cooking spray.

In a bowl, combine water and remaining ketchup; pour over meat loaves. Bake, uncovered, at 325° for 70 minutes or until meat is no longer pink and a meat thermometer reads 160°. **Yield:** 12 servings.

Nutritional Analysis: *One serving equals 267 calories, 10 g fat (4 g saturated fat), 70 mg cholesterol, 853 mg sodium, 21 g carbohydrate, 2 g fiber, 24 g protein.*
Diabetic Exchanges: *3 lean meat, 1-1/2 starch.*

Mexican Lasagna

(Pictured below)

I was hungry for something different, so I gave my Italian-style lasagna a Mexican accent. It's packed with tempting seasonings, and the cheese, green onions and ripe olives make an attractive topping.
—*Sheree Swistun, Selkink, Manitoba*

1 pound lean ground beef
1 can (16 ounces) fat-free refried beans
2 teaspoons dried oregano
1 teaspoon ground cumin
3/4 teaspoon garlic powder
9 uncooked lasagna noodles
1 jar (16 ounces) salsa
2 cups water
2 cups (16 ounces) reduced-fat sour cream
1 can (2-1/4 ounces) sliced ripe olives, drained
1 cup (4 ounces) shredded reduced-fat Mexican-blend cheese
1/2 cup thinly sliced green onions

In a nonstick skillet, cook beef over medium heat until no longer pink; drain. Add the refried beans, oregano, cumin and garlic powder; heat through.

Place three noodles in a 13-in. x 9-in. x 2-in. baking dish coated with nonstick cooking spray; cover with half of the meat mixture. Repeat layers. Top with remaining noodles. Combine salsa and water; pour over noodles.

Cover and bake at 350° for 60-70 minutes or until noodles are tender. Spread with sour cream. Sprinkle with olives, cheese and onions. **Yield:** 9 servings.

Nutritional Analysis: *One serving (1 piece) equals 341 calories, 13 g fat (7 g saturated fat), 49 mg cholesterol, 680 mg sodium, 31 g carbohydrate, 4 g fiber, 24 g protein.*
Diabetic Exchanges: *2 starch, 2 lean meat, 1-1/2 fat.*

and a fourth of the cheese mixture. Repeat layers of pasta, sauce and cheese mixture. Top with remaining sauce. Sprinkle with remaining Parmesan cheese and oregano. Cover and bake at 350° for 1 hour or until heated through. **Yield:** 2 casseroles (6 servings each).

Nutritional Analysis: One serving (about 1-1/3 cups) equals 324 calories, 11 g fat (6 g saturated fat), 38 mg cholesterol, 796 mg sodium, 30 g carbohydrate, 3 g fiber, 26 g protein.
Diabetic Exchanges: 1-1/2 lean meat, 1 starch, 1 vegetable, 1 fat.

Baked Ziti

(Pictured above)

This comforting Italian dish features a from-scratch spaghetti sauce, ziti pasta and a generous combination of cheeses.
—Kim Neer, Kalamazoo, Michigan

    1 pound lean ground beef
    2 medium onions, chopped
    3 garlic cloves, minced
    1 jar (28 ounces) reduced-sodium meatless
        spaghetti sauce
    1 can (28 ounces) diced tomatoes, undrained
    1 can (12 ounces) tomato paste
  3/4 cup water
    2 tablespoons minced fresh parsley
    1 tablespoon Worcestershire sauce
    2 teaspoons dried basil
1-1/2 teaspoons dried oregano, divided
    1 pound uncooked medium tube pasta
    1 carton (15 ounces) reduced-fat ricotta cheese
    2 cups (8 ounces) shredded part-skim mozzarella
        cheese
  1/2 cup grated Parmesan cheese, *divided*
  1/2 cup egg substitute
  1/2 teaspoon salt
  1/2 teaspoon pepper

In a large saucepan, cook beef, onions and garlic over medium heat until meat is no longer pink; drain. Stir in spaghetti sauce, tomatoes, tomato paste, water, parsley, Worcestershire sauce, basil and 1 teaspoon oregano. Cover and simmer for 3 hours, stirring occasionally. Cook pasta according to package directions; drain. In a bowl, combine ricotta, mozzarella, 1/4 cup Parmesan cheese, egg substitute, salt and pepper.

In two greased 13-in. x 9-in. x 2-in. baking dishes coated with nonstick cooking spray, spread 1 cup of meat sauce. In each dish, layer a fourth of the pasta, 1 cup meat sauce

Steak and Vegetables

(Pictured at right)

Soy sauce flavors this colorful combination of garden-fresh veggies and tender strips of sirloin. Served over rice, it's a hearty meal-in-one.
—Melanie Bowman, Midland, Texas

    1 tablespoon cornstarch
    1 teaspoon reduced-sodium beef bouillon
        granules
    1 cup water
  1/4 cup reduced-sodium soy sauce
   10 ounces boneless beef sirloin steak
    1 medium green pepper, julienned
    1 medium onion, halved and sliced
    1 garlic clove, minced
    2 teaspoons canola oil
    2 medium tomatoes, cut into eighths
    1 can (8 ounces) sliced water chestnuts, drained
  1/8 teaspoon pepper
    4 cups hot cooked rice

In a bowl, combine the cornstarch, bouillon, water and soy sauce; set aside. Cut steak thinly across the grain, then cut slices in half; set aside. In a nonstick skillet or wok, stir-fry green pepper, onion and garlic in oil for 4 minutes; remove and set aside. Add meat; stir-fry for 4-6 minutes.

Stir cornstarch mixture and add to pan. Bring to a boil; cook and stir for 1 minute or until thickened. Add tomatoes, water chestnuts and green pepper mixture; cook and stir until heated through. Sprinkle with pepper. Serve over rice. **Yield:** 4 servings.

Nutritional Analysis: One serving (1-1/2 cups meat mixture with 1 cup rice) equals 469 calories, 15 g fat (5 g saturated fat), 46 mg cholesterol, 678 mg sodium, 62 g carbohydrate, 5 g fiber, 21 g protein.
Diabetic Exchanges: 3 lean meat, 2 vegetable, 2 starch, 2 fat.

 Good-for-You Gravy

To make a lighter gravy, brown flour in a skillet. Cool slightly, then add some instant beef, chicken or vegetable bouillon granules and warm water. Cook and stir until thickened, then add salt and pepper if necessary.   —Elva Gamble, Detroit, Michigan

Stir in the tomatoes, beans, tomato paste, chilies and seasonings. Drain macaroni; add to beef mixture.

Transfer to a 13-in. x 9-in. x 2-in. baking dish coated with nonstick cooking spray. Cover and bake at 375° for 25-30 minutes or until bubbly. Uncover; sprinkle with cheese. Bake 5-8 minutes longer or until cheese is melted. **Yield:** 10 servings.

Nutritional Analysis: One serving (1 cup) equals 343 calories, 13 g fat (3 g saturated fat), 45 mg cholesterol, 812 mg sodium, 25 g carbohydrate, 6 g fiber, 32 g protein.
Diabetic Exchanges: 3 lean meat, 1-1/2 starch, 1 fat, 1/2 vegetable.

Chili Mac Casserole

(Pictured above)

This nicely spiced entree uses several of my family's favorite ingredients, including macaroni, kidney beans, tomatoes and cheese. Just add a green salad for a complete meal.
—Marlene Wilson, Rolla, North Dakota

   1 cup uncooked elbow macaroni
   2 pounds lean ground beef
   1 medium onion, chopped
   2 garlic cloves, minced
   1 can (28 ounces) diced tomatoes, undrained
   1 can (16 ounces) kidney beans, rinsed and drained
   1 can (6 ounces) tomato paste
   1 can (4 ounces) chopped green chilies
1-1/2 teaspoons salt
   1 teaspoon chili powder
1/2 teaspoon ground cumin
1/2 teaspoon pepper
   2 cups (8 ounces) shredded reduced-fat Mexican-blend cheese

Cook macaroni according to package directions. Meanwhile, in a large nonstick skillet, cook the beef, onion and garlic over medium heat until meat is no longer pink; drain.

Zesty Meatballs

Molasses adds a touch of sweetness to the tangy sauce that covers these moist meatballs. Serve them over egg noodles for a flavorful, family-pleasing meal.
—Debbie Segate, Grande Prairie, Alberta

1/3 cup finely chopped onion
   2 egg whites, lightly beaten
1/4 cup fat-free milk
   2 teaspoons prepared mustard
1/2 teaspoon salt
3/4 cup graham cracker crumbs (about 12 squares)
3/4 pound lean ground beef
3/4 pound lean ground turkey
BARBECUE SAUCE:
1/2 cup packed brown sugar
   3 tablespoons cornstarch
1/2 cup cider vinegar
1/2 cup ketchup
1/2 cup molasses
1/4 cup orange juice concentrate
   2 tablespoons Dijon mustard
   2 tablespoons reduced-sodium soy sauce
1/4 teaspoon hot pepper sauce
   6 cups hot cooked yolk-free noodles

Place onion in a small microwave-safe bowl; cover and microwave on high for 2 minutes or until tender. In a large bowl, combine the egg whites, milk, mustard, salt, cracker crumbs and onion. Crumble beef and turkey over mixture and mix well. Shape into 1-1/4-in. balls. Place 1 in. apart on 15-in. x 10-in. x 1-in. baking pans coated with nonstick cooking spray. Bake at 375° for 15-18 minutes or until meat is no longer pink.

Meanwhile, in a large saucepan, combine brown sugar and cornstarch. Stir in vinegar until smooth. Add the ketchup, molasses, orange juice concentrate, mustard, soy sauce and hot pepper sauce. Bring to a boil; cook and stir for 2 minutes or until thickened. Add meatballs; heat through. Serve over noodles. **Yield:** 6 servings.

Nutritional Analysis: One serving (6 meatballs and 1/3 cup sauce with 1 cup of noodles) equals 672 calories, 13 g fat (4 g saturated fat), 66 mg cholesterol, 1,050 mg sodium, 105 g carbohydrate, 4 g fiber, 34 g protein.
Diabetic Exchanges: 7 starch, 2 lean meat.

Chicken & Turkey Entrees

You don't have to eat like a bird—or forego flavor—in order to trim down on fat and calories. A simple solution is to choose chicken and turkey. Your family will flock to the table for these enticing entrees.

Chicken Parmigiana (page 140)

Creamy Braised Chicken

(Pictured below)

A smooth and delicate cream sauce gives special taste to these tender chicken breasts accompanied by sweet pearl onions and sauteed mushrooms. This dish is so rich tasting, you'll want to serve it to company.
—Pat Patty, Spring, Texas

1/2 pound pearl onions
　1 cup thinly sliced onion
1/2 cup thinly sliced carrot
1/2 cup thinly sliced celery
　1 tablespoon plus 2 teaspoons butter *or* stick margarine, *divided*
　6 boneless skinless chicken breast halves (1-1/2 pounds)
　1 cup chardonnay *or* other dry white wine *or* reduced-sodium chicken broth
1-1/3 cups reduced-sodium chicken broth
　1 tablespoon minced fresh parsley
　1 teaspoon salt
　1 teaspoon dried thyme
1/8 teaspoon white pepper
　1 bay leaf
　3 tablespoons all-purpose flour
1/2 cup fat-free evaporated milk
1/2 pound fresh mushrooms, quartered

In a Dutch oven or large kettle, bring 6 cups water to a boil. Add pearl onions; boil for 3 minutes. Drain and rinse in cold water; peel and set aside. In the same pan, saute sliced onion, carrot and celery in 1 tablespoon butter until tender. Remove vegetables; set aside.

Add chicken to the pan; brown on both sides. Remove and keep warm. Add wine; simmer until reduced to 1/2 cup. Stir in broth and seasonings. Return chicken to pan; cover and simmer for 5 minutes or until juices run clear. Remove chicken to a serving platter; keep warm. Combine flour and milk until smooth; gradually stir into pan. Bring to a boil; cook and stir for 2 minutes or until thickened. Return vegetables to pan. Remove from the heat; cover and set aside.

In a nonstick skillet, saute reserved pearl onions in remaining butter until tender. Remove and set aside. In the same pan, saute mushrooms until tender. Add the onions and mushrooms to serving platter. Discard bay leaf from sauce; spoon over chicken and vegetables. **Yield:** 6 servings.

Nutritional Analysis: One serving (1 chicken breast half with 2/3 cup sauce) equals 273 calories, 5 g fat (3 g saturated fat), 75 mg cholesterol, 748 mg sodium, 18 g carbohydrate, 2 g fiber, 31 g protein.
Diabetic Exchanges: 3-1/2 lean meat, 1-1/2 vegetable, 1 fat.

Herbed Turkey Breast

This is a family favorite that's also popular with company. The herbs tucked under the skin give the turkey a wonderful aroma as it's roasting, and the lemon juice adds a subtle hint of citrus.
—Alicia Glover, Sterling, Alaska

　1 bone-in turkey breast (8-1/2 pounds)
　3 tablespoons lemon juice, *divided*
　2 tablespoons olive *or* canola oil, *divided*
　2 garlic cloves, minced
1-1/4 teaspoons salt
　1 teaspoon grated lemon peel
　1 teaspoon dried thyme
3/4 teaspoon pepper
1/2 teaspoon rubbed sage

Loosen skin from turkey with fingers, leaving skin attached along bottom edges. In a small bowl, combine 1 tablespoon lemon juice, 1 tablespoon oil, garlic and seasonings. Spread under turkey skin. Combine remaining lemon juice and oil; set aside. Place turkey on a rack in a shallow roasting pan. Bake, uncovered, at 350° for 2-1/2 to 3 hours or until a meat thermometer reads 170°, basting every 15-20 minutes with lemon mixture. Let stand for 10 minutes. Discard skin before carving. **Yield:** 16 servings.

Nutritional Analysis: One serving equals 158 calories, 3 g fat (1 g saturated fat), 79 mg cholesterol, 246 mg sodium, 1 g carbohydrate, trace fiber, 31 g protein.
Diabetic Exchange: 3 lean meat.

Chicken Fajitas

For a zippy meal, give this quick and easy stir-fry idea a try. Tender chicken and colorful pepper strips are wrapped in tortillas for a tasty meal.
—*Eleanor Martens, Rosenort, Manitoba*

  1/3 cup lemon juice
    2 tablespoons reduced-sodium soy sauce
    2 tablespoons Worcestershire sauce
    1 tablespoon canola oil
    2 garlic cloves, minced
    1 teaspoon dried oregano
    1 teaspoon ground cumin
  3/4 pound boneless skinless chicken breasts, cut into 1/4-inch strips
    1 *each* medium green, sweet red and yellow pepper, cut into 1/2-inch strips
    2 small onions, cut into 1/2-inch strips
   12 flour tortillas (8 inches), warmed
    6 tablespoons reduced-fat sour cream
    6 tablespoons salsa

In a bowl, combine the lemon juice, soy sauce, Worcestershire sauce, oil, garlic, oregano and cumin; set aside 2 tablespoons. Pour remaining marinade into a large resealable plastic bag. Add chicken, peppers and onions. Seal bag and turn to coat; refrigerate for 2 hours, turning occasionally.

Drain and discard marinade. In a nonstick skillet or wok, stir-fry chicken and vegetables in reserved marinade for 3-4 minutes or until chicken juices run clear. Spoon onto tortillas. Top with sour cream and salsa. Roll up. **Yield:** 6 servings.

Nutritional Analysis: One serving (2 fajitas) equals 392 calories, 12 g fat (4 g saturated fat), 53 mg cholesterol, 477 mg sodium, 43 g carbohydrate, 6 g fiber, 30 g protein.
Diabetic Exchanges: 3 lean meat, 1-1/2 starch, 1-1/2 fat, 1-1/2 vegetable.

Turkey Spaghetti Pie

(Pictured above)

This turkey-based entree is a tasty change from traditional spaghetti. Its saucy goodness really comes through when it's reheated.
—*Anita Cunningham, Blaine, Washington*

    6 ounces uncooked spaghetti
    5 tablespoons grated Parmesan cheese
  1/2 cup egg substitute
  3/4 pound lean ground turkey breast
    1 medium onion, chopped
  1/2 medium green pepper, chopped
1-1/2 cups meatless spaghetti sauce
    1 cup fat-free cottage cheese
  1/2 cup shredded part-skim mozzarella cheese

Cook spaghetti according to package directions. Drain well and cool to room temperature. In a bowl, combine the spaghetti, Parmesan cheese and egg substitute. Transfer to a 9-in. pie plate coated with nonstick cooking spray and form into a crust; set aside.

In a nonstick skillet over medium heat, cook turkey, onion and green pepper until turkey is no longer pink; drain. Add spaghetti sauce; heat through. Spread cottage cheese over crust; top with turkey mixture.

Bake, uncovered, at 350° for 20 minutes. Sprinkle with mozzarella cheese. Bake 5 minutes longer or until cheese is melted. Let stand for 5 minutes before cutting. **Yield:** 6 servings.

Nutritional Analysis: One serving (1 wedge) equals 274 calories, 11 g fat (4 g saturated fat), 57 mg cholesterol, 710 mg sodium, 19 g carbohydrate, 2 g fiber, 25 g protein.
Diabetic Exchanges: 3 lean meat, 1 starch, 1 vegetable.

Shedding Light on Chicken

WHITE MEAT CHICKEN is a great source of lean protein, provides B vitamins and other essential nutrients your body needs and is lower in saturated fat than many meats.

To help reduce fat when fixing chicken, the American Dietetic Association offers these suggestions:

- Prepare boneless skinless chicken breasts or thighs using low-fat cooking methods like stir-frying and grilling.
- Instead of adding oil when cooking, use a nonstick pan or cooking spray to prevent sticking.
- Roast, bake, oven-fry or grill chicken pieces—preferably on a rack—to allow fat to drip off during cooking.
- Remove the skin from chicken after cooking instead of before. A thin membrane between the skin and the flesh of chicken holds moisture in the meat while it cooks, yet it keeps fat out. The result is juicy chicken with less fat.

Zesty Apricot Turkey

Grilled turkey is bound to be the centerpiece of any picnic. The poultry's fruity coating gets a little kick from hot pepper sauce...and would be a nice complement to other meats, too.
—Wendy Moylan, Crystal Lake, Illinois

1/3 cup reduced-sugar apricot preserves
1 tablespoon white wine vinegar *or* cider vinegar
1 tablespoon honey
1/2 teaspoon grated lemon peel
1 garlic clove, minced
1/8 teaspoon hot pepper sauce
1 boneless skinless turkey breast half (1 pound)

In a microwave-safe dish, combine the first six ingredients. Microwave, uncovered, until the preserves are melted, about 1-2 minutes on high. Stir to blend. Set aside half to serve with turkey.

Grill turkey, covered, over indirect medium heat for 3 minutes on each side. Brush with remaining apricot sauce. Grill 7-10 minutes longer or until juices run clear and a meat thermometer reads 170°. Slice; serve with the reserved apricot sauce. **Yield:** 4 servings.

Nutritional Analysis: One serving equals 193 calories, 1 g fat (trace saturated fat), 70 mg cholesterol, 62 mg sodium, 17 g carbohydrate, 1 g fiber, 28 g protein.
Diabetic Exchanges: 3 lean meat, 1/2 fruit.

Glazed Herb Chicken

(Pictured above right)

The orange flavor really comes through in the sauce that nicely coats this grilled chicken. I like to garnish it with fresh orange segments and a sprinkling of green chives for a pretty look.
—Jill Smith, Irmo, South Carolina

1 can (14-1/2 ounces) chicken broth
3/4 cup orange juice concentrate
2 tablespoons red wine vinegar *or* cider vinegar
2 teaspoons grated orange peel
2 garlic cloves, minced
1/2 teaspoon dried minced onion
1/8 to 1/4 teaspoon cayenne pepper
1/8 teaspoon dried thyme
1/8 teaspoon ground allspice
4 boneless skinless chicken breast halves (1 pound)
1 tablespoon cornstarch
1/4 cup honey
1 medium navel orange, peeled and sectioned
3 cups hot cooked rice
2 teaspoons minced chives

In a bowl, combine the first nine ingredients. Remove 1 cup for sauce; cover and refrigerate. Place the chicken in a large resealable plastic bag; add the remaining marinade. Seal bag and turn to coat; refrigerate for 2-8 hours, turning occasionally. Drain and discard marinade.

Grill chicken, uncovered, over medium heat for 4 minutes on each side or until juices run clear. Meanwhile, in a saucepan, combine the cornstarch and reserved marinade until smooth. Stir in the honey. Bring to a boil; cook and stir for 2 minutes or until thickened.

Serve chicken with orange sections over rice; spoon sauce over top. Sprinkle with chives. **Yield:** 4 servings.

Nutritional Analysis: One serving (1 chicken breast half with 1/4 cup sauce) equals 276 calories, 2 g fat (1 g saturated fat), 66 mg cholesterol, 912 mg sodium, 37 g carbohydrate, 2 g fiber, 28 g protein.
Diabetic Exchanges: 3 lean meat, 1-1/2 starch.

Broccoli Chicken Stir-Fry

Chinese Five Spice gives this stir-fry an authentic Oriental flavor. I make this speedy supper often.
—Lucy Duncan, Willis, Virginia

1 pound boneless skinless chicken breasts, cut into 1-inch pieces
1 tablespoon canola oil
2 cups broccoli florets
1 small sweet red pepper, julienned
1 can (8 ounces) sliced water chestnuts, drained
1 package (6 ounces) frozen snow peas, thawed
1 small onion, cut into thin wedges
2 garlic cloves, minced
1 teaspoon Chinese Five Spice (recipe on page 82)
1 can (14-1/2 ounces) chicken broth
2 tablespoons cornstarch

2 tablespoons cold water
4 cups hot cooked rice

In a large nonstick skillet or wok, stir-fry chicken in oil for 8 minutes or until lightly browned and juices run clear. Remove and keep warm. In the same skillet, stir-fry the broccoli, red pepper, water chestnuts, snow peas, onion and garlic for 6-8 minutes or until crisp-tender.

Return chicken to the pan; sprinkle with Chinese Five Spice. Add broth; bring to a boil. Combine cornstarch and cold water until smooth; stir into skillet. Cook and stir for 2 minutes or until thickened. Serve over rice. **Yield:** 4 servings.

Nutritional Analysis: One serving (1-1/2 cups chicken mixture with 1 cup rice) equals 459 calories, 6 g fat (1 g saturated fat), 66 mg cholesterol, 504 mg sodium, 65 g carbohydrate, 6 g fiber, 35 g protein.
Diabetic Exchanges: 3 lean meat, 2-1/2 starch, 2 vegetable, 1 fat.

Spicy Chicken and Peppers

My husband didn't think he could eat chicken prepared any way but fried—until he was coaxed into trying this colorful combination. Chili powder gives this skillet dish a little kick.
—Ruth Ann Toppins, Huntington, West Virginia

1 pound boneless skinless chicken breasts, cut into 1-inch strips
1-1/2 cups julienned green peppers
1 cup chopped onion
2 garlic cloves, minced
1 tablespoon olive *or* canola oil
1 can (15 ounces) tomato sauce
1 can (14-1/2 ounces) diced tomatoes, drained
2 teaspoons Italian seasoning
1-1/2 teaspoons sugar
1-1/2 teaspoons chili powder
1/4 teaspoon salt
1/4 teaspoon pepper
4 cups cooked no-yolk noodles
Fresh parsley

In a nonstick skillet, cook the chicken, green peppers, onion and garlic in oil until chicken juices run clear. Stir in the tomato sauce, tomatoes and seasonings. Bring to a boil. Reduce heat; cook, uncovered, for 5 minutes or until thickened. Serve over noodles. Garnish with parsley. **Yield:** 4 servings.

Nutritional Analysis: One serving (1-1/4 cups chicken mixture with 1 cup noodles) equals 548 calories, 4 g fat (1 g saturated fat), 66 mg cholesterol, 1,069 mg sodium, 85 g carbohydrate, 9 g fiber, 42 g protein.
Diabetic Exchanges: 4 lean meat, 3 starch, 2 vegetable, 1/2 fat.

Crunchy Baked Chicken

(Pictured below)

One bite of tender chicken in a crunchy golden coating explains why I give this recipe such a workout. Besides serving it at home for the two of us, I make a big batch for our senior group at church.
—Essie Malatt, Converse, Indiana

3/4 cup fat-free Western salad dressing
1/2 teaspoon chili powder
1/4 teaspoon salt
8 bone-in chicken breast halves (10 ounces *each*), skin removed
2-1/2 cups crushed cornflakes
DIPPING SAUCE (not shown):
1/4 cup chopped green pepper
1/4 cup chopped onion
3/4 cup fat-free Western salad dressing
1/2 teaspoon chili powder
1/4 teaspoon salt

In a shallow bowl, combine the salad dressing, chili powder and salt. Dip chicken in the mixture, then roll in cornflakes. Place in a 15-in. x 10-in. x 1-in. baking pan coated with nonstick cooking spray. Bake, uncovered, at 350° for 35-40 minutes or until chicken juices run clear.

Meanwhile, for sauce, combine green pepper and onion in a microwave-safe bowl. Microwave on high for 1-1/2 minutes. Stir in remaining ingredients. Cover and cook 30-60 seconds longer or until heated through. Serve with chicken. **Yield:** 8 servings.

Editor's Note: This recipe was tested in an 850-watt microwave.

Nutritional Analysis: One serving (1 chicken breast half with 2 tablespoons sauce) equals 278 calories, 1 g fat (trace saturated fat), 66 mg cholesterol, 888 mg sodium, 38 g carbohydrate, 1 g fiber, 29 g protein.
Diabetic Exchanges: 3-1/2 lean meat, 1 starch.

Turkey Lo Mein

I substituted turkey for pork in this classic Chinese recipe. It was a hit at our church potluck. My husband and two children love it, too.
—Leigh Lundy, York, Nebraska

    1 pound ground turkey breast
    1 cup thinly sliced carrots
    1 medium onion, chopped
1/2 teaspoon garlic powder
    2 teaspoons canola oil
    2 packages (3 ounces *each*) ramen noodles
1-1/2 cups water
    6 cups shredded cabbage
    1 cup frozen peas, thawed
1/4 cup reduced-sodium soy sauce

In a large nonstick skillet over medium heat, cook turkey, carrots, onion and garlic powder in oil until turkey is no longer pink. Break noodles. Add noodles, contents of seasoning packets and water to turkey mixture. Bring to a boil. Reduce heat; cover and simmer for 3-5 minutes. Add cabbage, peas and soy sauce; cook and stir until cabbage is crisp-tender and noodles are tender, about 1 minute. **Yield:** 8 servings.

Nutritional Analysis: One serving (1 cup) equals 239 calories, 10 g fat (3 g saturated fat), 45 mg cholesterol, 640 mg sodium, 23 g carbohydrate, 3 g fiber, 15 g protein.
Diabetic Exchanges: 2 lean meat, 1 starch, 1 fat.

Savory Spinach Chicken Roll-Ups

The herb-flavored chicken stays tender and moist in this entree developed by our Test Kitchen.

    1 package (10 ounces) fresh spinach
1/4 cup chopped fresh mushrooms
    1 green onion, finely chopped
    1 to 2 garlic cloves, minced
    2 teaspoons olive *or* canola oil
    1 egg, lightly beaten
1/4 cup crumbled feta cheese
1/4 cup dry bread crumbs
3/4 teaspoon dried rosemary, crushed, *divided*
1/4 teaspoon salt
    4 boneless skinless chicken breast halves
       (1 pound)
1/2 teaspoon *each* dried basil and dried thyme
1/4 teaspoon pepper

In a large saucepan, place spinach in a steamer basket over 1 in. of boiling water. Cover and steam for 2-3 minutes or just until wilted. When cool enough to handle, squeeze spinach dry and finely chop. In a nonstick skillet, saute the mushrooms, onion and garlic in oil until tender. Add spinach; cook and stir for 2 minutes. Transfer to a bowl. Add the egg, cheese, bread crumbs, 1/4 teaspoon rosemary and salt; mix well.
    Flatten chicken to 1/4-in. thickness. Combine basil,

thyme, pepper and remaining rosemary; rub over one side of chicken. Spread spinach mixture over plain side; roll up. Secure with toothpicks. In a large saucepan, place roll-ups in a steamer basket over 1 in. of boiling water. Cover and steam for 12-15 minutes or until chicken is no longer pink. **Yield:** 4 servings.

Nutritional Analysis: One serving (1 roll-up) equals 235 calories, 8 g fat (3 g saturated fat), 127 mg cholesterol, 456 mg sodium, 9 g carbohydrate, 2 g fiber, 32 g protein.
Diabetic Exchanges: 3 lean meat, 1 vegetable, 1 fat.

Smoked Sausage Stir-Fry

(Pictured at right)

A dish needs to look as good as it tastes. This eye-catching stir-fry is a prime example. The colorful peppers and tomatoes contrast nicely with the sausage—and the whole thing is delicious!
—Sandi Towne, Sauk Village, Illinois

    1 pound fully cooked smoked turkey sausage,
       cut into 1/2-inch slices
    2 tablespoons olive *or* canola oil
1/2 cup julienned green pepper
1/2 cup julienned sweet red pepper
    1 small onion, sliced and separated into rings
1-1/2 teaspoons garlic powder
1-1/2 teaspoons dried basil
1-1/2 teaspoons dried oregano
1/4 teaspoon pepper
    2 medium tomatoes, cut into wedges
    4 cups hot cooked rice

In a nonstick skillet or wok, stir-fry sausage in oil over medium heat until lightly browned, about 10 minutes. Add the peppers, onion and seasonings. Cover and cook for 10 minutes or until the vegetables are crisp-tender, stirring occasionally. Add the tomatoes; cook 1 minute longer. Serve over rice. **Yield:** 4 servings.

Nutritional Analysis: One serving (3/4 cup sausage mixture with 1 cup rice) equals 421 calories, 8 g fat (3 g saturated fat), 51 mg cholesterol, 981 mg sodium, 64 g carbohydrate, 2 g fiber, 20 g protein.
Diabetic Exchanges: 3 lean meat, 2-1/2 starch, 1 fat.

🍎 Ground Turkey Trick

- When cooking with ground turkey in recipes for lasagna or spaghetti sauce, I increase the amount of seasonings and leave the mixture in the refrigerator overnight. The turkey seems to pick up more of the flavor. —*Kathy Mason Lima, Ohio*

- If a recipe calls for ground beef or pork, I replace half of it with ground turkey. This cuts down on the fat in the dish without sacrificing the taste my family loves. —*Diane Bulanda Bedford, Ohio*

Chicken with Raspberry Sauce

(Pictured below)

This tender marinated chicken gets a hint of sweetness when drizzled with a fruity sauce. It's always a hit with rice pilaf and a salad.
—Amy Ammann, Long Valley, New Jersey

3/4 cup seedless raspberry preserves, divided
1/2 cup raspberry vinegar (recipe on page 84)
1/2 cup unsweetened pineapple juice
1/4 cup reduced-sodium soy sauce
2 tablespoons balsamic vinegar
1 garlic clove, minced
2 teaspoons dried basil
1/2 teaspoon salt
1/2 teaspoon chili powder
1/2 teaspoon curry powder
6 boneless skinless chicken breast halves (1-1/2 pounds)
2 teaspoons cornstarch
1/4 cup unsweetened raspberries

In a bowl, combine 1/2 cup preserves, raspberry vinegar, pineapple juice, soy sauce, balsamic vinegar, garlic and seasonings; mix well. Remove 1 cup for sauce; cover and refrigerate.

Place the chicken in a large resealable plastic bag; add remaining marinade. Seal bag and turn to coat; refrigerate for at least 3 hours. Drain and discard marinade. Grill chicken, uncovered, over medium heat for 4 minutes on each side or until juices run clear.

In a small saucepan, combine cornstarch and reserved marinade until blended. Bring to a boil; cook and stir for 2 minutes or until thickened. Add remaining preserves; mix well. Drizzle over chicken. Garnish with raspberries. **Yield:** 6 servings.

Nutritional Analysis: One serving (1 chicken breast half with 1/4 cup sauce) equals 209 calories, 1 g fat (trace saturated fat), 66 mg cholesterol, 432 mg sodium, 20 g carbohydrate, 1 g fiber, 27 g protein.
Diabetic Exchanges: *3-1/2 lean meat, 1/2 fruit.*

Juicy Turkey Burgers

The way to a healthy heart for my husband is through luscious low-fat recipes. He enjoys these grilled turkey burgers with their herb flavor and garden-fresh garnish. They make an ideal summer sandwich or in-hand meal for when we're on the run.
—Trina Hopsecger, Elkhart, Indiana

1 medium apple, peeled and finely shredded
1/2 cup cooked brown rice
2 tablespoons grated onion
2 garlic cloves, minced
1-1/2 teaspoons rubbed sage
1 teaspoon salt
1/2 teaspoon pepper
1/2 teaspoon dried thyme
1/4 teaspoon ground allspice
1/4 teaspoon cayenne pepper
1 pound ground turkey breast
2 tablespoons minced fresh parsley
6 whole wheat hamburger buns, split
6 lettuce leaves
6 tomato slices

If grilling the burgers, coat grill rack with nonstick cooking spray before starting the grill. In a bowl, combine the first 10 ingredients. Crumble turkey over mixture and mix well. Shape into six 1/2-in.-thick patties.

Grill, covered, over indirect medium heat or broil 6 in. from the heat for 6-7 minutes on each side or until a meat thermometer reads 165°. Sprinkle with parsley. Serve on buns with lettuce and tomato. **Yield:** 6 servings.

Nutritional Analysis: One burger equals 265 calories, 9 g fat (2 g saturated fat), 60 mg cholesterol, 663 mg sodium, 28 g carbohydrate, 3 g fiber, 18 g protein.
Diabetic Exchanges: *2 starch, 2 lean meat.*

Light Grilling Made Fuss-Free

- The reduced-fat Italian dressing you pour on your salad makes a speedy and savory marinade. Place chicken, meat, pork or vegetables in a resealable plastic bag. Add the dressing and marinate in the refrigerator for 30 minutes or more. Be sure to discard the marinade before grilling.
- Try spicing up your backyard barbecue with fat-free salsa. It's wonderful for basting poultry and meats, and it adds a bit of pizzazz.

Nutritional Analysis: One serving (2 tacos) equals 371 calories, 6 g fat (1 g saturated fat), 66 mg cholesterol, 599 mg sodium, 44 g carbohydrate, 4 g fiber, 36 g protein.
Diabetic Exchanges: 3-1/2 very lean meat, 2 starch, 2 vegetable, 1 fat.

Spiced Orange Chicken

Orange juice along with zesty herbs and spices dress up this chicken that's especially nice served over rice.
—Carolyn Grasse-Bachman, Lancaster, Pennsylvania

    6 boneless skinless chicken breast halves (1-1/2
        pounds)
    2 cups orange juice, *divided*
    1 tablespoon dried minced onion
1-1/2 teaspoons dried parsley flakes
    1/2 teaspoon salt
    1/2 teaspoon paprika
    1/4 teaspoon ground ginger
    1/4 teaspoon pepper
Dash ground cinnamon
Dash ground nutmeg
    2 tablespoons cornstarch
    1/4 cup water
    6 cups hot cooked rice

Place chicken in a large nonstick skillet; add 1 cup of orange juice. Sprinkle with the seasonings. Bring to a boil. Reduce heat; cover and simmer for 20-25 minutes or until the chicken juices run clear. Remove chicken and keep warm.
   Combine cornstarch, water and remaining orange juice until smooth; stir into cooking juices. Bring to a boil; cook and stir for 2 minutes or until thickened. Serve over chicken and rice. **Yield:** 6 servings.

Nutritional Analysis: One serving (1 chicken breast half with 1/3 cup sauce and 1 cup rice) equals 381 calories, 2 g fat (1 g saturated fat), 66 mg cholesterol, 272 mg sodium, 56 g carbohydrate, 1 g fiber, 31 g protein.
Diabetic Exchanges: 3 lean meat, 2 starch, 1 fruit.

Lemon Chicken Tacos

(Pictured above)

These tempting tacos are low in fat but full of zippy flavor. I often modify the recipe to our tastes by adding more tomato and green onion and a bit of cheddar cheese. It's a keeper!
—Lisa Giegel, Spokane, Washington

    1 pound boneless skinless chicken breasts, cut
        into 1/2-inch cubes
    2 tablespoons plus 1 teaspoon lemon juice,
        divided
    1 large onion, sliced
    1 green onion, sliced
    2 garlic cloves, minced
    2 teaspoons olive *or* canola oil
    1/2 teaspoon ground cumin
    1/2 teaspoon salt
    1/4 teaspoon pepper
    2 plum tomatoes, seeded and chopped
    1/4 cup minced fresh cilantro *or* parsley
    8 flour tortillas (8 inches), warmed
    1 cup shredded lettuce
    1/2 cup salsa

Place chicken in a large resealable plastic bag; add 2 tablespoons lemon juice. Seal bag and turn to coat; refrigerate for 1-2 hours.
   In a nonstick skillet, saute the onions and garlic in oil until tender. Add the chicken, cumin, salt and pepper. Cook and stir for 4 minutes or until juices run clear. Remove from the heat; stir in the tomatoes, cilantro and remaining lemon juice. Spoon onto tortillas; top with lettuce. Serve with salsa. **Yield:** 4 servings.

Baked Chicken Breast

This quick-to-fix chicken dish from our Test Kitchen is sure to put a feather in your cap at dinnertime!

    4 chicken breast quarters (10 ounces *each*)
    1 teaspoon Salt Substitute (recipe on page 93)
    1 teaspoon canola oil

Loosen chicken skin; rub salt substitute under skin and over skin if desired. Place skin side up in an ungreased 15-in. x 10-in. x 1-in. baking pan. Brush with oil. Bake, uncovered, at 325° for 40-50 minutes or until juices run clear. **Yield:** 4 servings.

Nutritional Analysis: One serving (4 ounces cooked chicken, skin removed) equals 203 calories, 5 g fat (1 g saturated fat), 99 mg cholesterol, 95 mg sodium, trace carbohydrate, trace fiber, 36 g protein.
Diabetic Exchange: 4 lean meat.

Spinach-Stuffed Chicken

(Pictured above)

These moist chicken rolls get their appealing look from a golden crumb coating and wonderful spinach and onion filling. They're good right out of the oven, but you can also serve them chilled for an elegant lunch.
—*Mary Jones, St. Louis, Missouri*

6 cups torn fresh spinach (5 ounces)
1/2 cup chopped onion
1/2 cup chopped fresh mushrooms
1 garlic clove, minced
1 tablespoon olive *or* canola oil
1/2 teaspoon dried oregano
1/2 teaspoon salt
1/4 teaspoon pepper
6 boneless skinless chicken breast halves (1-1/2 pounds)
1/2 cup dry bread crumbs
3 tablespoons grated Parmesan cheese
1/2 teaspoon paprika
1/4 cup egg substitute
1 tablespoon water
2 tablespoons butter *or* stick margarine, melted

In a large nonstick skillet, cook spinach in 1/2 in. of water over medium heat just until wilted, about 2 minutes. Drain and set spinach aside. In the same skillet, saute the onion, mushrooms and garlic in oil until tender. Stir in the seasonings; add spinach and set aside.

Flatten chicken to 1/4-in. thickness. Spread spinach mixture down the center of each chicken breast. Fold one side over filling and roll up tightly; secure with a toothpick. In a shallow bowl, combine bread crumbs, Parmesan cheese and paprika. In another bowl, combine egg substitute and water. Dip each roll-up in egg mixture, then roll in crumb mixture.

Place, seam side down, in a 13-in. x 9-in. x 2-in. baking pan coated with nonstick cooking spray. Drizzle with butter. Bake, uncovered, at 350° for 20-25 minutes or until juices run clear. Discard toothpicks. **Yield:** 6 servings.

Nutritional Analysis: One stuffed chicken breast equals 260 calories, 9 g fat (4 g saturated fat), 78 mg cholesterol, 497 mg sodium, 11 g carbohydrate, 1 g fiber, 32 g protein.
Diabetic Exchanges: 4 lean meat, 1/2 starch.

Chicken Stroganoff

When I prepare this meal, I often tell people it's beef Stroganoff. Because of its convincing appearance and taste, they're surprised when I later confide that it's actually chicken.
—*Lori Borrowman, Schenectady, New York*

1 pound fresh mushrooms, sliced
1 large onion, chopped
2 tablespoons butter *or* stick margarine
1-1/2 pounds boneless skinless chicken breasts, cut into 2-inch strips
1/4 cup browning sauce
1-1/3 cups reduced-sodium beef broth, *divided*
1 cup white wine *or* additional reduced-sodium beef broth
2 tablespoons ketchup
2 garlic cloves, minced
1 teaspoon salt
3 tablespoons all-purpose flour
1 cup (8 ounces) fat-free sour cream
6 cups cooked no-yolk noodles

In a large nonstick skillet, saute mushrooms and onion in butter until tender. Remove and set aside. In the same skillet, cook the chicken with browning sauce until browned. Add 1 cup broth, wine or additional broth, ketchup, garlic and salt. Bring to a boil. Reduce heat; cover and simmer for 15 minutes.

Combine flour and remaining 1/3 cup broth until smooth; stir into chicken mixture. Add reserved mushroom mixture. Bring to a boil; cook and stir for 2 minutes or until thickened. Reduce heat to low. Stir in sour cream; heat through (do not boil). Serve over noodles. **Yield:** 6 servings.

Nutritional Analysis: One serving (1 cup chicken mixture with 1 cup noodles) equals 535 calories, 7 g fat (3 g saturated fat), 80 mg cholesterol, 1,339 mg sodium, 66 g carbohydrate, 4 g fiber, 41 g protein.
Diabetic Exchanges: 3-1/2 lean meat, 3-1/2 starch, 1 vegetable, 1 fat.

Bean and Sausage Rigatoni

Cutting the fat in this casserole I revised didn't make it any less hearty. I tested it on a friend with a good appetite, and he loved it! Served with a fresh

green salad and crusty French bread, it makes a balanced meal. The smoked turkey sausage is delicious.
—Irene Heath, Hastings, Michigan

1 can (15 ounces) great northern beans, rinsed and drained
1 can (14-1/2 ounces) stewed tomatoes
1 package (10 ounces) frozen chopped spinach, thawed and drained
8 ounces rigatoni *or* penne pasta, cooked and drained
1/2 pound reduced-fat fully cooked smoked turkey kielbasa, halved and sliced
5 tablespoons tomato paste
1/4 cup chicken broth
1-1/2 teaspoons Italian seasoning
1/4 cup shredded Parmesan cheese

In a bowl, combine the first eight ingredients; transfer to a 2-qt. baking dish coated with nonstick cooking spray. Sprinkle with Parmesan cheese. Bake, uncovered, at 375° for 15-20 minutes or until heated through. **Yield:** 8 servings.

Nutritional Analysis: One serving (1 cup) equals 249 calories, 3 g fat (1 g saturated fat), 15 mg cholesterol, 537 mg sodium, 42 g carbohydrate, 5 g fiber, 14 g protein.
Diabetic Exchanges: 2 starch, 2 vegetable, 1 lean meat.

Turkey Fried Rice

My husband, our two young sons and I enjoy this deliciously different fried rice dish. The brown rice makes it extra nutritious...and it's a great way to use up leftover cooked turkey.
—Lorna Plett, Riverton, Manitoba

2 cups reduced-sodium chicken broth
1 cup uncooked brown rice
2 cups cubed cooked turkey breast
3 tablespoons reduced-sodium soy sauce
1 egg, lightly beaten
1 small onion, chopped
1/4 cup chopped green pepper
1/4 cup chopped celery
1 tablespoon canola oil
1 cup shredded romaine

In a saucepan, bring broth to a boil. Stir in rice. Reduce heat; cover and simmer for 45-50 minutes or until liquid is absorbed and rice is tender. Remove from the heat; cool. Cover and refrigerate overnight.

In a bowl, combine turkey and soy sauce; cover and refrigerate. In a large nonstick skillet, cook and stir the egg over medium heat until completely set. Remove and set aside. In the same skillet, saute onion, green pepper and celery in oil until tender. Add rice and turkey; cook and stir over medium heat for 6-8 minutes. Add lettuce and reserved egg; cook and stir for 1-2 minutes. Serve immediately. **Yield:** 4 servings.

Nutritional Analysis: One serving (1 cup) equals 367 calories, 10 g fat (2 g saturated fat), 106 mg cholesterol, 994 mg sodium, 40 g carbohydrate, 2 g fiber, 28 g protein.
Diabetic Exchanges: 3 lean meat, 2-1/2 starch.

Pepperoni Pizza Pasta

(Pictured below)

Adding pizzazz to platters is a simple process. Bow tie pasta and colorful peppers make this dish look as good as it tastes. Quick and easy to toss together, it's an impressive addition to the dinner table or any buffet...for as long as it lasts!
—Suzan Suskie, Whitesboro, New York

8 ounces uncooked bow tie pasta
1 large onion, chopped
1-1/2 cups julienned green pepper
1-1/2 cups julienned sweet red pepper
2 garlic cloves, minced
1 tablespoon olive *or* canola oil
1 can (14-1/2 ounces) stewed tomatoes
1-1/2 teaspoons dried basil
4 ounces turkey pepperoni, halved and sliced
1 cup diced fresh tomatoes
3/4 teaspoon salt
1/4 teaspoon pepper
4 ounces part-skim mozzarella cheese, diced
Crushed red pepper flakes, optional

Cook pasta according to package directions. Meanwhile, in a large nonstick skillet, saute the onion, peppers and garlic in oil until vegetables are crisp-tender. Add stewed tomatoes and basil. Bring to a boil. Reduce heat; cover and simmer for 10 minutes, stirring occasionally.

Stir in the pepperoni, diced tomatoes, salt and pepper; simmer for 2 minutes. Drain pasta; add to the tomato mixture. Add cheese and toss well. Sprinkle with pepper flakes if desired. **Yield:** 9 servings.

Nutritional Analysis: One serving (1 cup) equals 213 calories, 6 g fat (2 g saturated fat), 22 mg cholesterol, 585 mg sodium, 29 g carbohydrate, 3 g fiber, 12 g protein.
Diabetic Exchanges: 1-1/2 starch, 1 lean meat, 1 vegetable.

Chicken Broccoli Stir-Fry

Julienned carrots and broccoli florets brighten this delectable dish. This is a guilt-free meal... the fat content is so minimal, there's no reason not to enjoy dessert afterward!
—Kris Lundberg, Baldwin, Wisconsin

1 pound boneless skinless chicken breasts, cut
   into thin strips
2 teaspoons canola oil
2 medium carrots, julienned
2 cups broccoli florets
3-1/4 cups water, *divided*
3 teaspoons chicken bouillon granules
1 tablespoon reduced-sodium soy sauce
1/2 teaspoon ground ginger
1/4 cup cornstarch
4 cups hot cooked rice

In a large nonstick skillet or wok, stir-fry chicken in oil until no longer pink. Remove and keep warm. Stir-fry the carrots and broccoli for 3-4 minutes or until crisp-tender. Remove and keep warm.

Add 3 cups water to the pan; bring to a boil. Add bouillon; stir until dissolved. Reduce heat. Add soy sauce, ginger, chicken and vegetables; cook for 5 minutes or until heated through. Combine the cornstarch and remaining water until smooth; stir into pan. Bring to a boil; cook and stir for 2 minutes or until thickened. Serve over rice. **Yield:** 4 servings.

Nutritional Analysis: *One serving (1 cup chicken mixture with 1 cup rice) equals 421 calories, 4 g fat (1 g saturated fat), 66 mg cholesterol, 1,123 mg sodium, 59 g carbohydrate, 2 g fiber, 33 g protein.*
Diabetic Exchanges: *3 starch, 2-1/2 lean meat, 2 vegetable.*

let, stir-fry chicken and garlic in oil until chicken juices run clear. Remove and keep warm. Add broth, peas, carrots, cream cheese and lemon juice to the skillet; cook and stir until cheese is melted. Drain pasta. Add pasta, chicken and salt to vegetable mixture; heat through. Sprinkle with Parmesan cheese. **Yield:** 4 servings.

Nutritional Analysis: *One serving (1-1/2 cups) equals 399 calories, 11 g fat (4 g saturated fat), 64 mg cholesterol, 824 mg sodium, 42 g carbohydrate, 4 g fiber, 33 g protein.*
Diabetic Exchanges: *3 lean meat, 2 starch, 1 vegetable, 1 fat.*

Bow Tie Lemon Chicken

(Pictured above right)

The zesty flavor of lemon brightens every bite of this creamy chicken and pasta dish. With two small sons and a farmer husband who has a second full-time job, I rely on my collection of speedy recipes.
—Rebecca Snapp, Cynthiana, Kentucky

4-2/3 cups uncooked bow tie pasta
12 ounces boneless skinless chicken breasts, cut
   into 1-inch strips
1/2 teaspoon salt-free lemon-pepper seasoning
2 garlic cloves, minced
1 tablespoon canola oil
1 cup chicken broth
1 cup frozen peas, thawed
2/3 cup shredded carrots
1/4 cup cubed reduced-fat cream cheese
2 teaspoons lemon juice
1/2 teaspoon salt
1/3 cup shredded Parmesan cheese

Cook pasta according to package directions. Meanwhile, sprinkle chicken with lemon-pepper. In a large nonstick skil-

Italian Turkey Sandwiches

I hope you enjoy these tasty turkey sandwiches as much as our family does. The recipe makes plenty, so it's great for potlucks. Leftovers are just as good reheated the next day.
—Carol Riley, Galva, Illinois

1 bone-in turkey breast (5-1/2 pounds), skin
   removed
1/2 cup chopped green pepper
1 medium onion, chopped
1/4 cup chili sauce
3 tablespoons white vinegar
2 tablespoons dried oregano *or* Italian seasoning
4 teaspoons beef bouillon granules
11 kaiser *or* hard sandwich rolls, split

Place the turkey breast, green pepper and onion in a 5-qt. slow cooker coated with nonstick cooking spray. Combine the chili sauce, vinegar, oregano and bouillon; pour over turkey and vegetables. Cover and cook on low for 5-6 hours or until meat juices run clear and vegetables are tender.

Remove turkey with a slotted spoon, reserving cooking liquid. Shred the turkey with two forks; return to cooking juices. Spoon 1/2 cup onto each roll. **Yield:** 11 servings.

Nutritional Analysis: One serving (1 sandwich) equals 364 calories, 4 g fat (1 g saturated fat), 102 mg cholesterol, 576 mg sodium, 33 g carbohydrate, trace fiber, 46 g protein.
Diabetic Exchanges: 3-1/2 lean meat, 2 starch.

Chicken and Asparagus Bundles

(Pictured below)

My husband is a big asparagus fan, so I had to try this recipe. It's a mainstay when I want something unusual but simple for guests. For variety, you can leave off the sauce and serve the bundles chilled for lunch.
—*Donna Lohnes, Wooster, Ohio*

    4 **boneless skinless chicken breast halves (1 pound)**
  20 **fresh asparagus spears (about 1 pound), trimmed**
4-1/2 **teaspoons olive *or* canola oil**
    2 **teaspoons lemon juice**
  1/2 **teaspoon dried basil**
  1/4 **teaspoon dried thyme**
  1/4 **teaspoon pepper**
  1/8 **teaspoon salt**
  1/4 **cup chopped green onions**
    2 **teaspoons cornstarch**
    1 **cup chicken broth**

Flatten chicken breasts slightly. Wrap each around five asparagus spears; secure with toothpicks. Place in a 13-in. x 9-in. x 2-in. baking dish coated with nonstick cooking spray. Combine the oil, lemon juice and seasonings; pour over bundles. Cover asparagus tips with foil.

Cover and bake at 350° for 15 minutes. Uncover; sprinkle with the onions. Bake 12-15 minutes longer or until the chicken juices run clear and asparagus is crisp-tender. Remove bundles to a serving platter and keep warm.

In a saucepan, combine cornstarch and broth until smooth; stir in pan juices. Bring to a boil; cook and stir for 2 minutes or until thickened. Remove toothpicks from bundles; top with sauce. **Yield:** 4 servings.

Nutritional Analysis: One serving (1 bundle with about 1/3 cup sauce) equals 207 calories, 7 g fat (1 g saturated fat), 66 mg cholesterol, 316 mg sodium, 6 g carbohydrate, 2 g fiber, 29 g protein.
Diabetic Exchanges: 3 lean meat, 1 vegetable, 1 fat.

Chicken Curry

A host of spices lends an authentic flavor to this ethnic entree. The mother of one of my friends is from India...and she shared the secret ingredients for making this wonderful curry.
—*Trisha Kuster, Macomb, Illinois*

1-1/2 **pounds boneless skinless chicken breasts, cubed**
  1/4 **cup chopped onion**
    2 **tablespoons canola oil**
    1 **can (28 ounces) crushed tomatoes with Italian herbs**
    1 **teaspoon curry powder**
  1/2 **teaspoon *each* salt, pepper and cayenne pepper**
  1/2 **teaspoon *each* garlic powder, paprika and chili powder**
  1/2 **teaspoon *each* ground turmeric, ginger and cloves**
    6 **cups hot cooked rice**

In a saucepan, saute the chicken and onion in oil until the chicken is browned. Stir in the tomatoes and seasonings. Bring to a boil. Reduce the heat; cover and simmer for 30 minutes or until chicken juices run clear. Serve over rice. **Yield:** 6 servings.

Nutritional Analysis: One serving (3/4 cup chicken mixture with 1 cup rice) equals 411 calories, 7 g fat (1 g saturated fat), 66 mg cholesterol, 715 mg sodium, 55 g carbohydrate, 3 g fiber, 32 g protein.
Diabetic Exchanges: 3 starch, 2-1/2 lean meat, 1 vegetable.

Ready-Made Meal

When I buy chicken breasts, I remove the skin and put the number I need for a meal in a freezer bag. I add marinade right in with the meat. Then all I have to do is pull a bag from the freezer, thaw it in the refrigerator and discard the marinade before cooking. I have seasoned chicken ready to bake or grill. —*Moira Elsley, Mindemoya, Ontario*

Turkey Manicotti

The addition of wholesome bulgur gives extra nutrition to this Italian entree. It's so zesty and flavorful, your family will never realize it's good for them.
—Mary Gunderson, Conrad, Iowa

1/4 cup bulgur*
2/3 cup boiling water
3/4 pound lean ground turkey
1-1/2 cups 2% small-curd cottage cheese
1 teaspoon dried basil
1 teaspoon dried oregano
1/2 teaspoon salt
1/4 teaspoon pepper
14 uncooked manicotti shells
1 jar (28 ounces) meatless spaghetti sauce
1/2 cup water
1 cup (4 ounces) shredded part-skim mozzarella cheese

Place the bulgur in a bowl; stir in boiling water. Cover and let stand for 30 minutes or until the liquid is absorbed. Drain and squeeze dry.

In a nonstick skillet, cook turkey over medium heat until no longer pink; drain. Add the cottage cheese, basil, oregano, salt, pepper and bulgur; mix well. Stuff into uncooked manicotti shells. Arrange in a 13-in. x 9-in. x 2-in. baking dish coated with nonstick cooking spray.

Combine spaghetti sauce and water; pour over shells. Cover and bake at 350° for 1 hour and 15 minutes or until shells are tender and sauce is bubbly. Uncover; sprinkle with mozzarella cheese. Bake 5 minutes longer or until cheese is melted. **Yield:** 7 servings.

*Editor's Note: Look for bulgur in the cereal, rice or organic food aisle of your grocery store.

Nutritional Analysis: One serving (2 stuffed shells) equals 418 calories, 13 g fat (5 g saturated fat), 51 mg cholesterol, 986 mg sodium, 49 g carbohydrate, 6 g fiber, 27 g protein.
Diabetic Exchanges: 3 lean meat, 3 starch, 1/2 fat.

Turkey Quesadillas

(Pictured above right)

Loaded with garden-fresh vegetables, this Mexican specialty is sure to be popular with the whole family. Plus, it's a snap to prepare on a busy weeknight.
—Wendy Greinke, Round Rock, Texas

1 pound lean ground turkey
1 cup chopped red onion
1 to 2 garlic cloves, minced
2 cups julienned zucchini
1 cup salsa
1 cup frozen corn
1 cup julienned sweet red pepper
1 can (4 ounces) chopped green chilies
2 tablespoons minced fresh cilantro *or* parsley
1/2 teaspoon dried oregano
1/2 teaspoon ground cumin
1/4 teaspoon salt
1/8 teaspoon cayenne pepper
8 flour tortillas (8 inches)

2 cups (8 ounces) shredded reduced-fat Mexican-blend cheese *or* cheddar cheese

In a nonstick skillet, cook turkey, onion and garlic over medium heat until meat is no longer pink; drain. Add zucchini, salsa, corn, red pepper and chilies. Reduce heat; cover and simmer until vegetables are tender. Stir in the seasonings.

For each quesadilla, place one tortilla in an ungreased nonstick skillet. Sprinkle with 1-1/2 cups turkey mixture and 1/4 cup cheese; cover with another tortilla. Cook over medium heat, carefully turning once, until lightly browned on both sides and cheese begins to melt. Cut into eight wedges. **Yield:** 4 quesadillas (8 wedges each).

Nutritional Analysis: One serving (4 wedges) equals 349 calories, 13 g fat (5 g saturated fat), 55 mg cholesterol, 771 mg sodium, 37 g carbohydrate, 3 g fiber, 24 g protein.
Diabetic Exchanges: 2 starch, 2 lean meat, 1-1/2 fat.

Twisty Pasta Primavera With Chicken

I frequently turn to this tasty meal-in-one dish to feed my family when time is short. For a fun variation, try multicolored spirals.
—Elaine Anderson, Aliquippa, Pennsylvania

2 quarts water
2-1/2 cups uncooked spiral pasta
2 cups chopped broccoli
3/4 cup sliced carrots
1 cup (4 ounces) shredded part-skim mozzarella cheese

2 cups cubed cooked chicken breast
1 can (10-3/4 ounces) reduced-fat reduced-sodium condensed cream of broccoli soup, undiluted
1 cup fat-free milk
1/4 cup grated Parmesan cheese
1/8 teaspoon garlic powder
1/8 teaspoon pepper

In a large saucepan, bring water to a boil. Add pasta; cook for 4 minutes. Add broccoli and carrots; cook 4-5 minutes longer or until pasta is tender. Drain and place in a bowl. Add mozzarella cheese and chicken.

In another saucepan, combine the remaining ingredients. Bring to a boil; cook and stir until blended. Pour over pasta mixture and toss gently. Serve immediately. **Yield:** 6 servings.

Nutritional Analysis: One serving (1-1/3 cups) equals 345 calories, 8 g fat (4 g saturated fat), 57 mg cholesterol, 433 mg sodium, 38 g carbohydrate, 3 g fiber, 29 g protein.
Diabetic Exchanges: 3 lean meat, 2 starch, 1 vegetable.

Herbed Lime Chicken

When we have friends over during the summer, I usually serve this grilled chicken. It's tender, moist and bursting with the tangy taste of lime. I'm often asked for the recipe.
—Kay Alliman, Biggsville, Illinois

1 bottle (16 ounces) fat-free Italian salad dressing
1/2 cup lime juice
1 lime, halved and sliced
3 garlic cloves, minced
1 teaspoon dried thyme
4 boneless skinless chicken breast halves (1 pound)

In a bowl, combine the first five ingredients. Remove 1/2 cup for basting; cover and refrigerate. Pour remaining marinade into a large resealable plastic bag; add chicken. Seal bag and turn to coat; refrigerate for 8-10 hours.

Drain and discard marinade. Grill chicken, uncovered, over medium heat for 5 minutes. Turn chicken; baste with the reserved marinade. Grill 5-7 minutes longer or until juices run clear, basting occasionally. **Yield:** 4 servings.

Nutritional Analysis: One serving equals 162 calories, 2 g fat (1 g saturated fat), 67 mg cholesterol, 718 mg sodium, 8 g carbohydrate, trace fiber, 27 g protein.
Diabetic Exchange: 4 very lean meat.

Chicken Lasagna

(Pictured at right)

For a cooking class several years ago, I lightened up a classic lasagna and created this chicken version. It was preferred over the traditional dish in taste-tests in my class and by my family and friends as well.
—Dena Stapelman, Laurel, Nebraska

10 uncooked lasagna noodles
1 pound boneless skinless chicken breasts
1 can (14-1/2 ounces) diced tomatoes, undrained
1 can (12 ounces) tomato paste
1-1/2 cups sliced fresh mushrooms
1/4 cup chopped onion
1 tablespoon dried basil
1-3/4 teaspoons salt, *divided*
1/8 teaspoon garlic powder
3 cups 2% small-curd cottage cheese
1/2 cup egg substitute
1/2 cup grated Parmesan cheese
1/3 cup minced fresh parsley
1/2 teaspoon pepper
2 cups (8 ounces) shredded part-skim mozzarella cheese

Cook noodles according to package directions. Meanwhile, broil chicken 6 in. from the heat until juices run clear; let stand for 15 minutes or until cool enough to handle. Shred chicken with two forks. Drain noodles; set aside.

In a large nonstick skillet, combine the shredded chicken, tomatoes, tomato paste, mushrooms, onion, basil, 3/4 teaspoon salt and garlic powder. Bring to a boil. Reduce heat; cover and simmer for 25-30 minutes. In a bowl, combine the cottage cheese, egg substitute, Parmesan cheese, parsley, pepper and remaining salt.

In a 13-in. x 9-in. x 2-in. baking dish coated with nonstick cooking spray, place half of the noodles, overlapping them. Layer with half of the cheese mixture, chicken mixture and mozzarella. Repeat layers. Cover and bake at 375° for 25-30 minutes or until bubbly. Uncover; bake 5 minutes longer. Let stand for 15 minutes before cutting. **Yield:** 12 servings.

Nutritional Analysis: One piece equals 240 calories, 7 g fat (4 g saturated fat), 43 mg cholesterol, 1,038 mg sodium, 17 g carbohydrate, 2 g fiber, 28 g protein.
Diabetic Exchanges: 2 lean meat, 1 starch, 1 fat.

Chicken Rice Casserole

Corn and red pepper bring color to this nicely seasoned chicken and rice bake.
—Mary Louise Chubb, Perkasie, Pennsylvania

      6 boneless skinless chicken breast halves (1-1/2 pounds)
      1 tablespoon canola oil
    3/4 cup chopped sweet red pepper
    3/4 cup chopped green pepper
    1/2 cup chopped onion
    1/2 cup chopped fresh mushrooms
      1 garlic clove, minced
      2 cups uncooked instant brown rice
      2 cups chicken broth
  1-1/2 cups frozen corn, thawed
    1/4 teaspoon salt
    1/8 teaspoon pepper
    1/4 cup slivered almonds, toasted
      2 tablespoons minced parsley

In a large skillet, brown chicken in oil for 4 minutes on each side. Remove and keep warm. In the same skillet, saute peppers, onion, mushrooms and garlic until tender. Stir in the rice, broth, corn, salt and pepper; bring to a boil.

Transfer to an 11-in. x 7-in. x 2-in. baking dish coated with nonstick cooking spray. Top with chicken. Cover and bake at 350° for 20 minutes. Uncover; bake 5 minutes longer or until chicken juices run clear. Sprinkle with almonds and parsley. **Yield:** 6 servings.

Nutritional Analysis: One serving (1 chicken breast half with 1 cup rice mixture) equals 351 calories, 8 g fat (1 g saturated fat), 66 mg cholesterol, 493 mg sodium, 37 g carbohydrate, 4 g fiber, 33 g protein.
Diabetic Exchanges: 3 lean meat, 2 starch, 1 vegetable.

Chicken Parmigiana

(Pictured above and on page 125)

A nicely seasoned breading coats the tender chicken breasts in this attractive entree. When I have extra time, I make my own herbed tomato sauce instead of using prepared spaghetti sauce.
—Rhonda Schiel, Magnolia, Texas

    1/2 cup dry bread crumbs
      3 tablespoons grated Parmesan cheese
    3/4 teaspoon Italian seasoning
    1/2 teaspoon garlic powder
    1/2 teaspoon salt
    1/4 cup egg substitute
      4 boneless skinless chicken breast halves (1 pound)
      1 jar (26 ounces) meatless spaghetti sauce
    3/4 cup shredded part-skim mozzarella cheese
    1/4 cup shredded Parmesan cheese

In a shallow bowl, combine the bread crumbs, grated Parmesan cheese, Italian seasoning, garlic powder and salt. In another bowl, beat egg substitute. Dip chicken in egg substitute, then roll in crumbs. Place in a 13-in. x 9-in. x 2-in. baking dish coated with nonstick cooking spray.

Bake, uncovered, at 375° for 10 minutes. Turn chicken; bake for 10 minutes. Pour spaghetti sauce over chicken; bake for 5 minutes. Sprinkle with cheeses; bake 10 minutes longer or until chicken juices run clear. **Yield:** 4 servings.

Nutritional Analysis: One serving equals 412 calories, 15 g fat (5 g saturated fat), 88 mg cholesterol, 1,420 mg sodium, 32 g carbohydrate, 5 g fiber, 37 g protein.
Diabetic Exchanges: 4 lean meat, 2 starch, 1/2 fat.

Creamed Turkey with Bow Ties

I created this dish for a church supper one night when I didn't have a lot on hand in my fridge or pantry. It was a hit! Now I fix it often for my large family.
—Cindy Evans, Sedalia, Missouri

      1 package (12 ounces) bow tie pasta
    12 green onions, chopped
      6 celery ribs, chopped
    1/2 pound fresh mushrooms, sliced
      2 tablespoons butter *or* stick margarine
  2-1/2 cups cubed cooked turkey breast
      1 can (14-1/2 ounces) chicken broth
      1 can (10-3/4 ounces) reduced-fat reduced-sodium cream of chicken soup, undiluted
    1/4 cup fat-free sour cream
Pepper to taste

Cook pasta according to package directions. Meanwhile, in a skillet, saute the onions, celery and mushrooms in butter until tender. Reduce heat. Add the turkey, broth, soup and sour cream; heat through (do not boil). Season with pepper. Drain pasta; top with turkey mixture. **Yield:** 6 servings.

Nutritional Analysis: One serving equals 290 calories, 6 g fat (3 g saturated fat), 78 mg cholesterol, 764 mg sodium, 27 g carbohydrate, 3 g fiber, 29 g protein.
Diabetic Exchanges: 2-1/2 lean meat, 2 starch.

Favorite Casserole Recipe Made Lighter

IT'S ALMOST impossible to resist a hearty helping of a rich and comforting casserole. "This versatile recipe for Chicken a la King Casserole was given to me by my sister-in-law when I was a new bride 37 years ago," says Eleanor McElroy of Kernersville, North Carolina.

"It has been enjoyed by our family and guests and at potluck suppers more times than I can count. Folks love the chicken and noodles in a delectable cheese sauce."

Our Test Kitchen home economists prepared Eleanor's recipe using reduced-fat soup, fat-free evaporated milk, reduced-fat process cheese, less butter and no added salt.

Makeover Chicken a la King is still deliciously creamy, and it's a crowd-pleaser!

Chicken a la King Casserole

- 8 ounces uncooked wide egg noodles
- 1 can (10-3/4 ounces) condensed cream of chicken soup, undiluted
- 2/3 cup evaporated milk
- 1/2 teaspoon salt
- 6 ounces cubed process cheese (Velveeta)
- 2 cups diced cooked chicken
- 1 cup diced celery
- 1/4 cup diced green pepper
- 1/4 cup diced pimientos
- 3/4 cup dry bread crumbs
- 3 tablespoons butter *or* margarine, melted
- 1/4 cup slivered almonds

Cook noodles according to package directions. Meanwhile, in a large saucepan, combine the soup, milk and salt. Cook and stir over medium heat for 2 minutes. Reduce heat; stir in cheese until melted. Add chicken, celery, green pepper and pimientos.

Drain noodles; add to chicken mixture and mix well. Transfer to a greased shallow 2-qt. baking dish. Cover and bake at 400° for 20 minutes. Toss bread crumbs and butter; sprinkle over the top. Sprinkle with almonds. Bake, uncovered, for 10-15 minutes or until heated through and golden. **Yield:** 8 servings.

Nutritional Analysis: One serving (1 cup) equals 444 calories, 22 g fat (10 g saturated fat), 98 mg cholesterol, 948 mg sodium, 36 g carbohydrate, 2 g fiber, 25 g protein.

Makeover Chicken a la King Casserole

(Pictured at right)

- 8 ounces uncooked wide egg noodles
- 1 can (10-3/4 ounces) reduced-fat reduced-sodium condensed cream of chicken soup, undiluted
- 2/3 cup fat-free evaporated milk
- 6 ounces cubed reduced-fat process cheese (Velveeta)
- 2 cups cubed cooked chicken breast
- 1 cup sliced celery
- 1/4 cup chopped green pepper
- 1 jar (2 ounces) diced pimientos, drained
- 1/3 cup dry bread crumbs
- 1 tablespoon butter *or* stick margarine, melted
- 1/4 cup slivered almonds

Cook noodles according to package directions. Meanwhile, in a large saucepan, combine the soup and milk. Cook and stir over medium heat for 2 minutes. Reduce heat; stir in cheese until melted. Add the chicken, celery, green pepper and pimientos.

Drain noodles; add to chicken mixture and mix well. Transfer to a shallow 2-qt. baking dish coated with non-stick cooking spray. Cover and bake at 400° for 20 minutes. Toss bread crumbs and butter; sprinkle over the top. Sprinkle with almonds. Bake, uncovered, for 10-15 minutes or until heated through and golden. **Yield:** 8 servings.

Nutritional Analysis: One serving (1 cup) equals 306 calories, 9 g fat (3 g saturated fat), 72 mg cholesterol, 405 mg sodium, 31 g carbohydrate, 2 g fiber, 24 g protein. *Diabetic Exchanges:* 2 starch, 2 lean meat, 1 fat.

Turkey Tomato Pizza

(Pictured below)

I got this recipe from a party my husband and I attended. Now it's a hit at get-togethers at our house. Friends and family appreciate the different twist on ordinary pizza.
—Michelle Beal, Westminster, Maryland

- 1 tube (10 ounces) refrigerated pizza crust
- 2 teaspoons sesame seeds
- 1/4 cup reduced-fat mayonnaise
- 1/4 teaspoon grated lemon peel
- 1 cup (4 ounces) shredded reduced-fat Mexican-blend cheese *or* part-skim mozzarella
- 1 teaspoon dried basil
- 1/4 pound thinly sliced deli turkey, julienned
- 3 bacon strips, cooked and crumbled
- 2 small tomatoes, thinly sliced
- 1 cup (4 ounces) shredded reduced-fat Swiss cheese
- 2 tablespoons thinly sliced green onions

Unroll the pizza crust onto a 15-in. x 10-in. x 1-in. baking pan coated with nonstick cooking spray. Flatten dough and build up edges slightly. Prick dough several times with a fork; sprinkle with sesame seeds. Bake at 425° for 10-12 minutes or until lightly browned.

Combine the mayonnaise and lemon peel; spread over crust. Sprinkle with Mexican or mozzarella cheese and basil. Top with turkey, bacon, tomatoes and Swiss cheese. Bake for 7-9 minutes or until the crust is golden brown and cheese is melted. Sprinkle with onions. **Yield:** 6 servings.

Nutritional Analysis: One serving equals 284 calories, 11 g fat (4 g saturated fat), 27 mg cholesterol, 865 mg sodium, 27 g carbohydrate, 1 g fiber, 19 g protein.
Diabetic Exchanges: 2 meat, 1-1/2 starch, 1 vegetable, 1 fat.

Mediterranean Chicken Fettuccine

Herbed tomato sauce enhances the tender, moist chicken in this delectable dish. Crumbled feta cheese and tangy green olives bring home the essence of Mediterranean flavor. If you use fresh herbs, add them to the skillet during the last 15 minutes of cooking. This dish is excellent made the day before and reheated.
—Cynthia McGraw, Florissant, Missouri

- 6 skinless chicken thighs (about 6 ounces *each*)
- 1 tablespoon olive *or* canola oil
- 1 cup chopped onion
- 1 cup chopped celery
- 3 garlic cloves, minced
- 1 can (28 ounces) crushed tomatoes, undrained
- 1 cup dry red wine *or* chicken broth
- 2 teaspoons dried oregano
- 2 teaspoons dried basil
- 1 teaspoon sugar
- 1/2 teaspoon pepper
- 1/4 teaspoon salt
- 2 bay leaves
- 8 ounces uncooked fettuccine
- 1 cup (4 ounces) crumbled feta cheese
- 1/4 cup sliced stuffed olives

In a large nonstick skillet, brown chicken in oil. Remove and keep warm. In the same skillet, saute onion, celery and garlic until tender. Add tomatoes, wine or broth, oregano, basil, sugar, pepper, salt, bay leaves and chicken; bring to a boil. Reduce heat; cover and simmer for 25-30 minutes, stirring occasionally.

Meanwhile, cook fettuccine according to package directions. Uncover chicken mixture; simmer 10 minutes longer or until chicken juices run clear. Discard bay leaves. Drain fettuccine; top with chicken and sauce. Sprinkle with feta cheese and olives. **Yield:** 6 servings.

Nutritional Analysis: One serving (one chicken thigh and 2/3 cup sauce with 2/3 cup pasta) equals 427 calories, 16 g fat (6 g saturated fat), 86 mg cholesterol, 953 mg sodium, 36 g carbohydrate, 4 g fiber, 29 g protein.
Diabetic Exchanges: 3 lean meat, 2 starch, 1 vegetable, 1 fat.

Nutritional Analysis: One serving (1 chicken breast half) equals 205 calories, 6 g fat (1 g saturated fat), 66 mg cholesterol, 272 mg sodium, 11 g carbohydrate, trace fiber, 27 g protein.
Diabetic Exchanges: 3 lean meat, 1/2 starch.

Zesty Mustard Chicken

(Pictured below)

Whether you're grilling a broiler chicken or chicken breasts, consider this lip-smacking glaze. There are only four ingredients in the honey-mustard sauce, so you can whip it up in minutes.
—Michael Everidge, Morristown, Tennessee

1/2 cup prepared mustard
1/2 cup honey
  1 tablespoon salt-free seasoning blend
  1 tablespoon Worcestershire sauce
  1 broiler/fryer chicken (3 pounds), cut in half

In a bowl, combine the first four ingredients; mix well. Carefully loosen the skin of the chicken; spoon some of the mustard sauce under the skin.

Coat grill rack with nonstick cooking spray before starting the grill. Place chicken skin side up on grill rack. Grill, covered, over indirect medium heat for 20 minutes. Turn; grill 20-30 minutes longer or until juices run clear, basting occasionally with remaining mustard sauce. Remove chicken skin; cut into serving-size pieces. **Yield:** 6 servings.

Nutritional Analysis: One serving equals 261 calories, 7 g fat (2 g saturated fat), 72 mg cholesterol, 334 mg sodium, 25 g carbohydrate, 1 g fiber, 25 g protein.
Diabetic Exchanges: 3 lean meat, 1-1/2 starch.

Caribbean Chicken

(Pictured above)

You'd be hard-pressed to find a marinade that's this flavorful from any store! Add or subtract the jalapenos to suit your gang's taste, and you'll be grilling a new family favorite before you know it.
—Rusty Collins, Orlando, Florida

1/2 cup lemon juice
1/3 cup honey
  3 tablespoons canola oil
  6 green onions, sliced
  3 jalapeno peppers, seeded and chopped*
  3 teaspoons dried thyme
3/4 teaspoon salt
1/4 teaspoon ground allspice
1/4 teaspoon ground nutmeg
  6 boneless skinless chicken breast halves (1-1/2 pounds)

Place the first nine ingredients in a blender or food processor; cover and process until smooth. Pour 1/2 cup into a small bowl for basting; cover and refrigerate. Pour remaining marinade into a large resealable plastic bag; add chicken. Seal bag and turn to coat; refrigerate for up to 6 hours.

Drain and discard marinade. Coat grill rack with nonstick cooking spray before starting the grill. Grill chicken, covered, over medium heat for 4-6 minutes on each side or until juices run clear, basting frequently with the reserved marinade. **Yield:** 6 servings.

*Editor's Note: When cutting or seeding hot peppers, use rubber or plastic gloves to protect your hands. Avoid touching your face.

Herb-Rubbed Turkey

(Pictured above)

Seasoned for the holidays, this tender bird with its tasty herb rub is perfect for topping the table at your next gathering. The recipe's from our Test Kitchen staff.

```
    1 turkey (10 to 12 pounds)
    1 tablespoon each salt, dried thyme and
      marjoram
    2 teaspoons dried rosemary, crushed
1-1/2 teaspoons rubbed sage
  3/4 teaspoon celery seed, crushed
  3/4 teaspoon pepper
    2 medium carrots, cut into pieces
    1 medium onion, cut into wedges
    1 celery rlb wlth leaves, cut into pieces
ROASTED GARLIC GRAVY:
    2 whole garlic bulbs
    3 teaspoons olive or canola oil, divided
    2 celery ribs, cut into pieces
    1 medium onion, cut into wedges
    1 medium carrot, cut into pieces
6-1/4 cups water, divided
   10 black peppercorns
    2 whole cloves
    3 sprigs fresh parsley
    2 bay leaves
    1 teaspoon dried thyme
  1/2 teaspoon dried rosemary, crushed
  1/4 cup cornstarch
  1/4 teaspoon salt
Pepper to taste
```

Remove giblets from turkey; set aside. Loosen skin around turkey breast, leg and thigh. Combine seasonings; rub un-der skin, in body and neck cavities and over skin if de-sired. Place vegetables in the cavities. Skewer openings; tie drumsticks together. Place breast side up on a rack in a roasting pan. Lightly coat with nonstick cooking spray. Roast, uncovered, at 325° for 3 to 3-1/2 hours or until a meat thermometer reads 180° (cover loosely with foil if browning too quickly). Baste with pan drippings if desired.

Remove papery skin from garlic bulbs (do not peel or separate cloves). Brush with 1 teaspoon oil. Wrap in heavy-duty foil. Roast at 325° for 1 hour or until garlic is soft. Cool for 10-15 minutes. Cut top off heads, leaving root end intact. Squeeze garlic into a bowl. Mash to a smooth paste; set aside.

To make broth, cut reserved gizzard and heart into sev-eral pieces. (Save liver for another use or discard.) In a Dutch oven, saute neck, gizzard and heart in remaining oil over medium-high heat until no longer pink. Add the veg-etables; cook until browned. Gradually add 6 cups of wa-ter, stirring to loosen browned bits. Tie peppercorns, cloves and herbs in a cheesecloth bag; add to pan. Bring to a boil. Reduce heat; simmer, uncovered, for 2 hours or until broth is reduced by half. Discard giblets and spice bag. Cool broth; strain, discarding vegetables.

When turkey is done, cover and let stand for 20 minutes. Pour drippings and any loosened browned bits into a mea-suring cup; skim fat. Add enough broth to measure 3 cups. In a saucepan, combine the cornstarch and remaining wa-ter until smooth. Add broth, salt, pepper and 2 table-spoons roasted garlic. Bring to a boil; cook and stir for 2 min-utes or until thickened. Remove and discard turkey skin and vegetables in cavities before carving. Serve with gravy. **Yield:** 12 servings plus leftovers.

Nutritional Analysis: One serving (3 ounces cooked turkey, skin removed, with 1/4 cup gravy) equals 190 calories, 6 g fat (2 g saturated fat), 66 mg cholesterol, 542 mg sodium, 6 g carbohy-drate, 1 g fiber, 26 g protein.
Diabetic Exchanges: 3 lean meat, 1/2 starch.

Pinto Beans with Kielbasa

Sauced-up sausage, tomatoes, green pepper and onion accompany two kinds of beans in this warm main dish. Serve hearty helpings with a salad and rolls for a filling supper.
—*Gloria Slater, Seaford, Delaware*

```
    1 large onion, chopped
    1 medium green pepper, chopped
    1 tablespoon olive or canola oil
1-1/2 pounds reduced-fat smoked turkey kielbasa,
      cut into 1-inch pieces
    1 can (15-1/2 ounces) great northern beans,
      rinsed and drained
    1 can (15-1/2 ounces) pinto beans, rinsed and
      drained
    1 can (14-1/2 ounces) stewed tomatoes
    1 can (10 ounces) diced tomatoes and green
      chilies
    1 can (8 ounces) tomato sauce
  1/2 teaspoon garlic powder
  1/4 teaspoon pepper
```

In a Dutch oven, saute the onion and green pepper in oil until tender. Add the remaining ingredients; bring to a boil. Reduce heat; cover and simmer until heated through. **Yield:** 8 servings.

Nutritional Analysis: One serving (1 cup) equals 287 calories, 5 g fat (1 g saturated fat), 30 mg cholesterol, 1,363 mg sodium, 42 g carbohydrate, 7 g fiber, 19 g protein.
Diabetic Exchanges: 2 starch, 2 vegetable, 1-1/2 lean meat.

Chicken Stir-Fry with a Twist

It's easy to blend a savory sauce for this delightful chicken dish. The brown sugar, balsamic vinegar, soy sauce and ginger get added zip from chili sauce and cayenne pepper. Served over rice, this stir-fry makes a memorable meal.
—Candy Gruman, Tucson, Arizona

1 cup sliced celery
1 cup julienned carrots
1 cup chopped onion
4 tablespoons canola oil, *divided*
2/3 cup *each* julienned green, sweet red and yellow pepper
3/4 pound boneless skinless chicken breasts, cut into bite-size pieces
1/2 pound fresh mushrooms, sliced
1 can (8 ounces) sliced water chestnuts, drained
1-1/2 cups chicken broth
2 tablespoons reduced-sodium soy sauce
2 tablespoons balsamic vinegar
1 tablespoon chili sauce
2 teaspoons brown sugar
2 garlic cloves, minced
1/4 teaspoon ground ginger *or* 1 teaspoon grated fresh gingerroot
1/8 teaspoon cayenne pepper
2 tablespoons cornstarch
1/4 cup white wine *or* additional chicken broth
3 cups hot cooked rice

In a large skillet, saute celery, carrots and onion in 3 tablespoons oil for 2 minutes. Add peppers; cook for 2-3 minutes or until crisp-tender. Remove with a slotted spoon to paper towels. Add chicken, mushrooms and remaining oil; stir-fry for 4 minutes. Stir in water chestnuts; cook 2-3 minutes longer or until heated through. Remove with a slotted spoon to paper towels.

Drain skillet; add the broth, soy sauce, vinegar, chili sauce, brown sugar, garlic, ginger and cayenne. Combine cornstarch and wine or broth until smooth; stir into broth mixture. Bring to a boil; cook and stir for 2 minutes or until thickened. Reduce heat; return vegetables and chicken to pan. Cook for 5 minutes or until heated through. Serve over rice. **Yield:** 6 servings.

Nutritional Analysis: One serving (1 cup chicken mixture with 1/2 cup rice) equals 342 calories, 11 g fat (1 g saturated fat), 34 mg cholesterol, 529 mg sodium, 41 g carbohydrate, 4 g fiber, 18 g protein.
Diabetic Exchanges: 2 starch, 2 vegetable, 2 lean meat, 1 fat.

Penne Sausage Bake

(Pictured below)

This hearty pasta dish was inspired by the delicious sausage rolls served at our favorite Italian restaurant. I serve it frequently for supper since it's easy to prepare and my husband thinks it's great!
—Vicky Benscoter, Birmingham, Alabama

1 package (1 pound) penne *or* medium tube pasta
1 medium green pepper, chopped
1 small onion, chopped
1 tablespoon olive *or* canola oil
1 pound turkey Italian sausage links, casings removed
3 cups fat-free meatless spaghetti sauce
1-1/2 cups (6 ounces) shredded part-skim mozzarella cheese
1/4 cup grated Parmesan cheese

Cook pasta according to package directions; drain. In a large skillet, saute green pepper and onion in oil for 6-7 minutes. Add sausage; cook and stir until sausage is no longer pink. Drain. Stir in the spaghetti sauce and pasta.

Transfer to a 3-qt. baking dish coated with nonstick cooking spray. Cover and bake at 350° for 15-20 minutes. Uncover; sprinkle with cheeses. Bake 5-10 minutes longer or until cheese is melted. **Yield:** 9 servings.

Nutritional Analysis: One serving (1 cup) equals 276 calories, 11 g fat (4 g saturated fat), 40 mg cholesterol, 948 mg sodium, 25 g carbohydrate, 1 g fiber, 18 g protein.
Diabetic Exchanges: 2 lean meat, 1-1/2 starch, 1 fat.

Lemon Turkey with Couscous Stuffing

(Pictured above)

For a special-occasion main dish that's perfect for a small family gathering, try this moist tender turkey breast with its unusual dressing. Lemon and garlic flavor the meat, while raisins and shredded carrot add sweetness and color to the couscous stuffing.
—Kathi Graham, Naperville, Illinois

　1 bone-in turkey breast (4 to 4-1/2 pounds)
　2 teaspoons olive *or* canola oil
　1 teaspoon lemon juice
　1 garlic clove, minced
　1/2 teaspoon grated lemon peel
　1/4 teaspoon salt
　1/8 teaspoon pepper
STUFFING:
　1-1/2 cups boiling water
　1 cup uncooked couscous
　1 medium carrot, shredded
　1/2 cup raisins
　1/3 cup chicken broth
　1/4 cup slivered almonds, toasted
　2 tablespoons minced fresh parsley

Carefully loosen turkey skin, leaving it attached at the back. Combine oil, lemon juice, garlic, lemon peel, salt and pepper; spread under turkey skin. Place turkey to one side in a shallow roasting pan coated with nonstick cooking spray.

For stuffing, in a bowl, pour boiling water over couscous. Cover and let stand for 5 minutes or until water is absorbed. Add the remaining ingredients; toss to combine. Spoon stuffing into other side of pan, shaping into an 8-in. x 5-in. x 2-in. mound. Cover pan and bake at 350° for 45 minutes.

Uncover turkey; leave stuffing covered. Bake 40-50 minutes longer or until a meat thermometer reads 170°. Let stand for 15 minutes before slicing. Serve with stuffing. **Yield:** 8 servings.

Nutritional Analysis: One serving (4 ounces cooked turkey, skin removed, with 1/2 cup stuffing) equals 303 calories, 4 g fat (1 g saturated fat), 94 mg cholesterol, 181 mg sodium, 26 g carbohydrate, 2 g fiber, 38 g protein.
Diabetic Exchanges: 4 very lean meat, 1 starch, 1/2 fruit.

Plum-Glazed Chicken Kabobs

These creative kabobs make a great first impression. I brought them to a neighborhood dinner when we moved to our new home. People couldn't wait 'til dinner and started snatching them as soon as I walked in the door. They just couldn't resist the tantalizing aroma.
—Nancy Morrison, Midlothian, Virginia

　1 cup plum jam
　3 tablespoons reduced-sodium soy sauce
　1 tablespoon sherry *or* chicken broth
　1/4 teaspoon garlic powder
　1/4 teaspoon ground ginger
　1 pound boneless skinless chicken breasts, cubed
　1 can (20 ounces) pineapple chunks, drained
　1 large green pepper, cut into 1-inch pieces
　1 teaspoon cornstarch
　3 cups cooked rice

In a saucepan, combine the first five ingredients; heat on low until jam is melted. In a large resealable plastic bag, combine the chicken, pineapple and green pepper; add plum mixture. Seal bag and turn to coat; refrigerate for at least 2 hours.

Place cornstarch in a small saucepan; drain marinade into saucepan. Stir until smooth. Bring to a rolling boil over medium heat; cook and stir for 1 minute or until thickened. Remove from the heat; set aside.

On 12 metal or soaked wooden skewers, alternately thread chicken, pineapple and green pepper. Place skewers on a broiler pan 3-4 in. from the heat. Broil for 3 minutes, turning once. Baste with plum glaze. Broil 4-6 minutes longer or until chicken juices run clear, turning and basting frequently. Serve over hot rice with any remaining glaze. **Yield:** 4 servings.

Nutritional Analysis: One serving (3 skewers with 3/4 cup rice) equals 615 calories, 2 g fat (trace saturated fat), 66 mg cholesterol, 570 mg sodium, 108 g carbohydrate, 2 g fiber, 31 g protein.

Pork & Ham Favorites

Today's pork is leaner and more delicious than ever before. So it's ideal for people who are eating a little lighter. Plus, pork's pure versatility and quick cooking time make it a mealtime mainstay.

Roasted Pork Tenderloin and Vegetables (page 148)

Roasted Pork Tenderloin And Vegetables

(Pictured on page 147)

There are no complicated steps to follow when preparing this medley of tender pork and veggies. Just season with herbs, then pop in the oven for less than an hour.
—Diane Martin, Brown Deer, Wisconsin

- 2 pork tenderloins (3/4 pound *each*)
- 2 pounds red potatoes, quartered
- 1 pound carrots, halved and cut into 2-inch pieces
- 1 medium onion, cut into wedges
- 1 tablespoon olive *or* canola oil
- 2 teaspoons dried rosemary, crushed
- 1 teaspoon rubbed sage
- 1/2 teaspoon salt
- 1/4 teaspoon pepper

Place the pork in a shallow roasting pan coated with non-stick cooking spray; arrange the potatoes, carrots and onion around pork. Drizzle with oil. Combine the seasonings; sprinkle over the meat and vegetables. Bake, uncovered, at 450° for 30-40 minutes or until a meat thermometer reads 160°, stirring vegetables occasionally. **Yield:** 6 servings.

Nutritional Analysis: One serving (3 ounces cooked meat with 1 cup vegetables) equals 331 calories, 7 g fat (2 g saturated fat), 67 mg cholesterol, 299 mg sodium, 40 g carbohydrate, 5 g fiber, 28 g protein.
Diabetic Exchanges: 3 lean meat, 2 starch, 1 vegetable.

Spicy Pork 'n' Peanuts

I add a sprinkling of peanuts to this nicely spiced stir-fry that showcases savory pork tenderloin. If your family prefers less heat, simply decrease the amount of red pepper flakes.
—Pam Beil, Bradford, Rhode Island

- 1 pound pork tenderloin, cubed
- 1/3 cup reduced-sodium soy sauce, *divided*
- 3 tablespoons sugar
- 4 teaspoons cornstarch
- 1/2 cup chicken broth
- 3 tablespoons lemon juice
- 1/4 to 1/2 teaspoon crushed red pepper flakes
- 1 small onion, julienned
- 2 garlic cloves, minced
- 1 tablespoon olive *or* canola oil
- 2 small sweet red peppers, julienned
- 2 small sweet yellow peppers, julienned
- 1/4 cup unsalted dry roasted peanuts
- 6 cups hot cooked rice

Place pork in a bowl and drizzle with 2 tablespoons soy sauce; set aside. In another bowl, combine sugar and corn-starch. Stir in the broth, lemon juice, red pepper flakes and remaining soy sauce until blended; set aside.

In a nonstick skillet or wok, stir-fry pork, onion and garlic in oil for 4 minutes. Add peppers; stir-fry for 4-5 minutes. Stir cornstarch mixture and add to pan. Bring to a boil;

cook and stir for 1 minute or until thickened. Stir in peanuts. Serve over rice. **Yield:** 6 servings.

Nutritional Analysis: One serving (1-1/3 cups meat mixture with 1 cup rice) equals 432 calories, 9 g fat (2 g saturated fat), 49 mg cholesterol, 713 mg sodium, 63 g carbohydrate, 3 g fiber, 25 g protein.
Diabetic Exchanges: 3 starch, 2-1/2 meat, 1 fat.

Pork Chops with Mango Relish

(Pictured below)

A delicate marinade flavors these pork chops with the fragrant seasonings of India and tenderizes the meat at the same time. The colorful relish would be delicious alongside any grilled entree. It's also a tasty substitute for butter on baked potatoes!
—Linda Lacek, Winter Park, Florida

- 2 tablespoons fat-free plain yogurt
- 2 teaspoons honey
- 2 garlic cloves, minced
- 1 teaspoon white wine vinegar *or* cider vinegar
- 1/2 teaspoon ground cumin
- 1/4 teaspoon salt
- 1/4 teaspoon ground turmeric
- 1/8 teaspoon ground cloves
- 1/8 teaspoon ground cinnamon
- 1/8 teaspoon cayenne pepper
- Dash ground ginger *or* 1/2 teaspoon minced fresh gingerroot
- 4 boneless pork loin chops (4 ounces *each*)
- MANGO RELISH:
- 1 large mango *or* 2 small peaches, peeled and diced
- 3/4 cup chopped red onion
- 3/4 cup chopped seeded tomatoes

4 teaspoons chopped seeded jalapeno pepper*
2 teaspoons lime juice
1/4 teaspoon salt

In a large resealable plastic bag, combine the first 11 ingredients. Add pork. Seal bag and turn to coat; refrigerate for at least 2 hours. Meanwhile, combine the relish ingredients in a bowl. Let stand at room temperature for 1 hour; refrigerate until serving.

Drain and discard marinade. If using the grill, coat grill rack with nonstick cooking spray before starting the grill. Grill pork chops, covered, over medium heat or broil 3-4 in. from the heat for 6-10 minutes on each side or until a meat thermometer reads 160°. Serve with mango relish. **Yield:** 4 servings.

*Editor's Note: When cutting or seeding hot peppers, use rubber or plastic gloves to protect your hands. Avoid touching your face.

Nutritional Analysis: One serving (1 pork chop with 1/2 cup relish) equals 217 calories, 6 g fat (2 g saturated fat), 57 mg cholesterol, 350 mg sodium, 18 g carbohydrate, 2 g fiber, 24 g protein.
Diabetic Exchanges: 3 lean meat, 1 fruit.

Lemon-Rosemary Pork Tenderloin

(Pictured above)

This moist tender pork is seasoned with a wonderful herb and lemon rub I created. Even my husband, who is a chef, thinks this dish is special enough for company.
—*Carol Birkemeier, Nashville, Indiana*

1 medium onion, finely chopped
2 tablespoons olive *or* canola oil
1 tablespoon lemon juice
1 teaspoon minced fresh rosemary *or* 1/4 teaspoon dried rosemary, crushed
1 teaspoon minced fresh thyme *or* 1/4 teaspoon dried thyme
1 teaspoon grated lemon peel
1 garlic clove, minced
1/2 teaspoon salt
1/2 teaspoon pepper
2 pork tenderloins (1 pound *each*)

Combine the first nine ingredients; rub over tenderloins. Place on a rack in a shallow roasting pan. Bake, uncovered, at 400° for 45-50 minutes or until a meat thermometer reads 160°. Cover with foil; let stand for 10 minutes before slicing. **Yield:** 8 servings.

Nutritional Analysis: One serving equals 176 calories, 7 g fat (2 g saturated fat), 74 mg cholesterol, 204 mg sodium, 2 g carbohydrate, trace fiber, 24 g protein.
Diabetic Exchange: 3 lean meat.

Marinated Pork Loin

This tender, juicy pork is one of my favorite entrees to serve to guests. The pork slices marinate overnight, so all I have to do the next day is broil them. Paired with a vegetable or salad, this dish is sure to please.
—Jean Heady, Naples, Florida

1/2 cup reduced-sodium chicken broth
1/2 cup ketchup
2 tablespoons cider vinegar
2 tablespoons Worcestershire sauce
2 tablespoons brown sugar
2 garlic cloves, minced
1/2 teaspoon salt
1/4 teaspoon pepper
1/8 teaspoon cayenne pepper
1 boneless pork loin roast (2 pounds)

In a saucepan, combine the first nine ingredients. Bring to a boil. Reduce heat; simmer, uncovered, for 5 minutes. Remove from the heat; cool slightly. Place 2/3 cup marinade in a bowl for basting; cover and chill. Pour remaining marinade into a large resealable plastic bag. Cut pork into five slices, about 1 in. each; add to bag. Seal and turn to coat; refrigerate overnight.

Drain and discard marinade. Place pork on a broiler pan coated with nonstick cooking spray. Broil 4 in. from the heat for 10 minutes on each side or until juices run clear, brushing with reserved marinade and turning occasionally. **Yield:** 5 servings.

Nutritional Analysis: One serving (1 slice) equals 310 calories, 10 g fat (3 g saturated fat), 100 mg cholesterol, 570 mg sodium, 14 g carbohydrate, trace fiber, 40 g protein.
Diabetic Exchanges: 4-1/2 lean meat, 1/2 fruit, 1/2 fat.

Asparagus-Stuffed Pork Tenderloin

(Pictured above)

Asparagus looks lovely tucked inside this juicy pork tenderloin. The robust seasoning rub dresses up an eye-catching entree.
—Tonya Farmer, Iowa City, Iowa

1/4 teaspoon *each* onion powder, garlic powder, chili powder, salt, seasoned salt and poultry seasoning
1/8 teaspoon cayenne pepper
1 pork tenderloin (1 pound)
1 cup water
7 to 10 fresh asparagus spears, trimmed

In a small bowl, combine the seasonings; set aside. Cut a lengthwise slit down the center of pork tenderloin to within 1/2 in. of bottom; open so meat lies flat. Cover with plastic wrap; pound to flatten evenly. Remove plastic. Rub 1/2 teaspoon seasoning mix over inside of tenderloin.

In a large nonstick skillet, bring water to a boil. Add asparagus; cover and cook for 2 minutes. Drain asparagus and immediately place in ice water; drain and pat dry. Place asparagus lengthwise over tenderloin.

Fold meat over asparagus, starting with a long side, and secure with kitchen string. Rub remaining seasoning over meat. Grill, covered, over indirect medium heat for 20-25 minutes or until a meat thermometer reads 160°, turning occasionally. Let stand for 5 minutes before slicing. **Yield:** 4 servings.

Nutritional Analysis: One serving equals 201 calories, 6 g fat (2 g saturated fat), 90 mg cholesterol, 299 mg sodium, 2 g carbohydrate, 1 g fiber, 33 g protein.
Diabetic Exchanges: 3 lean meat, 1 vegetable.

🍎 Broiling Basics

- Select thin and tender cuts of meat that are uniform in size. Use lean cuts that cook quickly such as pork chops, chicken breasts, fish fillets and steaks.
- Preheat the oven for a short time to allow food to cook at an optimum temperature. If you're using an electric oven, leave the door ajar.
- Trim excess fat from meats and remove skin from poultry. Doing so is healthier and reduces excess spattering of fat.
- Position the meat 4 to 6 inches from the heat source. When broiling a thicker cut of meat, lower the oven rack to ensure the inside cooks at the same rate as the outside.
- To make sure meats are cooked properly, check the internal temperature with a meat thermometer.
- For easy cleanup, use aluminum foil to line the inside of your broiler pan. But don't line the rack with foil, because it will trap any fat drippings close to the meat.

Favorite Casserole Recipe Made Lighter

THERE'S nothing like a creamy meal-in-one casserole to draw compliments.

Dixie Terry from Marion, Illinois shares her tempting recipe for colorful Ham 'n' Potato Bake below. "With meat, potatoes and other vegetables, this comforting casserole is a welcome addition to a buffet meal. It's one of my favorite potluck dishes," Dixie says.

Like to steer your family toward a lighter version of Dixie's popular main dish? Our home economists rolled up their sleeves and came up with a delicious alternative.

In Makeover Ham 'n' Potato Bake, they replaced the whole milk with fat-free evaporated milk and used reduced-fat cheddar cheese in place of the sharp cheddar.

Ham 'n' Potato Bake

2 pounds red potatoes, peeled and cubed
1 cup chopped onion
1/2 cup chopped green pepper
1/2 cup chopped sweet red pepper
1 tablespoon vegetable oil
1/3 cup all-purpose flour
1/4 teaspoon *each* pepper and dried thyme
2-1/4 cups milk
1 cup plus 2 tablespoons shredded sharp cheddar cheese, *divided*
2 tablespoons Dijon mustard
1-1/2 pounds fully cooked ham slices, cut into strips
1 package (16 ounces) frozen sliced carrots, cooked and drained
1/4 cup minced fresh parsley

Cook potatoes in water until tender; drain. In a large skillet, saute onion and peppers in oil until tender. Stir in flour, pepper and thyme until blended. Gradually add milk. Bring to a boil; cook and stir for 2 minutes or until thickened. Reduce heat; stir in 1 cup cheese and mustard until cheese is melted.

Fold in potatoes, ham, carrots and parsley. Transfer to a greased 3-qt. baking dish. Cover and bake at 400° for 20 minutes. Uncover; bake 10 minutes longer. Sprinkle with remaining cheese. **Yield:** 10 servings.

Nutritional Analysis: One serving (1-1/4 cups) equals 380 calories, 18 g fat (8 g saturated fat), 63 mg cholesterol, 854 mg sodium, 32 g carbohydrate, 4 g fiber, 22 g protein.

Makeover Ham 'n' Potato Bake

(Pictured at right)

2 pounds red potatoes, peeled and cubed
1 cup chopped onion
1/2 cup chopped green pepper
1/2 cup chopped sweet red pepper
1 tablespoon canola oil
1/3 cup all-purpose flour
1/4 teaspoon *each* pepper and dried thyme
2 cans (12 ounces *each*) fat-free evaporated milk
1 cup plus 2 tablespoons shredded reduced-fat cheddar cheese, *divided*
2 tablespoons Dijon mustard
1-1/2 pounds fully cooked lean ham slices, cut into strips
1 package (16 ounces) frozen sliced carrots, cooked and drained
1/4 cup minced fresh parsley

Cook potatoes in water until tender; drain. In a large nonstick skillet, saute onion and peppers in oil until tender. Stir in flour, pepper and thyme until blended. Gradually add milk. Bring to a boil; cook and stir for 2 minutes or until thickened. Reduce heat; stir in 1 cup cheese and mustard until cheese is melted.

Fold in the potatoes, ham, carrots and parsley. Transfer to a 3-qt. baking dish coated with nonstick cooking spray. Cover and bake at 400° for 20 minutes. Uncover; bake 10 minutes longer. Sprinkle with the remaining cheese. **Yield:** 10 servings.

Nutritional Analysis: One serving (1-1/4 cups) equals 316 calories, 6 g fat (2 g saturated fat), 26 mg cholesterol, 1,046 mg sodium, 38 g carbohydrate, 4 g fiber, 27 g protein.
Diabetic Exchanges: 2-1/2 lean meat, 2 starch, 1/2 fat.

Honey-Dijon Pork Tenderloin

Pork tenderloin gets gussied up with a sweet honey, Dijon mustard and sesame seed marinade in this easy-to-fix low-fat entree. This is our family's favorite way to fix pork during grilling season.
—Barbara Blake, West Brattleboro, Vermont

    1 cup reduced-calorie *or* nonalcoholic beer
    6 tablespoons sesame seeds
    6 tablespoons honey
1/4 cup Dijon mustard
    4 garlic cloves, minced
    1 teaspoon coarsely ground pepper
    2 pork tenderloins (1 pound *each*)

In a bowl, combine the first six ingredients; mix well. Remove 1/2 cup for basting; cover and refrigerate. Pour remaining marinade into a large resealable plastic bag; add the pork. Seal bag and turn to coat; refrigerate for at least 2 hours.

Drain pork and discard marinade. Coat grill rack with nonstick cooking spray before starting the grill. Grill pork, covered, over medium heat for 20-25 minutes or until a meat thermometer reads 160°, turning and basting with reserved marinade occasionally. Or bake, uncovered, at 350° for 25-30 minutes or until a meat thermometer reads 160°, basting occasionally. **Yield:** 8 servings.

Nutritional Analysis: One serving (3 ounces cooked pork) equals 206 calories, 7 g fat (1 g saturated fat), 67 mg cholesterol, 192 mg sodium, 11 g carbohydrate, trace fiber, 25 g protein.
Diabetic Exchanges: 3 lean meat, 1/2 starch.

Grilled Pork with Hot Mustard

(Pictured above)

I love Chinese food, and this soy-marinated pork tenderloin is one of my favorites. It's terrific served warm or cold, especially when dipped in the zippy mustard sauce.
—Kyle Spencer, Havre, Montana

1/4 cup reduced-sodium soy sauce
    2 tablespoons dry red wine *or* chicken broth
    1 tablespoon brown sugar
    1 tablespoon honey
1/2 teaspoon ground cinnamon
    2 pork tenderloins (3/4 pound *each*)
HOT MUSTARD:
1/4 cup Dijon mustard
    1 tablespoon honey
    1 teaspoon prepared horseradish
    2 teaspoons sesame seeds, toasted

In a large resealable plastic bag, combine the first five ingredients; add pork. Seal bag and turn to coat; refrigerate for 8 hours or overnight.

Drain and discard marinade. Grill pork, covered, over indirect medium-hot heat for 12-15 minutes or until a meat thermometer reads 160°. Let pork stand for 5 minutes before slicing.

In a small bowl, combine the mustard, honey and horseradish. Slice pork; sprinkle with sesame seeds. Serve with hot mustard. **Yield:** 6 servings.

Nutritional Analysis: One serving equals 197 calories, 7 g fat (2 g saturated fat), 62 mg cholesterol, 408 mg sodium, 6 g carbohydrate, trace fiber, 26 g protein.
Diabetic Exchanges: 3 lean meat, 1/2 fat.

Green Chili Stew

I came up with this hearty pork stew when trying to duplicate the recipe we enjoyed at a local restaurant.
—Doris Johns, Hurst, Texas

1-1/2 pounds boneless pork loin roast, cut into
        3/4-inch cubes
    2 tablespoons olive *or* canola oil
    1 large onion, diced
    1 to 2 jalapeno peppers, seeded and chopped*
    3 garlic cloves, minced
1-1/2 teaspoons ground cumin
    1 teaspoon salt
1/4 teaspoon white pepper
    1 bay leaf
    5 medium potatoes, peeled and cubed
    3 cups water
    1 can (14-1/2 ounces) diced tomatoes, undrained
    3 cans (4 ounces *each*) chopped green chilies

In a Dutch oven or large saucepan, brown pork in oil. Add the onion, jalapenos, garlic, cumin, salt, pepper and bay leaf; saute until onion is tender. Add potatoes and water; bring to boil. Reduce heat; cover and simmer for 15-20 minutes or until potatoes are tender. Add tomatoes and chilies; simmer 10 minutes longer. Discard bay leaf before serving. **Yield:** 8 servings.

Editor's Note: When cutting or seeding hot peppers, use rubber or plastic gloves to protect your hands. Avoid touching your face.

Nutritional Analysis: One serving (1-1/3 cups) equals 253 calories, 8 g fat (2 g saturated fat), 47 mg cholesterol, 707 mg sodium, 24 g carbohydrate, 4 g fiber, 22 g protein.
***Diabetic Exchanges:** 2-1/2 meat, 1-1/2 vegetable, 1 starch.*

Indonesian Pork Tenderloin

Marinated in soy sauce, lime juice, red pepper and ginger, the meat takes on plenty of flavor—and is special enough for company.
—Pat Patty, Spring, Texas

3 tablespoons lime juice
3 tablespoons reduced-sodium soy sauce
3 tablespoons stir-fry sauce
3/4 teaspoon ground ginger *or* 4-1/2 teaspoons grated fresh gingerroot
1 teaspoon crushed red pepper flakes
3 garlic cloves, minced
1 pork tenderloin (1 pound)

In a bowl, combine the first six ingredients. Place the pork in a large resealable plastic bag; add half of the marinade. Seal bag and turn to coat; refrigerate for 2 hours, turning occasionally. Cover and refrigerate remaining marinade for basting.

Drain and discard marinade. Grill pork, covered, over hot heat for 15-20 minutes or until a meat thermometer reads 160° and juices run clear, basting occasionally with reserved marinade. **Yield:** 4 servings.

Nutritional Analysis: One serving equals 178 calories, 6 g fat (2 g saturated fat), 68 mg cholesterol, 486 mg sodium, 3 g carbohydrate, trace fiber, 27 g protein.
***Diabetic Exchange:** 3 lean meat.*

🍎 Use Ginger Gingerly

SPICING UP food with gingerroot is easy. More cooks are warming to this versatile, ancient seasoning, which has been found in ethnic cuisines for thousands of years. Keep these facts in mind next time you're shopping:

- Gingerroot is a knobby, fibrous rhizome that has a smooth light brown skin and white flesh. It's found in the produce department of grocery stores.
- Look for gingerroot with the least amount of knots and branching.
- Ginger can be used in many forms—fresh, ground or crystallized. It's available year-round.
- Gingerroot is a good match for curry, soy sauce, meat, poultry, vegetables, soups, chutneys, fish and cheese recipes. It's also tasty in baked fruit dishes, cakes, sweet breads, puddings, cookies and beverages.
- Gingerroot should be stored in a cool dry place. It may be refrigerated in plastic wrap for up to a week...or frozen for up to 3 months.

Ham Mushroom Fettuccine

ok but not a favorite!

(Pictured below)

I like the fact that I can make this creamy pasta toss in about half an hour, yet it tastes like I spent hours in the kitchen. It's also a great way to use up leftover ham.
—Michelle Armistead, Keyport, New Jersey

12 ounces uncooked fettuccine
3/4 pound fully cooked lean ham, cubed
2 tablespoons olive *or* canola oil
1 medium onion, finely chopped
1/2 pound fresh mushrooms, sliced
1 tablespoon all-purpose flour
1/2 teaspoon dried rosemary, crushed
1/4 teaspoon pepper
1-1/4 cups fat-free evaporated milk
1/2 cup frozen peas, thawed
2 tablespoons reduced-fat sour cream

Cook fettuccine according to package directions. Meanwhile, in a large skillet, saute ham in oil until lightly browned. Remove with a slotted spoon and set aside.

Add onion to skillet; saute for 4 minutes. Add mushrooms; saute 3 minutes longer. Stir in the flour, rosemary and pepper until blended. Gradually add milk. Bring to a boil; cook and stir for 2 minutes or until thickened. Reduce heat; add peas and sour cream. Cook 2 minutes longer. Drain fettuccine; stir into the mushroom mixture. Add ham; heat through. **Yield:** 6 servings.

Nutritional Analysis: One serving (1-1/3 cups) equals 334 calories, 8 g fat (1 g saturated fat), 29 mg cholesterol, 876 mg sodium, 46 g carbohydrate, 3 g fiber, 21 g protein.
***Diabetic Exchanges:** 2 starch, 2 lean meat, 1 fat, 1/2 vegetable.*

Pork Chops with Pears

I'm always on the lookout for ways to "spice up" and "trim down" traditional meals. In this case, pears bring a sweet change of taste to tender pork chops, while fragrant rosemary complements the entree. It's so simple, I can put it together fast after I get home from aerobics class.
—Vicki Herron, Portland, Maine

2 teaspoons butter *or* stick margarine
3 small firm pears, peeled and thinly sliced
1-1/2 teaspoons sugar
4 boneless pork loin chops (4 ounces *each* and
   1/3 inch thick)
1/4 teaspoon salt
1/8 teaspoon pepper
1 tablespoon cornstarch
1 cup chicken broth
1 tablespoon balsamic vinegar
1/2 teaspoon dried rosemary, crushed

In a large nonstick skillet, melt butter. Add pears; sprinkle with sugar. Cook and stir for 2-3 minutes or until softened. Remove pears to a serving platter and keep warm. Sprinkle pork chops with salt and pepper. In the same skillet, cook chops, uncovered, for 6-8 minutes on each side or until browned and juices run clear. Remove to the platter and keep warm.

Combine cornstarch and broth until smooth; add vinegar and rosemary. Stir into skillet. Bring to a boil; cook and stir for 2 minutes or until thickened. Serve with pork chops and pears. **Yield:** 4 servings.

Nutritional Analysis: *One serving (1 chop and 3/4 of a pear with about 1/4 cup sauce) equals 233 calories, 7 g fat (3 g saturated fat), 77 mg cholesterol, 458 mg sodium, 17 g carbohydrate, 4 g fiber, 25 g protein.*
Diabetic Exchanges: *2 lean meat, 1-1/2 fat, 1 fruit.*

Barbecued Pork Potpie

(Pictured above right)

I cook a roast the day before—or use leftover pork—when I prepare this casserole. A lattice topping made with refrigerated corn bread twists gives it a lovely look.
—Joan East, Leawood, Kansas

1 cup chopped onion
3/4 cup finely chopped celery
1 cup chopped sweet red pepper
1 large Anaheim pepper, seeded and chopped*
2 garlic cloves, minced
1 tablespoon canola oil
1 teaspoon ground cumin
1 teaspoon ground coriander
1/4 cup white wine vinegar *or* cider vinegar
1 can (14-1/2 ounces) reduced-sodium chicken
   broth
1 bottle (12 ounces) chili sauce
3 tablespoons brown sugar
1 square (1 ounce) unsweetened chocolate,
   grated
1 tablespoon Worcestershire sauce
2 tablespoons cornstarch

6 cups cubed cooked pork loin roast (2 pounds)
1 tube (11-1/2 ounces) refrigerated corn bread
   twists

In a large nonstick skillet, saute the onion, celery, peppers and garlic in oil until tender. Add cumin and coriander; cook and stir over medium heat for 2 minutes. Add vinegar and cook for 2 minutes.

Set aside 1/2 cup broth. Add chili sauce, brown sugar, chocolate, Worcestershire sauce and remaining broth to vegetable mixture. Bring to a boil. Reduce heat; simmer, uncovered, for 10-15 minutes, stirring occasionally.

Combine cornstarch and reserved broth until smooth; stir into vegetable mixture. Bring to a boil; cook and stir for 1-2 minutes or until slightly thickened. Stir in pork. Transfer to a 13-in. x 9-in. x 2-in. baking dish coated with nonstick cooking spray.

Roll out corn bread dough and cut into strips; twist and place over filling in a lattice design. Bake, uncovered, at 375° for 10-15 minutes or until golden brown. Let stand for 15 minutes before serving. **Yield:** 12 servings.

***Editor's Note:** When cutting or seeding hot peppers, use rubber or plastic gloves to protect your hands. Avoid touching your face.

Nutritional Analysis: *One serving (2/3 cup) equals 332 calories, 13 g fat (4 g saturated fat), 66 mg cholesterol, 1,059 mg sodium, 28 g carbohydrate, 1 g fiber, 25 g protein.*
Diabetic Exchanges: *2-1/2 lean meat, 1-1/2 starch, 1-1/2 fat.*

Greek Pork Wraps

(Pictured at right)

If you like gyros, you'll love these strips of grilled pork wrapped in tortillas. It's become a popular summer

dish in my home ever since a co-worker gave me the idea for the creamy cucumber dressing.
—Christine London, Kansas City, Missouri

1/4 cup lemon juice
2 tablespoons olive *or* canola oil
1 tablespoon prepared mustard
1-3/4 teaspoons minced garlic, *divided*
1 teaspoon dried oregano
1 pork tenderloin (1 pound)
1 cup chopped peeled cucumber
1 cup reduced-fat plain yogurt
1/4 teaspoon salt
1/4 teaspoon dill weed
8 flour tortillas (6 inches)
1/2 cup chopped green onions

In a large resealable plastic bag, combine the lemon juice, oil, mustard, 1-1/4 teaspoons garlic and oregano; add the pork. Seal bag and turn to coat; refrigerate for 2 hours.

In a bowl, combine the cucumber, yogurt, salt, dill and remaining garlic; cover and refrigerate until serving.

Drain and discard marinade. Coat grill rack with nonstick cooking spray before starting the grill for indirect medium-hot heat. Grill tenderloin, uncovered, over direct-heated area for 5 minutes, turning once. Move to indirect-heated area; cover and cook 10-15 minutes longer or until a meat thermometer reads 160°. Let stand for 5 minutes.

Meanwhile, wrap tortillas in foil; place on grill for 2-3 minutes or until warmed, turning once. Slice tenderloin into strips; place on tortillas. Top each with 3 tablespoons yogurt sauce and 1 tablespoon green onions. **Yield:** 4 servings.

Nutritional Analysis: *One serving (2 wraps) equals 402 calories, 14 g fat (2 g saturated fat), 77 mg cholesterol, 718 mg sodium, 34 g carbohydrate, 1 g fiber, 34 g protein.*
Diabetic Exchanges: *3 lean meat, 2 starch, 1/2 milk.*

Pork and Noodles

My family loves this mixed medley with its hint of ginger. They always ask for seconds, so leftovers are rare.
—Jacquelynn McCown, Palm Beach Gardens, Florida

6 tablespoons reduced-sodium soy sauce, *divided*
Dash ground ginger *or* 1/4 to 1/2 teaspoon minced fresh gingerroot
2 garlic cloves, minced
1 pound boneless pork loin, cut into 2-inch strips
4 ounces uncooked thin spaghetti
3 teaspoons canola oil, *divided*
4 cups thinly sliced napa (Chinese) cabbage
2 large onions, sliced
1 cup thinly sliced carrots
1/3 cup sweet white wine *or* chicken broth
4-1/2 teaspoons sugar
1/4 teaspoon crushed red pepper flakes

In a resealable plastic bag, combine 2 tablespoons of soy sauce, ginger and garlic; add pork. Seal bag and turn to coat; refrigerate for 30 minutes. Cook pasta according to package directions; drain.

In a large nonstick skillet or wok, stir-fry pork in 2 teaspoons oil for 3 minutes. Remove and keep warm. Stir-fry the cabbage, onions and carrots in remaining oil for 2-4 minutes or until crisp-tender. Add the wine or broth, sugar, red pepper flakes and remaining soy sauce. Cook over medium-high heat for 1 minute. Add spaghetti and pork; toss to coat. **Yield:** 6 servings.

Nutritional Analysis: *One serving (1 cup) equals 276 calories, 7 g fat (2 g saturated fat), 50 mg cholesterol, 663 mg sodium, 29 g carbohydrate, 3 g fiber, 21 g protein.*
Diabetic Exchanges: *2 lean meat, 2 vegetable, 1 starch, 1/2 fat.*

Herbed Pork Chops

Expect to get plenty of compliments on these fast, flavor-packed chops. They're tender and juicy.
—Billi Jo Sylvester, New Smyrna Beach, Florida

1 teaspoon salt-free garlic seasoning blend
1/2 teaspoon dried basil
1/2 teaspoon dried oregano
1/2 teaspoon minced fresh parsley
1/4 teaspoon dried rosemary, crushed
1/4 teaspoon salt
2 bone-in pork loin chops (6 ounces *each*)
1 teaspoon olive *or* canola oil
1 garlic clove, minced
1 tablespoon lemon juice

In a small bowl, combine the first six ingredients. Rub over both sides of pork chops. In a nonstick skillet, heat oil and garlic over medium-high heat. Add pork chops. Cook for 4-5 minutes on each side or until juices run clear. Remove from the heat; drizzle with lemon juice. Cover and let stand for 2 minutes before serving. **Yield:** 2 servings.

Nutritional Analysis: *One serving equals 184 calories, 8 g fat (2 g saturated fat), 70 mg cholesterol, 367 mg sodium, 2 g carbohydrate, 1 g fiber, 25 g protein.*
Diabetic Exchanges: *3 lean meat, 1/2 fat.*

to the broth mixture. Return to a boil; cook and stir for 1-2 minutes or until thickened. Serve with the pork chops. **Yield:** 6 servings.

Nutritional Analysis: One serving (1 pork chop with 2 tablespoons sauce) equals 200 calories, 5 g fat (2 g saturated fat), 71 mg cholesterol, 884 mg sodium, 11 g carbohydrate, trace fiber, 26 g protein.
Diabetic Exchange: 3-1/2 lean meat.

Honey-Lime Pork Chops

(Pictured above)

I really appreciate how easy it is to prepare these juicy pork chops. Marinating them overnight seasons them wonderfully. They're sure to be requested often by family and friends.
—Janice Mitchell, Aurora, Colorado

1/2 cup lime juice
1/2 cup reduced-sodium soy sauce
2 tablespoons honey
2 garlic cloves, minced
6 boneless pork loin chops (4 ounces *each*)
SAUCE:
3/4 cup reduced-sodium chicken broth
1 garlic clove, minced
1-1/2 teaspoons honey
1/2 teaspoon lime juice
1/8 teaspoon browning sauce
Dash pepper
2 teaspoons cornstarch
2 tablespoons water

In a large resealable plastic bag, combine the lime juice, soy sauce, honey and garlic. Add pork chops. Seal bag and turn to coat; refrigerate for 8 hours or overnight. Drain and discard marinade. Grill chops, covered, over medium heat or broil 4 in. from the heat for 6-7 minutes on each side or until juices run clear.

For sauce, combine the broth, garlic, honey, lime juice, browning sauce and pepper in a small saucepan. Bring to a boil. Combine the cornstarch and water until smooth; stir in-

Pork and Cabbage With Spaghetti

This all-in-one dinner featuring fresh veggies and tender pork is a family favorite. Serving it with pasta is a bit different. My granddaughter regularly asks for "vegetable spaghetti".
—Marjorie Frazier, Summerville, South Carolina

1 package (8 ounces) spaghetti
1 pound pork tenderloin, cut into thin strips
1 medium onion, cut into thin wedges
2 garlic cloves, minced
1/8 teaspoon crushed red pepper flakes
3 teaspoons canola oil, *divided*
2 cups shredded cabbage
2 celery ribs, sliced
1 cup sliced carrots
1 medium green pepper, julienned
1 medium sweet red pepper, julienned
1/3 cup reduced-sodium soy sauce

Cook spaghetti according to package directions. Meanwhile, in a nonstick skillet or wok, saute the pork, onion, garlic and pepper flakes in 2 teaspoons oil until meat is no longer pink. Remove and keep warm.

In the same skillet, saute cabbage, celery, carrots and peppers in remaining oil until crisp-tender. Drain spaghetti; add to vegetable mixture. Stir in soy sauce and pork mixture. Cook for 5 minutes or until heated through. **Yield:** 6 servings.

Nutritional Analysis: One serving (1-1/2 cups) equals 302 calories, 6 g fat (1 g saturated fat), 48 mg cholesterol, 604 mg sodium, 38 g carbohydrate, 5 g fiber, 23 g protein.
Diabetic Exchanges: 2-1/2 lean meat, 1-1/2 starch, 1 fat.

Pork Chop Veggie Medley

(Pictured below)

I couldn't wait for dinner when my grandmother prepared this delicious pork chop dish topped with colorful vegetables. Now I fix it for my family—it's one of the meals regularly requested by my husband.
—Shirley Hulin, Los Osos, California

- 2 medium onions, thinly sliced
- 2 garlic cloves, minced
- 1 tablespoon olive *or* canola oil
- 6 boneless pork loin chops (3/4 inch thick and 4 ounces *each*)
- 1/2 teaspoon salt
- 1/4 teaspoon pepper
- 1/3 cup water
- 1 can (28 ounces) diced tomatoes, undrained
- 1 package (10 ounces) frozen corn
- 3 small zucchini, thinly sliced
- 4 cups hot cooked rice

In a large nonstick skillet, saute onions and garlic in oil for 2-3 minutes. Add the pork chops; brown on both sides and sprinkle with salt and pepper. Remove chops and onions with a slotted spoon; keep warm. Add water to drippings; bring to a boil, scraping any browned bits from pan. Return chops and onions to pan; add the tomatoes. Bring to a boil. Reduce heat; cover and simmer for 25-30 minutes or until meat is tender.

Stir in corn and zucchini; cover and simmer 10-15 minutes longer or until the vegetables are tender. Serve over rice. **Yield:** 6 servings.

Nutritional Analysis: *One serving (1 pork chop and 1 cup vegetable mixture with 2/3 cup rice) equals 418 calories, 9 g fat (3 g saturated fat), 62 mg cholesterol, 455 mg sodium, 52 g carbohydrate, 5 g fiber, 32 g protein.*
Diabetic Exchanges: *3 lean meat, 2-1/2 starch, 2 vegetable.*

Asparagus Ham Dinner

(Pictured above)

I've been making this low-fat meal for my family for years now, and it's always well received. With asparagus, tomato, pasta and chunks of ham, it's a tempting blend of tastes and textures.
—Rhonda Zavodny, David City, Nebraska

- 2 cups uncooked spiral pasta
- 3/4 pound fresh asparagus, cut into 1-inch pieces
- 1 medium sweet yellow pepper, julienned
- 1 tablespoon olive *or* canola oil
- 3 cups diced fresh tomatoes (about 6 medium)
- 6 ounces reduced-sodium fully cooked ham, cubed
- 1/4 cup minced fresh parsley
- 1/2 teaspoon salt
- 1/2 teaspoon dried oregano
- 1/2 teaspoon dried basil
- 1/8 to 1/4 teaspoon cayenne pepper
- 1/4 cup shredded Parmesan cheese

Cook pasta according to package directions. Meanwhile, in a nonstick skillet, saute asparagus and yellow pepper in oil until tender. Add tomatoes and ham; heat through. Drain pasta; add to the vegetable mixture. Stir in seasonings. Sprinkle with Parmesan cheese. **Yield:** 6 servings.

Nutritional Analysis: *One serving (1-1/3 cups) equals 238 calories, 6 g fat (1 g saturated fat), 18 mg cholesterol, 522 mg sodium, 33 g carbohydrate, 3 g fiber, 14 g protein.*
Diabetic Exchanges: *2 lean meat, 2 vegetable, 1 starch.*

Orange-Ginger Pork Chops

Basting chops with this tangy sauce makes them extremely tender and savory. My family requests this dish for the terrific taste. I make it for them often because it's on the lighter side.
—Lynette Randleman, Cheyenne, Wyoming

  1 teaspoon ground ginger *or* 4 teaspoons
    minced fresh gingerroot
  1 garlic clove, minced
  1 tablespoon canola oil
1/2 cup sherry *or* chicken broth
1/4 cup honey
1/4 cup reduced-sodium soy sauce
  1 tablespoon sesame seeds
  1 tablespoon grated orange peel
3/4 teaspoon hot pepper sauce
  4 bone-in pork loin chops (6 ounces *each*)
  1 teaspoon cornstarch
  2 tablespoons water

In a saucepan, cook ginger and garlic in oil for 1 minute; remove from the heat. Stir in the sherry or broth, honey, soy sauce, sesame seeds, orange peel and hot pepper sauce; mix well. Pour 1/2 cup into a small bowl; set aside. Pour remaining marinade into a large resealable plastic bag; add pork chops. Seal bag and turn to coat; refrigerate for at least 1 hour.

Meanwhile, in a saucepan, combine cornstarch and water until smooth; add reserved marinade. Bring to a boil; cook and stir for 1 minute or until thickened.

Drain and discard marinade from the pork. Coat grill rack with nonstick cooking spray before starting the grill. Grill chops, covered, over medium heat for 4 minutes. Turn; baste with sauce. Grill 15-20 minutes longer or until juices run clear, basting occasionally. Serve with any remaining sauce. **Yield:** 4 servings.

Nutritional Analysis: One serving (1 pork chop) equals 243 calories, 9 g fat (2 g saturated fat), 58 mg cholesterol, 501 mg sodium, 15 g carbohydrate, trace fiber, 22 g protein.
Diabetic Exchanges: 3 lean meat, 1 starch.

Sweet 'n' Sour Pork Chops

(Pictured above)

Featuring a twist of citrus, these tender chops have earned a spot on my family's list of favorite dinners. To save time, I bake a double batch and freeze some.
—Margaret Pache, Mesa, Arizona

  6 boneless pork loin chops (1-1/2 pounds)
  2 teaspoons canola oil
1/2 cup packed brown sugar
1/3 cup balsamic vinegar
  1 tablespoon reduced-sodium soy sauce
  1 teaspoon molasses
  1 teaspoon grated orange peel
  2 teaspoons cornstarch
  1 tablespoon water
  2 large navel oranges, peeled and sectioned
  4 cups hot cooked rice

In a large nonstick skillet, brown pork chops on both sides in oil. Remove and keep warm. In the same pan, combine brown sugar, vinegar, soy sauce, molasses and orange peel until blended. Return meat to pan; cover and simmer for 15 minutes or until tender. Remove chops; keep warm. Combine cornstarch and water until smooth; stir into pan juices. Bring to a boil; cook and stir for 2 minutes or until thickened. Add orange segments; cook for 1 minute. Serve over pork and rice. **Yield:** 6 servings.

Nutritional Analysis: One serving (1 pork chop with 2 tablespoons sauce and 3/4 cup rice) equals 381 calories, 7 g fat (2 g saturated fat), 71 mg cholesterol, 173 mg sodium, 52 g carbohydrate, 2 g fiber, 27 g protein.
Diabetic Exchanges: 3 lean meat, 2 fruit, 1-1/2 starch.

Fish & Seafood Fare

Fabulous fish dinners and sensational seafood entrees can add appetizing variety to any cook's healthy menu planning. You'll quickly get hooked on these from-the-sea favorites swimming in fantastic flavor!

Flavorful Catfish Fillets and Spicy Scallop Fettuccine (page 164)

Seafood Stew

A friend who lives in Florida shared the recipe for this flavorful stew that's seasoned with chili powder and orange juice concentrate. My husband really enjoys it, so I make it often.
—*Carolyn Hayes, Marion, Illinois*

2-1/2 cups chicken broth
  1/2 cup uncooked long grain rice
    2 teaspoons chili powder
    2 garlic cloves, minced
    1 can (14-1/2 ounces) diced tomatoes, undrained
  3/4 cup julienned green pepper
  3/4 cup julienned sweet red *or* yellow pepper
  1/2 cup thinly sliced onion
    8 ounces orange roughy *or* red snapper fillets, cut into 1-inch pieces
    4 ounces uncooked medium shrimp, peeled and deveined
  3/4 cup orange juice concentrate

In a saucepan, bring broth to a boil. Add the rice, chili powder and garlic; return to a boil. Reduce heat; cover and simmer for 15-20 minutes or until rice is tender. Add the tomatoes, peppers and onion. Cover and cook over medium heat until vegetables are tender. Add fish, shrimp and orange juice concentrate. Cover and simmer for 2-4 minutes or until the fish flakes easily with a fork and the shrimp turn pink. **Yield:** 6 servings.

Nutritional Analysis: One serving (1 cup) equals 208 calories, 2 g fat (trace saturated fat), 36 mg cholesterol, 578 mg sodium, 35 g carbohydrate, 3 g fiber, 13 g protein.
***Diabetic Exchanges:** 2 lean meat, 1 starch, 1 vegetable.*

Stuffed Fish Fillets

(Pictured at right)

These fillets are bursting with fresh vegetables. I discovered this memorable recipe 40 years ago in college. It's remained a staple at our house.
—*Mildred Doucette, Sun City West, Arizona*

    2 small carrots, shredded
    1 small onion, minced
    5 tablespoons butter *or* stick margarine, *divided*
    4 slices bread, cubed
  3/4 cup diced canned tomatoes, drained
    1 jar (4-1/2 ounces) sliced mushrooms, drained
  1/2 small cucumber, chopped
1-1/4 teaspoons salt, *divided*

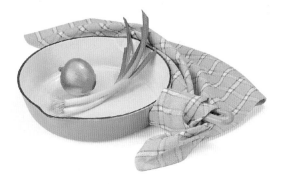

  1/4 teaspoon dill weed
  1/8 teaspoon pepper
    8 sole *or* orange roughy fillets (4 ounces *each*)
  1/8 teaspoon paprika
    8 lemon wedges

In a large nonstick skillet, saute carrots and onion in 3 tablespoons of butter until tender. Remove from the heat. Stir in bread cubes, tomatoes, mushrooms, cucumber, 1 teaspoon salt, dill and pepper.

Place four fillets in a 13-in. x 9-in. x 2-in. baking dish coated with nonstick cooking spray. Top each with 1 cup stuffing and another fillet. Sprinkle with paprika and remaining salt. Dot with remaining butter. Bake, uncovered, at 350° for 25-30 minutes or until fish flakes easily with a fork. Cut in half; serve with lemon. **Yield:** 8 servings.

Nutritional Analysis: One serving (half of a stuffed fillet) equals 233 calories, 9 g fat (5 g saturated fat), 74 mg cholesterol, 798 mg sodium, 14 g carbohydrate, 2 g fiber, 24 g protein.
***Diabetic Exchanges:** 2 lean meat, 1 starch, 1 fat.*

Salmon with Citrus Salsa

(Pictured at right)

I make each meal from scratch, which results in a lot of hit-or-miss attempts, but this grilled salmon is a surefire winner! It makes a perfect light supper.
—*Nancy Shirvani, Terryville, Connecticut*

  1/2 cup raspberry vinegar (recipe on page 84)
  1/4 cup reduced-sodium soy sauce
    2 tablespoons minced fresh cilantro *or* parsley
1-1/2 teaspoons ground ginger *or* 2 tablespoons minced fresh gingerroot
    1 tablespoon olive *or* canola oil
  1/2 teaspoon hot pepper sauce
  1/8 teaspoon pepper
    4 salmon fillets (6 ounces *each*)
CITRUS SALSA:
  3/4 cup pink grapefruit segments, cut into bite-size pieces
  1/2 cup orange segments, cut into bite-size pieces
    1 tablespoon raspberry vinegar
    1 tablespoon honey
    1 teaspoon minced fresh cilantro *or* parsley
  1/8 teaspoon ground ginger *or* 1 teaspoon minced fresh gingerroot
  1/8 teaspoon hot pepper sauce

In a large resealable plastic bag, combine the first seven ingredients; add salmon. Seal bag and turn to coat; refrigerate for 2 hours. Meanwhile, in a bowl, combine salsa ingredients. Cover and refrigerate until serving.

Drain and discard marinade. Coat grill rack with nonstick cooking spray before starting grill. Place salmon, skin side down, on grill. Grill, covered, over medium heat for 15-20 minutes or until fish flakes easily with a fork. Serve with salsa. **Yield:** 4 servings.

Nutritional Analysis: One serving (1 fillet with 3 tablespoons salsa) equals 361 calories, 19 g fat (4 g saturated fat), 112 mg cholesterol, 241 mg sodium, 12 g carbohydrate, 1 g fiber, 35 g protein.
***Diabetic Exchanges:** 4-1/2 lean meat, 1 fruit, 1 fat.*

Crumb-Topped Salmon

(Pictured at right)

My family of fishermen keeps me supplied with the star ingredient for this well-loved recipe. Often we catch enough to share and sometimes send some of our delicious Northwest salmon to Michigan for my sister to enjoy.
—Perlene Hoekema, Lynden, Washington

  1-1/2 cups soft bread crumbs
      2 tablespoons minced fresh parsley
      1 tablespoon minced fresh thyme *or* 1 teaspoon dried thyme
      2 garlic cloves, minced
      1 teaspoon grated lemon peel
  1/2 teaspoon salt
  1/4 teaspoon lemon-pepper seasoning
  1/4 teaspoon paprika
      4 salmon fillets (6 ounces *each*)
Refrigerated butter-flavored spray*

In a bowl, combine the first eight ingredients; set aside. Pat salmon dry. Place, skin side down, in a 13-in. x 9-in. x 2-in. baking dish coated with nonstick cooking spray. Spritz salmon with butter-flavored spray; cover with crumb mixture. Spritz crumbs with butter-flavored spray. Bake, uncovered, at 350° for 15-20 minutes or until fish flakes with a fork. **Yield:** 4 servings.

***Editor's Note:** This recipe was tested with I Can't Believe It's Not Butter Spray.

Nutritional Analysis: One salmon fillet equals 371 calories, 19 g fat (4 g saturated fat), 113 mg cholesterol, 525 mg sodium, 12 g carbohydrate, 1 g fiber, 36 g protein.
Diabetic Exchanges: 4 lean meat, 2-1/2 fat, 1/2 starch.

🍎 Salmon Savvy

AN ABUNDANT supply of salmon—fresh, frozen and canned—is making this hearty, easy-to-prepare fish a savory staple on family menus.

Here are some buying, storing and cooking tips from the Alaska Seafood Marketing Institute:

- Look for solidly frozen packages stored below the chill line in the freezer case of your grocery store.
- Do not buy salmon with freezer burns or icy white discoloration.
- Until you are ready to use it, keep salmon firmly frozen, wrapped in moisture-proof paper or in an airtight container. For best quality, store it at 0° or lower for up to 4 months.
- To thaw, place the wrapped package in the refrigerator overnight on a plate or a shallow pan to catch the drips. Allow 8 to 10 hours to thaw completely.
- You need not remove the soft edible bones in canned salmon. They are a rich source of calcium for folks of all ages, including children who have dairy product allergies.
- Red sockeye is the premier canned salmon. Deep-red with a firm texture, it's a great choice for salads or entrees where color is key to an attractive presentation.
- Milder, softer-textured pink salmon is perfect for pasta, soups, sandwiches and casseroles. Most abundant, pink salmon is less costly than red.

Haddock with Citrus Salsa

I'd prepared old favorites for 30 years when the latest emphasis on health-conscious cooking led me to find new recipes, like this mouth-watering way to serve fish.
—Sally Roberts, Port St. Lucie, Florida

      4 medium navel oranges, peeled and sectioned
  1/2 cup chopped red onion
  1/4 cup lime juice
  1/4 cup minced fresh cilantro *or* parsley
  1/4 teaspoon crushed red pepper flakes
      1 garlic clove, minced
      1 teaspoon grated orange peel
  3/4 teaspoon salt, *divided*
  1-1/8 teaspoons pepper, *divided*
      2 teaspoons ground coriander
      2 teaspoons ground cumin
      1 pound haddock fillets

For salsa, in a bowl, combine the oranges, onion, lime juice, cilantro, pepper flakes, garlic, orange peel, 1/4 teaspoon salt and 1/8 teaspoon pepper. Cover and chill. Combine coriander, cumin and remaining salt and pepper; rub over both sides of fillets. Grill, covered, over medium-hot heat or broil 4-6 in. from the heat for 5-6 minutes on each side or until fish flakes easily with a fork. Serve with citrus salsa. **Yield:** 4 servings.

Nutritional Analysis: One serving (1/4 of the fish with 1/2 cup salsa) equals 179 calories, 1 g fat (trace saturated fat), 65 mg cholesterol, 520 mg sodium, 20 g carbohydrate, 4 g fiber, 23 g protein.
Diabetic Exchanges: 3 lean meat, 1/2 fruit.

Basil Shrimp Fettuccine

(Pictured below)

Garlic and basil add fresh flavor to the light sauce that coats this colorful combination of firm shrimp, bright pepper chunks and tender pasta. It's a fast favorite that tastes like you fussed.
—Cathy Carroll, Bossier City, Louisiana

    8 ounces uncooked fettuccine
  1/2 cup chopped onion
  1/4 cup *each* chopped sweet yellow and red pepper
    1 to 2 garlic cloves, minced
    2 tablespoons olive *or* canola oil
  1/4 cup all-purpose flour
    1 can (12 ounces) fat-free evaporated milk
  1/2 teaspoon salt
  1/4 teaspoon white pepper
  1/8 teaspoon cayenne pepper
    1 pound uncooked shrimp, peeled and deveined
    2 tablespoons minced fresh basil *or* 2 teaspoons dried basil

Cook pasta according to package directions. Meanwhile, in a nonstick skillet, saute the onion, peppers and garlic in oil until tender. In a small bowl, combine flour and milk until smooth. Add to vegetable mixture. Stir in the seasonings. Bring to a boil; cook and stir for 2 minutes or until thickened.

Reduce heat; add shrimp and basil. Simmer, uncovered, for 3 minutes or until shrimp turn pink. Drain pasta; place in a large bowl. Add shrimp mixture and toss to coat. **Yield:** 6 servings.

Nutritional Analysis: One serving (1-1/4 cups) equals 306 calories, 7 g fat (1 g saturated fat), 115 mg cholesterol, 465 mg sodium, 37 g carbohydrate, 2 g fiber, 24 g protein.
Diabetic Exchanges: 2 starch, 2 lean meat, 1 fat.

Seafood Lasagna Roll-Ups

Imitation crabmeat makes a great filling for these saucy low-fat seafood spirals. They're delicious, healthy and very easy to prepare. You can assemble the roll-ups ahead of time, then refrigerate them until ready to bake.
—Juanita Patterson, New Castle, Indiana

    1 package (8 ounces) imitation crabmeat, chopped
1-1/2 cups 1% cottage cheese, drained
  1/3 cup dry bread crumbs
    5 tablespoons grated Parmesan cheese, *divided*
    1 egg, lightly beaten
  1/2 cup egg substitute
    1 tablespoon dried parsley flakes
  1/4 teaspoon onion powder
  1/4 teaspoon garlic powder
    6 lasagna noodles, cooked and drained
    2 cups meatless spaghetti sauce, *divided*

In a bowl, combine the crab, cottage cheese, bread crumbs, 4 tablespoons Parmesan cheese, egg, egg substitute, parsley, onion powder and garlic powder. Spread 1/3 cup on each noodle; roll up tightly. Spread 1/2 cup spaghetti sauce in a 9-in. square baking dish. Place roll-ups, seam side down, in dish. Top with remaining sauce.

Cover and bake at 350° for 30 minutes. Uncover; bake 25 minutes longer. Sprinkle with remaining Parmesan cheese. **Yield:** 6 servings.

Nutritional Analysis: One serving (1 roll-up) equals 326 calories, 8 g fat (3 g saturated fat), 50 mg cholesterol, 1,116 mg sodium, 40 g carbohydrate, 4 g fiber, 22 g protein.
Diabetic Exchanges: 3 lean meat, 2 starch.

Basil-Tomato Tuna Steaks

Be prepared to reel in raves when you place this fabulous fish dish on the table. It's moist and flavorful, topped off with basil, tomato and cheese. My husband requests it on a regular basis all year long.
—Jan Parker, Englewood, Florida

    1 tablespoon olive *or* canola oil
    4 tuna *or* salmon steaks (1 pound)
  1/2 teaspoon salt
  1/8 teaspoon pepper
  1/3 cup loosely packed fresh basil leaves
    1 medium tomato, chopped
  1/4 cup shredded part-skim mozzarella cheese

In a large nonstick skillet, heat oil over medium heat. Add the tuna steaks; cook for 3 minutes on each side or until fish flakes easily with a fork. Transfer to a broiler pan. Sprinkle fish with salt and pepper. Cover with basil leaves. Top with tomato and cheese. Broil 4-6 in. from the heat for 2 minutes or until the cheese is melted. **Yield:** 4 servings.

Nutritional Analysis: One serving equals 171 calories, 6 g fat (2 g saturated fat), 57 mg cholesterol, 371 mg sodium, 2 g carbohydrate, trace fiber, 27 g protein.
Diabetic Exchange: 3 lean meat.

Apricot-Glazed Shrimp

My husband has always been a beef and pork man, but after some 50 years, I've finally gotten him to eat seafood. Sometimes I substitute cubed pork for the shrimp, and that's excellent, too.
—Aletha Graves, Bellingham, Washington

  2 teaspoons cornstarch
1/2 cup chicken broth
  3 tablespoons apricot preserves
  1 tablespoon reduced-sodium soy sauce
  1 teaspoon sesame seeds, toasted
  1 medium green pepper, julienned
  1 medium sweet red pepper, julienned
1/4 cup sliced green onions
  1 garlic clove, minced
  2 teaspoons canola oil
1/2 pound uncooked medium shrimp, peeled and
      deveined
1/2 cup sliced water chestnuts
1-1/2 cups hot cooked rice

In a bowl, combine the cornstarch, broth, preserves, soy sauce and sesame seeds until blended; set aside. In a large nonstick skillet or wok, stir-fry the peppers, onions and garlic in oil for 5 minutes or until crisp-tender. Add shrimp and water chestnuts; stir-fry until shrimp turn pink. Stir broth mixture; add to the pan. Bring to a boil; cook and stir for 1-2 minutes or until thickened. Serve over rice. **Yield:** 2 servings.

Nutritional Analysis: One serving (1 cup stir-fry mixture with 3/4 cup rice) equals 471 calories, 8 g fat (1 g saturated fat), 172 mg cholesterol, 724 mg sodium, 70 g carbohydrate, 4 g fiber, 30 g protein.

Flavorful Catfish Fillets

(Pictured at right and on page 159)

This is the best catfish ever! The cornmeal and herb coating keeps the fillets moist and gives them traditional appeal without the fat that comes from frying.
—Ellen Munnik, Chesterfield, Michigan

1/4 cup 1% buttermilk
  2 teaspoons Dijon mustard
1/2 cup cornmeal
  1 teaspoon *each* salt, onion powder, garlic
      powder and paprika
1/2 teaspoon dried thyme
1/2 teaspoon pepper
1/4 to 1/2 teaspoon cayenne pepper
  1 pound catfish fillets
Lemon wedges, optional

In a shallow bowl, whisk buttermilk and mustard until smooth. In another bowl, combine the cornmeal and seasonings. Dip fillets into buttermilk mixture, then into cornmeal mixture. Place 1 in. apart on a wire rack coated with nonstick cooking spray.

Place rack on a baking sheet. Broil 4 in. from the heat for 3-4 minutes on each side or until fish flakes easily with a fork. Serve with lemon if desired. **Yield:** 4 servings.

Nutritional Analysis: One serving equals 295 calories, 13 g fat (3 g saturated fat), 75 mg cholesterol, 751 mg sodium, 16 g carbohydrate, 2 g fiber, 27 g protein.
Diabetic Exchanges: 4 lean meat, 1 starch.

Spicy Scallop Fettuccine

(Pictured at right and on page 159)

This attractive savory stir-fry stars succulent, quick-cooking scallops. It may seem that timing is everything when you first try this recipe, but you'll soon realize you can pretty much just throw it together. It's well worth it!
—Dot Christiansen, Bettendorf, Iowa

  8 ounces uncooked fettuccine
  2 large carrots, thinly sliced
  1 tablespoon olive *or* canola oil
  2 cups frozen sugar snap peas
  3 green onions, sliced
  3 garlic cloves, minced
  1 tablespoon butter *or* stick margarine
1/2 cup white wine *or* chicken broth
1/3 cup water
  2 teaspoons dried tarragon
  1 teaspoon chicken bouillon granules
1/8 to 1/4 teaspoon cayenne pepper
  1 pound fresh *or* frozen bay scallops, thawed
  2 tablespoons cornstarch
  2 tablespoons cold water
1/4 cup shredded Parmesan cheese

Cook fettuccine according to package directions. Meanwhile, in a large nonstick skillet, saute carrots in oil for 4 minutes. Add the peas, onions and garlic; saute 3 minutes longer or until carrots are tender. Remove vegetables and keep warm. Drain fettuccine and toss with butter; keep warm.

In the skillet, combine wine or broth, water, tarragon, bouillon and cayenne. Bring to a boil; add scallops. Reduce heat; simmer, uncovered, for 1 minute. Combine cornstarch and cold water until smooth; stir into skillet. Bring to a boil; cook and stir for 2 minutes or until sauce is thickened and scallops are opaque. Add pasta and vegetables; heat through. Sprinkle with Parmesan. **Yield:** 6 servings.

Nutritional Analysis: One serving (1 cup) equals 422 calories, 10 g fat (4 g saturated fat), 50 mg cholesterol, 741 mg sodium, 49 g carbohydrate, 5 g fiber, 30 g protein.
Diabetic Exchanges: 3 lean meat, 2 starch, 1-1/2 fat, 1 vegetable.

Scallops with Linguine

A mild garlic sauce adds extra zest to this delightful combination of linguine, tender bay scallops and bright carrots. Plus, this recipe is perfectly sized for two.
—Paula Jones, Brooksville, Florida

    1 tablespoon cornstarch
    1 cup chicken broth
    2 tablespoons white wine *or* additional chicken
      broth
    1 garlic clove, minced
1-1/2 teaspoons butter *or* stick margarine
  3/4 cup sliced fresh mushrooms
  1/4 cup sliced green onions
  1/4 cup grated carrot
  1/2 pound bay scallops
1-1/2 teaspoons minced fresh parsley
    1 cup hot cooked linguine
    2 lemon wedges

In a bowl, combine the first three ingredients until smooth; set aside. In a nonstick skillet or wok, stir-fry garlic in butter. Add mushrooms, onions and carrot; stir-fry for 3 minutes or until crisp-tender. Stir cornstarch mixture and add to skillet. Bring to a boil; cook and stir for 2 minutes or until thickened. Reduce heat. Add scallops and parsley; cook until scallops turn opaque. Serve with linguine and lemon. **Yield:** 2 servings.

Nutritional Analysis: *One serving (about 1/2 cup scallop mixture with 1/2 cup linguine) equals 279 calories, 5 g fat (2 g saturated fat), 45 mg cholesterol, 688 mg sodium, 31 g carbohydrate, 3 g fiber, 25 g protein.*
Diabetic Exchanges: *2 starch, 2 lean meat.*

Snappy Eggplant Spaghetti

(Pictured above right)

This recipe I adapted from an old Italian cookbook offers a flavorful taste of my roots. My family loves it with garlic bread.
—Brett Russo, Walterboro, South Carolina

    1 medium onion, chopped
    1 garlic clove, minced
    2 tablespoons olive *or* canola oil
3-1/2 cups tomato juice
    1 small eggplant, peeled and cubed
    1 medium green pepper, chopped
   16 large pitted ripe olives, finely chopped
  1/4 cup minced fresh parsley
    2 tablespoons minced fresh basil *or* 2 teaspoons
      dried basil
    1 teaspoon salt
  1/4 teaspoon crushed red pepper flakes
    1 package (1 pound) spaghetti
    1 pound fresh *or* frozen red snapper *or* grouper,
      cut into 1-inch cubes

In a large saucepan or Dutch oven, saute onion and garlic in oil until tender. Add tomato juice; bring to a boil. Reduce heat; cover and simmer for 10 minutes. Add the eggplant, green pepper, olives, parsley, basil, salt and red pepper flakes. Cover and simmer for 20 minutes.

Meanwhile, cook spaghetti according to package directions. Add fish to eggplant mixture; cover and simmer 10 minutes longer. Drain spaghetti; top with fish mixture. **Yield:** 8 servings.

Nutritional Analysis: *One serving (3/4 cup fish mixture with 1 cup spaghetti) equals 225 calories, 5 g fat (1 g saturated fat), 21 mg cholesterol, 781 mg sodium, 28 g carbohydrate, 4 g fiber, 16 g protein.*
Diabetic Exchanges: *2 lean meat, 1 starch, 1 vegetable.*

Poached Orange Roughy With Tarragon Sauce

A flavorful herb-flecked sauce enhances the mild, poached-to-perfection fish fillet in this recipe from our Test Kitchen.

    4 cups water
    1 cup dry white wine *or* vegetable broth
  1/4 cup chopped celery
  1/4 cup chopped carrot
    2 tablespoons chopped onion
    2 tablespoons lemon juice
    7 whole peppercorns
    1 bay leaf
    2 teaspoons dried tarragon, *divided*
    4 orange roughy *or* red snapper fillets (4 ounces
      each)
  1/8 teaspoon *each* salt and white pepper
    2 tablespoons 2% milk
    1 egg yolk

Poaching Pointers

- For poaching, the water temperature should be at 160°-180°. The surface of the liquid should merely suggest the hint of a bubble.
- Bring the liquid (water, stock or wine) to a boil first, then reduce the heat to poaching temperature before adding food.
- Using a fat skimmer or metal spatula, lower food into cooking liquid. It should be completely submerged.
- Most foods can be poached in a large skillet—but don't poach food in a cast-iron skillet. The metal lends an off-taste.

In a large nonstick skillet, combine the first eight ingredients. Add 1-1/2 teaspoons tarragon. Bring to a boil. Reduce heat; add fillets and poach, uncovered, until fish is firm and flakes easily with a fork (about 8-10 minutes per inch of fillet thickness). Remove to a warm serving platter.

Strain 1 cup of cooking liquid; place in a saucepan. Add salt and pepper. Bring to a boil; cook until liquid is reduced to about 1/3 cup. Remove from the heat. In a small bowl, beat milk and egg yolk. Stir 1 tablespoon reduced liquid into egg mixture; return all to the pan, stirring constantly. Stir in remaining tarragon. Bring to a gentle boil over low heat; cook and stir for 1 minute or until thickened. Spoon over fish. **Yield:** 4 servings.

Nutritional Analysis: One serving (1 fish fillet with 2 tablespoons sauce) equals 106 calories, 2 g fat (1 g saturated fat), 76 mg cholesterol, 152 mg sodium, 1 g carbohydrate, trace fiber, 18 g protein.
Diabetic Exchange: 3 very lean meat.

Tomato-Dill Shrimp Stew

Here in the Northwest, we have a seemingly endless supply of seafood, so we're always searching for creative new recipes. This thick hearty stew was a big hit when I served it one year on Father's Day. My dad loved it! And so did everyone else.
—Jennie Benjaminson, Renton, Washington

1 large onion, chopped
4 garlic cloves, minced
1 tablespoon olive *or* canola oil
3 cups diced fresh tomatoes
1 can (8 ounces) tomato sauce
3 tablespoons minced fresh dill *or* 2 teaspoons dill weed
2 teaspoons Dijon mustard
1 teaspoon honey
1/2 teaspoon salt
1 pound cooked medium shrimp, peeled and deveined
4 ounces crumbled feta cheese
1 cup minced fresh parsley

In a large saucepan, saute onion and garlic in oil for 5 minutes. Stir in the tomatoes, tomato sauce, dill, mustard, honey and salt. Bring to a boil. Reduce heat; simmer, un-

covered, for 20 minutes. Add the shrimp, cheese and parsley; simmer 5 minutes longer. **Yield:** 4 servings.

Nutritional Analysis: One serving (1 cup) equals 306 calories, 11 g fat (5 g saturated fat), 246 mg cholesterol, 1,282 mg sodium, 21 g carbohydrate, 4 g fiber, 31 g protein.
Diabetic Exchanges: 4 very lean meat, 1-1/2 starch, 1 fat.

Zippy Shrimp

(Pictured below)

Delicate shrimp picks up fabulous flavor when it's sauteed in chicken broth mixed with garlic and ripe olives in this entree from our Test Kitchen.

1-1/4 cups chicken *or* vegetable broth
10 medium pitted ripe olives, finely chopped
1 red chili pepper, finely chopped*
2 tablespoons lemon juice
1 tablespoon minced fresh rosemary *or* 1 teaspoon dried rosemary, crushed
4 garlic cloves, minced
2 teaspoons Worcestershire sauce
1 teaspoon paprika
1/2 teaspoon salt
1/4 to 1/2 teaspoon pepper
2 pounds fresh *or* frozen uncooked shrimp, peeled and deveined

In a large nonstick skillet, combine the first 10 ingredients. Bring to a boil; cook until mixture is reduced by half. Add shrimp. Simmer, uncovered, for 3-4 minutes or until shrimp turn pink, stirring occasionally. **Yield:** 8 servings.

Editor's Note: When cutting or seeding hot peppers, use rubber or plastic gloves to protect your hands. Avoid touching your face.

Nutritional Analysis: One serving (1/2 cup) equals 141 calories, 3 g fat (trace saturated fat), 172 mg cholesterol, 520 mg sodium, 3 g carbohydrate, trace fiber, 24 g protein.
Diabetic Exchange: 4 very lean meat.

Linguine with Seafood Sauce

Shrimp and clams give such an elegant touch to this easy-to-fix linguine dish that people will think you fussed. I'm a day-care provider with a husband and two hungry boys to cook for. When I'm pressed for time, I rely on this tried-and-true recipe that everyone likes.
—Karen Fitzgerald, Mt. Airy, Maryland

    4 green onions, sliced
    1 garlic clove, minced
    2 tablespoons butter *or* stick margarine
    1 pound cooked medium shrimp, peeled and deveined
    1 can (6-1/2 ounces) chopped clams, undrained
    1 cup chicken broth
  1/2 cup white wine *or* additional chicken broth
    2 tablespoons lemon juice
  1/2 cup minced fresh parsley
    1 teaspoon dried basil
    1 teaspoon dried oregano
  1/2 teaspoon salt
  1/4 teaspoon pepper
  12 ounces uncooked linguine
    2 tablespoons cornstarch
    2 tablespoons cold water
  1/4 cup reduced-fat sour cream

In a large nonstick skillet, saute onions and garlic in butter for 4-5 minutes or until tender. Stir in the next 10 ingredients. Bring to a boil. Reduce heat; simmer, uncovered, for 5 minutes. Meanwhile, cook linguine according to package directions.

Combine cornstarch and water until smooth; gradually add to seafood mixture. Bring to a boil; cook and stir for 2 minutes or until thickened. Drain linguine; toss with sour cream. Place in a serving bowl; add seafood sauce and toss to coat. **Yield:** 6 servings.

Nutritional Analysis: One serving (1-1/3 cups) equals 337 calories, 8 g fat (3 g saturated fat), 139 mg cholesterol, 632 mg sodium, 38 g carbohydrate, 2 g fiber, 26 g protein.
Diabetic Exchanges: 2-1/2 starch, 2 lean meat, 1/2 fat.

Mediterranean Baked Fish

(Pictured at right)

The mouth-watering aroma of this herbed fish dish baking is sure to lure guests to your kitchen. It makes a lovely and colorful presentation for company. In a pinch, you can use dried herbs and canned diced tomatoes to replace the fresh ingredients.
—Ellen De Munnik, Chesterfield, Michigan

    1 cup thinly sliced leeks (white portion only)
    2 garlic cloves, minced
    2 teaspoons olive *or* canola oil
  12 large fresh basil leaves
1-1/2 pounds orange roughy fillets
    1 teaspoon salt
    2 plum tomatoes, sliced
    1 can (2-1/4 ounces) sliced ripe olives, drained

    1 medium lemon
  1/8 teaspoon pepper
    4 fresh rosemary sprigs

In a nonstick skillet, saute the leeks and garlic in oil until tender; set aside. Coat a 13-in. x 9-in. x 2-in. baking dish with nonstick cooking spray. Arrange the basil in a single layer in dish; top with fish fillets. Sprinkle with salt. Top with the leek mixture.

Arrange tomatoes and olives over fish. Thinly slice half of the lemon; place over the top. Squeeze juice from remaining lemon over all. Sprinkle with pepper. Cover and bake at 425° for 15-20 minutes or until fish flakes easily with a fork. Garnish with rosemary. **Yield:** 4 servings.

Nutritional Analysis: One serving equals 186 calories, 6 g fat (1 g saturated fat), 34 mg cholesterol, 857 mg sodium, 9 g carbohydrate, 3 g fiber, 26 g protein.
Diabetic Exchanges: 3 lean meat, 1 vegetable.

Orzo Shrimp Stew

(Pictured at right)

Since my husband and I really enjoy seafood, I don't skimp on shrimp in this recipe! This mildly seasoned stew has other satisfying ingredients, too, like broccoli, tomatoes and pasta.
—Lisa Stinger, Hamilton, New Jersey

2-1/2 cups reduced-sodium chicken broth
    5 cups broccoli florets
    1 can (14-1/2 ounces) diced tomatoes, undrained
    1 cup uncooked orzo
    1 pound uncooked medium shrimp, peeled and deveined
  3/4 teaspoon salt
  1/4 teaspoon pepper
    2 teaspoons dried basil
    2 tablespoons butter *or* stick margarine

In a large nonstick skillet or saucepan, bring broth to a boil. Add broccoli, tomatoes and orzo. Reduce heat; simmer, uncovered, for 5 minutes, stirring occasionally. Add the shrimp, salt and pepper. Cover and cook for 4-5 minutes or until shrimp turn pink and orzo is tender. Stir in basil and butter. **Yield:** 4 servings.

Nutritional Analysis: One serving (1-3/4 cups) equals 401 calories, 10 g fat (5 g saturated fat), 190 mg cholesterol, 919 mg sodium, 45 g carbohydrate, 4 g fiber, 35 g protein.
Diabetic Exchanges: 3 lean meat, 2-1/2 starch, 1 vegetable.

Basil-Marinated Fish

(Pictured below)

Our Test Kitchen combined basil vinegar, oil, a sprinkling of herbs and a little zesty lemon peel to make a delightfully mild and pleasant marinade for orange roughy or halibut.

1/4 cup basil vinegar (recipe on page 84)
2 tablespoons olive *or* canola oil
1 tablespoon *each* chopped fresh basil, thyme, oregano and parsley *or* 1 teaspoon *each* dried basil, thyme, oregano and parsley flakes
2 garlic cloves, minced
1 teaspoon grated lemon peel
1/2 teaspoon salt
1/4 teaspoon pepper
2 orange roughy *or* halibut fillets (1 pound)

In a large resealable plastic bag, combine the vinegar, oil, herbs, garlic, lemon peel, salt and pepper. Add fillets; seal bag and turn to coat. Refrigerate for 30 minutes, turning once or twice. Drain and discard marinade.

Coat the grill rack with nonstick cooking spray before starting the grill. Grill the fillets, covered, over medium-hot heat for 7-10 minutes or until fish flakes easily with a fork. **Yield:** 4 servings.

Nutritional Analysis: One serving equals 145 calories, 8 g fat (1 g saturated fat), 23 mg cholesterol, 366 mg sodium, 2 g carbohydrate, trace fiber, 17 g protein.
Diabetic Exchange: 4 very lean meat.

Salmon with Orange-Kiwi Salsa

My husband has very selective tastes, so when he raved about this wonderful marinated baked salmon at a dinner party, I knew I had to have the recipe. The citrusy salsa is as pretty as it is tasty.
—Maria Davis, Flower Mound, Texas

1/2 cup white wine *or* chicken broth
1/2 cup unsweetened red grapefruit juice
4 garlic cloves, minced
1 to 2 teaspoons dill weed
4 salmon fillets (6 ounces *each*)
SALSA:
1 cup chopped orange
1 cup chopped kiwifruit
1 large onion, chopped
1 jalapeno pepper, seeded and diced*

In a large resealable plastic bag, combine the first four ingredients; add salmon. Seal bag and turn to coat; refrigerate for 2 hours. In a bowl, combine salsa ingredients. Cover and refrigerate until serving.

Drain marinade and place in a saucepan. Bring to a boil; boil for 1 minute. Place salmon in a 13-in. x 9-in. x 2-in. baking dish. Pour marinade over salmon. Cover and bake at 375° for 20-25 minutes or until fish flakes easily with a fork. Serve with salsa. **Yield:** 4 servings.

***Editor's Note:** When cutting or seeding hot peppers, use rubber or plastic gloves to protect your hands. Avoid touching your face.*

Nutritional Analysis: One serving (1 fillet with 1/2 cup salsa) equals 294 calories, 7 g fat (2 g saturated fat), 80 mg cholesterol, 90 mg sodium, 21 g carbohydrate, 3 g fiber, 36 g protein.
Diabetic Exchanges: 5 very lean meat, 1 fruit, 1 vegetable, 1 fat.

Tuna-Filled Shells

(Pictured above right)

Hot tuna's a hit when you mix it with sizable pasta shells and a cheesy sauce. Dill also complements the fish nicely in this creamy comfort food. It's a great change of pace from the traditional tuna casserole.
—Connie Staal, Greenbrier, Arkansas

12 jumbo pasta shells
5 teaspoons all-purpose flour
2 cups 2% milk
1 teaspoon dill weed
1/2 teaspoon salt
1 celery rib, diced
1 small onion, diced
1 tablespoon canola oil
2 slices white bread, crumbled
1 can (12 ounces) light water-packed tuna, drained and flaked
1/2 cup reduced-fat ranch salad dressing
1/2 cup shredded part-skim mozzarella cheese

Cook pasta shells according to package directions. Meanwhile, in a saucepan, combine the flour, milk, dill and salt until smooth. Bring to a boil; cook and stir for 2 minutes or until thickened. Pour 1-1/4 cups sauce into a 2-qt. baking

dish; set aside.

In a nonstick skillet, saute celery and onion in oil until tender. Add bread. Stir in the tuna, salad dressing and cheese; mix well. Drain shells; stuff with tuna mixture. Place over sauce. Drizzle with remaining sauce. Cover and bake at 350° for 25-30 minutes or until bubbly and heated through. **Yield:** 6 servings.

Nutritional Analysis: One serving (2 filled shells) equals 291 calories, 9 g fat (3 g saturated fat), 34 mg cholesterol, 733 mg sodium, 27 g carbohydrate, 1 g fiber, 24 g protein.
Diabetic Exchanges: 2 starch, 2 lean meat, 1/2 fat.

Caesar Salmon Fillets

Not only is this my husband's favorite meal, but it's a dish dinner guests enjoy as well. The delicate taste is a wonderful reminder that it is as delicious as it is healthy.
—Joan Garneau, Ellenton, Florida

4 salmon fillets (6 ounces *each*)
1/2 cup fat-free Caesar salad dressing
1/4 cup reduced-sodium soy sauce
1 garlic clove, minced

Place salmon fillets in a large resealable plastic bag; add the salad dressing. Seal bag and turn to coat; refrigerate for at least 2 hours.

Drain and discard marinade. Coat grill rack with nonstick cooking spray before starting the grill. Place salmon skin side down on grill rack. Grill, covered, over medium heat for 5 minutes. In a small bowl, combine the soy sauce and garlic; brush over salmon. Grill 10-15 minutes longer or until the fish flakes easily with a fork, basting occasionally. **Yield:** 4 servings.

Nutritional Analysis: One serving (1 fillet) equals 322 calories, 18 g fat (4 g saturated fat), 112 mg cholesterol, 880 mg sodium, 2 g carbohydrate, trace fiber, 35 g protein.
Diabetic Exchange: 5 lean meat.

Sunshine Halibut

(Pictured below)

Seasoned with garlic, onion and citrus, these fish fillets are moist and tasty, and they look especially pretty on a colorful bed of shredded carrots. This delightful main dish tastes like you fussed, but it can be made in a snap.
—Jalayne Luckett, Marion, Illinois

1/3 cup chopped onion
1 garlic clove, minced
2 tablespoons minced fresh parsley
1/2 teaspoon grated orange peel
4 halibut steaks (4 ounces *each*)
1/4 cup orange juice
1 tablespoon lemon juice
1/4 teaspoon salt
1/4 teaspoon lemon-pepper seasoning

In a nonstick skillet coated with nonstick cooking spray, saute onion and garlic until tender; remove from the heat. Stir in parsley and orange peel. Place halibut in an 8-in. square baking dish coated with nonstick cooking spray. Top with onion mixture. Combine orange and lemon juices; pour over fish. Sprinkle with salt and lemon-pepper. Cover and bake at 400° for 15-20 minutes or until fish flakes easily with a fork. **Yield:** 4 servings.

Nutritional Analysis: One serving equals 142 calories, 3 g fat (trace saturated fat), 36 mg cholesterol, 237 mg sodium, 4 g carbohydrate, trace fiber, 24 g protein.
Diabetic Exchanges: 3 very lean meat, 1 vegetable.

Broccoli-Stuffed Sole

(Pictured below)

My husband isn't big on seafood, but he dives into this dish. Lemon enhances the mild-tasting sole, and the broccoli and cheese stuffing makes this fish special enough for company.
—Edna Lee, Greeley, Colorado

   2 tablespoons butter *or* stick margarine, melted
   1 to 2 tablespoons lemon juice
   1 teaspoon salt
1/4 teaspoon pepper
   1 package (10 ounces) frozen chopped broccoli, thawed and drained
   1 cup cooked rice
   1 cup (4 ounces) shredded reduced-fat cheddar cheese
   8 sole *or* whitefish fillets (4 ounces *each*)
Paprika

In a small bowl, combine the butter, lemon juice, salt and pepper. In another bowl, combine the broccoli, rice, cheese and half of the butter mixture. Spoon 1/2 cup onto each fillet. Roll up and place seam side down in a baking dish coated with nonstick cooking spray. Pour remaining butter mixture over roll-ups.

Bake, uncovered, at 350° for 25 minutes or until fish flakes easily with a fork. Baste with pan drippings; sprinkle with paprika. **Yield:** 8 servings.

Nutritional Analysis: *One serving (1 stuffed fillet) equals 190 calories, 6 g fat (3 g saturated fat), 64 mg cholesterol, 478 mg sodium, 8 g carbohydrate, 1 g fiber, 26 g protein.*
Diabetic Exchanges: *3 lean meat, 1 vegetable.*

Creole Catfish Fillets

I rub catfish fillets with a pleasant mixture of seasonings before cooking them quickly on the grill. The moist fish gets plenty of flavor when served with a spicy sauce and fresh lemon wedges.
—Dave Bremstone, Plantation, Florida

   3 tablespoons reduced-fat plain yogurt
   2 tablespoons finely chopped onion
   1 tablespoon fat-free mayonnaise
   1 tablespoon Dijon mustard
   1 tablespoon ketchup
1/2 teaspoon dried thyme
1/4 teaspoon grated lemon peel
   1 teaspoon paprika
1/2 teaspoon onion powder
1/4 teaspoon salt
1/8 teaspoon cayenne pepper
   4 catfish fillets (4 ounces *each*)
   4 lemon wedges

In a bowl, combine the first seven ingredients. Cover and refrigerate until serving. In another bowl, combine the paprika, onion powder, salt and cayenne; rub over both sides of fillets. Grill, covered, in a grill basket coated with nonstick cook-

Tasty Toppings for Fish

- For an easy, delicious and different way to prepare fish, combine fat-free ranch dressing and picante sauce, then spread over the fillets. Wrap them in foil and grill or bake until the fish flakes with a fork. *—Mrs. Russell Bennett, Harlingen, Texas*
- Here's a great way to serve orange roughy. Spread a little prepared mustard over fresh fillets, then sprinkle with Worcestershire sauce and a Cajun seasoning blend. Simply broil or grill them...they taste fabulous.
—Christel Tuba
St. Louis, Missouri

ing spray over medium-hot heat, or broil 6 in. from the heat for 5-6 minutes on each side or until fish flakes easily with a fork. Serve with lemon wedges and yogurt sauce. **Yield:** 4 servings.

Nutritional Analysis: One serving (1 fillet with about 1 tablespoon sauce) equals 182 calories, 9 g fat (2 g saturated fat), 54 mg cholesterol, 382 mg sodium, 5 g carbohydrate, 1 g fiber, 19 g protein.
Diabetic Exchanges: 3 lean meat, 1/2 fat.

Chunky Cod Stir-Fry

Making the most of fish is what this dish is all about! Chunks of cod are nicely accented by a zesty sauce.
—Dorothy Collette, Bourbonnais, Illinois

  2 teaspoons cornstarch
1/3 cup chicken broth
  2 tablespoons sherry *or* additional chicken broth
  2 tablespoons reduced-sodium soy sauce
1/8 teaspoon crushed red pepper flakes
  1 garlic clove, minced
  1 tablespoon canola oil
  1 package (16 ounces) frozen Oriental mixed vegetables, thawed
  1 small sweet red pepper, julienned
  1 pound cod fillets, cut into 1-inch cubes
1/4 cup chopped peanuts
  4 cups hot cooked rice

In a bowl, combine the first five ingredients until blended; set aside. In a nonstick skillet or wok, stir-fry garlic in oil for 30 seconds. Add mixed vegetables; stir-fry for 2 minutes. Add red pepper; stir-fry for 2 minutes or until crisp-tender. Remove and keep warm. Add half of the cod to skillet; gently stir-fry for 3-5 minutes or until fish flakes easily with a fork. Remove and keep warm. Repeat with remaining cod.

Stir reserved broth mixture and add to skillet. Bring to a boil; cook and stir for 2 minutes or until thickened. Return vegetables and fish to the pan. Add peanuts. Gently stir to coat. Cover and cook for 1 minute or until heated through. Serve over rice. **Yield:** 4 servings.

Nutritional Analysis: One serving (1-1/2 cups fish mixture with 1 cup rice) equals 484 calories, 12 g fat (2 g saturated fat), 49 mg cholesterol, 1,117 mg sodium, 62 g carbohydrate, 3 g fiber, 29 g protein.
Diabetic Exchanges: 3 starch, 3 lean meat, 1 vegetable, 1 fat.

Shrimp Kabobs

(Pictured above right)

My family always asks me to prepare these tangy and juicy kabobs during our beach getaways. They fit perfectly with our healthy lifestyle.
—Cheryl Williams, Evington, Virginia

  1 can (8 ounces) tomato sauce
  1 cup chopped onion
1/2 cup water
1/4 cup packed brown sugar
1/4 cup lemon juice

  3 tablespoons Worcestershire sauce
  2 tablespoons canola oil
  2 tablespoons prepared mustard
1/2 teaspoon salt
1/2 teaspoon pepper
  1 can (20 ounces) unsweetened pineapple chunks
  1 pound uncooked medium shrimp, peeled and deveined (about 32)
  1 medium green pepper, cut into chunks
  1 medium onion, cut into chunks
  3 cups hot cooked rice

In a saucepan, combine the first 10 ingredients. Bring to a boil. Reduce heat; simmer, uncovered, for 15 minutes.

Drain pineapple, reserving 2 tablespoons juice (save remaining juice for another use); set pineapple aside. Stir reserved juice into sauce. Pour half into a bowl for basting; cover and refrigerate. Pour remaining sauce into a large resealable plastic bag; add shrimp. Seal bag and turn to coat; refrigerate for 2-3 hours.

Drain and discard marinade. Alternately thread shrimp, pineapple, green pepper and onion on eight metal or soaked wooden skewers.

Coat grill rack with nonstick cooking spray before starting the grill. Grill kabobs, covered, over medium heat for 5 minutes on each side or until shrimp turn pink, basting occasionally with reserved sauce. Serve over rice. **Yield:** 4 servings.

Nutritional Analysis: One serving (2 kabobs with 3/4 cup rice) equals 428 calories, 6 g fat (1 g saturated fat), 161 mg cholesterol, 775 mg sodium, 71 g carbohydrate, 4 g fiber, 23 g protein.
Diabetic Exchanges: 3 lean meat, 2-1/2 starch, 2 vegetable, 1 fruit, 1 fat.

Lime Fish Tacos

(Pictured below)

The secret to getting my family to eat fish is tucked inside these tempting tacos. The tastes and textures in this unusual entree blend in a surprisingly pleasing way. Lime adds a zippy twist to the flaky fillets and the creamy sauce.
—Tammy Hayden, Carmichael, California

1 pound red snapper *or* orange roughy fillets
1 garlic clove, minced
2 tablespoons butter *or* stick margarine
7 teaspoons lime juice, *divided*
1/4 teaspoon white pepper
2 tablespoons reduced-fat sour cream
2 tablespoons fat-free mayonnaise
Dash hot pepper sauce
7 flour tortillas (8 inches), warmed
1 cup shredded lettuce
1 cup chopped fresh tomato

Remove skin from fish and cut fish into 1-in. cubes. In a nonstick skillet, saute garlic in butter and 5 teaspoons lime juice for 30 seconds. Add fish and pepper. Cook for 6-8 minutes over medium heat until fish flakes easily with a fork. Meanwhile, combine the sour cream, mayonnaise, hot pepper sauce and remaining lime juice.

Place a spoonful of fish on each tortilla. Top each with lettuce, tomato and sour cream sauce; fold over. **Yield:** 7 servings.

Nutritional Analysis: *One taco equals 238 calories, 7 g fat (3 g saturated fat), 24 mg cholesterol, 366 mg sodium, 28 g carbohydrate, 1 g fiber, 15 g protein.*
Diabetic Exchanges: *2 starch, 1-1/2 lean meat.*

🍎 In the Limelight

LIKE lemons, their citrusy cousins, limes are too tart to eat on their own—but they add zing to sweet and savory dishes and provide a healthy dose of vitamin C.

Grown in tropical and subtropical climates, two main varieties of limes are widely available. Solid green Persian limes are similar in size and shape to lemons, while Mexican limes are smaller and tarter with thin yellow-green skin. Key limes, a type of Mexican lime, are small and round and produce the juice used in Key lime pie.

One of the most versatile fruit juices for cooking, lime juice gives a lift to marinades for chicken, pork and fish. Since it mixes well with strong flavors, lime is used extensively in Mexican cooking—in soups, salads and seafood dishes. In addition, lime is sublime in beverages, marmalades, desserts and ice cream.

Look for brightly colored, smooth-skinned limes that are firm and unblemished. They can be refrigerated for up to 2 weeks. Sweetened or unsweetened, bottled or frozen lime juice is available in most grocery stores.

Marinated Orange Roughy

This recipe—from a seafood cookbook my husband bought me before we were married—is a longtime favorite. I have literally worn out the page it's printed on. The citrus-flavored fillets are broiled to a golden brown...then topped with toasted sesame seeds for a fun crunch.
—Robin Guth, Endicott, New York

1-1/2 pounds orange roughy *or* other whitefish fillets
1/2 cup orange juice
1/4 cup ketchup
2 tablespoons canola oil
2 tablespoons reduced-sodium soy sauce
2 tablespoons lemon juice
1/4 teaspoon pepper
1 tablespoon sesame seeds, toasted

Cut fillets into four pieces if necessary; set aside. In a bowl, combine the orange juice, ketchup, oil, soy sauce, lemon juice and pepper; mix well. Remove 1/4 cup for basting; cover and refrigerate. Pour remaining marinade into a large resealable plastic bag; add fillets. Seal bag and turn to coat; refrigerate for 2 hours, turning once or twice.

Drain and discard marinade. Place fillets on a broiler pan coated with nonstick cooking spray. Broil 4-6 in. from the heat for 5-6 minutes on each side or until fish flakes easily with a fork, basting occasionally with reserved marinade. Sprinkle with sesame seeds. **Yield:** 4 servings.

Nutritional Analysis: *One serving equals 181 calories, 5 g fat (trace saturated fat), 34 mg cholesterol, 349 mg sodium, 4 g carbohydrate, trace fiber, 25 g protein.*
Diabetic Exchanges: *4 very lean meat, 1 fat.*

Meatless Main Dishes

You won't find any meat in these main dishes
...but you won't miss it either. This hearty
vegetarian fare is so delightfully satisfying,
even your most ardent meat-and-potatoes
lovers will give it rave reviews.

Roasted Red Pepper Lasagna (page 176)

Black Bean Enchiladas

(Pictured above)

Picante sauce gives lots of zip to the tasty filling in these meatless enchiladas from our Test Kitchen. Each generous serving is packed with fresh-tasting ingredients—and fiber, too.

1 large onion, chopped
1 medium green pepper, chopped
2 tablespoons chicken broth
2 cans (15 ounces *each*) black beans, rinsed and drained, *divided*
1-1/2 cups picante sauce, *divided*
12 flour tortillas (6 inches)
2 medium tomatoes, chopped
1/2 cup shredded reduced-fat cheddar cheese
1/2 cup shredded part-skim mozzarella cheese
3 cups shredded lettuce
6 tablespoons fat-free sour cream

In a nonstick skillet, cook and stir onion and green pepper in broth for 2-3 minutes or until tender. Mash one can of black beans. Add to the skillet with 3/4 cup of picante sauce and remaining beans; heat through.

Spoon 1/4 cup mixture down the center of each tortilla. Roll up and place, seam side down, in a 13-in. x 9-in. x 2-in. baking dish coated with nonstick cooking spray. Combine tomatoes and remaining picante sauce; spoon over enchiladas.

Cover and bake at 350° for 15 minutes. Uncover; sprinkle with cheeses. Bake 5 minutes longer. To serve, place 1/2 cup lettuce on each plate and top with two enchiladas. Garnish each serving with 1 tablespoon sour cream. **Yield:** 6 servings.

Nutritional Analysis: One serving (2 enchiladas) equals 404 calories, 9 g fat (1 g saturated), 7 mg cholesterol, 1,477 mg sodium, 60 g carbohydrate, 9 g fiber, 21 g protein.
Diabetic Exchanges: 3 lean meat, 2-1/2 starch, 1 fat.

Roasted Red Pepper Lasagna

(Pictured on page 175)

A friend gave me this recipe, and it quickly became a family favorite. It's rich and creamy, and the roasted red peppers give it such a wonderful flavor.
—Deborah Johnson, Cody, Wyoming

4 medium sweet red peppers
9 lasagna noodles
4 garlic cloves, minced
1 tablespoon olive *or* canola oil
1 can (28 ounces) crushed tomatoes
2 tablespoons minced fresh parsley
1 teaspoon sugar
1 teaspoon dried basil
1/2 teaspoon pepper
1/4 cup butter *or* stick margarine
1/3 cup all-purpose flour
1/2 teaspoon salt
1/4 teaspoon ground nutmeg
2-1/2 cups fat-free milk
1 cup shredded Parmesan cheese

Cut each pepper into quarters; remove seeds. Place peppers, cut side down, on a foil-lined baking sheet. Broil 4 in. from the heat for 20-25 minutes or until skin is blistered and blackened. Immediately place peppers in a bowl; cover and let stand for 15-20 minutes. Peel off and discard skin. Cut peppers into 1/4-in. strips.

Cook lasagna noodles according to package directions; drain. In a saucepan, cook red peppers and garlic in oil for 1 minute; add the tomatoes, parsley, sugar, basil and pepper. Simmer, uncovered, for 20 minutes. In a saucepan, melt butter. Stir in flour, salt and nutmeg until smooth. Gradually add milk. Bring to a boil; cook and stir for 2 minutes or until thickened.

Spread 1 cup pepper sauce in a 13-in. x 9-in. x 2-in. baking dish coated with nonstick cooking spray. Top with three noodles, 1-1/2 cups pepper sauce, 1 cup white sauce and 1/3 cup Parmesan cheese. Repeat layers. Top with remaining noodles, white sauce and pepper sauce. Bake, uncovered, at 350° for 30-35 minutes or until bubbly. Sprinkle with remaining cheese. Let stand for 15 minutes before cutting. **Yield:** 9 pieces.

Nutritional Analysis: One piece equals 229 calories, 8 g fat (5 g saturated fat), 19 mg cholesterol, 386 mg sodium, 31 g carbohydrate, 3 g fiber, 9 g protein.
Diabetic Exchanges: 2 starch, 1 lean meat, 1/2 fat.

Pasta Primavera

Generous servings of this pretty pasta toss are sure to fill up your family. Broccoli, peppers, squash and more provide the lively color.
—Beverly Little, Marietta, Georgia

8 ounces uncooked linguine
1 medium carrot, thinly sliced
1/2 cup chopped onion
1/2 cup julienned sweet red pepper

Fat Substitutions

IT CAN take a little experimenting on your part, but if you're patient, you'll find that there are some good alternatives to the traditional fat that's called for in most recipes.

Once you find a suitable substitute, be sure to mark your recipe card so you'll remember what worked well the next time you prepare that dish.

- Try replacing part of the oil and fat called for in recipes with applesauce.
- Plain low-fat yogurt and reduced-fat sour cream are great stand-ins for sour cream.
- Consider substituting buttermilk or 2% milk for whole milk or cream.
- When sauteing meat and vegetables, use chicken or vegetable broth, apple juice, flavored vinegar, water or wine in place of the butter, margarine or cooking oil.
- In some recipes, you can just add less fat than the recipe calls for. Start by cutting the butter, margarine or oil in half, then reduce it a little more the next time you make the recipe.

1/2 cup julienned sweet yellow pepper
1 medium zucchini, thinly sliced
1 medium yellow summer squash, thinly sliced
1 cup broccoli florets
1 pound thin fresh asparagus, cut into 3-inch pieces
8 ounces fresh mushrooms, sliced
1/3 cup all-purpose flour
2 cups cold water
2 teaspoons chicken bouillon granules
1/2 cup white wine *or* chicken broth
1/4 teaspoon salt
1/4 cup minced fresh basil *or* 4 teaspoons dried basil
6 tablespoons grated Parmesan cheese

Cook pasta according to package directions. Meanwhile, in a nonstick skillet coated with nonstick cooking spray, combine carrot, onion, peppers, zucchini, summer squash and broccoli. Cover and cook over medium-low heat for 10 minutes. Add asparagus and mushrooms; cook 5 minutes longer.

In a saucepan, combine flour and water until smooth. Add the bouillon. Bring to a boil; cook and stir for 2 minutes or until slightly thickened. Add wine or broth and salt; stir well. Pour over vegetables. Drain pasta and add to vegetable mixture. Add basil; toss to coat. Sprinkle with Parmesan cheese. **Yield:** 6 servings.

Nutritional Analysis: *One serving (1-1/2 cups) equals 168 calories, 3 g fat (1 g saturated fat), 5 mg cholesterol, 614 mg sodium, 26 g carbohydrate, 4 g fiber, 9 g protein.*
Diabetic Exchanges: *2 vegetable, 1-1/2 starch.*

Fresh Marinara Sauce

(Pictured below)

My family loves this zesty meatless sauce served over bow tie pasta. When tomatoes and carrots are ripe and plentiful, I double the recipe and store it in the freezer for future use.
—Martha Robinson, Homer, Michigan

3 large carrots, finely chopped
2 large onions, chopped
6 garlic cloves, minced
1/3 cup olive *or* canola oil
15 medium tomatoes (about 6 pounds), peeled and chopped
1/3 cup chopped fresh basil *or* 2 tablespoons dried basil
3 tablespoons chopped fresh oregano *or* 1 tablespoon dried oregano
1-1/2 teaspoons salt
1/4 teaspoon pepper
7 cups hot cooked penne *or* bow tie pasta

In a large saucepan or Dutch oven, saute the carrots, onions and garlic in oil until tender. Add the tomatoes and seasonings; bring to a boil. Reduce heat; simmer, uncovered, for 1 to 1-1/2 hours or until thickened and reduced by half, stirring occasionally. Serve over pasta. **Yield:** 7 servings.

Nutritional Analysis: *One serving (1 cup sauce with 1 cup pasta) equals 400 calories, 12 g fat (2 g saturated fat), 0 cholesterol, 558 mg sodium, 65 g carbohydrate, 7 g fiber, 11 g protein.*
Diabetic Exchanges: *3 starch, 2-1/2 vegetable, 2 fat.*

Zucchini Crust Pizza

(Pictured above)

My mother-in-law shared the recipe for this unique pizza with me. Its quiche-like zucchini crust makes it just right for brunch, lunch or a light supper.
—*Ruth Denomme, Englehart, Ontario*

3 cups shredded zucchini
3/4 cup egg substitute
1/3 cup all-purpose flour
1/2 teaspoon salt
2 cups (8 ounces) shredded part-skim mozzarella cheese
2 small tomatoes, halved and thinly sliced
1/2 cup chopped onion
1/2 cup julienned green pepper
1 teaspoon dried oregano
1/2 teaspoon dried basil
3 tablespoons shredded Parmesan cheese

In a bowl, combine zucchini and egg substitute; mix well. Add flour and salt; stir well. Spread onto the bottom of a 12-in. pizza pan coated with nonstick cooking spray. Bake at 450° for 8 minutes. Reduce heat to 350°. Sprinkle with mozzarella, tomatoes, onion, green pepper, oregano, basil and Parmesan cheese. Bake for 15-20 minutes or until onion is tender and cheese is melted. **Yield:** 6 slices.

Nutritional Analysis: One slice equals 190 calories, 8 g fat (5 g saturated fat), 24 mg cholesterol, 431 mg sodium, 13 g carbohydrate, 2 g fiber, 17 g protein.
Diabetic Exchanges: 2 lean meat, 2 vegetable, 1/2 fat.

Three-Bean Cassoulet

Brimming with a trio of bean varieties, this recipe is as easy as one, two, three. You can serve it as a satisfying meatless main dish or on the side.
—*Carol Berigan, Golden, Colorado*

2 cans (14-1/2 ounces *each*) stewed tomatoes
1 can (19 ounces) garbanzo beans *or* chickpeas, rinsed and drained
1 can (15-1/2 ounces) great northern beans, rinsed and drained
1 can (15 ounces) butter beans, rinsed and drained
1 cup finely chopped carrots
1 cup finely chopped onion
2 garlic cloves, minced
1 bay leaf
2 teaspoons dried parsley flakes
1 teaspoon dried basil
1/2 teaspoon dried thyme
1/2 teaspoon salt
1/8 teaspoon pepper

In an ungreased 3-qt. baking dish, combine all ingredients. Cover and bake at 350° for 60-70 minutes or until vegetables are tender, stirring occasionally. Discard bay leaf before serving. **Yield:** 9 servings.

Nutritional Analysis: One serving (3/4 cup) equals 197 calories, 1 g fat (trace saturated fat), 0 cholesterol, 687 mg sodium, 41 g carbohydrate, 9 g fiber, 10 g protein.
Diabetic Exchanges: 2 starch, 2 vegetable.

Tasty Lentil Tacos

(Pictured below)

When my husband's cholesterol numbers rose,
I quickly lowered the fat in our family's diet.
Finding dishes that were healthy for him and yummy
for our five children was a challenge. This fun
taco recipe was a huge hit with everyone.
—Michelle Thomas, Bangor, Maine

```
   1 cup finely chopped onion
   1 garlic clove, minced
   1 teaspoon canola oil
   1 cup dry lentils, rinsed
   1 tablespoon chili powder
   2 teaspoons ground cumin
   1 teaspoon dried oregano
2-1/2 cups chicken broth
   1 cup salsa
  12 taco shells
1-1/2 cups shredded lettuce
   1 cup chopped fresh tomato
1-1/2 cups (6 ounces) shredded reduced-fat cheddar
     cheese
   6 tablespoons fat-free sour cream
```

In a large nonstick skillet, saute the onion and garlic in oil until tender. Add the lentils, chili powder, cumin and oregano; cook and stir for 1 minute. Add broth; bring to a boil. Reduce heat; cover and simmer for 25-30 minutes or until the lentils are tender. Uncover; cook for 6-8 minutes or until mixture is thickened. Mash lentils slightly. Stir in salsa. Spoon about 1/4 cup into each taco shell. Top with lettuce, tomato, cheese and sour cream. **Yield:** 6 servings.

Nutritional Analysis: One serving (2 tacos) equals 364 calories, 11 g fat (4 g saturated fat), 17 mg cholesterol, 815 mg sodium, 45 g carbohydrate, 9 g fiber, 22 g protein.
Diabetic Exchanges: 2-1/2 lean meat, 2 starch, 1-1/2 fat.

The Lowdown on Lentils

- The lentil is a cousin of the bean, and both are part of the legume family.
- Lentils are shaped like a lens. In fact, "lens" is the Latin word for lentil.
- Choose plump-looking lentils. Discard if they are shriveled or spotted.
- Drain off cooking liquid as soon as lentils are done or they'll continue to cook.

Meatless Spaghetti Sauce

Garden vegetables and a generous sprinkling
of herbs liven up this spaghetti sauce.
—Bruce Emery, Huntington Beach, California

```
   2 cups diced onions
   2 cups diced green peppers
   1 cup diced celery
   2 garlic cloves, minced
   1 tablespoon olive or canola oil
   4 cups diced fresh tomatoes
   2 cups sliced fresh mushrooms
   1 can (15 ounces) tomato sauce
   2 cans (6 ounces each) tomato paste
1/2 cup burgundy wine or water
   2 tablespoons sugar
   1 tablespoon red wine vinegar or cider vinegar
   2 tablespoons minced fresh basil or 2 teaspoons
     dried basil
   1 tablespoon minced fresh oregano or 1
     teaspoon dried oregano
   1 tablespoon minced fresh parsley
   1 bay leaf
   1 teaspoon salt
   1 teaspoon dried rosemary, crushed
1/4 teaspoon pepper
  10 cups hot cooked spaghetti
```

In a large soup kettle or Dutch oven, saute the onions, green peppers, celery and garlic in oil until tender. Add the tomatoes, mushrooms, tomato sauce, tomato paste, wine or water, sugar, vinegar and seasonings. Bring to a boil. Reduce heat; cover and simmer for 1-1/2 hours. Discard bay leaf. Serve over spaghetti. **Yield:** 10 servings.

Nutritional Analysis: One serving (3/4 cup sauce with 1 cup spaghetti) equals 320 calories, 3 g fat (trace saturated fat), 0 cholesterol, 536 mg sodium, 63 g carbohydrate, 7 g fiber, 11 g protein.
Diabetic Exchanges: 2-1/2 starch, 2-1/2 vegetable, 1 lean meat.

Angel Hair Pasta with Garden Vegetables

(Pictured below)

This family favorite is especially fun to make when the garden is full of fresh vegetables. It's quick to fix, delicious and always different—just choose the vegetables that have ripened that day!
—June Barrus, Springville, Utah

8 ounces uncooked angel hair pasta
1 cup *each* snow peas, sliced fresh mushrooms and thinly sliced carrots
1 cup chopped sweet yellow, red *or* green pepper
1/3 cup chopped fresh basil
2 garlic cloves, minced
2 tablespoons olive *or* canola oil
2 teaspoons cornstarch
1 cup chicken broth
1/4 teaspoon salt
3 medium tomatoes, peeled and chopped
1/4 cup grated Parmesan cheese

Cook pasta according to package directions. Meanwhile, in a nonstick skillet, saute the snow peas, mushrooms, carrots, yellow pepper, basil and garlic in oil for 2-3 minutes. Combine cornstarch, broth and salt until smooth; stir into the vegetable mixture. Bring to a boil. Reduce heat; cook and stir for 3-5 minutes or until vegetables are crisp-tender.

Remove from the heat; stir in tomatoes. Drain pasta; divide between four plates. Top with vegetable mixture; sprinkle with Parmesan cheese. **Yield:** 4 servings.

***Nutritional Analysis:** One serving (2 cups) equals 333 calories, 11 g fat (2 g saturated fat), 5 mg cholesterol, 714 mg sodium, 49 g carbohydrate, 5 g fiber, 14 g protein.*
***Diabetic Exchanges:** 2 starch, 2 vegetable, 1-1/2 fat, 1 lean meat.*

Very Veggie Lasagna

People often tell me you can't call something "lasagna" if it doesn't have meat. Then they try this dish and ask for the recipe.
—Kim Bender, Aurora, Colorado

2 cups (16 ounces) 1% cottage cheese
1 carton (15 ounces) reduced-fat ricotta cheese
2 tablespoons minced fresh parsley
1 jar (26 ounces) meatless spaghetti sauce
9 uncooked lasagna noodles
2 medium carrots, shredded
1-1/2 cups broccoli florets
4 ounces fresh mushrooms, sliced
1 small zucchini, thinly sliced
1 small yellow summer squash, thinly sliced
2 cups fresh spinach
2 cups (8 ounces) shredded part-skim mozzarella cheese

In a bowl, combine the cottage cheese, ricotta and parsley. Spread 1/2 cup spaghetti sauce in a 13-in. x 9-in. x 2-in. baking dish coated with nonstick cooking spray. Top with three noodles and a third of the cheese mixture. Sprinkle with half of the carrots, broccoli, mushrooms, zucchini and squash. Top with a third of the remaining sauce.

Arrange half of the spinach over spaghetti sauce; sprinkle with a third of the mozzarella cheese. Repeat layers of noodles, cheese mixture, vegetables, sauce, spinach and mozzarella. Top with the remaining noodles, cheese mixture, sauce and mozzarella.

Cover tightly and bake at 350° for 45 minutes. Uncover; bake 15 minutes longer or until noodles are tender. Let stand for 15 minutes before cutting. **Yield:** 12 servings.

***Nutritional Analysis:** One serving (1 piece) equals 234 calories, 7 g fat (4 g saturated fat), 26 mg cholesterol, 572 mg sodium, 25 g carbohydrate, 4 g fiber, 19 g protein.*
***Diabetic Exchanges:** 2 lean meat, 1-1/2 starch.*

Mushroom Broccoli Pizza

(Pictured above right)

I wouldn't say I'm a vegetarian, but I do like meatless entrees. Since I enjoy gardening, I often cook with homegrown veggies.
—Kathleen Kelly, Days Creek, Oregon

1 package (1/4 ounce) active dry yeast
3/4 cup warm water (110° to 115°)
1 teaspoon olive *or* canola oil
1/2 teaspoon sugar
1/2 cup whole wheat flour
1/2 teaspoon salt
1-1/2 cups all-purpose flour
TOPPINGS:
3 cups broccoli florets
1 cup sliced fresh mushrooms
1/4 cup chopped onion
4 garlic cloves, minced
1 tablespoon olive *or* canola oil
1/2 cup pizza sauce

Bean and Veggie Pitas

A zippy Dijon dressing pulls together the satisfying flavors in this Tex-Mex treat. My husband, Eric, loves it! We like to top these sandwiches with a bit of shredded cheddar cheese.
—*Renée Flott, Emporia, Kansas*

    2 cups thinly sliced red cabbage
1-1/2 cups canned red beans, rinsed and drained
    1 can (10 ounces) diced tomatoes and green
        chilies, drained
    1 cup fresh *or* frozen corn
  1/2 cup diced zucchini
  1/2 cup diced yellow summer squash
  1/4 cup finely chopped onion
    1 tablespoon minced fresh cilantro *or* parsley
    1 tablespoon lime juice
DIJON DRESSING:
    3 tablespoons olive *or* canola oil
    3 tablespoons red wine vinegar *or* cider vinegar
    3 tablespoons Dijon mustard
    2 tablespoons honey
    1 tablespoon lime juice
  1/4 teaspoon garlic powder
  1/4 teaspoon salt
  1/4 teaspoon ground cumin
  1/8 teaspoon cayenne pepper
    6 whole wheat pitas (6 inches), halved
   12 lettuce leaves

In a bowl, combine the first nine ingredients; set aside. In a jar with tight-fitting lid, combine the oil, vinegar, mustard, honey, lime juice, garlic powder, salt, cumin and cayenne; shake well. Line pita halves with lettuce; fill each with about 1/3 cup vegetable mixture. Drizzle with dressing. **Yield:** 6 servings.

Nutritional Analysis: One serving (2 filled pita halves with about 1-1/2 tablespoons dressing) equals 464 calories, 10 g fat (1 g saturated fat), 0 cholesterol, 885 mg sodium, 81 g carbohydrate, 7 g fiber, 20 g protein.
Diabetic Exchanges: 3 starch, 2 lean meat, 2 fat, 1 vegetable.

    4 plum tomatoes, sliced lengthwise
  1/4 cup chopped fresh basil
1-1/2 cups (6 ounces) shredded part-skim mozzarella
        cheese
  1/3 cup shredded Parmesan cheese

In a bowl, dissolve yeast in warm water. Add oil and sugar; mix well. Combine the whole wheat flour and salt; stir into yeast mixture until smooth. Stir in enough all-purpose flour to form a soft dough. Turn onto a floured surface; knead until smooth and elastic, about 6-8 minutes. Place in a greased bowl, turning once to grease top. Cover and let rise in a warm place until doubled, about 1-1/2 hours.

Punch dough down. Press onto the bottom and 1 in. up the sides of a 12-in. pizza pan coated with nonstick cooking spray. Prick dough several times with a fork. Bake at 425° for 6-8 minutes.

In a saucepan, bring 1 in. of water to a boil. Place broccoli in a steamer basket over water; cover and steam for 5-6 minutes or until crisp-tender. Transfer broccoli to a colander. Rinse with cold water; drain and set aside.

In a nonstick skillet, saute mushrooms, onion and garlic in oil until mushrooms are tender. Spread pizza sauce over crust. Sprinkle with mushroom mixture. Arrange tomatoes and broccoli on top. Sprinkle with basil and cheeses. Bake at 425° for 12-14 minutes or until crust is golden and cheese is melted. **Yield:** 6 slices.

Nutritional Analysis: One serving (1 slice) equals 283 calories, 9 g fat (4 g saturated fat), 19 mg cholesterol, 492 mg sodium, 39 g carbohydrate, 4 g fiber, 15 g protein.
Diabetic Exchanges: 2 starch, 2 lean meat, 1/2 fat.

Drain spaghetti; add to tomato mixture and toss to coat. Sprinkle with mozzarella cheese, basil and Parmesan; toss. Spoon into peppers. Place in a 3-qt. microwave-safe baking dish. Cover and microwave on high for 3-5 minutes or until heated through. **Yield:** 6 servings.

Editor's Note: This recipe was tested in an 850-watt microwave.

Nutritional Analysis: One serving (1 filled pepper) equals 172 calories, 6 g fat (3 g saturated fat), 10 mg cholesterol, 645 mg sodium, 23 g carbohydrate, 4 g fiber, 9 g protein.

Diabetic Exchanges: 2 vegetable, 1 starch, 1 fat.

Five-Veggie Stir-Fry

An assortment of vegetables sprouts up in this marvelous medley. Orange juice lends a hint of citrus to the mildly seasoned sauce.
—Rachel Thompson, Midlothian, Virginia

    2 tablespoons cornstarch
    2 tablespoons sugar
1/2 teaspoon ground ginger
    1 cup orange juice
1/4 cup reduced-sodium soy sauce
    2 garlic cloves, minced
    2 large carrots, sliced
    2 cups broccoli florets
    2 cups cauliflowerets
    4 teaspoons olive *or* canola oil, *divided*
    1 cup quartered fresh mushrooms
    1 cup fresh *or* frozen snow peas
    4 cups hot cooked rice

In a small bowl, combine the cornstarch, sugar and ginger. Stir in orange juice, soy sauce and garlic until blended; set aside. In a nonstick skillet or wok, stir-fry the carrots, broccoli and cauliflower in 3 teaspoons of oil for 4-5 minutes. Add mushrooms, peas and remaining oil; stir-fry for 3 minutes. Stir orange juice mixture and add to the pan. Bring to a boil; cook and stir until thickened. Serve over rice. **Yield:** 4 servings.

Nutritional Analysis: One serving (1 cup vegetable mixture with 1 cup rice) equals 382 calories, 5 g fat (1 g saturated fat), 0 cholesterol, 648 mg sodium, 74 g carbohydrate, 3 g fiber, 9 g protein.

Diabetic Exchanges: 3 starch, 2 vegetable, 1 lean meat, 1 fat.

Pasta-Filled Peppers

(Pictured above)

Pretty bell peppers provide a rainbow of colorful "cups" for serving up this fresh-tasting tomato-herb pasta dish. Spaghetti noodles are the unusual "stuffing" ingredient in the recipe. I managed to make a lighter version of a family favorite that's as tasty as the original.
—Connie Krause, Virginia Beach, Virginia

    6 medium sweet red, green *or* yellow peppers
    6 ounces uncooked spaghetti
3/4 cup diced onion
    2 garlic cloves, minced
    2 teaspoons canola oil
1-3/4 cups diced fresh tomatoes
    1 tablespoon all-purpose flour
3/4 teaspoon salt
1-1/4 cups chicken broth
3/4 cup shredded part-skim mozzarella cheese
1/4 cup minced fresh basil
    3 tablespoons grated Parmesan cheese

Place whole peppers on a broiler pan; broil 6 in. from the heat for 10-15 minutes or until skins are blistered and blackened, turning often. Immediately place peppers in a bowl; cover and let stand for 10 minutes. Peel off and discard charred skins. Carefully cut tops off peppers and discard; remove seeds. Set peppers aside.

Cook spaghetti according to package directions. Meanwhile, in a large nonstick skillet, saute onion and garlic in oil until tender. Add tomatoes; cook for 1 minute. In a bowl, combine flour, salt and broth until smooth. Stir into tomato mixture. Bring to a boil; cook and stir for 1 minute or until slightly thickened.

Vegetarian Jambalaya

This make-ahead main or side dish has all the flavor and boldness of traditional jambalaya. If there's any left over, roll it up in a flour tortilla and add your favorite topping.
—LynnMarie Frucci, Pullman, Washington

1 medium onion, finely chopped
1 cup chopped celery
1 cup chopped green pepper
1 cup sliced fresh mushrooms
2 garlic cloves, minced
1 teaspoon olive *or* canola oil
3 cups chopped fresh tomatoes
2 cups water
1 cup uncooked long grain rice
2 tablespoons reduced-sodium soy sauce
1 tablespoon minced fresh parsley
1/4 teaspoon salt
1/4 teaspoon paprika
1/8 teaspoon cayenne pepper
1/8 teaspoon chili powder
1/8 teaspoon pepper
6 tablespoons reduced-fat sour cream

In a large nonstick skillet, saute the onion, celery, green pepper, mushrooms and garlic in oil until tender. Stir in the tomatoes, water, rice, soy sauce, parsley, salt, paprika, cayenne, chili powder and pepper.

Transfer to a 2-1/2-qt. baking dish coated with nonstick cooking spray. Cover and bake at 350° for 65-70 minutes or until rice is tender and liquid is absorbed. Top each serving with 1 tablespoon sour cream. **Yield:** 6 servings.

Nutritional Analysis: One serving (1 cup) equals 187 calories, 3 g fat (1 g saturated fat), 5 mg cholesterol, 339 mg sodium, 36 g carbohydrate, 3 g fiber, 5 g protein.
Diabetic Exchanges: 2 vegetable, 1-1/2 starch, 1/2 fat.

Roasted Vegetable Ziti Bake

(Pictured at right)

This fresh-tasting and well-seasoned entree is a real crowd-pleaser. I combine roasted vegetables, zesty sauce and just the right touch of melted cheese to create this pasta dish, which is deliciously filling.
—Helen Carpenter, Albuquerque, New Mexico

1 pound eggplant, peeled and cut into 1-inch cubes
1 large red onion, cut into 1-inch pieces
2 medium sweet yellow peppers, cut into 1-inch pieces
1 tablespoon olive *or* canola oil
1/2 teaspoon salt
SAUCE:
1-1/2 cups chopped onions
2 teaspoons olive *or* canola oil
6 garlic cloves, minced
1/2 teaspoon crushed red pepper flakes
1/2 teaspoon fennel seed, crushed
1 can (28 ounces) crushed tomatoes
1 can (14-1/2 ounces) diced tomatoes, undrained
1/4 cup minced fresh parsley
1-1/4 teaspoons salt
1/2 teaspoon pepper
1/4 teaspoon sugar
1/8 teaspoon dried thyme
1 package (16 ounces) ziti *or* other small tube pasta
4 cups chopped fresh spinach
1 cup (4 ounces) shredded part-skim mozzarella cheese

In a 15-in. x 10-in. x 1-in. baking pan coated with nonstick cooking spray, combine the eggplant, red onion and yellow peppers. Drizzle with oil; sprinkle with salt. Bake, uncovered, at 400° for 35-45 minutes or until edges of peppers begin to brown, stirring every 10 minutes.

Meanwhile, in a saucepan, saute onions in oil until tender. Add garlic, red pepper flakes and fennel; cook and stir for 1 minute. Add the tomatoes, parsley, salt, pepper, sugar and thyme. Bring to a boil. Reduce heat; simmer, uncovered, for 15 minutes. Cook pasta according to package directions; drain.

In two greased 2-qt. baking dishes, spread 1/2 cup sauce each. In each dish, layer a fourth of the pasta, a fourth of the roasted vegetables and 1/2 cup sauce. Top with 2 cups spinach and 1/2 cup sauce. Top with remaining roasted vegetables, pasta and sauce.

Cover and bake at 350° for 30 minutes. Uncover; sprinkle with cheese. Bake 10-15 minutes longer or until heated through and cheese is melted. **Yield:** 12 servings.

Nutritional Analysis: One serving (1 cup) equals 230 calories, 5 g fat (1 g saturated fat), 5 mg cholesterol, 497 mg sodium, 40 g carbohydrate, 4 g fiber, 10 g protein.
Diabetic Exchanges: 2 starch, 2 vegetable, 1 fat.

Meatless Lasagna

This saucy lasagna is one of my specialties. It's packed with fresh-tasting vegetables, such as zucchini, mushrooms, carrots and peppers. The colorful casserole is a great way to celebrate the bounty of summertime.
—Sharon Allen, Allentown, Pennsylvania

  9 uncooked lasagna noodles
1/2 cup chopped onion
  2 garlic cloves, minced
  2 cups diced zucchini
1-1/2 cups sliced fresh mushrooms
  1 cup thinly sliced carrots
1/2 cup diced green pepper
1/2 cup diced sweet red pepper
  1 can (28 ounces) crushed tomatoes
1-1/2 cups water
  1 can (6 ounces) tomato paste
  1 teaspoon sugar
  1 teaspoon dried basil
1/2 teaspoon salt
1/2 teaspoon dried rosemary, crushed
1/4 teaspoon pepper
  1 carton (15 ounces) reduced-fat ricotta cheese
1-1/2 cups (6 ounces) shredded part-skim mozzarella cheese, *divided*
1/4 cup grated Romano cheese

Cook lasagna noodles according to package directions. Meanwhile, in a large saucepan coated with nonstick cooking spray, saute onion and garlic for 3 minutes. Add the zucchini, mushrooms, carrots and peppers; cook and stir until tender, about 5 minutes. Stir in the tomatoes, water, tomato paste and seasonings. Bring to a boil. Reduce heat; cover and simmer for 20 minutes. Remove 2 cups sauce and set aside.

Drain noodles; set aside. Combine the ricotta, 1 cup mozzarella and Romano cheese. In an ungreased 13-in. x 9-in. x 2-in. baking dish, layer a third of the remaining sauce, three noodles and half of the cheese mixture. Repeat layers. Top with remaining sauce and noodles. Spread reserved sauce over top.

Cover and bake at 350° for 45 minutes. Uncover; sprinkle with remaining mozzarella. Bake 5-10 minutes longer or until cheese is melted. Let stand for 15 minutes before cutting. **Yield:** 8 servings.

Nutritional Analysis: One piece equals 244 calories, 9 g fat (5 g saturated fat), 32 mg cholesterol, 672 mg sodium, 26 g carbohydrate, 4 g fiber, 17 g protein.
Diabetic Exchanges: *2 vegetable, 2 lean meat, 1 starch.*

Meatless Meat Exchanges

WONDERING WHY we list meat in the Diabetic Exchanges in this chapter when we feature only meatless recipes here?

When our registered dietitians calculate the meat exchanges in recipes, they are referring to protein foods. One meat exchange is equal to about 7 grams of protein. Other forms of protein that are calculated as "meat exchanges" include cheeses, eggs, beans, peas, lentils, etc.

That's why you'll sometimes see meat exchanges listed, even though all the recipes are meatless.

Citrus Veggie Stir-Fry

(Pictured at right)

Crunchy cashews and a citrus-seasoned sauce will stir your appetite for this colorful vegetable medley. My husband requests the meatless entree often, so it's on the menu at least once a month.
—Dorothy Swanson, St. Louis, Missouri

  1 tablespoon cornstarch
  1 cup orange juice
  2 tablespoons balsamic vinegar
  2 garlic cloves, minced
  1 teaspoon grated orange peel
1/2 teaspoon ground ginger
1/8 teaspoon hot pepper sauce
  1 cup sliced carrots
  1 cup julienned sweet red pepper
  1 cup julienned green pepper
  1 tablespoon canola oil
  1 cup sliced fresh mushrooms
  2 cups fresh *or* frozen snow peas
1/2 cup sliced green onions
1/3 cup salted cashews
  4 cups hot cooked rice

In a bowl, combine the first seven ingredients until blended; set aside. In a large nonstick skillet or wok, stir-fry carrots and peppers in oil for 5 minutes. Add mushrooms and snow peas; stir-fry for 6 minutes. Add green onions; stir-fry for 3 minutes or until the vegetables are crisp-tender.

Stir orange juice mixture and add to pan. Bring to a boil; cook and stir for 2 minutes or until thickened. Stir in cashews. Serve with rice. **Yield:** 4 servings.

Nutritional Analysis: One serving (1 cup vegetable mixture with 1 cup rice) equals 400 calories, 10 g fat (1 g saturated fat), 0 cholesterol, 97 mg sodium, 71 g carbohydrate, 5 g fiber, 9 g protein.
Diabetic Exchanges: *4 starch, 2 vegetable, 1/2 fat.*

Linguine with Fresh Tomatoes

(Pictured at right)

This garlic and basil pasta recipe is a wonderful way to use your bounty of late-summer tomatoes. Ideal as a light supper when coupled with salad and breadsticks, it also makes a great side dish for grilled chicken.
—Susan Jones, Downers Grove, Illinois

8 ounces uncooked linguine
3 medium tomatoes, chopped
6 green onions, sliced
1/2 cup grated Parmesan cheese
1/4 cup minced fresh basil *or* 4 teaspoons dried basil
2 garlic cloves, minced
1 teaspoon salt
1/2 teaspoon pepper
3 tablespoons butter *or* stick margarine

Cook pasta according to package directions. Meanwhile, in a large serving bowl, combine the tomatoes, onions, Parmesan cheese, basil, garlic, salt and pepper. Drain pasta and toss with butter. Add to tomato mixture; toss to coat. **Yield:** 6 servings.

Nutritional Analysis: One serving (1 cup) equals 211 calories, 9 g fat (5 g saturated fat), 22 mg cholesterol, 680 mg sodium, 26 g carbohydrate, 2 g fiber, 8 g protein.
Diabetic Exchanges: 2 fat, 1-1/2 starch.

Nutritional Analysis: One serving (1 cup) equals 289 calories, 7 g fat (4 g saturated fat), 21 mg cholesterol, 535 mg sodium, 34 g carbohydrate, 15 g fiber, 26 g protein.
Diabetic Exchanges: 2 starch, 2 lean meat, 1/2 fat.

Baked Lentils with Cheese

Onions, garlic, tomatoes, green pepper and several herbs and spices give a hearty punch to this cheesy bean dish. These are the only beans my family will eat anymore.
—Pamela Ulrich, Charlottesville, Virginia

2-1/4 cups water
1-3/4 cups dry lentils, rinsed
1 cup chopped onion
2 medium carrots, thinly sliced
1/2 cup thinly sliced celery
2 garlic cloves, minced
1 teaspoon salt
1/4 teaspoon pepper
1/8 teaspoon dried marjoram
1/8 teaspoon rubbed sage
1/8 teaspoon dried thyme
1 bay leaf
2 cups chopped fresh tomatoes
1/2 cup finely chopped green pepper
2 tablespoons minced fresh parsley
2-1/2 cups (10 ounces) shredded reduced-fat cheddar cheese

In a 13-in. x 9-in. x 2-in. baking dish, combine the first 12 ingredients. Cover and bake at 350° for 45 minutes. Stir in the tomatoes and green pepper. Cover and bake 15 minutes longer. Sprinkle with parsley and cheese. Bake, uncovered, for 5-10 minutes or until cheese is melted. Discard bay leaf before serving. **Yield:** 8 servings.

Zesty Rice 'n' Bean Casserole

A savory mix of seasonings adds zip to this satisfying dish that's loaded with beans, rice, vegetables and cheese. We enjoy it as a light entree with garlic bread and fresh spinach salad.
—Daphne Blandford, Gander, Newfoundland

2 medium green peppers, chopped
1-1/2 cups sliced fresh mushrooms
1 medium onion, chopped
2 garlic cloves, minced
1/2 cup water
1 teaspoon canola oil
1 can (28 ounces) diced tomatoes, undrained
1 can (16 ounces) kidney beans, rinsed and drained
3/4 cup uncooked long grain rice
2 teaspoons ground cumin
1 teaspoon chili powder
1/4 teaspoon cayenne pepper
1 cup (4 ounces) shredded part-skim mozzarella cheese, *divided*

In a large nonstick skillet, saute the green peppers, mushrooms, onion and garlic in water and oil until onion is tender. Add the tomatoes, beans, rice and seasonings. Bring to a boil. Reduce heat; cover and simmer for 25 minutes or until rice is tender and most of the liquid is absorbed. Remove from the heat; stir in 1/2 cup cheese.

Transfer to a 2-1/2-qt. baking dish coated with nonstick cooking spray. Sprinkle with remaining cheese. Bake, uncovered, at 350° for 15-20 minutes or until cheese is melted. **Yield:** 8 servings.

Nutritional Analysis: One serving (1 cup) equals 195 calories, 3 g fat (2 g saturated fat), 8 mg cholesterol, 392 mg sodium, 33 g carbohydrate, 7 g fiber, 10 g protein.
Diabetic Exchanges: 1-1/2 starch, 1 lean meat, 1 vegetable.

Zucchini Crepes

(Pictured below)

By keeping a few of these tender well-stuffed crepes in the freezer, I can easily reheat them when vegetarian friends stop by unexpectedly.
—Patricia Moyer, Island Pond, Vermont

1 cup all-purpose flour
2 eggs
1/2 cup egg substitute
1-1/2 cups fat-free milk
3/4 teaspoon salt
FILLING:
1 large onion, chopped
1 medium green pepper, chopped
1 cup sliced fresh mushrooms
1 tablespoon canola oil
1 medium zucchini, shredded and squeezed dry
2 medium tomatoes, chopped and seeded
1-1/2 cups (6 ounces) shredded reduced-fat cheddar cheese, divided
1/4 teaspoon salt

1/4 teaspoon dried oregano
1/8 teaspoon pepper
1-1/2 cups meatless spaghetti sauce

In a bowl, whisk together flour, eggs, egg substitute, milk and salt until smooth. Cover and refrigerate for 1 hour.

Heat an 8-in. nonstick skillet coated with nonstick cooking spray; pour about 1/4 cup batter into center of skillet. Lift and tilt pan to evenly coat bottom. Cook until top appears dry; turn and cook 15-20 seconds longer. Remove to a wire rack. Repeat with remaining batter, adding nonstick cooking spray as needed. When cool, stack crepes with waxed paper or paper towels in between.

In a skillet, saute the onion, green pepper and mushrooms in oil until tender. Add zucchini; saute 2-3 minutes longer. Remove from the heat; stir in tomatoes, 1 cup of cheese, salt, oregano and pepper. Spoon onto crepes and roll up. Arrange in a 13-in. x 9-in. x 2-in. baking dish coated with nonstick cooking spray.

Spread spaghetti sauce over crepes. Cover and bake at 350° for 15-20 minutes. Sprinkle with remaining cheese. Bake, uncovered, 5 minutes longer or until cheese is melted. **Yield:** 6 servings.

Nutritional Analysis: One serving (2 filled crepes) equals 264 calories, 7 g fat (2 g saturated fat), 78 mg cholesterol, 900 mg sodium, 33 g carbohydrate, 3 g fiber, 18 g protein.
Diabetic Exchanges: 2 lean meat, 1-1/2 starch, 1 vegetable.

Southern Okra Bean Stew

When this spicy stew's simmering on the stove, my family has a hard time waiting for dinner. It's much like a thick tomato-based soup with a hearty mix of okra, brown rice and beans. Everyone leaves the table feeling satisfied...and eager to have it again soon.
—Beverly McDowell, Athens, Georgia

4 cups water
1 can (28 ounces) diced tomatoes, undrained
1-1/2 cups chopped green peppers
1 large onion, chopped
3 garlic cloves, minced
1 teaspoon Italian seasoning
1 teaspoon chili powder
1/2 to 1 teaspoon hot pepper sauce
3/4 teaspoon salt
1 bay leaf
4 cups cooked brown rice
2 cans (16 ounces each) kidney beans, rinsed and drained
3 cans (8 ounces each) tomato sauce
1 package (16 ounces) frozen sliced okra

In a large Dutch oven or soup kettle, combine the first 10 ingredients. Bring to a boil. Reduce heat; simmer, uncovered, for 5 minutes. Add the rice, beans, tomato sauce and okra. Simmer, uncovered, for 8-10 minutes or until the vegetables are tender. Discard bay leaf before serving. **Yield:** 11 servings.

Nutritional Analysis: One serving (1-1/2 cups) equals 198 calories, 1 g fat (trace saturated fat), 0 cholesterol, 926 mg sodium, 41 g carbohydrate, 7 g fiber, 8 g protein.
Diabetic Exchanges: 2 vegetable, 1-1/2 starch, 1 very lean meat.

Vegetarian Cabbage Rolls

(Pictured below)

Zucchini is a fun change of pace in these cabbage rolls. This marvelous meatless entree comes from my grandmother, who cooks a lot with grains.
—Michelle Dougherty, Lewiston, Idaho

1-1/2 cups chopped fresh mushrooms
1 cup diced zucchini
3/4 cup chopped green pepper
3/4 cup chopped sweet red pepper
3/4 cup vegetable broth
1/2 cup bulgur*
1 teaspoon dried basil
1/2 teaspoon dried marjoram
1/2 teaspoon dried thyme
1/4 teaspoon pepper
1 large head cabbage
6 tablespoons shredded Parmesan cheese, divided
2 teaspoons lemon juice
1 can (8 ounces) tomato sauce
1/8 teaspoon hot pepper sauce

In a large saucepan, combine the first 10 ingredients. Bring to a boil over medium heat. Reduce heat; cover and simmer for 5 minutes. Remove from the heat; let stand for 5 minutes.

Meanwhile, cook cabbage in boiling water just until leaves fall off head. Set aside eight large leaves for rolls (re-

frigerate remaining cabbage for another use). Cut out the thick vein from each leaf, making a V-shaped cut. Overlap cut ends before filling. Stir 4 tablespoons Parmesan cheese and lemon juice into vegetable mixture. Place a heaping 1/3 cupful on each cabbage leaf; fold in sides. Starting at an unfolded edge, roll to completely enclose filling.

Combine tomato sauce and hot pepper sauce; pour 1/3 cup into a 2-qt. baking dish. Place cabbage rolls in dish; spoon remaining sauce over top. Cover and bake at 400° for 15 minutes or until heated through. Sprinkle with remaining Parmesan cheese. **Yield:** 4 servings.

*Editor's Note: Look for bulgur in the cereal, rice or organic food aisle of your grocery store.

Nutritional Analysis: *One serving (2 cabbage rolls) equals 142 calories, 3 g fat (1 g saturated fat), 5 mg cholesterol, 675 mg sodium, 25 g carbohydrate, 6 g fiber, 8 g protein.*
Diabetic Exchanges: *2 vegetable, 1 starch.*

Pinto Bean Stew

(Pictured above right)

This thick, hearty stew is chock-full of beans and vegetables and makes a wonderful supper on cold winter days. I sometimes serve it over rice for a fun change of pace. It also freezes well.
—Gina Passantino, Amherst, New York

1 cup dry pinto beans
2 cups cold water
1/2 cup chopped carrot
2 garlic cloves, minced
3/4 teaspoon chili powder
1/2 teaspoon salt
Dash cayenne pepper
1 package (16 ounces) frozen corn, thawed
1 large onion, chopped
1 medium green pepper, chopped
1 can (14-1/2 ounces) diced tomatoes, undrained
2 to 3 teaspoons balsamic vinegar
1/4 teaspoon sugar

Place beans in a large saucepan; add water to cover by 2 in. Bring to a boil; boil for 2 minutes. Remove from the heat; cover and let stand for 1 hour. Drain and rinse beans, discarding liquid. Return beans to the pan; add cold water, carrot, garlic, chili powder, salt and cayenne. Bring to a boil. Reduce heat; cover and simmer for 45 minutes or until beans are almost tender.

In a nonstick skillet coated with nonstick cooking spray;

- **1 small onion, quartered**
- **1 garlic clove, minced**
- **1 jar (28 ounces) meatless spaghetti sauce,** *divided*
- **1-1/2 cups (6 ounces) shredded mozzarella cheese**

Cook pasta shells according to package directions. Meanwhile, place the chickpeas and egg whites in a food processor or blender; cover and process until smooth. Add the ricotta, parsley, Parmesan, onion and garlic; cover and process until well blended. Pour 1-1/4 cups of spaghetti sauce into an ungreased 13-in. x 9-in. x 2-in. baking dish; set aside.

Drain pasta shells; stuff with chickpea mixture. Place over sauce. Drizzle with remaining sauce. Bake, uncovered, at 350° for 30 minutes. Sprinkle with mozzarella cheese. Bake 5-10 minutes longer or until cheese is melted and sauce is bubbly. **Yield:** 6 servings.

Nutritional Analysis: One serving (3 stuffed shells) equals 508 calories, 19 g fat (9 g saturated fat), 42 mg cholesterol, 1,066 mg sodium, 58 g carbohydrate, 8 g fiber, 27 g protein.

saute the corn, onion and green pepper until tender. Add to the bean mixture. Cover and cook for 45 minutes. Stir in the tomatoes, vinegar and sugar. Cook 5 minutes longer or until heated through. **Yield:** 6 servings.

Nutritional Analysis: One serving (1 cup) equals 214 calories, 1 g fat (trace saturated fat), 0 cholesterol, 309 mg sodium, 45 g carbohydrate, 10 g fiber, 10 g protein.
***Diabetic Exchanges:** 2 starch, 1 very lean meat, 1 vegetable.*

Chickpea-Stuffed Shells

(Pictured at right)

I never guessed my picky eaters would agree to try chickpeas, but they gobble them up when I disguise them this way. This pasta dish receives raves from my husband, young son and daughter and dinner guests, too. No one can guess my secret ingredient is nutritious legumes!
—Susan Brown, Saugerties, New York

- **18 uncooked jumbo pasta shells**
- **1 can (15 ounces) chickpeas** *or* **garbanzo beans, rinsed and drained**
- **2 egg whites**
- **1 carton (15 ounces) reduced-fat ricotta cheese**
- **1/2 cup minced fresh parsley**
- **1/3 cup grated Parmesan cheese**

Reduce heat; add cashews and sesame oil. Cook 2 minutes longer or until heated through. Serve over rice. **Yield:** 4 servings.

Nutritional Analysis: One serving (about 2/3 cup asparagus mixture with 1 cup rice) equals 406 calories, 13 g fat (2 g saturated fat), 0 cholesterol, 847 mg sodium, 64 g carbohydrate, 8 g fiber, 12 g protein.
Diabetic Exchanges: 3 starch, 2 vegetable, 2 fat, 1/2 lean meat.

Five-Cheese Stuffed Shells

These yummy stuffed pasta shells will make any luncheon special. I experimented with various cheeses, herbs and spices until I found that just-right blend. Try adding chopped walnuts for extra protein and a little crunch.
—*Wendy Lee Guerin, Fridley, Minnesota*

 20 uncooked jumbo pasta shells
  2 cups cooked chopped spinach
  1 cup fat-free cottage cheese
  1 cup part-skim ricotta cheese
  4 slices reduced-fat provolone cheese, finely
   chopped
 1/2 cup shredded Parmesan cheese
 1/2 cup shredded Romano cheese
  1 egg, lightly beaten
  2 garlic cloves, minced
  1 teaspoon Italian seasoning
 1/2 teaspoon salt
Dash pepper
  1 jar (26 ounces) meatless spaghetti sauce

Cook pasta shells according to package directions; drain. In a large bowl, combine the next 11 ingredients; spoon into shells. Arrange in a 13-in. x 9-in. x 2-in. baking dish coated with nonstick cooking spray. Pour spaghetti sauce over all. Cover and bake at 350° for 40-45 minutes or until heated through. **Yield:** 10 servings.

Nutritional Analysis: One serving (2 stuffed shells) equals 226 calories, 8 g fat (4 g saturated fat), 42 mg cholesterol, 849 mg sodium, 24 g carbohydrate, 1 g fiber, 16 g protein.
Diabetic Exchanges: 2 lean meat, 1-1/2 vegetable, 1 starch.

Asparagus Cashew Stir-Fry

(Pictured above)

When I'm in the mood for Chinese food, I turn to this snappy recipe. The colorful nutty dish is sure to stir your creativity...substitute broccoli for the asparagus or add carrots and mushrooms.
—*Christine Sherrill, Herndon, Virginia*

  1 pound fresh asparagus, trimmed and cut into
   1-inch pieces
 1/2 cup chopped green onions
 1/2 cup chopped sweet red pepper
  1 garlic clove, minced
  1 teaspoon canola oil
  2 tablespoons cornstarch
1-1/2 cups vegetable broth
  3 tablespoons reduced-sodium soy sauce
 1/4 teaspoon ground ginger *or* 3/4 to 1 teaspoon
   minced fresh gingerroot
 1/2 cup cashews
  1 teaspoon sesame oil
  4 cups hot cooked brown rice

In a large nonstick skillet, saute the asparagus, onions, red pepper and garlic in oil until tender. Combine the cornstarch, broth, soy sauce and ginger until blended; add to the skillet. Bring to a boil; cook and stir for 2 minutes or until thickened.

From the Bread Basket

Is your family getting enough grains?
It's easy to ingrain the goodness of wheat,
oats, rye and more into your meal plans
when you present an incredible assortment
of breads, rolls and muffins.

Country Raisin Rye Bread (page 192)

Nutritional Analysis: One slice equals 134 calories, 2 g fat (trace saturated fat), trace cholesterol, 298 mg sodium, 26 g carbohydrate, 2 g fiber, 4 g protein.
Diabetic Exchange: 1-1/2 starch.

Country Raisin Rye Bread

(Pictured on page 191)

The recipe for this delicious bread came from my aunt. I made just a few changes to it—and it's been a favorite ever since. The dark rustic loaves are moist and tender with a delicate rye and sweet molasses flavor.
—Carolyn Rose Sykora, Bloomer, Wisconsin

2 cups whole wheat flour, *divided*
2 cups rye flour, *divided*
1 tablespoon active dry yeast
1 teaspoon salt
2 cups water
1/2 cup plus 1 teaspoon olive *or* **canola oil,** *divided*
1/2 cup molasses
1/2 cup honey
2-1/2 to 2-3/4 cups all-purpose flour
1 cup raisins

In a mixing bowl, combine 1 cup whole wheat flour, 1 cup rye flour, yeast and salt. In a saucepan, heat water, 1/2 cup oil, molasses and honey to 120°-130°. Add to dry ingredients; stir just until moistened. Stir in remaining whole wheat and rye flours and enough all-purpose flour to form a medium stiff dough.

Turn onto a floured surface; sprinkle with raisins. Knead until smooth and elastic, about 8-10 minutes. Grease a bowl with the remaining oil. Place dough in bowl, turning once to grease top. Cover and let rise in a warm place until doubled, about 1-1/2 hours.

Punch dough down; turn onto a lightly floured surface. Divide into four pieces; shape each into a round loaf. Place 4 in. apart on two baking sheets coated with nonstick cooking spray. Cover and let rise until doubled, about 45 minutes. Bake at 325° for 35-40 minutes or until golden brown. **Yield:** 4 loaves (8 slices each).

Nutritional Analysis: One slice equals 159 calories, 4 g fat (1 g saturated fat), 0 cholesterol, 151 mg sodium, 29 g carbohydrate, 3 g fiber, 3 g protein.
Diabetic Exchanges: 1 fruit, 1 starch, 1/2 fat.

Seven-Grain Bread

(Pictured above)

Flavorful and slightly chewy, this lovely loaf is the best thing to come out of my bread machine. We like to start our day with a nice warm slice full of good-for-you grains.
—Lise Thomson, Magrath, Alberta

1-2/3 cups water (70° to 80°)
3 tablespoons nonfat dry milk powder
2 tablespoons shortening
2 tablespoons honey
2 teaspoons salt
2-1/2 cups all-purpose flour
1 cup whole wheat flour
3/4 cup five-grain cereal
1-1/4 teaspoons active dry yeast

In bread machine pan, place all ingredients in order suggested by manufacturer. Select basic bread setting. Choose crust color and loaf size if available. Bake according to bread machine directions (check dough after 5 minutes of mixing; add 1 to 2 tablespoons of water or flour if needed). **Yield:** 1 loaf, 16 slices (about 2 pounds).

Orange-Raisin Toasting Bread

This tasty no-knead bread is so easy, it almost makes itself. With raisins and a hint of orange flavor, it's wonderful toasted for breakfast or any time of the day with tea. I like to keep some on hand to share when friends stop by our ranch.
—Virginia Doyle, Pinedale, Wyoming

3 cups all-purpose flour, *divided*
2 teaspoons sugar
1 package (1/4 ounce) active dry yeast
1 teaspoon salt
1/8 teaspoon baking powder

🍎 **Using Applesauce in Bread Recipes**

I use unsweetened applesauce instead of butter in bread machine recipes. My bread comes out just the same as if I had used butter. —*Ronda VanDerslice Columbus, Nebraska*

1-1/4 cups orange juice
1/4 cup butter *or* stick margarine
1 teaspoon grated orange peel
1/2 cup raisins
Cornmeal

In a mixing bowl, combine 1-1/2 cups flour, sugar, yeast, salt and baking powder. In a saucepan, heat orange juice and butter to 120°-130°. Add to dry ingredients; beat on low speed for 30 seconds. Beat on high for 3 minutes. Add orange peel. Stir in remaining flour (batter will be thick). Stir in raisins (do not knead).

Coat an 8-in. x 4-in. x 2-in. loaf pan with nonstick cooking spray and sprinkle with cornmeal; spoon batter into pan. Cover and let rise in a warm place until doubled, about 45 minutes. Bake at 375° for 35-40 minutes or until golden brown. Remove from pan to a wire rack. **Yield:** 1 loaf (12 slices).

Nutritional Analysis: One slice equals 183 calories, 4 g fat (2 g saturated fat), 10 mg cholesterol, 240 mg sodium, 33 g carbohydrate, 1 g fiber, 4 g protein.
Diabetic Exchanges: *2 starch, 1/2 fat.*

Blueberry Corn Muffins

These tender corn muffins are bursting with juicy blueberries. For a different fruity flavor, I sometimes substitute chopped apples for the berries.
—Genevieve Fairchild, Chester, Iowa

1/4 cup butter *or* stick margarine, softened
1/4 cup sugar
1/4 cup packed brown sugar
1 egg
1 cup all-purpose flour
1/2 cup cornmeal
2 teaspoons baking powder
1/4 teaspoon salt
1/4 teaspoon ground nutmeg
1/2 cup 2% milk
1 cup fresh *or* frozen blueberries*

In a mixing bowl, cream butter and sugars. Add egg; mix well. Combine the flour, cornmeal, baking powder, salt and nutmeg; add to creamed mixture alternately with milk just until moistened. Fold in blueberries. Coat muffin cups with nonstick cooking spray or use paper liners; fill two-thirds full with batter. Bake at 400° for 18-22 minutes or until a toothpick comes out clean. Cool for 5 minutes before removing from pan to a wire rack. **Yield:** 1 dozen.

*Editor's Note: If using frozen blueberries, do not thaw before adding to batter.

Nutritional Analysis: One muffin equals 146 calories, 5 g fat (3 g saturated fat), 29 mg cholesterol, 141 mg sodium, 23 g carbohydrate, 1 g fiber, 3 g protein.
Diabetic Exchanges: *1 starch, 1 fruit.*

Raspberry Chocolate Chip Muffins

(Pictured below)

Yummy chocolate and luscious berries create bursts of sweetness in these treats. My family enjoys the muffins even before they're done baking because they make the kitchen smell heavenly!
—Carol Schwammel, Antioch, California

1-2/3 cups all-purpose flour
3/4 cup quick-cooking oats
2/3 cup sugar
2 teaspoons baking powder
1 teaspoon baking soda
1/4 teaspoon ground cinnamon
1 egg, lightly beaten
3/4 cup fat-free milk
1/3 cup canola oil
2 tablespoons orange juice
1 teaspoon vanilla extract
3/4 cup fresh *or* frozen unsweetened raspberries*
1/2 cup miniature semisweet chocolate chips

In a large bowl, combine the first six ingredients. Combine the egg, milk, oil, orange juice and vanilla; stir into dry ingredients just until moistened. Fold in raspberries and chocolate chips. Fill paper-lined muffin cups or cups coated with nonstick cooking spray two-thirds full.

Bake at 375° for 20-25 minutes or until a toothpick comes out clean. Cool for 5 minutes before removing from pan to a wire rack. **Yield:** 1 dozen.

*Editor's Note: If using frozen berries, do not thaw before adding to batter.

Nutritional Analysis: One muffin equals 232 calories, 9 g fat (2 g saturated fat), 20 mg cholesterol, 163 mg sodium, 34 g carbohydrate, 2 g fiber, 4 g protein.
Diabetic Exchanges: *2 starch, 1 fat, 1/2 fruit.*

Cheesy Biscuit Triangles

I've always loved crescent rolls, but not all the fat that comes with them. I decided to come up with my own lighter recipe—and this cheesy version was the result. Everyone at my house enjoys these...and I know your family will, too!
—Suzette Jones, Tulsa, Oklahoma

2 cups all-purpose flour
3 teaspoons baking powder
1/2 teaspoon salt
1/2 teaspoon dried oregano, *divided*
1/2 teaspoon dried basil, *divided*
2 egg whites
1 egg
1 cup (4 ounces) crumbled feta cheese
1/2 cup reduced-fat ricotta cheese
1/3 cup 1% buttermilk
1/4 cup reduced-fat sour cream

In a bowl, combine the flour, baking powder, salt, 1/4 teaspoon oregano and 1/4 teaspoon basil. Set one egg white aside. In a bowl, combine the egg, cheeses, buttermilk, sour cream and remaining egg white; mix well. Stir into the dry ingredients just until moistened.

On a lightly floured surface, roll dough into a 12-in. x 9-in. rectangle. Cut into twelve 3-in. squares; cut each diagonally in half. Place triangles on baking sheets coated with nonstick cooking spray. Beat reserved egg white; brush over tops. Sprinkle with remaining oregano and basil. Bake at 425° for 12-15 minutes or until golden brown. **Yield:** 2 dozen.

Nutritional Analysis: One serving (2 biscuits) equals 128 calories, 4 g fat (3 g saturated fat), 32 mg cholesterol, 360 mg sodium, 17 g carbohydrate, 1 g fiber, 6 g protein.
Diabetic Exchanges: *1 starch, 1 fat.*

mix well. Stir into dry ingredients just until moistened. Fold in walnuts.

Spoon into a 9-in. x 5-in. x 3-in. baking pan coated with nonstick cooking spray. Bake at 350° for 60-65 minutes or until a toothpick inserted near the center comes out clean. Cool for 15 minutes before removing from pan to a wire rack. **Yield:** 1 loaf (12 slices).

Nutritional Analysis: One slice equals 208 calories, 8 g fat (1 g saturated fat), trace cholesterol, 239 mg sodium, 31 g carbohydrate, 3 g fiber, 5 g protein.
Diabetic Exchanges: *2 starch, 1 fat.*

Whole Wheat Pumpkin Nut Bread

(Pictured above right)

Nicely spiced with cloves, cinnamon and pumpkin, this bread is a family favorite. You can substitute raisins or chocolate chips for the walnuts.
—Jean-Marie Hirsch, East Rochester, New York

1 cup whole wheat flour
1 cup sugar
2/3 cup all-purpose flour
1 teaspoon baking soda
1 teaspoon ground cinnamon
1/2 teaspoon baking powder
1/2 teaspoon salt
1/2 teaspoon ground cloves
1 cup cooked *or* canned pumpkin
1/2 cup egg substitute
1/3 cup water
1/4 cup canola oil
1/2 cup chopped walnuts

In a bowl, combine the first eight ingredients. In another bowl, combine the pumpkin, egg substitute, water and oil;

Orange Date Muffins

Anyone who likes dates and the flavor of orange will think these moist muffins are a treat. I get compliments each time I serve them.
—Rosella Peters, Gull Lake, Saskatchewan

1-1/4 cups whole wheat flour
1 cup all-purpose flour
3/4 cup packed brown sugar
3 teaspoons baking powder
1/2 teaspoon salt
2 eggs
1 cup orange juice
1/3 cup butter *or* stick margarine, melted
3/4 cup chopped dates
1/3 cup chopped walnuts
1 teaspoon grated orange peel

In a bowl, combine the dry ingredients. Combine eggs, orange juice and butter; mix well. Stir into dry ingredients just until moistened. Fold in dates, walnuts and orange peel. Coat muffin cups with nonstick cooking spray or use paper liners; fill two-thirds full with batter.

Bake at 400° for 15-20 minutes or until a toothpick comes out clean. Cool for 5 minutes before removing from pan to a wire rack. **Yield:** 1 dozen.

Dilly Yeast Muffins

I simply snip fresh dill from my herb garden to add savory flavor to these light and golden no-knead muffins. Cottage cheese makes them moist.
—Diane Armstrong, Elm Grove, Wisconsin

2 packages (1/4 ounce *each*) active dry yeast
1/4 cup warm water (110° to 115°)
  1 cup small-curd 2% cottage cheese
  1 egg, beaten
  1 tablespoon butter *or* stick margarine, softened
  2 tablespoons finely chopped onion
  4 teaspoons snipped fresh dill *or* 1 teaspoon dill weed
  1 tablespoon sugar
  1 teaspoon salt
1/4 teaspoon baking soda
2-1/4 cups all-purpose flour

In a mixing bowl, dissolve yeast in warm water. Heat the cottage cheese to 110°-115°; add to yeast mixture. Add egg, butter, onion, dill, sugar, salt and baking soda; beat well. Beat in 1 cup flour. Stir in the remaining flour (do not knead). Cover and let rise in a warm place until doubled, about 30 minutes.

Stir batter down. Fill muffin cups coated with nonstick cooking spray half full. Cover and let rise until batter reaches top of cups, about 30 minutes. Bake at 350° for 20-22 minutes or until golden brown. Serve warm. **Yield:** 17 muffins.

Blueberry Cheese Danish

(Pictured at right)

A layer of blueberries is the sweet surprise hidden inside this pretty pastry. The recipe comes from our Test Kitchen staff.

3/4 cup 1% cottage cheese
1/3 cup sugar
1/3 cup 1% milk
1/4 cup canola oil
  1 teaspoon vanilla extract
  2 cups all-purpose flour
  2 teaspoons baking powder
1/2 teaspoon salt
FILLING:
  4 ounces reduced-fat cream cheese
1/4 cup sugar
  1 egg, *separated*
  1 teaspoon grated lemon peel
  1 teaspoon vanilla extract
  1 cup fresh *or* frozen blueberries*
  1 tablespoon water
GLAZE:
1/2 cup confectioners' sugar
  2 teaspoons lemon juice

In a blender or food processor, cover and process cottage cheese until smooth. Add sugar, milk, oil and vanilla; process until smooth. Combine the flour, baking powder and salt; add to cheese mixture. Process just until dough forms a ball (dough will be sticky). Turn onto a floured surface; knead 4-5 times. Place in a bowl; cover and refrigerate for 30 minutes.

In a mixing bowl, beat cream cheese and sugar until smooth. Add egg yolk, lemon peel and vanilla; mix well. Turn dough onto a 17-in. x 13-in. piece of parchment paper. Roll into a 16-in. x 12-in. rectangle. Transfer with paper to a baking sheet.

Spread cream cheese mixture lengthwise in a 3-1/2-in.-wide strip down center of dough; sprinkle with blueberries. On each long side, cut 1-in.-wide strips about 3-3/4 in. into center. Fold alternating strips at an angle across berries. Pinch ends to seal and tuck under. Beat egg white and water; brush over dough.

Bake at 400° for 20-22 minutes or until golden brown. Remove to a wire rack. Combine glaze ingredients; drizzle over warm pastry. Refrigerate leftovers. **Yield:** 10 servings.

*Editor's Note: If using frozen blueberries, do not thaw.

Sunflower Wheat Rolls

(Pictured below)

My husband, Milt, gave me a bread machine for Christmas, and it certainly has been a time-saver. With some trial and error, we came up with this recipe. Quite often, we are asked to bring the golden rolls to family gatherings or potlucks. We get compliments every time.
—Roxann Field, Hutchinson, Minnesota

1 cup water (70° to 80°)
1/4 cup canola oil
1/4 cup honey
1 egg
1 teaspoon salt
2-1/2 cups bread flour
1 cup whole wheat flour
1/4 cup toasted wheat germ
1/4 cup wheat bran
1/4 cup sunflower kernels
1 tablespoon poppy seeds
2-1/2 teaspoons active dry yeast

In bread machine pan, place all ingredients in the order suggested by manufacturer. Select dough setting (check dough after 5 minutes of mixing; add 1 to 2 tablespoons of water or flour if needed). When the cycle is completed, turn dough onto a lightly floured surface. Punch down; cover and let stand for 10 minutes.

Divide dough into 20 pieces; shape each into a ball. Place 2 in. apart on baking sheets coated with nonstick cooking spray. Cover and let rise in a warm place until doubled, about 45 minutes. Bake at 375° for 12 minutes or until golden brown. Remove from pans to cool on wire racks. **Yield:** 20 rolls.

Editor's Note: If your bread machine has a timer feature, we recommend you do not use it for this recipe.

Nutritional Analysis: One roll equals 142 calories, 5 g fat (trace saturated fat), 11 mg cholesterol, 122 mg sodium, 22 g carbohydrate, 2 g fiber, 4 g protein.
Diabetic Exchanges: 1 starch, 1 fat.

Golden Oatmeal Bread

Slice into this old-fashioned loaf and savor the subtle oat flavor, crunchy pecans and sweet raisins, with just a hint of cinnamon. The recipe was developed by our Test Kitchen.

1 cup all-purpose flour
3/4 cup plus 1 tablespoon quick-cooking oats, *divided*
1/2 cup whole wheat flour
1/2 cup sugar
2 teaspoons baking powder
3/4 teaspoon baking soda
1/2 teaspoon ground cinnamon
3/4 cup unsweetened applesauce
1 egg
1-1/2 teaspoons vanilla extract
1/3 cup golden raisins
1/3 cup chopped pecans, toasted

In a large bowl, combine all-purpose flour, 3/4 cup of oats, whole wheat flour, sugar, baking powder, baking soda and cinnamon. In another bowl, combine the applesauce, egg and vanilla; stir into dry ingredients just until moistened. Fold in raisins and pecans.

Pour into an 8-in. x 4-in. x 2-in. loaf pan coated with nonstick cooking spray. Sprinkle with remaining oats. Bake at 325° for 50-55 minutes or until a toothpick inserted near the center comes out clean. Cool for 10 minutes before removing from pan to wire rack. **Yield:** 1 loaf (10 slices).

Nutritional Analysis: One slice equals 188 calories, 4 g fat (1 g saturated fat), 21 mg cholesterol, 149 mg sodium, 35 g carbohydrate, 3 g fiber, 4 g protein.
Diabetic Exchanges: 2 starch, 1/2 fat.

Nutty Whole Wheat Bread

My recipe box is quickly gaining in grains. Moist and nutty, this whole wheat bread has excellent flavor and always bakes up golden and tender. You may want to make a couple loaves at a time. It never lasts long at our house!
—Rosadene Herold, Lakeville, Indiana

2-1/4 cups all-purpose flour
1-1/4 cups whole wheat flour
3/4 cup finely chopped walnuts
2 tablespoons brown sugar
1 package (1/4 ounce) quick-rise yeast
1 teaspoon salt
1 cup water
1/3 cup reduced-fat plain yogurt
2 tablespoons butter *or* stick margarine

In a mixing bowl, combine 1 cup all-purpose flour, whole wheat flour, walnuts, brown sugar, yeast and salt. In a saucepan, heat the water, yogurt and butter to 120°-130°.

Add to dry ingredients; beat until smooth. Stir in enough remaining all-purpose flour to form a soft dough. Turn onto a floured surface; knead until smooth and elastic, about 4 minutes (do not let rise).

Shape dough into a ball; place on a baking sheet coated with nonstick cooking spray. Cover and let rest in a warm place for 20 minutes. Bake at 400° for 25-30 minutes or until golden brown. Remove from pan to cool on a wire rack. **Yield:** 1 loaf (16 slices).

Nutritional Analysis: One slice equals 156 calories, 6 g fat (1 g saturated fat), 4 mg cholesterol, 167 mg sodium, 23 g carbohydrate, 2 g fiber, 4 g protein.
Diabetic Exchanges: 1-1/2 starch, 1/2 fat.

Butternut Squash Rolls

My grandma loves these light moist rolls, and so do my nieces and nephews. They are a great way to use leftover squash—or to get non-squash lovers to eat this delicious vegetable!
—Angela Leschisin, Turtle Lake, Wisconsin

1 tablespoon active dry yeast
1/4 cup warm water (110° to 115°)
1 teaspoon sugar
2/3 cup warm fat-free milk (110° to 115°)
1 cup mashed cooked butternut squash
1/3 cup butter *or* stick margarine, melted
1/3 cup packed brown sugar
1 teaspoon salt
2 cups whole wheat flour
2 to 2-1/2 cups all-purpose flour

In a mixing bowl, dissolve yeast in warm water. Add sugar; let stand for 5 minutes. Stir in the milk, squash, butter, brown sugar and salt. Add whole wheat flour. Beat on medium speed for 2 minutes. Stir in enough all-purpose flour to form a soft dough.

Turn onto a floured surface; knead until smooth and elastic, about 10 minutes. Place in a bowl coated with nonstick cooking spray, turning once to coat top. Cover and let rise in a warm place until doubled, about 1 hour.

Punch dough down and turn onto a floured surface; divide into 20 pieces. Shape each piece into a ball. Place 2 in. apart on baking sheets coated with nonstick cooking spray. With a sharp knife, make shallow slashes on top of rolls. Cover and let rise until doubled, about 45 minutes.

Bake at 400° for 11-13 minutes or until golden brown. Remove from pans to wire racks to cool. **Yield:** 20 rolls.

Nutritional Analysis: One roll equals 147 calories, 4 g fat (2 g saturated fat), 8 mg cholesterol, 156 mg sodium, 26 g carbohydrate, 2 g fiber, 4 g protein.
Diabetic Exchanges: 1-1/2 starch, 1/2 fat.

🍎 Sour Cream Substitution

One day when I was making my favorite banana bread recipe, I didn't have the sour cream it called for. I substituted an equal amount of low-fat strawberry yogurt and the bread was scrumptious!
—Fran Hoard, Kalamazoo, Michigan

Spinach-Stuffed Bread

(Pictured above)

Slices of this golden loaf swirled with spinach and cheese disappear in a hurry. They're a tasty accompaniment to most any meal or make a hearty appetizer.
—Terry Byrne, Warwick, New York

1 loaf (1 pound) frozen bread dough
1 medium onion, chopped
1 to 2 garlic cloves, minced
2 teaspoons olive *or* canola oil
1 package (10 ounces) frozen chopped spinach, thawed and squeezed dry
2 cups (8 ounces) shredded reduced-fat cheddar *or* part-skim mozzarella cheese

Thaw bread dough according to package directions; let rise until doubled. Meanwhile, in a skillet, saute onion and garlic in oil until tender. Stir in spinach.

On a lightly floured surface, roll dough into a 14-in. x 10-in. rectangle. Spread the spinach mixture to within 1/2 in. of edges; sprinkle with cheese. Roll up jelly-roll style, starting with a long side; pinch seam to seal. Place seam side down on a baking sheet coated with nonstick cooking spray; tuck ends under.

Bake at 350° for 25-30 minutes or until golden brown. Remove from pan to a wire rack; let stand for 10 minutes before slicing. Serve warm. **Yield:** 6 servings.

Nutritional Analysis: One serving (2 slices) equals 340 calories, 11 g fat (4 g saturated fat), 20 mg cholesterol, 687 mg sodium, 45 g carbohydrate, 4 g fiber, 21 g protein.
Diabetic Exchanges: 2 starch, 2 lean meat, 1-1/2 fat.

Nutritional Analysis: One slice equals 134 calories, 4 g fat (1 g saturated fat), 2 mg cholesterol, 240 mg sodium, 20 g carbohydrate, 1 g fiber, 4 g protein.
Diabetic Exchange: 1-1/2 starch.

Southwestern Corn Bread

I found this recipe in a cookbook and lightened it up with skim milk, less oil, egg whites and reduced-fat cheese.
—*Tena Edyvean, Rapid City, South Dakota*

1 can (15-1/4 ounces) whole kernel corn, drained
1 cup all-purpose flour
1 cup cornmeal
1/2 teaspoon baking soda
1/2 teaspoon salt
1 egg
2 egg whites
3/4 cup fat-free milk
1/4 cup canola oil
1 cup (4 ounces) shredded reduced-fat cheddar cheese
1 can (4 ounces) chopped green chilies

Place corn in a food processor or blender; cover and process until coarsely chopped. Set aside. In a bowl, combine the flour, cornmeal, baking soda and salt. In a small bowl, combine the egg, egg whites, milk and oil. Stir into dry ingredients just until moistened. Add the cheese, chilies and corn. Pour into a 9-in. square baking dish coated with nonstick cooking spray. Bake at 350° for 40-45 minutes or until a toothpick inserted near the center comes out clean. Serve warm. **Yield:** 9 servings.

Nutritional Analysis: One serving equals 243 calories, 10 g fat (3 g saturated fat), 33 mg cholesterol, 598 mg sodium, 30 g carbohydrate, 3 g fiber, 10 g protein.
Diabetic Exchanges: 2 starch, 2 fat.

Peppered Focaccia

(Pictured above)

A busy college student, I make this lightened-up version of flat Italian bread often because it's so easy to prepare. Focaccia goes great with soup or pasta. And by adding tomatoes and onions, I can turn it into a light supper.
—*Sarah McClanahan, Raleigh, North Carolina*

2-3/4 to 3 cups all-purpose flour
2 tablespoons sugar
1 package (1/4 ounce) quick-rise yeast
1-1/2 teaspoons salt, *divided*
1 cup water
4 tablespoons olive *or* canola oil, *divided*
1/2 medium green pepper, thinly sliced
1/2 medium sweet red pepper, thinly sliced
1/2 cup shredded part-skim mozzarella cheese
1 teaspoon crushed red pepper flakes, optional
1/2 teaspoon dried basil
1/2 teaspoon dried oregano
1/2 teaspoon garlic powder
1/2 teaspoon pepper

In a mixing bowl, combine 1-1/2 cups flour, sugar, yeast and 1/2 teaspoon salt. In a saucepan, heat water and 2 tablespoons oil to 120°-130°. Add to dry ingredients; beat on low speed just until moistened. Beat on medium until batter is elastic and pulls away from sides of bowl. Stir in enough remaining flour to form a soft dough (do not knead). Cover and let rest for 10 minutes.

Divide dough in half. Press each portion into a 12-in. pizza pan coated with nonstick cooking spray. Brush with remaining oil; top with peppers and cheese. Sprinkle with pepper flakes if desired, basil, oregano, garlic powder, pepper and remaining salt. Let rest for 10 minutes. Bake at 425° for 12-15 minutes or until golden brown. **Yield:** 2 focaccias (8 slices each).

Orange Chocolate Chip Bread

I was first inspired to try this recipe one year when our orange tree was teeming with fruit.
—*Misti Konsavage, Thonotosassa, Florida*

1 cup fat-free milk
1/4 cup orange juice
1/3 cup sugar
1 egg
1 tablespoon finely grated orange peel
3 cups reduced-fat biscuit/baking mix
1/2 cup miniature semisweet chocolate chips

In a large bowl, combine the milk, orange juice, sugar, egg and orange peel. Stir in baking mix just until moistened. Stir in chocolate chips. Pour into a 9-in. x 5-in. x 3-in. loaf pan coated with nonstick cooking spray. Bake at 350° for 45-50 minutes or until a toothpick inserted near the center comes out clean. Cool for 10 minutes before removing from pan to a wire rack. **Yield:** 1 loaf (16 slices).

Nutritional Analysis: One slice equals 139 calories, 3 g fat (1 g saturated fat), 14 mg cholesterol, 274 mg sodium, 25 g carbohydrate, 1 g fiber, 3 g protein.
Diabetic Exchanges: 1 starch, 1 fruit.

Dazzling Desserts

It used to be that the words "rich", "creamy" and "yummy" were never spoken in the same sentence as "low fat", especially when the conversation turned to desserts. But now you can have your cake and eat it, too!

German Chocolate Torte and Orange Delight (page 204)

Spice Bars

These bars smell so good while they are baking—the spicy aroma brings everyone to the kitchen in a hurry!
—Brooke Pike, Pierre, South Dakota

6 tablespoons 1% buttermilk
1/3 cup packed brown sugar
1/4 cup molasses
3 tablespoons butter *or* stick margarine, melted
1 egg
1 teaspoon vanilla extract
1-1/4 cups all-purpose flour
3/4 teaspoon ground cinnamon, *divided*
1-1/4 teaspoons Chinese Five Spice (recipe on page 82)
1/2 teaspoon baking powder
1/4 teaspoon baking soda
1/4 teaspoon salt
1/3 cup raisins
1 tablespoon confectioners' sugar

In a mixing bowl, combine the buttermilk, brown sugar, molasses, butter, egg and vanilla; mix well. Combine the flour, 1/2 teaspoon cinnamon, Chinese Five Spice, baking powder, baking soda and salt; add to buttermilk mixture and beat until smooth. Stir in raisins.

Pour into a 9-in. square baking pan coated with nonstick cooking spray. Bake at 350° for 18-20 minutes or until a toothpick inserted near the center comes out clean. Cool on a wire rack. Combine confectioners' sugar and remaining cinnamon; sprinkle over bars. **Yield:** 1 dozen.

Nutritional Analysis: One bar equals 139 calories, 4 g fat (2 g saturated fat), 26 mg cholesterol, 134 mg sodium, 25 g carbohydrate, 1 g fiber, 2 g protein.
Diabetic Exchanges: 1-1/2 starch, 1/2 fat.

Lemon Angel Cake Roll

(Pictured at right)

Every time I make this sunny cake roll, people comment on its fresh flavor and festive look. It goes over big at church dinners.
—Diana Hardwick, Holdenville, Oklahoma

1 package (16 ounces) angel food cake mix
3/4 cup plus 1 tablespoon confectioners' sugar, *divided*
1 package (8 ounces) reduced-fat cream cheese, softened
1/4 cup lemon juice

2 teaspoons grated lemon peel
1 carton (8 ounces) frozen reduced-fat whipped topping, thawed, *divided*
12 drops liquid yellow food coloring, optional
24 whole strawberries

Line a 15-in. x 10-in. x 1-in. baking pan with waxed paper; coat paper with nonstick cooking spray. Set aside. Prepare cake mix according to package directions. Spread batter evenly in prepared pan. Bake at 350° for 25-30 minutes or until golden brown.

Turn cake onto a kitchen towel lightly dusted with confectioners' sugar. Gently peel off waxed paper. Dust with 1/4 cup confectioners' sugar. Roll up cake in the towel, jelly-roll style, starting with a short side. Cool completely on a wire rack.

For filling, beat cream cheese and 1/2 cup confectioners' sugar. Stir in lemon juice and peel. Fold in whipped topping and food coloring if desired. Unroll cake; spread with filling to within 1 in. of edges. Roll up again; dust with remaining confectioners' sugar. Refrigerate for 1-2 hours. Cut into slices. Garnish with strawberries. **Yield:** 12 servings.

Nutritional Analysis: One serving (1 slice with 2 strawberries) equals 270 calories, 6 g fat (4 g saturated fat), 11 mg cholesterol, 335 mg sodium, 48 g carbohydrate, 1 g fiber, 6 g protein.
Diabetic Exchanges: 2 starch, 1 fruit, 1 fat.

Double Chocolate Cupcakes

(Pictured at right)

This recipe proves you don't have to fudge on chocolate to make a light and luscious treat. These moist cupcakes are chock-full of sweet flavor, but low in saturated fat.
—Linda Utter, Sidney, Montana

2 tablespoons butter *or* stick margarine, softened
3/4 cup sugar
1 egg
1 egg white
1/2 cup plus 2 tablespoons 1% buttermilk
1/3 cup water
1 tablespoon white vinegar
1 teaspoon vanilla extract
1-1/2 cups all-purpose flour
1/4 cup baking cocoa
1 teaspoon baking soda
1/2 teaspoon salt
1/3 cup miniature semisweet chocolate chips

In a mixing bowl, cream butter and sugar. Add egg and egg white, one at a time, beating well after each addition. Beat on high speed until light and fluffy. Stir in buttermilk, water, vinegar and vanilla. Combine the flour, cocoa, baking soda and salt; add to batter just until moistened. Stir in chocolate chips.

Fill muffin cups coated with nonstick cooking spray three-fourths full. Bake at 375° for 15-18 minutes or until a toothpick comes out clean. Cool for 5 minutes before removing from pans to wire racks. **Yield:** 14 cupcakes.

Nutritional Analysis: One cupcake equals 139 calories, 2 g fat (1 g saturated fat), 1 mg cholesterol, 221 mg sodium, 29 g carbohydrate, 1 g fiber, 3 g protein.
Diabetic Exchanges: 1-1/2 starch, 1/2 fat.

Marbled Chocolate Cheesecake Bars

(Pictured above)

Chocolate and cream cheese are swirled in these yummy bars to create a sensation that's sure to please your sweet tooth...and fool it at the same time! This dessert tastes so rich, it's hard to believe it's low in fat.
—Jean Komlos, Plymouth, Michigan

   3/4 cup water
   1/3 cup butter (no substitutes)
1-1/2 squares (1-1/2 ounces) unsweetened chocolate
   2 cups all-purpose flour
1-1/2 cups packed brown sugar
   1 teaspoon baking soda
   1/2 teaspoon salt
   1 egg
   1 egg white
   1/2 cup reduced-fat sour cream
CREAM CHEESE MIXTURE:
   1 package (8 ounces) reduced-fat cream cheese, softened
   1/3 cup sugar
   1 egg white
   1 tablespoon vanilla extract
   1 cup (6 ounces) miniature semisweet chocolate chips

In a small saucepan, combine the water, butter and chocolate. Cook and stir over low heat until melted; stir until smooth. Cool.

In a mixing bowl, combine the flour, brown sugar, baking soda and salt. Add egg, egg white and sour cream; beat on low speed just until combined. Stir in chocolate mixture until smooth. In another mixing bowl, beat cream cheese, sugar, egg white and vanilla; set aside.

Spread chocolate batter into a 15-in. x 10-in. x 1-in. baking pan coated with nonstick cooking spray. Drop the cream cheese mixture by tablespoonfuls over batter; cut through batter with a knife to swirl. Sprinkle with chocolate chips.

Bake at 375° for 20-25 minutes or until a toothpick inserted near the center comes out clean. Cool on a wire rack. **Yield:** about 4 dozen.

Nutritional Analysis: One bar equals 95 calories, 4 g fat (2 g saturated fat), 10 mg cholesterol, 90 mg sodium, 15 g carbohydrate, trace fiber, 2 g protein.
Diabetic Exchanges: 1 starch, 1/2 fat.

Apricot Noodle Kugel

Kugel—traditionally served on the Jewish Sabbath— is a baked pudding usually made with potatoes or noodles and served as a side dish. Sweet versions make delicious desserts.
—Martha Chayet, Manchester, Massachusetts

   1 package (8 ounces) reduced-fat cream cheese
   1/2 cup sugar
   1/4 cup packed brown sugar
   1 egg
   3/4 cup egg substitute
   1 cup fat-free evaporated milk
   3/4 cup reduced-fat sour cream
   3/4 cup apricot nectar
   1/2 cup part-skim ricotta cheese
   2 tablespoons butter *or* stick margarine, melted
   2 tablespoons baking fat replacement*
   1 teaspoon vanilla extract
   8 ounces fettuccine, cooked and drained
   1 jar (8 ounces) apricot jam, warmed
TOPPING:
   1/2 cup cornflakes, crushed
   1/4 cup sugar
   1/4 cup packed brown sugar
   1 teaspoon ground cinnamon
   1/4 teaspoon ground nutmeg
   2 tablespoons butter *or* stick margarine, melted

In a mixing bowl, beat cream cheese and sugars until smooth. Add the next nine ingredients; mix well. Add fet-

tuccine; mix gently. Pour into a 13-in. x 9-in. x 2-in. baking dish coated with nonstick cooking spray. Top with jam; cut through noodle mixture with a knife to swirl.

In a bowl, combine the first five topping ingredients; sprinkle with butter and toss to coat. Sprinkle topping over kugel. Bake, uncovered, at 325° for 60-70 minutes or until a knife inserted near the center comes out clean. **Yield:** 12 servings.

Editor's Note: This recipe was tested with Smucker's Baking Healthy. Look for it in the baking aisle of your grocery store.

Nutritional Analysis: One serving (1 piece) equals 347 calories, 11 g fat (6 g saturated fat), 48 mg cholesterol, 234 mg sodium, 54 g carbohydrate, 1 g fiber, 10 g protein.
Diabetic Exchanges: 2-1/2 starch, 2 fat, 1 lean meat.

Mock Ice Cream Sandwiches

(Pictured below)

As a busy lawyer, I can't take my sweet time making ice cream treats. So my girlfriend and I came up with this one. The recipe cuts down on fat but not on flavor. I usually keep a batch in the freezer.
—Tony Kern, Milwaukee, Wisconsin

2 cups fat-free whipped topping
1/2 cup miniature semisweet chocolate chips
8 whole chocolate graham crackers

In a bowl, combine whipped topping and chocolate chips. Break or cut graham crackers in half. Spread whipped topping mixture over half of the crackers; top with remaining crackers. Wrap in plastic wrap and freeze for at least 1 hour. **Yield:** 8 sandwiches.

Nutritional Analysis: One sandwich equals 180 calories, 7 g fat (3 g saturated fat), 0 cholesterol, 88 mg sodium, 28 g carbohydrate, 1 g fiber, 2 g protein.
Diabetic Exchanges: 2 starch, 1/2 fat.

Watermelon Ice

(Pictured above)

For a different way to serve watermelon, try this make-ahead frozen dessert. It's so refreshing on a summer day...and you don't have to worry about seeds while you're enjoying it.
—Kaaren Jurack, Virginia Beach, Virginia

1 teaspoon unflavored gelatin
2 tablespoons water
4 cups seeded cubed watermelon, *divided*
2 tablespoons lime juice
2 tablespoons honey

In a microwave-safe bowl, sprinkle gelatin over water; let stand for 2 minutes. Microwave on high for 40 seconds; stir. Let stand for 2 minutes or until gelatin is dissolved. Pour into a blender or food processor; add 1 cup watermelon, lime juice and honey. Cover and process until smooth. Add remaining melon, a cup at a time, and process until smooth.

Pour into a 9-in. square dish; freeze until almost firm. Transfer to a chilled bowl; beat with an electric mixer until mixture is bright pink. Pour into serving dishes; freeze until firm. Remove from the freezer 15-20 minutes before serving. **Yield:** 4 servings.

Nutritional Analysis: One serving (3/4 cup) equals 85 calories, 1 g fat (trace saturated fat), 0 cholesterol, 5 mg sodium, 20 g carbohydrate, 1 g fiber, 2 g protein.
Diabetic Exchange: 1-1/2 fruit.

Apricot Oat Bars

*With an oat-filled crust and golden crumb
topping, these apricot-filled bars are sweet and chewy.
Snackers can't resist my fruity treats.*
—Dorothy Myrick, Kent, Washington

1 cup quick-cooking oats
1 cup all-purpose flour
2/3 cup packed brown sugar
1/4 teaspoon baking soda
1/4 teaspoon salt
1/4 cup canola oil
3 tablespoons unsweetened apple juice
1 jar (10 ounces) 100% apricot spreadable fruit

In a bowl, combine the oats, flour, brown sugar, baking soda and salt. Drizzle with oil and apple juice; stir until moistened. Set aside 1/2 cup for topping. Press remaining oat mixture into an 11-in. x 7-in. x 2-in. baking pan coated with nonstick cooking spray. Spread the apricot fruit spread to within 1/4 in. of edges. Sprinkle with reserved oat mixture. Bake at 325° for 30-35 minutes or until golden brown. **Yield:** 16 bars.

Nutritional Analysis: One bar equals 151 calories, 4 g fat (trace saturated fat), 0 cholesterol, 24 mg sodium, 28 g carbohydrate, 1 g fiber, 2 g protein.
Diabetic Exchanges: *1 starch, 1 fat, 1/2 fruit.*

German Chocolate Torte

(Pictured at right and on page 199)

*I made this cake for my stepdaughter's birthday,
and everyone loved it. It has just half the fat of
a classic German chocolate cake.*
—Lois Maxwell, Alexandria, Louisiana

1 package (4 ounces) German sweet chocolate
1/2 cup water
2 cups sugar
3/4 cup baking fat replacement*
1/4 cup canola oil
4 eggs, *separated*
2-1/4 cups all-purpose flour
1 teaspoon baking soda
1/2 teaspoon salt
1 cup 1% buttermilk
1 teaspoon vanilla extract
1/4 teaspoon butter flavoring
FROSTING:
3 egg yolks
1 cup fat-free evaporated milk
1 cup sugar
1/2 cup marshmallow creme
1 teaspoon vanilla extract
1/4 teaspoon butter flavoring
1-1/3 cups flaked coconut
3/4 cup chopped pecans

In a microwave-safe bowl, combine chocolate and water. Microwave on high for 1-1/2 to 2 minutes or until chocolate is melted; stir until smooth. In a mixing bowl, combine sugar, fat replacement and oil. Add egg yolks, one at a time, beating well after each. Add melted chocolate; beat well. Combine flour, baking soda and salt; add to chocolate mixture alternately with buttermilk. Stir in vanilla and butter flavoring. In another mixing bowl, beat egg whites until stiff peaks form; fold into batter.

Pour into three 9-in. round baking pans coated with nonstick cooking spray. Bake at 350° for 30 minutes or until a toothpick inserted near the center comes out clean. Cool for 10 minutes before removing from pans to wire racks to cool completely.

For frosting, combine egg yolks, milk, sugar and marshmallow creme in a saucepan. Cook and stir over medium heat until thickened, about 15 minutes. Remove from the heat; stir in vanilla and butter flavoring. Fold in coconut and pecans. Cool completely. Spread between layers and over top of cooled cake. **Yield:** 16 slices.

***Editor's Note:** This recipe was tested with Smucker's Baking Healthy.*

Nutritional Analysis: One slice equals 432 calories, 14 g fat (4 g saturated fat), 94 mg cholesterol, 233 mg sodium, 73 g carbohydrate, 1 g fiber, 6 g protein.

Orange Delight

(Pictured at right and on page 199)

*I'm a college student who was introduced to the kitchen
when I was very young. My favorite thing is baking
desserts—because I like the sweet reward at the end.*
—Michael Gagliardi, Bell Canyon, California

1 cup vanilla wafer crumbs (about 32 wafers)
2 tablespoons butter *or* stick margarine, melted
3/4 cup orange juice
1/3 cup sugar
2 envelopes unflavored gelatin
1 carton (15 ounces) reduced-fat ricotta cheese
16 ounces fat-free reduced-sugar vanilla yogurt
1 teaspoon grated orange peel
1/8 teaspoon orange extract, optional
1 can (15 ounces) mandarin oranges, drained
2 tablespoons reduced-sugar orange marmalade

In a bowl, combine wafer crumbs and butter; press onto the bottom of an ungreased 9-in. springform pan. Bake at 375° for 10 minutes. Cool on a wire rack. In a saucepan, combine orange juice, sugar and gelatin; let stand for 5 minutes. Cook and stir over low heat until gelatin is dissolved. Cool for 10 minutes.

Meanwhile, in a blender or food processor, cover and process ricotta cheese until smooth. Add the yogurt, orange peel, extract if desired and gelatin mixture; cover and process until smooth. Set aside 1/3 cup oranges for garnish. Add remaining oranges to yogurt mixture. Spoon into the crust.

Chill for at least 6 hours or overnight. Just before serving, run a knife around edge of pan to loosen. Remove sides of pan. Arrange reserved oranges on top. Melt marmalade; spoon over top. Refrigerate leftovers. **Yield:** 10 slices.

Nutritional Analysis: One slice equals 249 calories, 8 g fat (4 g saturated fat), 23 mg cholesterol, 184 mg sodium, 35 g carbohydrate, trace fiber, 9 g protein.
Diabetic Exchanges: *1 starch, 1 lean meat, 1 fruit, 1 fat.*

Crispy Cereal Meringues

Topped with creamy chocolate ribbons, these meringues are rich-tasting but feather-light.
—Beverly Albrecht, Beatrice, Nebraska

    4 egg whites
1/4 teaspoon cream of tartar
1/4 teaspoon salt
    1 cup sugar
    2 cups chocolate-flavored crisp rice cereal
1/4 cup semisweet chocolate chips
1/2 teaspoon vegetable shortening

In a mixing bowl, beat egg whites, cream of tartar and salt until soft peaks form. Gradually add sugar, 1 tablespoon at a time, until stiff peaks form, about 6 minutes. Fold in cereal. Drop by rounded teaspoonfuls 1 in. apart onto baking sheets coated with nonstick cooking spray. Bake at 300° for 35-40 minutes or until firm to the touch. Remove to wire racks to cool.

In a microwave or heavy saucepan, melt chocolate chips with shortening. Transfer to a small resealable plastic bag; cut a small hole in the corner of bag. Drizzle melted chocolate over meringues. Place on waxed paper to harden. **Yield:** 64 cookies.

Nutritional Analysis: One serving (2 cookies) equals 43 calories, 1 g fat (trace saturated fat), 0 cholesterol, 43 mg sodium, 9 g carbohydrate, trace fiber, 1 g protein.
Diabetic Exchange: 1/2 starch.

Marshmallow Fudge

Chock-full of marshmallows and graham crackers, no one will believe that this tantalizing treat is low in fat.
—Holly Mann, Amherst, New Hampshire

1-1/3 cups semisweet chocolate chips
  2/3 cup fat-free sweetened condensed milk
    1 teaspoon vanilla extract
1-1/3 cups miniature marshmallows
    2 whole reduced-fat graham crackers, broken into bite-size pieces

Line an 8-in. square pan with foil and coat with nonstick cooking spray; set aside. In a heavy saucepan over low heat, melt chocolate chips with milk; stir until smooth. Remove from the heat; cool for 2 minutes. Stir in vanilla. Fold in the marshmallows and graham crackers. Pour into prepared pan. Refrigerate for 1 hour or until firm. Lift out of pan and remove foil; cut into 48 pieces. **Yield:** 4 dozen.

Nutritional Analysis: One piece equals 41 calories, 1 g fat (1 g saturated fat), trace cholesterol, 10 mg sodium, 7 g carbohydrate, trace fiber, 1 g protein.
Diabetic Exchange: 1/2 starch.

Sunny Sponge Cake

(Pictured above)

This golden cake has a light texture and mild flavor that makes it a pleasant ending to most any meal. The spongy interior is flecked with bits of orange peel.
—Candy Snyder, Salem, Oregon

    3 egg yolks
    1 cup sugar, *divided*
    2 teaspoons hot water
1/2 cup orange juice, warmed
1-1/4 teaspoons vanilla extract
  3/4 teaspoon grated orange peel
  1/4 teaspoon grated lemon peel
1-1/2 cups all-purpose flour
1-1/4 teaspoons baking powder
  1/4 teaspoon salt
    6 egg whites
  3/4 cup reduced-fat whipped topping

In a mixing bowl, beat egg yolks until slightly thickened. Gradually add 3/4 cup sugar and hot water, beating until thick and lemon-colored. Blend in the orange juice, vanilla and orange and lemon peels. Sift together the flour, baking powder and salt; add to egg yolk mixture.

In another mixing bowl, beat the egg whites until soft peaks form. Add the remaining sugar, 1 tablespoon at a time, beating until stiff peaks form. Fold a fourth of the egg whites into the batter; fold in remaining whites.

Spoon into an ungreased 10-in. tube pan. Bake at 350° for 20-25 minutes or until cake springs back when lightly touched. Immediately invert pan; cool completely. Cut into slices; serve with whipped topping. **Yield:** 12 servings.

Nutritional Analysis: One serving (1 slice with 1 tablespoon whipped topping) equals 160 calories, 2 g fat (1 g saturated fat), 53 mg cholesterol, 103 mg sodium, 31 gm carbohydrate, trace fiber, 4 g protein.
Diabetic Exchanges: 1-1/2 starch, 1/2 fruit.

Favorite Pear Cheesecake Recipe Made Lighter

FOR Jennifer Short of Omaha, Nebraska, there's no better way to savor the flavor of pears than in a creamy cheesecake. "My family has always had a fondness for pears, so desserts that feature them, such as this Pear Cheesecake, are popular at my house," she says.

For a slimmed-down version of Jennifer's fruity favorite, try our Test Kitchen's Makeover Pear Cheesecake. To trim the original recipe, our crew used reduced-fat graham cracker crumbs, less butter in the crust, reduced-fat cream cheese and fat-free milk in the filling.

Pear Cheesecake

1-1/2 cups graham cracker crumbs (about 24 squares)
1 cup sugar, *divided*
1/3 cup butter *or* margarine, melted
2 cans (15 ounces *each*) pear halves, drained
3 packages (8 ounces *each*) cream cheese, softened
3 tablespoons all-purpose flour
2 eggs
1/2 cup milk
2 tablespoons lemon juice
1-1/2 teaspoons grated lemon peel

In a small bowl, combine cracker crumbs, 1/4 cup sugar and butter. Press onto the bottom and 1-1/2 in. up the sides of a greased 9-in. springform pan; refrigerate for 30 minutes. Place pear halves cut side down on crust.

In a mixing bowl, beat cream cheese and remaining sugar until smooth. Add flour; beat well. Add eggs; beat on low speed just until combined. Add the milk, lemon juice and peel; beat just until blended. Pour over pears.

Bake at 350° for 45-50 minutes or until center is almost set. Cool on a wire rack for 10 minutes. Carefully run a knife around edge of pan to loosen; cool 1 hour longer. Chill overnight. Remove sides of pan. Refrigerate leftovers. **Yield:** 12 servings.

Nutritional Analysis: One slice equals 437 calories, 27 g fat (16 g saturated fat), 112 mg cholesterol, 330 mg sodium, 43 g carbohydrate, 2 g fiber, 7 g protein.

Makeover Pear Cheesecake

(Pictured at right)

1-1/4 cups reduced-fat graham cracker crumbs (about 20 squares)
3 tablespoons plus 3/4 cup sugar, *divided*
3 tablespoons butter *or* stick margarine, melted
2 medium ripe pears, peeled and sliced

3 packages (8 ounces *each*) reduced-fat cream cheese
3 tablespoons all-purpose flour
1 egg
1/4 cup egg substitute
1/2 cup fat-free milk
2 tablespoons lemon juice
1-1/2 teaspoons grated lemon peel

In a small bowl, combine cracker crumbs, 3 tablespoons sugar and butter. Press onto the bottom and 1-1/4 in. up the sides of a 9-in. springform pan coated with nonstick cooking spray; refrigerate for 30 minutes. Arrange pear slices over crust.

In a mixing bowl, beat cream cheese and remaining sugar until smooth. Add flour; beat well. Add egg and egg substitute; beat on low speed just until combined. Add the milk, lemon juice and peel; beat just until blended. Pour over pears.

Bake at 350° for 45-50 minutes or until center is set. Cool on a wire rack for 10 minutes. Carefully run a knife around edge of pan to loosen; cool 1 hour longer. Chill overnight. Remove sides of pan. Refrigerate leftovers. **Yield:** 12 servings.

Nutritional Analysis: One slice equals 272 calories, 14 g fat (8 g saturated fat), 57 mg cholesterol, 258 mg sodium, 9 g carbohydrate, 1 g fiber, 8 g protein.
Diabetic Exchanges: 2 fat, 1-1/2 starch, 1/2 fruit, 1/2 lean meat.

Blueberry Crumb Pie

Treating yourself to this indulgent dessert won't give you the blues later on! Even with a fabulous fruit filling and crumb topping, this light recipe keeps fat and calories to a minimum. Serve the pie warm, advises our Test Kitchen staff...and expect plenty of compliments!

1-1/4 cups all-purpose flour, *divided*
    5 tablespoons cold water
1-1/4 teaspoons lemon juice
1-1/4 teaspoons sugar
    1/4 teaspoon salt
    3 tablespoons plus 2 teaspoons shortening
FILLING:
4-1/2 cups fresh *or* frozen blueberries*
    1 cup (8 ounces) reduced-fat vanilla yogurt
    1/2 cup packed brown sugar
    3 tablespoons all-purpose flour
1-1/2 teaspoons vanilla extract
    1/4 teaspoon grated lemon peel
    1/2 cup graham cracker crumbs (about 12 squares)
    2 tablespoons sugar
    2 tablespoons butter *or* stick margarine, melted

In a bowl, whisk together 1/4 cup flour, water and lemon juice; set aside. In a large bowl, combine sugar, salt and remaining flour; cut in shortening until crumbly. Gradually add flour mixture, tossing with a fork until moistened. On a piece of plastic wrap, press dough into a 4-in. circle. Cover with a second sheet of plastic wrap; roll into a 12-in. circle. Freeze for 10 minutes.

Let stand for 1 minute; remove plastic wrap. Transfer pastry to pie plate; trim to 1/2 in. beyond edge of plate. Flute edges. Prick bottom and sides of pastry with a fork. Line shell with a double thickness of heavy-duty foil. Bake at 375° for 8 minutes. Remove foil; bake 5 minutes longer.

Place blueberries in crust. In a bowl, combine the yogurt, brown sugar, flour, vanilla and lemon peel; spread over blueberries. Combine graham cracker crumbs, sugar and butter; sprinkle over yogurt mixture. Bake at 375° for 35-40 minutes or until crumbs are lightly browned and filling is bubbly. **Yield:** 8 servings.

*Editor's Note: If using frozen berries, do not thaw before adding to pie.

Nutritional Analysis: One slice equals 313 calories, 9 g fat (3 g saturated fat), 9 mg cholesterol, 164 mg sodium, 55 g carbohydrate, 2 g fiber, 4 g protein.
Diabetic Exchanges: 2 starch, 1-1/2 fruit, 1-1/2 fat.

Tortilla Dessert Cups

(Pictured above right)

Diabetics and dessert lovers alike are "wowed" by these creamy treats. After finding out my mother had diabetes, I went on a search for good recipes like this. These bites taste so yummy.
—Susan Miller, Wakeman, Ohio

    3 tablespoons sugar
    2 teaspoons ground cinnamon
10 flour tortillas (6 inches)
    1 package (8 ounces) reduced-fat cream cheese, softened

    1 cup cold fat-free milk
    1 package (1 ounce) sugar-free instant white chocolate *or* vanilla pudding mix
    2 cups reduced-fat whipped topping
    1/4 cup milk chocolate chips, melted

In a small bowl, combine sugar and cinnamon. Coat one side of each tortilla with nonstick cooking spray; sprinkle with cinnamon-sugar. Turn tortillas over; repeat on the other side. Cut each tortilla into four wedges. For each dessert cup, place round edge of one tortilla wedge in the bottom of a muffin cup, shaping sides to fit cup. Place a second tortilla wedge in muffin cup, allowing bottom and sides to overlap. Bake at 350° for 10 minutes or until crisp and lightly browned. Cool completely in pan.

Meanwhile, for filling, beat cream cheese in a mixing bowl until smooth. In another mixing bowl, beat milk and pudding mix on low speed for 2 minutes. Beat in cream cheese on low until smooth. Fold in whipped topping. Cover and refrigerate for 1 hour. Carefully remove cups from pan. Pipe or spoon about 3 tablespoons filling into each cup. Drizzle or pipe with melted chocolate. Refrigerate for 5 minutes or until chocolate is set. Store in the refrigerator. **Yield:** 20 servings.

Nutritional Analysis: One serving (1 dessert cup) equals 130 calories, 4 g fat (2 g saturated fat), 5 mg cholesterol, 178 mg sodium, 19 g carbohydrate, trace fiber, 4 g protein.
Diabetic Exchange: 1-1/2 starch.

Triple Orange Fluff

A friend I used to work with brought this light, refreshing dessert to potlucks frequently—it always went over well. It's just slightly sweet...and so easy to make!
—Joy MacLaren, Winter Park, Florida

1 package (.3 ounce) sugar-free orange gelatin
1 cup boiling water

1 pint orange sherbet, softened
1 carton (8 ounces) frozen reduced-fat whipped topping, thawed
1 prepared angel food cake (16 ounces), torn into 1-inch pieces
1 can (15 ounces) mandarin oranges, drained

In a large bowl, dissolve gelatin powder in boiling water. Stir in sherbet. Refrigerate until partially set. Fold in whipped topping. Place cake pieces in a 13-in. x 9-in. x 2-in. dish. Arrange oranges over cake. Pour gelatin mixture over the top. Cover and refrigerate for 4 hours or until firm. **Yield:** 15 servings.

Nutritional Analysis: *One piece equals 167 calories, 3 g fat (2 g saturated fat), 2 mg cholesterol, 181 mg sodium, 33 g carbohydrate, 1 g fiber, 3 g protein.*
Diabetic Exchanges: *1-1/2 starch, 1/2 fruit.*

Chocolate Chip Cookies

(Pictured below)

As a high school home economics teacher, I like coming up with trimmed-down snacks for my class to try. The kids think these cookies deserve an A+.
—Linda Todd, Coldwater, Michigan

1/2 cup butter *or* stick margarine, softened
1 cup sugar
1 cup packed brown sugar
2 eggs
1/2 cup egg substitute
1/4 cup corn syrup
2 teaspoons vanilla extract
4 cups all-purpose flour
2 teaspoons baking soda
1 teaspoon salt
1-1/4 cups semisweet chocolate chips

In a mixing bowl, cream butter and sugars. Add eggs, one at a time, beating well after each addition. Beat in the egg substitute, corn syrup and vanilla. Combine the flour, baking soda and salt; gradually add to creamed mixture. Stir in chocolate chips.

Drop by rounded tablespoonfuls 2 in. apart onto ungreased baking sheets. Bake at 350° for 9-11 minutes or until lightly browned. Immediately remove to wire racks to cool. **Yield:** 5-1/2 dozen.

Nutritional Analysis: *One cookie equals 87 calories, 3 g fat (2 g saturated fat), 10 mg cholesterol, 97 mg sodium, 15 g carbohydrate, trace fiber, 1 g protein.*
Diabetic Exchange: *1 starch.*

Frosty Pumpkin Pie

(Pictured above)

This frozen treat is so delightful that no one will guess it's made with reduced-fat ingredients. My gang actually prefers a slice of this layered dessert to traditional pumpkin pie at Christmastime.
—Janet Jackson, Hopedale, Illinois

2 cups frozen reduced-fat vanilla yogurt, softened
1 reduced-fat graham cracker crust (9 inches)
1 cup cooked *or* canned pumpkin
1/2 cup sugar
1 teaspoon pumpkin pie spice
1/2 teaspoon salt
1/2 teaspoon ground ginger
1 carton (8 ounces) frozen reduced-fat whipped topping, thawed

Spread yogurt into crust. Freeze for 30 minutes. Meanwhile, in a bowl, combine the pumpkin, sugar, pumpkin pie spice, salt and ginger; mix well. Fold in the whipped topping. Spoon over frozen yogurt. Freeze for 6 hours or overnight. Remove from the freezer 20 minutes before cutting. **Yield:** 8 servings.

Nutritional Analysis: *One piece equals 282 calories, 7 g fat (5 g saturated fat), 3 mg cholesterol, 273 mg sodium, 47 g carbohydrate, 1 g fiber, 4 g protein.*
Diabetic Exchanges: *2 starch, 1 fruit, 1 fat.*

Ribbon Pudding Pie

(Pictured above)

Cool, smooth and creamy, this pretty pie is a slice of heaven for diabetics and anyone who likes an easy yet impressive dessert. The lovely pudding layers feature a yummy combination of vanilla, chocolate and butterscotch.
—*Doris Morgan, Verona, Mississippi*

4 cups cold fat-free milk, *divided*
1 package (1 ounce) sugar-free instant vanilla pudding mix
1 reduced-fat graham cracker crust (8 inches)
1 package (1 ounce) sugar-free instant butterscotch pudding mix
1 package (1.4 ounces) sugar-free instant chocolate pudding mix
1/2 cup reduced-fat whipped topping
2 tablespoons chopped pecans

In a mixing bowl, beat 1-1/3 cups milk and vanilla pudding mix on low speed for 2 minutes. Pour into graham cracker crust. In another bowl, beat 1-1/3 cups milk and butterscotch pudding mix for 2 minutes. Spoon evenly over the vanilla layer. Beat chocolate pudding mix and remaining milk for 2 minutes. Spread evenly over butterscotch layer. Spread with whipped topping. Sprinkle with pecans. Refrigerate for at least 30 minutes. **Yield:** 8 servings.

Nutritional Analysis: One serving (1 slice) equals 107 calories, 2 g fat (1 g saturated fat), 2 mg cholesterol, 512 mg sodium, 17 g carbohydrate, trace fiber, 5 g protein.
Diabetic Exchanges: 1 starch, 1/2 fruit.

Banana Spice Cake

This delicious spice cake is bursting with the fresh flavor of ripe bananas and zesty orange peel. I've packed lots of spices into my favorite healthy dessert.
—*Sharon Carroll, Whittier, California*

1 egg yolk
1/4 cup canola oil
1 cup mashed ripe bananas (about 3 medium)
2 cups cake flour
1-1/4 cups sugar, *divided*
1/2 cup all-purpose flour
2 teaspoons baking powder
2 teaspoons ground cinnamon
1-1/2 teaspoons baking soda
1 teaspoon ground nutmeg
1/2 teaspoon *each* **salt, ground cloves, ginger and allspice**
1/2 cup fat-free milk
1/4 cup orange juice concentrate
2 tablespoons fat-free plain yogurt
1 tablespoon grated orange peel
1 tablespoon vanilla extract
3 egg whites
1/4 teaspoon cream of tartar
GLAZE:
1 cup confectioners' sugar
1/4 teaspoon vanilla extract
1 to 2 tablespoons fat-free milk

In a mixing bowl, beat the egg yolk, oil and bananas. Combine the cake flour, 1 cup sugar, all-purpose flour, baking powder, cinnamon, baking soda, nutmeg, salt, cloves, ginger and allspice. In another bowl, combine the milk, orange juice concentrate, yogurt, orange peel and vanilla. Gradually add dry ingredients to banana mixture alternately with milk mixture.

In another mixing bowl, beat egg whites and cream of tartar until soft peaks form. Gradually add remaining sugar, beating until stiff peaks form. Fold into batter. Pour into a greased and floured 10-in. fluted tube pan. Bake at 350° for 48-52 minutes or until a toothpick comes out clean. Cool for 10 minutes before removing from pan to a wire rack.

Combine the glaze ingredients; drizzle over cooled cake. **Yield:** 16 servings.

Nutritional Analysis: One piece equals 216 calories, 4 g fat (trace saturated fat), 14 mg cholesterol, 238 mg sodium, 42 g carbohydrate, 1 g fiber, 3 g protein.
Diabetic Exchanges: 2 starch, 1 fruit.

Pleasing Pie Crusts

IT'S NOT a pie-in-the-sky idea. You *can* have a home-made pie, but without all the fat! Our Test Kitchen home economists have come up with deliciously different ways to lighten up the fat and calories in pie crusts.

Graham Cracker Crust

This light version has only about half the fat of a traditional graham cracker crust.

1-1/4 cups graham cracker crumbs (about 20 squares)
3 tablespoons sugar
3 tablespoons butter *or* stick margarine, melted
1 egg white

In a food processor, combine cracker crumbs, sugar and butter; pulse until blended. Add egg white; pulse until moistened. Press mixture onto the bottom and up the sides of a 9-in. pie plate. Bake at 375° for 8-10 minutes or until lightly browned. Cool completely before filling. **Yield:** 8 servings.

Nutritional Analysis: One serving (1/8 of pie crust) equals 130 calories, 5 g fat (3 g saturated fat), 12 mg cholesterol, 122 mg sodium, 19 g carbohydrate, 1 g fiber, 2 g protein.

Chocolate Brownie Crust

Soft and chewy, this fudgy crust will remind you of brownies the moment you bite into it. Fill with a light creamy pudding or low-fat mousse, then top with fresh fruit.

1-1/4 cups reduced-fat chocolate wafer crumbs (about 40 wafers)
2 tablespoons sugar
2 tablespoons butter *or* stick margarine, melted
1 egg white

In a food processor, combine wafer crumbs, sugar and butter; pulse until blended. Add egg white; pulse until moistened. Press mixture onto the bottom and up the sides of a 9-in. pie plate. Bake at 375° for 8-10 minutes or until lightly browned. Cool completely before filling. **Yield:** 8 servings.

Nutritional Analysis: One serving (1/8 of pie crust) equals 115 calories, 4 g fat (2 g saturated fat), 8 mg cholesterol, 102 mg sodium, 18 g carbohydrate, 0 fiber, 1 g protein.

Strawberry Chiffon Pie

(Pictured at right)

This scrumptious strawberry chiffon filling is so refreshing. Either of the crumb crusts on this page will showcase it nicely.

2-1/2 cups sliced unsweetened strawberries
1 envelope unflavored gelatin
2 tablespoons lemonade concentrate
1/4 cup sugar
3 egg whites, lightly beaten
1 tablespoon orange juice
1-1/2 cups reduced-fat whipped topping
1 Graham Cracker Crust *or* Chocolate Brownie Crust (recipes on this page)
4 large fresh strawberries, halved

Place sliced strawberries in a food processor or blender; cover and process until smooth. Set aside 1-1/2 cups for filling (discard remaining puree or save for another use). In a saucepan, soften gelatin in lemonade concentrate; let stand for 5 minutes. Stir in sugar and reserved strawberry puree. Cook and stir over medium heat until mixture comes to a boil and gelatin is dissolved. Remove from the heat.

Stir a small amount of filling into egg whites; return all to the pan, stirring constantly. Cook and stir over low heat for 3 minutes or until mixture is slightly thickened and a thermometer reaches 160° (do not boil). Remove from the heat; stir in orange juice. Cover and refrigerate for 2 hours, stirring occasionally. Fold in whipped topping; spoon into crust. Cover and refrigerate for 2 hours or until set. Just before serving, garnish with halved strawberries. **Yield:** 8 servings.

Nutritional Analysis: One piece (calculated with Graham Cracker Crust) equals 226 calories, 7 g fat (5 g saturated fat), 12 mg cholesterol, 145 mg sodium, 35 g carbohydrate, 2 g fiber, 4 g protein.
***Diabetic Exchanges:** 2 starch, 1 fruit.*

1 egg white
3 tablespoons water
3/4 teaspoon vanilla extract
1/3 cup all-purpose flour
1/3 cup whole wheat flour
2 teaspoons ground cinnamon
1/2 teaspoon baking soda
1/4 teaspoon salt
2 cups old-fashioned oats
1/2 cup raisins

In a mixing bowl, beat oil and sugars. Add egg white, water and vanilla; mix well. Combine the flours, cinnamon, baking soda and salt; add to creamed mixture. Stir in oats and raisins.

Drop by scant 1/4 cupfuls onto baking sheets coated with nonstick cooking spray; flatten slightly with the back of a spoon. Bake at 350° for 10-12 minutes or until golden brown. Cool for 1 minute before removing from pans to wire racks. **Yield:** 15 cookies.

Nutritional Analysis: One cookie equals 143 calories, 6 g fat (trace saturated fat), 0 cholesterol, 89 mg sodium, 21 g carbohydrate, 2 g fiber, 3 g protein.
Diabetic Exchanges: 1-1/2 starch, 1/2 fat.

Mile-High Lime Pie

(Pictured above)

Convenience items speed along the preparation of this light and fluffy make-ahead pie. The lime filling is very sweet, creamy and piles high in the crust.
—*Candi Smith, Blue Springs, Missouri*

1 can (14 ounces) fat-free sweetened condensed milk
1 cup (8 ounces) reduced-fat sour cream
1/3 cup plus 2 tablespoons lime juice
5 drops green food coloring, optional
1 carton (8 ounces) frozen reduced-fat whipped topping, thawed
1 reduced-fat graham cracker crust (8 inches)

In a bowl, combine the milk, sour cream, lime juice and food coloring if desired. Fold in whipped topping. Pour into the crust. Refrigerate for at least 12 hours. **Yield:** 8 servings.

Nutritional Analysis: One piece equals 355 calories, 9 g fat (6 g saturated fat), 12 mg cholesterol, 171 mg sodium, 57 g carbohydrate, trace fiber, 7 g protein.
Diabetic Exchanges: 3 starch, 1 fruit, 1/2 fat.

Chewy Oatmeal Raisin Cookies

Even picky preschoolers, like my son, devour these wholesome treats sprinkled with cinnamon and packed with raisins. With a glass of juice or milk, the cookies are also great as an on-the-go breakfast.
—*Trina Boitnott, Boones Mill, Virginia*

1/3 cup canola oil
1/3 cup packed brown sugar
2 tablespoons sugar

Pineapple-Coconut Angel Food Cake

(Pictured at right)

I found this recipe in a local paper and adapted it to suit my family's tastes. A friend who doesn't cook much took this cake to a family gathering, and they thought she was an overnight gourmet!
—*Donna Quinn, Salem, Wisconsin*

1 package (16 ounces) angel food cake mix
2 cans (8 ounces *each*) crushed pineapple, undrained
1 teaspoon coconut extract
1 package (8 ounces) reduced-fat cream cheese
2 tablespoons confectioners' sugar
1 teaspoon pineapple *or* orange extract
1-1/2 cups reduced-fat whipped topping
1/4 cup flaked coconut, toasted

🍎 Superb Slices

- Angel food cake is a great fat-free treat, but it's difficult to slice since it squashes easily under pressure. I use my electric knife to make perfect slices every time.
  —*Helen Westie Empire, Michigan*
- I've found that if I freeze the whole angel food cake overnight, it slices up really nice. Because it's frozen, the knife doesn't "squish" the cake.
  —*Sandy Fank, Olivia, Minnesota*

In a mixing bowl, combine the dry cake mix, pineapple and coconut extract. Beat on low speed for 30 seconds; beat on medium for 1 minute. Pour into an ungreased 10-in. tube pan. Bake at 350° for 35-40 minutes or until cake springs back when lightly touched. Immediately invert pan; cool completely. Carefully run a knife around sides of pan. Remove cake to a serving plate.

For topping, in a mixing bowl, beat cream cheese, sugar and pineapple extract until smooth. Fold in whipped topping. Spread over top and sides of cake. Sprinkle with coconut. **Yield:** 16 servings.

Nutritional Analysis: One piece equals 178 calories, 4 g fat (3 g saturated fat), 8 mg cholesterol, 254 mg sodium, 31 g carbohydrate, 1 g fiber, 4 g protein.
Diabetic Exchanges: 1-1/2 starch, 1 fruit.

Cool Mandarin Dessert

(Pictured above)

I've served this refreshing, pleasantly light citrus dessert for years. It is easy to make but looks so elegant. For special occasions, I put it in a crystal bowl to show off its pretty color.
—Sue Murphy, Greenwood, Michigan

1 can (11 ounces) mandarin oranges
2 packages (.3 ounce *each*) sugar-free orange
   gelatin
2 cups boiling water
1 pint orange sherbet
Fresh mint, optional

Drain oranges, reserving the juice; add enough water to juice to measure 1 cup. Refrigerate the oranges. In a large bowl, dissolve gelatin in boiling water. Stir in reserved juice. Add sherbet, stirring until dissolved. Refrigerate for 1 hour or until thickened.

Keep 10 orange segments refrigerated for garnish. Fold remaining oranges into gelatin mixture; cover and refrigerate overnight. Just before serving, garnish with reserved oranges and mint if desired. **Yield:** 10 servings.

Nutritional Analysis: One serving (1/2 cup) equals 134 calories, 1 g fat (trace saturated fat), 2 mg cholesterol, 462 mg sodium, 15 g carbohydrate, trace fiber, 7 g protein.
Diabetic Exchanges: 1 starch, 1 fruit.

Lemon Snack Cake

I love to experiment with lighter recipes and was pleased to come up with this moist lemon cake. A dollop of whipped topping gives the final touch to each sunny square.
—Rosalie Buyce, Winter Haven, Florida

      1/3 cup butter *or* stick margarine, softened
      3/4 cup sugar
        2 eggs
        2 teaspoons grated lemon peel
    1-1/2 teaspoons lemon extract
        1 teaspoon vanilla extract
    2-1/2 cups all-purpose flour
        1 teaspoon baking soda
      1/2 teaspoon baking powder
      1/4 teaspoon salt
        1 carton (8 ounces) fat-free lemon yogurt
  Reduced-fat whipped topping
  Additional lemon peel, optional

In a mixing bowl, cream butter and sugar. Add eggs, one at a time, beating well after each addition. Beat in lemon peel and extracts. Combine dry ingredients; add to the creamed mixture alternately with yogurt (batter will be thick).

Spread into a 13-in. x 9-in. x 2-in. baking pan coated with nonstick cooking spray. Bake at 350° for 20-25 minutes or until a toothpick inserted near the center comes out clean. Cool on a wire rack. Garnish with whipped topping and lemon peel if desired. **Yield:** 15 servings.

Nutritional Analysis: One serving (1 piece with 1 tablespoon whipped topping) equals 185 calories, 5 g fat (3 g saturated fat), 40 mg cholesterol, 207 mg sodium, 30 g carbohydrate, 1 g fiber, 4 g protein.
Diabetic Exchanges: 1 fruit, 1 starch, 1 fat.

Lemon Blueberry Cheesecake

(Pictured at right)

For a light, refreshing alternative to traditional cheesecake, try this no-bake treat that calls for gelatin and cottage cheese.
—Julia Klee, Alta, Iowa

        1 package (3 ounces) lemon gelatin
        1 cup boiling water
        2 tablespoons butter *or* stick margarine, melted
        1 tablespoon canola oil
        1 cup graham cracker crumbs (about 16 squares)
        1 carton (24 ounces) fat-free cottage cheese
      1/4 cup sugar
  TOPPING:
        2 tablespoons sugar
    1-1/2 teaspoons cornstarch
      1/4 cup water
    1-1/3 cups fresh *or* frozen blueberries, *divided*
        1 teaspoon lemon juice

In a bowl, dissolve gelatin in boiling water; cool. Combine butter and oil; add crumbs and blend well. Press onto the bottom of a 9-in. springform pan. Chill. In a blender, process cottage cheese and sugar until smooth. While processing, slowly add cooled gelatin. Pour into crust; chill overnight.

For topping, combine sugar and cornstarch in a saucepan; stir in water until smooth. Add 1 cup blueberries. Bring to a boil; cook and stir for 2 minutes or until thickened. Stir in lemon juice; cool slightly. Process in a blender until smooth. Refrigerate until completely cooled. Carefully run a knife around edge of pan to loosen cheesecake; remove sides of pan. Spread the blueberry mixture over the top. Top with remaining blueberries. Refrigerate leftovers. **Yield:** 12 servings.

Nutritional Analysis: One piece equals 171 calories, 4 g fat (1 g saturated fat), 8 mg cholesterol, 352 mg sodium, 27 g carbohydrate, 1 g fiber, 8 g protein.
Diabetic Exchanges: 1-1/2 starch, 1/2 fruit, 1/2 fat.

Cream-Filled Strawberries

(Pictured at right)

These plump berries filled with a creamy pudding mixture are so elegant-looking and luscious-tasting that they're perfect for parties or holiday gatherings.
—Karin Poroslay, Wesley Chapel, Florida

      18 large fresh strawberries
        1 cup cold fat-free milk
        1 package (1 ounce) sugar-free instant vanilla pudding mix
        2 cups reduced-fat whipped topping
      1/4 teaspoon almond extract

Remove stems from strawberries; cut a deep X in the top of each berry. Spread berries apart. In a bowl, whisk milk and pudding mix for 2 minutes. Fold in whipped topping and almond extract. Pipe or spoon about 5 teaspoons into each berry. Chill until serving. **Yield:** 18 strawberries.

Nutritional Analysis: One filled strawberry equals 36 calories, 1 g fat (1 g saturated fat), trace cholesterol, 73 mg sodium, 6 g carbohydrate, 1 g fiber, 1 g protein.
Diabetic Exchange: 1/2 fruit.

🍎 Creamy Cheesecake

I've found fat-free products to be less appealing in most cases than the regular versions. But fat-free cream cheese is one exception—it's almost as good. I have found, however, that it doesn't get as firm in cheesecake recipes.

To remedy that, I use one envelope of unflavored gelatin for every 8 ounces of fat-free cream cheese I use. The gelatin adds no flavor but firms up the cheesecake.   —Len Bloom, Wausau, Wisconsin

Frozen Strawberry Torte

(Pictured above)

I first tried this special dessert one day when I was expecting company and wanted to serve something other than strawberry shortcake. The berry mixture makes such a pretty filling and frosting...and it's an easy way to dress up a purchased pound cake.
—Linda Lamy, Mason, New Hampshire

2 cups fresh strawberries, *divided*
1/4 cup sugar
1/2 cup fat-free milk
3 drops red food coloring, optional
1 package (1 ounce) sugar-free instant vanilla pudding mix
2 cups reduced-fat whipped topping
1 loaf (13.6 ounces) reduced-fat pound cake

In a bowl, mash 1 cup strawberries with sugar; let stand for 30 minutes. Add milk and food coloring if desired. Sprinkle with pudding mix; stir until well blended. Fold in whipped topping. Split cake into three horizontal layers. Place bottom layer on a serving plate; spread with 1/2 cup strawberry mixture. Repeat layers. Top with third cake layer; spread remaining strawberry mixture over top and sides of cake.

Cover and freeze for at least 1 hour or overnight. Remove from the freezer 15 minutes before slicing. Garnish with remaining strawberries. **Yield:** 10 servings.

Nutritional Analysis: *One slice equals 175 calories, 2 g fat (1 g saturated fat), trace cholesterol, 301 mg sodium, 37 g carbohydrate, 1 g fiber, 2 g protein.*
Diabetic Exchanges: *1-1/2 starch, 1 fruit.*

Crinkle-Top Chocolate Cookies

When I baked these moist fudgy cookies for the first time, my three preschool children loved them! But I like them because they're lower in fat and easy to mix.
—Maria Groff, Ephrata, Pennsylvania

2 cups (12 ounces) semisweet chocolate chips, *divided*
2 tablespoons butter *or* stick margarine, softened
1 cup sugar
2 egg whites
1-1/2 teaspoons vanilla extract
1-1/2 cups all-purpose flour
1-1/2 teaspoons baking powder
1/4 teaspoon salt
1/4 cup water
1/2 cup confectioners' sugar

In a microwave or heavy saucepan, melt 1 cup chocolate chips. Stir until smooth; set aside. In a small mixing bowl, cream butter and sugar. Add egg whites and vanilla; beat well. Stir in melted chocolate. Combine the flour, baking powder and salt; gradually add to creamed mixture alternately with water. Stir in remaining chocolate chips. Cover and refrigerate for 2 hours or until easy to handle.

Shape dough into 1-in. balls. Roll in confectioners' sugar. Place 2 in. apart on baking sheets coated with nonstick cooking spray. Bake at 350° for 10-12 minutes or until set. Remove to wire racks to cool. **Yield:** 3-1/2 dozen.

Nutritional Analysis: *One cookie equals 84 calories, 3 g fat (2 g saturated fat), 1 mg cholesterol, 31 mg sodium, 15 g carbohydrate, 1 g fiber, 1 g protein.*
Diabetic Exchange: *1 starch.*

Favorite Brownie Recipe Made Lighter

GOT a craving for chocolate? Bake up a batch of scrumptious Deluxe Brownies!

"From the very first time I mixed up these doubly rich treats, my family was hooked," says Debbie Heine of Great Falls, Montana. "They're so fast and easy, I make them often for family gatherings and church potlucks."

To trim down Debbie's brownies, our Test Kitchen crew knew just what to do. They reduced the amount of butter, sugar, eggs and nuts in the original recipe, then added egg substitute and baking fat replacement.

The outcome? Makeover Deluxe Brownies won raves from our panel of taste-testers.

Deluxe Brownies

1-1/4 cups butter *or* margarine, softened
2-1/4 cups sugar
    5 eggs, lightly beaten
    2 teaspoons vanilla extract
1-1/2 cups all-purpose flour
    2/3 cup baking cocoa
    1 teaspoon salt
1-1/2 cups chopped pecans
FROSTING:
    1 cup sugar
    1/4 cup butter *or* margarine
    1/4 cup milk
    1/2 cup semisweet chocolate chips
    1/2 cup miniature marshmallows

In a mixing bowl, cream butter and sugar. Add eggs and vanilla; mix well. Combine dry ingredients; add to creamed mixture. Stir in pecans; spread in a greased 13-in. x 9-in. x 2-in. baking pan. Bake at 325° for 30-35 minutes or until a toothpick comes out with moist crumbs. Cool on a wire rack.

In a saucepan over low heat, cook and stir sugar, butter and milk until sugar is dissolved. Remove from the heat; stir in chips and marshmallows until melted. Chill until mixture reaches room temperature. Beat until frosting reaches spreading consistency. Spread over brownies. **Yield:** 2-1/2 dozen.

Nutritional Analysis: One brownie equals 265 calories, 16 g fat (7 g saturated fat), 61 mg cholesterol, 187 mg sodium, 31 g carbohydrate, 2 g fiber, 3 g protein.

Makeover Deluxe Brownies

(Pictured at right)

    1/3 cup butter *or* stick margarine, softened
1-3/4 cups sugar
    2 eggs

    3/4 cup egg substitute
    3/4 cup baking fat replacement*
    2 teaspoons vanilla extract
1-1/4 cups all-purpose flour
    1/2 cup baking cocoa
    1 teaspoon salt
    3/4 cup chopped pecans
FROSTING:
    1/2 cup sugar
    2 tablespoons 2% milk
    2 tablespoons butter *or* stick margarine
    1/4 cup semisweet chocolate chips
    1/4 cup miniature marshmallows

In a mixing bowl, cream butter and sugar. Add the next four ingredients; mix well. Combine dry ingredients; add to creamed mixture. Stir in pecans. Spread in a 13-in. x 9-in. x 2-in. baking pan coated with nonstick cooking spray. Bake at 325° for 30-35 minutes or until a toothpick comes out clean. Cool. In a saucepan over low heat, cook and stir sugar, milk and butter until sugar is dissolved. Remove from heat; stir in chips and marshmallows until melted. Spread over brownies. **Yield:** 2-1/2 dozen.

*Editor's Note:** This recipe was tested with Sunsweet Lighter Bake, available in the baking aisle of your grocery store.

Nutritional Analysis: One brownie equals 158 calories, 6 g fat (2 g saturated fat), 22 mg cholesterol, 126 mg sodium, 24 g carbohydrate, 1 g fiber, 2 g protein.
Diabetic Exchanges: 1-1/2 starch, 1 fat.

the pan, stirring constantly. Cook and stir over medium-low heat for 2-3 minutes or just until the sauce thickens slightly and reaches 160° (do not boil).

Remove from the heat. Stir in vanilla. Pour into a bowl; press a piece of waxed paper or plastic wrap over top of sauce. Refrigerate until serving.

Divide raspberry mixture between four dessert dishes; top with vanilla sauce. **Yield:** 4 servings.

Nutritional Analysis: One serving (1/2 cup raspberry mixture with 2 tablespoons vanilla sauce) equals 283 calories, 3 g fat (1 g saturated fat), 58 mg cholesterol, 129 mg sodium, 60 g carbohydrate, 9 g fiber, 6 g protein.
Diabetic Exchanges: 3 starch, 1 fruit.

Raspberry Dessert with Vanilla Sauce

(Pictured above)

This delicious fruity dessert comes from my German background. Mom always called it "Rote Grütz". We had a large raspberry patch, so she served it often in summer, when fresh berries were in season.
—Marie Baumgartner, Stoughton, Wisconsin

4 cups unsweetened raspberries, crushed
1/2 cup orange juice
1/4 cup quick-cooking tapioca
1/2 cup sugar
1/8 teaspoon salt
2 teaspoons cornstarch
1 tablespoon sugar
1 cup 2% milk
1 egg, lightly beaten
1 teaspoon vanilla extract

In a saucepan, combine the raspberries, orange juice and tapioca; let stand for 15 minutes. Stir in sugar and salt. Bring to a boil; cook and stir for 2 minutes or until thickened. Remove from the heat. Cover and refrigerate.

For vanilla sauce, combine the cornstarch and sugar in a saucepan; gradually stir in milk. Bring to a boil; cook and stir for 1-2 minutes or until thickened. Remove from the heat. Stir 1/2 cup of hot mixture into the egg; return all to

Fudgy White Chocolate Pudding Pie

This creamy luscious layered pie is a real treat. No one ever guesses that it's made with sugar-free pudding mixes. Whenever I serve it, I get compliments and requests for the recipe.
—Toni Preiner, Menahga, Minnesota

2 cups cold fat-free milk, *divided*
1 package (1.4 ounces) sugar-free instant chocolate fudge pudding mix
1 carton (8 ounces) frozen reduced-fat whipped topping, thawed, *divided*
1 reduced-fat graham cracker crust (8 inches)
1 package (1 ounce) sugar-free instant white chocolate *or* vanilla pudding mix
1/2 square (1/2 ounce) semisweet chocolate, shaved

In a bowl, whisk 1 cup milk and chocolate fudge pudding mix for 2 minutes or until slightly thickened. Fold in half of the whipped topping. Spread over crust.

In another bowl, whisk remaining milk and white chocolate pudding mix for 2 minutes or until slightly thickened. Fold in remaining whipped topping; spread over fudge pudding layer. Refrigerate for 4 hours or until set. Garnish with shaved chocolate. **Yield:** 8 servings.

Nutritional Analysis: One piece equals 208 calories, 7 g fat (5 g saturated fat), 1 mg cholesterol, 154 mg sodium, 28 g carbohydrate, trace fiber, 4 g protein.
Diabetic Exchanges: 2 starch, 1 fat.

Harvest Snack Cake

(Pictured above)

This tasty treat was my first successful attempt at baking light. The ginger, cinnamon and nutmeg give it a familiar spice cake flavor...and raisins and shredded carrots help keep it moist.
—Hilary Carroll, Dearborn, Michigan

 2 cups whole wheat flour
 1-1/4 cups packed brown sugar
 2 teaspoons baking soda
 3/4 teaspoon ground cinnamon
 1/2 teaspoon ground nutmeg
 1/8 to 1/4 teaspoon ground ginger
 2 eggs
 1/2 cup unsweetened applesauce
 1 teaspoon vanilla extract
 1-1/2 cups shredded carrots
 1 cup raisins

In a bowl, combine the flour, brown sugar, baking soda, cinnamon, nutmeg and ginger. Combine the eggs, applesauce and vanilla; stir into dry ingredients just until moistened. Fold in the carrots and raisins (batter will be thick). Spread evenly in a 13-in. x 9-in. x 2-in. baking pan coated with nonstick cooking spray. Bake at 350° for 30-35 minutes or until a toothpick inserted near the center comes out clean. Cool on a wire rack. **Yield:** 15 servings.

Nutritional Analysis: *One piece equals 170 calories, 1 g fat (trace saturated fat), 28 mg cholesterol, 191 mg sodium, 39 g carbohydrate, 3 g fiber, 3 g protein.*
Diabetic Exchanges: *1-1/2 starch, 1 fruit.*

Apple Cobbler

(Pictured below)

The pleasing aroma of apples and cinnamon wafting from the kitchen will whet your appetite for this yummy fall favorite.
—Vivian Haen, Menomonee Falls, Wisconsin

 1/3 cup sugar
 1 tablespoon cornstarch
 1/2 teaspoon ground cinnamon
 1/4 teaspoon ground nutmeg
 4 cups sliced peeled tart apples (about 4 large)
 1/3 cup orange juice
TOPPING:
 1 cup all-purpose flour
 1/3 cup plus 2 teaspoons sugar, *divided*
 1-1/2 teaspoons baking powder
 1/4 teaspoon salt
 1/4 cup cold butter *or* stick margarine
 1/2 cup fat-free milk

In a large bowl, combine the sugar, cornstarch, cinnamon and nutmeg. Add apples and orange juice; toss to coat. Transfer to an 11-in. x 7-in. x 2-in. baking dish coated with nonstick cooking spray.

For topping, combine the flour, 1/3 cup sugar, baking powder and salt. Cut in butter until the mixture resembles coarse crumbs. Stir in milk just until moistened. Drop eight mounds onto the apple mixture. Sprinkle with remaining sugar. Bake at 375° for 30-35 minutes or until a toothpick inserted into topping comes out clean. Serve warm if desired. **Yield:** 8 servings.

Nutritional Analysis: *One serving equals 253 calories, 6 g fat (4 g saturated fat), 16 mg cholesterol, 184 mg sodium, 49 g carbohydrate, 3 g fiber, 2 g protein.*
Diabetic Exchanges: *2-1/2 starch, 1 fruit.*

Mixed Berry Pizza

(Pictured above)

The fresh fruit shines through in this colorful dessert pizza. It's also a tempting appetizer at parties because it's a sweet change of pace from the usual savory dips.
—Gretchen Widner, Sun City West, Arizona

 1 tube (8 ounces) refrigerated reduced-fat
 crescent rolls
 11 ounces reduced-fat cream cheese
 1/2 cup apricot preserves
 2 tablespoons confectioners' sugar
 2 cups sliced fresh strawberries
 1 cup fresh blueberries
 1 cup fresh raspberries

Unroll crescent roll dough and place in a 15-in. x 10-in. x 1-in. baking pan coated with nonstick spray. Press onto the bottom and 1 in. up the sides of pan to form a crust; seal seams and perforations. Bake at 375° for 8-10 minutes or until golden. Cool completely.

In a mixing bowl, beat cream cheese until smooth. Beat in preserves and confectioners' sugar; spread over crust. Cover and refrigerate for 1-2 hours. Just before serving, arrange berries on top. Cut into 20 pieces. **Yield:** 20 pieces.

Nutritional Analysis: One piece equals 110 calories, 5 g fat (2 g saturated fat), 9 mg cholesterol, 143 mg sodium, 15 g carbohydrate, 1 g fiber, 3 g protein.
Diabetic Exchanges: 1 fruit, 1/2 starch.

Strawberry Raspberry Trifle

(Pictured at right)

A fantastic finale to any meal, this tantalizing trifle helped finish first in a local competition. It took top prize in the low-fat category of our Wisconsin Strawberry Festival recipe contest.
—Patricia Schroedl, Jefferson, Wisconsin

 3 cups cold fat-free milk
 2 packages (1 ounce *each*) sugar-free instant
 white chocolate pudding mix
 1 prepared angel food cake (14 ounces), cut into
 1-inch cubes
 3 cups sliced fresh strawberries
 3 cups fresh raspberries
 1 carton (8 ounces) reduced-fat frozen whipped
 topping, thawed
 3 whole strawberries, quartered

In a bowl, whisk milk and pudding mix for 2 minutes or until slightly thickened. Place a third of the cake cubes in a trifle bowl or 3-1/2-qt. glass serving bowl. Top with a third of the pudding, 1 cup sliced strawberries, 1-1/2 cups raspberries and a third of the whipped topping. Layer with a third of the cake and pudding, 1 cup strawberries and a third of the whipped topping.

Top with remaining cake, pudding, strawberries, raspberries and whipped topping. Garnish with quartered strawberries. Serve immediately or refrigerate. **Yield:** 14 servings.

Nutritional Analysis: One serving (1 cup) equals 170 calories, 3 g fat (2 g saturated fat), 1 mg cholesterol, 289 mg sodium, 32 g carbohydrate, 3 g fiber, 4 g protein.
Diabetic Exchanges: 1 starch, 1 fruit.

Fruity Sherbet Dessert

(Pictured at right)

Simple and refreshing, this dressed-up sherbet is a real treat in the heat of summer. I often serve it on special occasions, too, and in late winter, when everyone's eager for spring. With only four ingredients, it's a breeze to make.
—Rhonda Robertson, Casper, Wyoming

 1/2 gallon pineapple sherbet, softened
 2 packages (8 ounces *each*) frozen unsweetened
 raspberries, partially thawed
 2 medium firm bananas, diced
 1/2 teaspoon almond extract

Place sherbet in a bowl. Fold in remaining ingredients. Cover and freeze for at least 3 hours. **Yield:** 2-1/2 quarts (20 servings).

Nutritional Analysis: One serving (1/2 cup) equals 133 calories, 2 g fat (1 g saturated fat), 5 mg cholesterol, 37 mg sodium, 30 g carbohydrate, 2 g fiber, 1 g protein.
Diabetic Exchange: 2 fruit.

In a mixing bowl, beat the butter and sugar until crumbly, about 2 minutes. Add the vanilla. Combine the flour, baking powder and salt; add to butter mixture alternately with milk. Fold in cranberries.

Transfer to an 11-in. x 7-in. x 2-in. baking dish coated with nonstick cooking spray. Bake at 350° for 30-35 minutes or until top springs back when lightly touched. Cool on a wire rack.

For sauce, combine the sugar, cornstarch and salt in a saucepan. Gradually add water. Bring to a boil; cook and stir for 2 minutes or until thickened. Add the orange juice, butter, orange peel and extract; mix well. Serve warm sauce over cake. **Yield:** 12 servings.

Nutritional Analysis: One serving (1 piece with 2 tablespoons sauce) equals 233 calories, 4 g fat (2 g saturated fat), 10 mg cholesterol, 250 mg sodium, 49 g carbohydrate, 1 g fiber, 2 g protein.
Diabetic Exchanges: 1-1/2 starch, 1-1/2 fruit, 1/2 fat.

Cranberry Cake with Orange Sauce

(Pictured above)

I love the tart cranberry flavor of this cheery cake. Served with a warm citrus sauce, it makes a wonderful treat to share at get-togethers with family and friends.
—Shirley Debler, Columbus, Wisconsin

   2 tablespoons butter *or* stick margarine, softened
   1 cup sugar
   1 teaspoon vanilla extract
   2 cups cake flour
   3 teaspoons baking powder
1/2 teaspoon salt
   1 cup 2% milk
   2 cups fresh *or* frozen cranberries, chopped
ORANGE SAUCE:
 3/4 cup sugar
   2 teaspoons cornstarch
 1/4 teaspoon salt
1-1/2 cups water
   3 tablespoons orange juice
   4 teaspoons butter *or* stick margarine
1-1/2 teaspoons grated orange peel
 1/4 teaspoon orange extract

Honey Bun Cake

I take along recipe cards to hand out when I bring this moist, fluffy cake to school socials. It always goes quickly.
—Kathy Mayo, Winston-Salem, North Carolina

   1 package (18-1/4 ounces) yellow *or* white cake mix
   4 egg whites
   1 cup (8 ounces) reduced-fat sour cream
 2/3 cup unsweetened applesauce
 1/2 cup packed brown sugar
   2 teaspoons ground cinnamon
1-1/2 cups confectioners' sugar
   2 tablespoons fat-free milk
   1 teaspoon vanilla extract

In a mixing bowl, combine dry cake mix, egg whites, sour cream and applesauce. Beat on low speed until moistened. Beat on medium for 2 minutes. Pour half into a 13-in. x 9-in. x 2-in. baking pan coated with nonstick cooking spray. Combine brown sugar and cinnamon; sprinkle over batter. Cover with remaining batter; cut through with a knife to swirl. Bake at 325° for 35-40 minutes or until a toothpick comes out clean. For glaze, combine confectioners' sugar, milk and vanilla; drizzle over warm cake. Cool on a wire rack. **Yield:** 20 servings.

Nutritional Analysis: One piece equals 185 calories, 4 g fat (1 g saturated fat), 5 mg cholesterol, 198 mg sodium, 36 g carbohydrate, 1 g fiber, 2 g protein.
Diabetic Exchanges: 2 starch, 1/2 fat.

Low-Fat Dessert Idea

Try this idea for a quick dessert. Spritz a flour tortilla with refrigerated butter-flavored spray and sprinkle with a tablespoon of sugar and a couple dashes of cinnamon. Broil 2-3 inches from the heat until browned. It's sweet and satisfying.
—Kathy Vanderbilt, Goodyear, Arizona

Favorite Recipe Made Lighter

CARROT CAKE is a scrumptious treat that has been a favorite of families for generations. One delicious version comes from Mrs. Harold Podraza of Houston, Texas. For a slimmed-down version, try our Test Kitchen's Makeover Carrot Cake.

Carrot Cake

      2 cups sugar
  3/4 cup buttermilk
  3/4 cup vegetable oil
      3 eggs
      2 teaspoons vanilla extract
      2 cups all-purpose flour
      1 tablespoon ground cinnamon
      2 teaspoons baking soda
      1 teaspoon grated orange peel
  1/2 teaspoon salt
      2 cups grated carrots
1-1/3 cups flaked coconut
      1 cup chopped walnuts
      1 can (8 ounces) crushed pineapple, undrained
GLAZE:
      1 cup sugar
  1/2 cup butter *or* margarine
  1/2 cup buttermilk
      1 tablespoon light corn syrup
  1/2 teaspoon baking soda
      1 teaspoon vanilla extract
FROSTING:
      1 package (8 ounces) cream cheese, softened
  1/2 cup butter *or* margarine, softened
      1 teaspoon vanilla extract
      1 teaspoon orange juice
      1 teaspoon grated orange peel
      4 cups confectioners' sugar

In a mixing bowl, combine the first five ingredients; beat until smooth. Combine flour, cinnamon, baking soda, orange peel and salt; add to buttermilk mixture and mix well. Stir in carrots, coconut, nuts and pineapple. Pour into three greased and floured 9-in. cake pans. Bake at 350° for 35-40 minutes or until a toothpick comes out clean. Place pans on wire racks.

In a saucepan, combine the first five glaze ingredients. Bring to a boil; cook and stir for 4 minutes. Remove from the heat; add vanilla. Spread over warm cakes. Cool completely before removing from pans.

In a mixing bowl, combine the first five frosting ingredients; beat until fluffy. Beat in sugar. Place one cake glaze side up on a serving plate; spread with 1 cup frosting. Repeat layers. Frost top and sides of cake. **Yield:** 12 servings.

Nutritional Analysis: One piece equals 835 calories, 43 g fat (16 g saturated fat), 116 mg cholesterol, 625 mg sodium, 108 g carbohydrate, 2 g fiber, 9 g protein.

Makeover Carrot Cake

1-1/2 cups sugar
  1/2 cup 1% buttermilk
  1/4 cup canola oil
  1/4 cup baking fat replacement* *or* unsweetened applesauce
      2 eggs
  1/4 cup egg substitute
      2 teaspoons vanilla extract
2-1/4 cups all-purpose flour
      1 tablespoon ground cinnamon
1-1/2 teaspoons baking soda
      1 teaspoon grated orange peel
  1/2 teaspoon baking powder
  1/2 teaspoon salt
      2 cups finely shredded carrots
      1 can (8 ounces) crushed pineapple, drained
  1/2 cup chopped walnuts
GLAZE:
  1/4 cup sugar
      2 tablespoons butter *or* stick margarine
      2 tablespoons 1% buttermilk
      1 teaspoon light corn syrup
  1/4 teaspoon baking soda
  1/2 teaspoon vanilla extract
FROSTING:
      1 package (8 ounces) reduced-fat cream cheese
      2 tablespoons butter *or* stick margarine, softened
      1 teaspoon vanilla extract
      1 teaspoon orange juice
      1 teaspoon grated orange peel
      5 cups confectioners' sugar

In a mixing bowl, combine the first seven ingredients; beat until smooth. Combine flour, cinnamon, baking soda, orange peel, baking powder and salt; add to buttermilk mixture and mix well. Stir in carrots, pineapple and nuts. Pour into three 9-in. cake pans coated with nonstick cooking spray and floured. Bake at 350° for 30-35 minutes or until a toothpick comes out clean. Place pans on wire racks.

In a saucepan, combine the first five glaze ingredients. Bring to a boil; cook and stir for 1-2 minutes. Remove from the heat; add vanilla. Spread over warm cakes. Cool completely before removing from pans.

In a mixing bowl, combine the first five frosting ingredients; beat until fluffy. Beat in sugar. Place one cake glaze side up on a serving plate; spread with 1/3 cup frosting. Repeat layers. Frost top and sides of cake. Refrigerate. **Yield:** 12 servings.

*Editor's Note: This recipe was tested with Sunsweet Lighter Bake. Look for it in the baking aisle of your grocery store.

Nutritional Analysis: One piece equals 564 calories, 16 g fat (6 g saturated fat), 59 mg cholesterol, 458 mg sodium, 98 g carbohydrate, 2 g fiber, 8 g protein.

spoon. Bake at 275° for 45 minutes or until golden brown. Turn oven off; leave meringues in oven for 1-1/2 hours.

In a large saucepan, combine the milk, egg, 1/4 cup corn syrup and cocoa. Cook and stir over medium heat until mixture reaches 160° and coats a metal spoon. Remove from the heat. Add the chocolate and cream cheese; stir until melted.

In a small saucepan, sprinkle gelatin over 1/4 cup water; let stand for 1 minute. Cook and stir over low heat until gelatin is dissolved. Stir gelatin and vanilla into chocolate mixture. Cool.

In a heavy saucepan, combine egg whites, sugar, cream of tartar, and remaining corn syrup and water. Cook over low heat and beat with a hand mixer on low until mixture reaches 160°. Pour into a mixing bowl; beat on high until soft peaks form. Fold into chocolate mixture. Chill for 1-2 hours or until mixture mounds.

Just before serving, spoon the mousse into meringue cups; sprinkle with the peppermint candy pieces. **Yield:** 15 servings.

Nutritional Analysis: *One filled cup equals 201 calories, 4 g fat (2 g saturated fat), 19 mg cholesterol, 153 mg sodium, 40 g carbohydrate, 2 g fiber, 5 g protein.*
Diabetic Exchange: *2-1/2 starch.*

Chocolate Meringue Cups

(Pictured above)

Looking for something low in cholesterol that will satisfy your sweet tooth? Give this airy cloud of cocoa meringue and chocolate mousse a try! It's a bit fussy, but it's well worth the effort.
—Ellen Govertsen, Wheaton, Illinois

 4 egg whites
 1 teaspoon vanilla extract
 1/2 teaspoon salt
 1/2 teaspoon white vinegar
 1 cup sugar
 2 tablespoons baking cocoa
CHOCOLATE MOUSSE:
 1 cup fat-free milk
 1 egg
 1/4 cup plus 2 teaspoons corn syrup, *divided*
 1/4 cup baking cocoa
 3 squares (1 ounce *each*) semisweet chocolate, chopped
 4 ounces reduced-fat cream cheese
 2 teaspoons unflavored gelatin
 1/4 cup plus 1 tablespoon cold water, *divided*
 1 teaspoon vanilla extract
 4 egg whites
 3/4 cup sugar
 1/4 teaspoon cream of tartar
 15 peppermint candies, crushed

In a mixing bowl, beat egg whites until foamy. Add vanilla, salt and vinegar; beat on medium speed until soft peaks form. Gradually add sugar, 1 tablespoon at a time, beating on high until stiff peaks form. Sift cocoa over egg whites; fold in.

Drop 15 heaping tablespoonfuls onto parchment-lined baking sheets. Shape into 3-in. cups with the back of a

Pears with Spiced Caramel Sauce

(Pictured below)

With caramel sauce draping a tender poached pear, this dessert is pretty to look at but even sweeter to eat. Our Test Kitchen created the recipe.

 6 medium pears, stems attached
 5 cups water
 1 cup orange juice

1/2 cup sugar
4 whole cloves
2 cinnamon sticks (3 inches)
1/2 medium lemon
6 tablespoons fat-free caramel apple dip
Dash ground cloves

Core pears from bottom, leaving stems intact. Peel pears. Cut 1/4 in. from bottom to level if necessary. In a large saucepan, combine the next five ingredients. Squeeze juice from lemon; add juice and lemon to pan. Bring to a boil. Reduce heat. Add pears; poach, uncovered, for 15-20 minutes or until tender. Remove from the heat; cool pears in liquid.

In a microwave-safe bowl, combine caramel dip and ground cloves. Microwave, uncovered, on high for 20 seconds; stir. Cook 20 seconds longer or until heated through. To serve, drain pears and pat dry; drizzle with caramel sauce. **Yield:** 6 servings.

Nutritional Analysis: One serving (1 pear with 1 tablespoon caramel sauce) equals 174 calories, 1 g fat (trace saturated fat), trace cholesterol, 78 mg sodium, 44 g carbohydrate, 4 g fiber, 1 g protein.

Strawberry Almond Pastries

I try hard to avoid sugar, but I don't want to give up sweet treats altogether. Fruit spread provides wonderful flavor in desserts like these pastries. Made with convenient phyllo dough, they are light and crisp—flaky on the outside and chewy inside.
—Connie Moore, Medway, Ohio

6 sheets phyllo dough (18 inches x 14 inches)
1 jar (10 ounces) strawberry all-fruit spread
1/4 cup slivered almonds

Place one sheet of phyllo dough on a work surface with a long side facing you; spritz dough with nonstick cooking spray. Layer with two more sheets, spritzing in between. Spread half of the fruit spread over dough to within 1/2 in. of edges. Sprinkle with half of the almonds. Roll up, jelly-roll style, starting with a long side; moisten edges with water and press to seal. Cut into six pieces. Repeat with remaining ingredients.

Place pieces, cut side down, 1 in. apart on a baking sheet coated with nonstick cooking spray. Lightly spritz tops with cooking spray. Bake at 375° for 12-15 minutes or until golden brown. Remove to wire racks to cool. **Yield:** 1 dozen.

Nutritional Analysis: One pastry equals 101 calories, 2 g fat (trace saturated fat), 0 cholesterol, 51 mg sodium, 19 g carbohydrate, trace fiber, 1 g protein.
Diabetic Exchanges: 1 fruit, 1/2 starch.

Pumpkin Gingerbread

(Pictured at right)

If you enjoy gingerbread and pumpkin goodies, you'll like this spiced dessert I always fix around the holidays. My family and friends look forward to moist slices every year.
—Suzanne Loveland, Edinburg, Virginia

2 eggs
1/2 cup egg substitute
1 can (15 ounces) solid-pack pumpkin
1-1/2 cups honey
1/2 cup butter *or* stick margarine, melted
1/2 cup fat-free plain yogurt
1 cup wheat germ
3 cups all-purpose flour
2 teaspoons baking soda
2 teaspoons ground ginger
1 teaspoon ground cinnamon
1 teaspoon ground nutmeg
1/2 teaspoon salt
1/4 teaspoon ground cloves
ICING:
3/4 cup confectioners' sugar
2 teaspoons fat-free milk
1/4 teaspoon vanilla extract

In a large bowl, beat eggs and egg substitute. Stir in the pumpkin, honey, butter and yogurt until smooth. Stir in wheat germ. Combine the dry ingredients; gradually add to pumpkin mixture and mix well. Coat a 10-in. fluted tube pan with nonstick cooking spray and dust with flour; add batter.

Bake at 350° for 55-60 minutes or until a toothpick inserted near the center comes out clean. Cool for 10 minutes before removing from pan to a wire rack to cool completely. Combine icing ingredients until smooth; drizzle over cake. **Yield:** 16 servings.

Nutritional Analysis: One piece equals 299 calories, 7 g fat (4 g saturated fat), 42 mg cholesterol, 319 mg sodium, 55 g carbohydrate, 3 g fiber, 6 g protein.

Raspberry Peach Delight

This light dessert is a snap to make using prepared angel food cake. I sometimes layer it in a glass trifle bowl and top it with fresh raspberries for an elegant party dish.
—Alice Reed, Penfield, New York

- **1 prepared angel food cake (8 inches), cut into 1-inch cubes**
- **1 package (.3 ounce) sugar-free raspberry gelatin**
- **1 cup boiling water**
- **1 cup cold water**
- **1 can (16 ounces) reduced-sugar sliced peaches, well drained and halved**
- **3 cups cold fat-free milk**
- **1 package (1.5 ounces) sugar-free instant vanilla pudding mix**
- **1 carton (8 ounces) frozen reduced-fat whipped topping, thawed**

Arrange cake cubes in a 13-in. x 9-in. x 2-in. dish. In a small bowl, dissolve gelatin in boiling water; stir in cold water. Pour over cake. Arrange peaches over gelatin. In a bowl, whisk milk and pudding mix for 2 minutes. Let stand for 2 minutes or until soft set. Spoon over peaches. Top with whipped topping. Cover and refrigerate for at least 2 hours before cutting. **Yield:** 15 servings.

Nutritional Analysis: One piece equals 133 calories, 2 g fat (2 g saturated fat), 1 mg cholesterol, 260 mg sodium, 24 g carbohydrate, trace fiber, 3 g protein.
Diabetic Exchanges: 1 starch, 1 fruit.

Ginger Thins

(Pictured at right)

My family loves nibbling on these spiced cookies at Christmastime. A dollop of lemon sherbet complements these treats nicely.
—Eleanor Senske, Rock Island, Illinois

- **6 tablespoons butter (no substitutes), softened**
- **1/2 cup plus 2 tablespoons sugar, *divided***
- **2 tablespoons molasses**
- **1 tablespoon cold strong brewed coffee**
- **1-1/4 cups all-purpose flour**
- **3/4 teaspoon ground ginger**
- **1/2 teaspoon baking soda**
- **1/2 teaspoon ground cinnamon**
- **1/4 teaspoon ground cloves**
- **1/8 teaspoon salt**

In a mixing bowl, cream butter and 1/2 cup sugar; set remaining sugar aside. Add molasses and coffee to creamed mixture; mix well. Combine the remaining ingredients; add to creamed mixture. Mix well (dough will be soft). Cover and freeze for 15 minutes. Shape dough into a 7-in. roll; flatten to 1-in. thickness. Wrap in plastic wrap. Freeze for 8 hours or overnight.

Unwrap dough and cut into 1/8-in. slices; place 2 in. apart on parchment paper-lined baking sheets. Sprinkle with reserved sugar. Bake at 350° for 8-10 minutes or until firm. Remove to wire racks to cool. **Yield:** 3-1/2 dozen.

Nutritional Analysis: One serving (2 cookies) equals 81 calories, 3 g fat (2 g saturated fat), 8 mg cholesterol, 75 mg sodium, 12 g carbohydrate, trace fiber, 1 g protein.
Diabetic Exchange: 1 starch.

Mom's Pumpkin Pie

(Pictured at right)

My husband is on a restricted diet, so his mom shared the recipe for these pared-down pies. Now my family enjoys them at holidays.
—Carol Kloes, Arlington, Texas

- **2 cups all-purpose flour, *divided***
- **2 teaspoons sugar**
- **1/2 teaspoon salt**
- **6 tablespoons shortening**
- **6 tablespoons cold water**

FILLING:
- **1/2 cup egg substitute**
- **1 egg**
- **1 cup packed brown sugar**
- **1/2 cup sugar**
- **1 teaspoon salt**
- **1 teaspoon ground cinnamon**
- **1/2 teaspoon ground ginger**
- **1/4 teaspoon ground cloves**
- **2 cans (15 ounces *each*) solid-pack pumpkin**
- **2 cups fat-free evaporated milk**
- **2 cups reduced-fat whipped topping**

In a bowl, combine 1-1/2 cups flour, sugar and salt; cut in shortening until crumbly. In another bowl, whisk water and remaining flour until smooth; add to crumb mixture and toss until moistened. Divide pastry in half. Roll out each portion between two pieces of plastic wrap into an 11-in. circle. Freeze for 10 minutes.

Remove one sheet of plastic wrap from one pastry; transfer to a 9-in. pie plate coated with nonstick cooking spray. Remove remaining plastic wrap. Trim edges of pastry and flute. Repeat with remaining pastry.

In a large mixing bowl, beat the egg substitute, egg, sugars, salt and spices until smooth. Mix in pumpkin. Gradually beat in milk. Pour into crusts. Bake at 375° for 50-60 minutes or until a knife inserted near the center comes out clean. Garnish with whipped topping. **Yield:** 2 pies (8 servings each).

Nutritional Analysis: One serving (1 piece with 2 tablespoons whipped topping) equals 245 calories, 6 g fat (2 g saturated fat), 14 mg cholesterol, 282 mg sodium, 41 g carbohydrate, 3 g fiber, 6 g protein.
Diabetic Exchanges: 2-1/2 starch, 1 fat.

of pan to loosen. Cool 1 hour longer. Refrigerate overnight. Remove sides of pan. Top with strawberries and kiwi. Refrigerate leftovers. **Yield:** 12 servings.

Nutritional Analysis: One piece equals 300 calories, 8 g fat (5 g saturated fat), 26 mg cholesterol, 522 mg sodium, 42 g carbohydrate, 1 g fiber, 15 g protein.
Diabetic Exchanges: 2 fat-free milk, 1 fruit, 1 fat.

Light Lemon Cheesecake

(Pictured above)

My family loves cheesecake, but we don't care for the fat that usually comes with it. This pretty fruit-topped alternative offers a creamy texture and full flavor—without the guilt!
—Deborah Lobe, Olympia, Washington

  3/4 cup crushed reduced-fat cinnamon graham crackers (about 10 squares)
    3 packages (8 ounces *each*) fat-free cream cheese, cubed
    2 packages (8 ounces *each*) reduced-fat cream cheese, cubed
1-2/3 cups sugar
  1/8 teaspoon salt
    9 egg whites
  1/4 cup lemon juice
1-1/2 teaspoons vanilla extract
    1 teaspoon grated lemon peel
    8 strawberries, sliced
    2 medium kiwifruit, peeled and sliced

Sprinkle graham cracker crumbs on the bottom and up the sides of a 9-in. springform pan well coated with nonstick cooking spray; set aside. In a mixing bowl, beat cream cheese, sugar and salt until smooth. Add egg whites; beat on low speed just until combined, about 2 minutes. Stir in the lemon juice, vanilla and lemon peel.

Pour into prepared pan. Bake at 325° for 70-80 minutes or until center is almost set. Turn oven off; leave cheesecake in oven with door ajar for 30 minutes.

Remove from oven. Carefully run a knife around edge

Fudgy Peanut Butter Brownies

No one believes these fudgy brownies—with a hint of peanut butter—are actually low-fat. They're so full of flavor, they'll satisfy anyone's chocolate cravings.
—Martha Domeny, Overland Park, Kansas

    2 cups sugar
1-1/2 cups all-purpose flour
  3/4 cup baking cocoa
  1/2 teaspoon salt
  2/3 cup unsweetened applesauce
  3/4 cup egg substitute
    2 teaspoons vanilla extract
FILLING:
    3 ounces reduced-fat cream cheese, softened
  1/3 cup reduced-fat peanut butter
  1/4 cup sugar
  1/4 cup egg substitute
    1 teaspoon vanilla extract
FROSTING:
    1 cup confectioners' sugar
    3 tablespoons baking cocoa
    2 tablespoons 2% milk
    1 teaspoon vanilla extract
    1 teaspoon water

In a large bowl, combine the sugar, flour, cocoa and salt. Stir in the applesauce, egg substitute and vanilla; mix well. Pour about half of the batter into a 13-in. x 9-in. x 2-in. baking pan coated with nonstick cooking spray.

In a mixing bowl, combine filling ingredients; beat until smooth. Drop by tablespoonfuls onto batter. Spoon remaining batter over top; cut through batter with a knife to swirl peanut butter mixture. Bake at 325° for 20-25 minutes or until edges are firm and center is almost set.

Cool completely in pan on a wire rack. In a small bowl, combine frosting ingredients until smooth. Frost brownies. **Yield:** 20 brownies.

Nutritional Analysis: One brownie equals 201 calories, 3 g fat (1 g saturated fat), 3 mg cholesterol, 119 mg sodium, 40 g carbohydrate, 2 g fiber, 5 g protein.
Diabetic Exchanges: 2 starch, 1 fat.

Favorite Recipe Made Lighter

A RICH old-fashioned treat, Dark Chocolate Layer Cake comes from David Heppner of Brandon, Florida.

If you're looking for a fantastic chocolate finale to a meal but would like a little lighter version, try our Test Kitchen's Makeover Dark Chocolate Layer Cake.

Dark Chocolate Layer Cake

    3 cups sugar
2-1/2 cups all-purpose flour
1-1/2 cups baking cocoa
    2 teaspoons baking soda
    3/4 teaspoon baking powder
1-1/4 teaspoons salt
1-1/2 cups buttermilk
    3 eggs
    3/4 cup vegetable oil
    3 squares (1 ounce *each*) semisweet chocolate, melted
1-1/2 cups brewed coffee, cooled
    3/4 teaspoon vanilla extract
FROSTING:
    1 cup whipping cream
    2 tablespoons sugar
    2 tablespoons light corn syrup
    16 squares (1 ounce *each*) semisweet chocolate
    1/4 cup butter (no substitutes)

In a mixing bowl, combine dry ingredients. Add buttermilk, eggs, oil, chocolate, coffee and vanilla; mix until combined. Pour into three greased and floured 9-in. round baking pans. Bake at 350° for 30-35 minutes or until a toothpick comes out clean. Cool for 10 minutes before removing from pans to wire racks to cool completely.

For frosting, combine cream, sugar and corn syrup in a saucepan. Bring to a full boil over medium heat, stirring constantly. Remove from the heat; stir in chocolate and butter until melted. Transfer to a bowl. Refrigerate until spreadable, stirring occasionally. Spread frosting between layers and over top and sides of cake. Store in the refrigerator. **Yield:** 12 servings.

Nutritional Analysis: One slice equals 816 calories, 41 g fat (17 g saturated fat), 93 mg cholesterol, 569 mg sodium, 112 g carbohydrate, 11 g fiber, 11 g protein.

Makeover Dark Chocolate Layer Cake

(Pictured at right)

2-1/4 cups all-purpose flour
1-3/4 cups sugar
    3/4 cup baking cocoa
1-1/2 teaspoons baking soda
    1 teaspoon salt
    1/2 teaspoon baking powder

1-1/2 cups 1% buttermilk
    2 eggs
    1/3 cup canola oil
    1/4 cup egg substitute
    1/4 cup baking fat replacement*
    2 squares (1 ounce *each*) semisweet chocolate, melted
    1 cup brewed coffee, cooled
    3/4 teaspoon vanilla extract
FROSTING:
    2 squares (1 ounce *each*) semisweet chocolate
    2 tablespoons butter (no substitutes)
    2 tablespoons light corn syrup
    3 cups confectioners' sugar
    2 tablespoons baking cocoa
    1/4 cup 1% milk
    1 teaspoon vanilla extract
    1/4 cup fat-free whipped topping

In a mixing bowl, combine the dry ingredients. Add buttermilk, eggs, oil, egg substitute, baking fat replacement, chocolate, coffee and vanilla; mix until combined. Pour into three 9-in. round baking pans coated with nonstick cooking spray and floured. Bake at 350° for 25-30 minutes or until a toothpick comes out clean. Cool for 10 minutes before removing from pans to wire racks to cool completely.

For frosting, in a microwave, melt chocolate and butter. Stir in corn syrup. In a mixing bowl, combine sugar and cocoa; beat in chocolate mixture, milk and vanilla. Fold in whipped topping. Spread between layers and over top of cake. Store in the refrigerator. **Yield:** 12 servings.

Editor's Note: This recipe was tested with Smucker's Baking Healthy. Look for it in the baking aisle of your grocery store.

Nutritional Analysis: One slice equals 485 calories, 13 g fat (4 g saturated fat), 42 mg cholesterol, 446 mg sodium, 89 g carbohydrate, 4 g fiber, 7 g protein.

Chocolate-Glazed Brownies

(Pictured at right)

These moist and fudgy squares are bursting with such rich chocolate flavor, you'd never know they're low in fat. These brownies are ideal for taking to bake sales and family gatherings or sharing with co-workers. For various holidays, I like to dress them up with colorful candy sprinkles.
—Deb Anderson, Joplin, Missouri

1/3 cup butter *or* stick margarine, softened
1 cup sugar
3 egg whites
1 teaspoon vanilla extract
2/3 cup all-purpose flour
1/2 cup baking cocoa
1/2 teaspoon baking powder
1/4 teaspoon salt
CHOCOLATE GLAZE:
2/3 cup confectioners' sugar
2 tablespoons baking cocoa
1/4 teaspoon vanilla extract
3 to 4 teaspoons hot water
Candy sprinkles, optional

In a mixing bowl, cream butter and sugar. Add egg whites; beat well. Beat in vanilla. Combine the flour, cocoa, baking

🍎 Brownie Basics

TO MAKE brownies so magical they'll disappear right before your eyes, keep these brownie basics in mind:

- Use the pan size specified in the recipe. A different size can change the brownie's texture. To double-check the width of a pan, measure across the top from inside edge to inside edge.
- To ease cleanup, line your brownie pan with aluminum foil. Cooled brownies will lift right out and are easily cut.
- If brownie batter is overmixed, brownie texture may be less tender.
- Place pan in the center of the oven's middle rack to allow for even heat circulation.
- Overbaking brownies will cause them to dry out. Closely follow the recipe's recommended baking times.
- Cool baked brownies completely before cutting and removing them from the pan unless the recipe specifies differently. This helps prevent the bars from crumbling.
- For a simple brownie garnish, try sprinkling unfrosted bars with powdered sugar. Or top frosted bars with dried or candied fruit.
- To cut even squares or rectangles of brownies, use a ruler to measure and toothpicks to mark the lines.
- For a fun flavor variation in recipes calling for vanilla extract, try replacing it with almond or peppermint extract.

powder and salt; gradually add to creamed mixture. Spread into an 8-in. square baking pan coated with nonstick cooking spray. Bake at 350° for 20-25 minutes or until a toothpick inserted near the center comes out clean. Cool on a wire rack.

For glaze, in a small bowl, combine confectioners' sugar, cocoa, vanilla and enough water to achieve desired consistency. Spread over brownies. Decorate with candy sprinkles if desired. Cut into bars. **Yield:** 1 dozen.

Nutritional Analysis: One brownie equals 173 calories, 6 g fat (3 g saturated fat), 14 mg cholesterol, 124 mg sodium, 30 g carbohydrate, 2 g fiber, 2 g protein.
Diabetic Exchange: 2 starch.

Granola Blondies

(Pictured above)

A mix of tasty good-for-you ingredients makes these chewy blond brownies impossible to pass up. The granola adds crunch while dried fruit lends pleasing sweetness. I serve them to just about anybody who walks in our front door.
—Janet Farley, Snellville, Georgia

1 egg
1 egg white
1-1/4 cups packed brown sugar
1/4 cup canola oil
1 cup all-purpose flour

1 teaspoon baking powder
1/2 teaspoon salt
2 cups reduced-fat granola with raisins
1 cup dried cranberries *or* cherries

In a mixing bowl, combine the egg, egg white, brown sugar and oil; mix well. Combine the flour, baking powder and salt; stir into sugar mixture just until blended. Stir in granola and cranberries (batter will be thick).

Spread into a 9-in. square baking pan coated with nonstick cooking spray. Bake at 350° for 25-30 minutes or until golden and set. Cool on a wire rack. Cut into bars. **Yield:** 1 dozen.

Nutritional Analysis: One brownie equals 256 calories, 6 g fat (1 g saturated fat), 18 mg cholesterol, 173 mg sodium, 49 g carbohydrate, 2 g fiber, 3 g protein.
Diabetic Exchanges: 3 starch, 1/2 fat.

Meringue Candy Canes

These red-and-white striped treats get lots of compliments for their cute looks and minty taste. The seasonal confections are easy to make and so light that they melt in your mouth!
—Anne Lindway, Indianapolis, Indiana

3 egg whites
1/2 teaspoon cream of tartar
3/4 cup sugar
1/4 teaspoon peppermint extract
Red paste food coloring

In a mixing bowl, beat egg whites until foamy. Add cream of tartar; beat on medium speed until soft peaks form. Gradually add sugar, 1 tablespoon at a time, beating on high until stiff peaks form and sugar is dissolved, about 6 minutes. Beat in peppermint extract.

Cut a small hole in the corner of a pastry bag; insert star tip #21. On the inside of the bag, brush three evenly spaced 1/4-in. strips of red food coloring from the tip to three-fourths of the way to the top of the bag. Carefully fill bag with meringue.

Pipe 3-in. candy canes onto parchment-lined baking sheets. Bake at 225° for 25 minutes; rotate baking sheets to a different oven rack. Bake 25 minutes longer or until firm to the touch. Turn oven off; leave cookies in oven with door ajar for at least 1 hour or until cool. **Yield:** 4 dozen.

Nutritional Analysis: One cookie equals 13 calories, 0 fat (0 saturated fat), 0 cholesterol, 3 mg sodium, 3 g carbohydrate, 0 fiber, trace protein.
Diabetic Exchange: Free food.

Chocolate Mint Eclair Dessert

(Pictured at right)

My college roommate gave me this recipe, which I lightened up a little. You can try other pudding flavors, but I think the combination of mint and chocolate is perfect for the holidays.
—Renee Ratcliffe, Charlotte, North Carolina

23 whole chocolate graham crackers (5 inches x 2-1/2 inches)
3 cups cold fat-free milk
2 packages (3.3 to 3.4 ounces *each*) instant white chocolate *or* vanilla pudding mix
1/2 teaspoon mint *or* peppermint extract
3 to 4 drops green food coloring, optional
1 carton (8 ounces) frozen reduced-fat whipped topping, thawed
CHOCOLATE FROSTING:
1 tablespoon butter *or* stick margarine
2 tablespoons baking cocoa
2 tablespoons plus 1 teaspoon fat-free milk
1 teaspoon vanilla extract
1 cup confectioners' sugar

Coat a 13-in. x 9-in. x 2-in. dish with nonstick cooking spray. Break five whole graham crackers in half; line the bottom of pan with three half crackers and six whole crackers.

In a bowl, whisk milk and pudding mix for 2 minutes. Whisk in extract and food coloring if desired. Fold in whipped topping. Spread half over graham crackers. Top with another layer of three half and six whole crackers. Top with remaining pudding mixture and graham crackers (save remaining half cracker for another use). Cover and refrigerate for 2 hours.

For frosting, melt butter in a saucepan. Stir in cocoa and milk until blended. Remove from the heat; stir in vanilla and confectioners' sugar. Spread over dessert. Cover and refrigerate overnight. **Yield:** 15 servings.

Nutritional Analysis: One piece equals 244 calories, 7 g fat (3 g saturated fat), 3 mg cholesterol, 296 mg sodium, 41 g carbohydrate, 1 g fiber, 4 g protein.
Diabetic Exchanges: 2 starch, 1 fat, 1/2 fruit.

Meanwhile, drain raspberries, reserving juice. Set the berries aside. Add enough water to juice to measure 2 cups. In a saucepan, combine cornstarch and sugar; stir in the raspberry liquid until smooth. Bring to a boil; cook and stir for 2 minutes or until thickened. Cool completely. Fold in the sweetened raspberries.

To assemble, place one meringue on a serving plate; top with about 2/3 cup whipped topping and 3/4 cup raspberry filling. Repeat three times. Top with remaining meringue layer and whipped topping. Refrigerate for 1 hour before serving. Garnish with fresh berries. Cut with a serrated knife. **Yield:** 10 servings.

Nutritional Analysis: One piece equals 332 calories, 6 g fat (6 g saturated fat), 0 cholesterol, 59 mg sodium, 66 g carbohydrate, 3 g fiber, 3 g protein.

Peeling Peaches

Here's an easy way to peel fresh peaches. Place them in boiling water for just a moment or pour boiling water over them. Then pour very cold water over them and the skins will slide right off.
—*Mary Henderson, Kerrville, Texas*

Raspberry-Filled Meringue Torte

(Pictured above)

My family always asks for this impressive sweet during the holidays. I've relied on this light meringue recipe for as long as I can remember—it's a surefire success each and every time I serve it.
—*Rosemarie Cook, Haliburton, Ontario*

6 egg whites
1/4 teaspoon cream of tartar
1-1/2 cups sugar
1 cup flaked coconut
1/2 cup cornstarch
FILLING:
2 packages (10 ounces *each*) frozen sweetened raspberries, thawed
3 tablespoons cornstarch
2 tablespoons sugar
1 carton (8 ounces) frozen reduced-fat whipped topping, thawed
10 fresh raspberries

Line baking sheets with parchment paper and trace five 7-1/2-in. circles on paper; set aside.

In a large mixing bowl, beat the egg whites until foamy. Add cream of tartar; beat on medium speed until soft peaks form. Gradually add sugar, 1 tablespoon at a time, beating on high until stiff peaks form. Combine coconut and cornstarch; fold into meringue.

Spread meringue evenly over each circle on prepared pans. Bake at 300° for 30 minutes or until firm and lightly golden. Cool for 5 minutes. Gently remove meringues from baking sheets to wire racks to cool completely.

Blueberry-Peach Pound Cake

The fruit of my cake-baking labors is applauded all around the table at my house. Each golden piece is packed with fruit, so it makes for a refreshing snack.
—*Martha Domeny, San Diego, California*

2 tablespoons butter *or* stick margarine, softened
1-1/4 cups sugar
3 tablespoons unsweetened applesauce
3/4 cup egg substitute
1/4 cup 2% milk
2-1/2 cups cake flour
2 teaspoons baking powder
1/4 teaspoon salt
2-1/4 cups chopped fresh *or* frozen unsweetened peaches
2 cups fresh *or* frozen unsweetened blueberries*
3/4 cup reduced-fat whipped topping

In a mixing bowl, beat the butter, sugar and applesauce. Add egg substitute and milk. Combine the flour, baking powder and salt; add to the creamed mixture and mix until blended. Fold in peaches and blueberries. Pour into a 10-in. fluted tube pan coated with nonstick cooking spray.

Bake at 350° for 55-60 minutes or until a toothpick comes out clean. Cool for 10 minutes before removing from pan to a wire rack. Garnish slices with whipped topping. **Yield:** 12 servings.

*Editor's Note: If using frozen blueberries, do not thaw before adding to batter.

Nutritional Analysis: One serving (1 slice with 1 tablespoon whipped topping) equals 225 calories, 3 g fat (2 g saturated fat), 6 mg cholesterol, 138 mg sodium, 45 g carbohydrate, 2 g fiber, 4 g protein.
Diabetic Exchanges: 2 starch, 1 fruit.

Favorite Pie Recipe Made Lighter

WHAT'S for dessert? How about a scrumptious slice of Peanut Butter Pie?

"'Wow!' That's what I hear whenever I serve this creamy peanut butter pie with its chocolate cookie crust," says Elaine Sabacky of Litchfield, Minnesota. "Everyone seems to love the chocolate/peanut butter combination.

"But I'm wondering if it's possible to revise the recipe using less fat," she asks.

Our Test Kitchen crew knew just what to do. Using fat-free cream cheese, reduced-fat peanut butter, skim milk and fat-free frozen whipped topping, they trimmed down the fat in Elaine's popular pie.

The outcome? Makeover Peanut Butter Pie has just half the fat of the original, but our panel of taste-testers found it to be every bit as mouth-watering and sweetly satisfying. Any way you slice it, that's good news!

Peanut Butter Pie

- 1 package (3 ounces) cream cheese, softened
- 1/3 cup peanut butter
- 1 cup confectioners' sugar
- 1/4 cup milk
- 1 carton (8 ounces) frozen whipped topping, thawed
- 1 chocolate crumb crust (9 inches)
- 1/4 cup chopped peanuts

In a mixing bowl, beat cream cheese until fluffy. Mix in peanut butter and sugar. Gradually add milk; mix well. Fold in whipped topping. Spoon into crust. Refrigerate overnight. Garnish with peanuts. **Yield:** 8 slices.

Nutritional Analysis: One slice equals 410 calories, 26 g fat (11 g saturated fat), 13 mg cholesterol, 292 mg sodium, 38 g carbohydrate, 1 g fiber, 6 g protein.

🍎 Peanut Butter Tidbits

- Peanut butter was first introduced in 1890, when an unknown St. Louis physician encouraged the owner of a food products company to process and package ground peanut paste as a nutritious protein substitute.
- Although peanut butter is a good source of protein, niacin, phosphorus and magnesium, it's very high in fat. Two tablespoons have 16 grams of fat.

Makeover Peanut Butter Pie

(Pictured below)

- 3 ounces fat-free cream cheese, softened
- 1/3 cup reduced-fat peanut butter
- 1/2 cup confectioners' sugar
- 1/4 cup fat-free milk
- 1 carton (8 ounces) fat-free frozen whipped topping, thawed
- 1 chocolate crumb crust (9 inches)

In a mixing bowl, beat cream cheese until fluffy. Mix in peanut butter and sugar. Gradually add milk; mix well. Gently fold in whipped topping. Spoon into the crust. Refrigerate overnight. **Yield:** 8 slices.

Nutritional Analysis: One slice equals 280 calories, 12 g fat (3 g saturated fat), 2 mg cholesterol, 325 mg sodium, 35 g carbohydrate, 1 g fiber, 6 g protein.
Diabetic Exchanges: 2 starch, 1 fat, 1 fruit.

Applesauce Cake

This family favorite is so sweet, moist and tender, no one will know it's a low-fat cake.
—*Joanne Huff, Champaign, Illinois*

1/2 cup egg substitute
1-1/2 cups unsweetened applesauce
1 cup sugar
1/4 cup canola oil
2 cups all-purpose flour
2 teaspoons ground cinnamon
1-1/2 teaspoons baking soda
1 teaspoon ground nutmeg
1/2 teaspoon salt
1/2 cup raisins
1/2 cup chopped walnuts
FROSTING:
4 ounces reduced-fat cream cheese
1 cup confectioners' sugar
1/2 teaspoon vanilla extract

In a mixing bowl, beat egg substitute for 1 minute on medium speed. Add the applesauce, sugar and oil; mix well. Combine the dry ingredients; add to applesauce mixture and mix well. Stir in raisins and walnuts.

Pour into a 13-in. x 9-in. x 2-in. baking pan coated with nonstick cooking spray. Bake at 350° for 25-30 minutes or until a toothpick inserted near the center comes out clean. Cool on a wire rack.

In a mixing bowl, beat cream cheese until fluffy. Beat in confectioners' sugar and vanilla. Frost the cake. **Yield:** 20 servings.

Nutritional Analysis: One piece equals 186 calories, 6 g fat (1 g saturated fat), 3 mg cholesterol, 124 mg sodium, 30 g carbohydrate, 1 g fiber, 3 g protein.
Diabetic Exchanges: 1 starch, 1 fruit, 1 fat.

serted near the center comes out clean. Cool for 10 minutes before removing from pan to a wire rack to cool completely. Dust with confectioners' sugar. **Yield:** 12 servings.

Nutritional Analysis: One piece equals 266 calories, 9 g fat (3 g saturated fat), 62 mg cholesterol, 520 mg sodium, 41 g carbohydrate, 2 g fiber, 6 g protein.
Diabetic Exchanges: 2-1/2 starch, 1-1/2 fat.

Ultimate Chocolate Cake

(Pictured above right)

Semisweet chocolate chips add rich flavor to this moist chocolaty cake that's lower in fat. Slices of it are excellent for dessert or a snack.
—*Kay McMicken, Charlotte, North Carolina*

1 package (18-1/4 ounces) devil's food cake mix
1 package (1.4 ounces) sugar-free instant chocolate pudding mix
1 cup (8 ounces) fat-free sour cream
1/2 cup unsweetened applesauce
1/2 cup water
2 eggs
1/2 cup egg substitute
1/2 cup semisweet chocolate chips
1-1/2 teaspoons confectioners' sugar

In a mixing bowl, combine the first seven ingredients; mix well. Stir in chocolate chips. Coat a 10-in. fluted tube pan with nonstick cooking spray and dust with flour; add batter.

Bake at 350° for 45-50 minutes or until a toothpick in-

Frosted Zucchini Bars

I grow tons of zucchini in my garden—and this is a wonderful way to share it. These moist tender bars are topped with a yummy caramel cream cheese frosting. When I bring a plateful of them to work, they're always a hit!
—*Sandi Laskowski, Rapid City, South Dakota*

3 eggs
1-1/2 cups sugar
1/2 cup canola oil
1/4 cup baking fat replacement
1 teaspoon vanilla extract
2 cups all-purpose flour
2 teaspoons baking soda
1 teaspoon ground cinnamon
1/2 teaspoon baking powder
1/4 teaspoon salt
2 cups shredded zucchini
1 cup chopped dates
1/2 cup chopped walnuts

CARAMEL CREAM CHEESE FROSTING:
  10 caramels
   1 tablespoon water
   3 ounces reduced-fat cream cheese
2-1/2 cups confectioners' sugar
   1/8 teaspoon salt

In a mixing bowl, beat the eggs, sugar, oil, baking fat replacement and vanilla. Combine the dry ingredients; add to the egg mixture and mix well. Stir in zucchini, dates and walnuts. Spread into a 13-in. x 9-in. x 2-in. baking pan coated with nonstick cooking spray. Bake at 350° for 25-30 minutes or until a toothpick inserted near the center comes out clean. Cool on a wire rack.

In a saucepan, heat caramels and water over low heat until caramels are melted, stirring occasionally. In a mixing bowl, beat cream cheese and confectioners' sugar until smooth. Add caramel mixture and salt; mix well. Spread over cooled bars. **Yield:** 18 servings.

Editor's Note: This recipe was tested with Smucker's Baking Healthy (found in the baking aisle of grocery stores) and Hershey caramels.

Nutritional Analysis: One bar equals 323 calories, 11 g fat (2 g saturated fat), 38 mg cholesterol, 232 mg sodium, 55 g carbohydrate, 2 g fiber, 4 g protein.

Double Chocolate Biscotti

(Pictured below right)

Not fond of biscotti? Try this moister version from our Test Kitchen that's especially good with a hot cup of coffee. It has such a chocolaty taste and sweet drizzle on top that you won't even know it's been lightened up.

🍎 Cutting Calories Creatively

WITH a little help from your imagination, you can easily trim down your desserts. Keep the following tips in mind to create goodies that are light and low-calorie yet delicious:

- Sprinkle cakes and brownies with confectioners' sugar instead of spreading with canned frosting. Prepared frosting can pack as much as 140 calories in a mere 2 tablespoons. Confectioners' sugar, on the other hand, contains about 120 calories in 1/4 cup.
- Top off a slice of angel food cake with fresh fruit and a dollop of reduced-fat whipped topping or frozen yogurt.
- Skip the sweets and surprise dinner guests with a coffee or hot chocolate bar. They can fix their own steaming mug when you offer a variety of cocoas and coffees and flavored low-fat creamers. Don't forget a sugar substitute, reduced-fat whipped topping, and ground cinnamon and nutmeg.

   2 eggs
   1 teaspoon vanilla extract
   1/4 teaspoon almond extract
   1/2 cup sugar
   1 cup all-purpose flour
   1/2 cup finely chopped pecans
   1/4 cup baking cocoa
   1/4 teaspoon salt
   1/2 cup miniature semisweet chocolate chips
ICING:
 1-1/2 teaspoons miniature semisweet chocolate chips
   3 teaspoons fat-free milk
   1/2 cup confectioners' sugar
   1/8 teaspoon vanilla extract

In a mixing bowl, beat the eggs and extracts. Beat in sugar. Combine the flour, pecans, cocoa and salt; gradually add to egg mixture. Stir in chocolate chips.

On a baking sheet coated with nonstick cooking spray, shape dough into a 14-in. x 3-in. rectangle. Bake at 350° for 20-25 minutes or until lightly browned. Cool for 5 minutes.

Transfer to a cutting board; cut with a serrated knife into 1-in. slices. Place cut side down on baking sheets coated with nonstick cooking spray. Bake for 15-20 minutes or until firm. Remove to wire racks to cool.

For icing, melt chocolate chips. Stir in milk, confectioners' sugar and vanilla. Drizzle over cookies; let stand until hardened. **Yield:** about 1 dozen.

Nutritional Analysis: One cookie equals 181 calories, 7 g fat (2 g saturated fat), 37 mg cholesterol, 67 mg sodium, 27 g carbohydrate, 2 g fiber, 4 g protein.
Diabetic Exchanges: 2 starch, 1 fat.

thick). Remove from the heat. Stir in chocolate until melted. Stir a small amount of hot filling into egg yolks; return all to the pan, stirring constantly. Cool to room temperature.

Let egg whites stand at room temperature for 30 minutes. In a mixing bowl, beat egg whites until foamy. Add cream of tartar; beat on medium speed until soft peaks form. Gradually add remaining sugar, 1 tablespoon at a time, beating on high until stiff peaks form. Gently fold a fourth of the egg white mixture into chocolate mixture; fold in remaining egg white mixture.

Spoon batter into prepared dishes. Bake at 325° for 25-35 minutes or until a toothpick inserted near the center comes out clean. Cool on wire racks. Dust with confectioners' sugar. Refrigerate leftovers. **Yield:** 7 servings.

Nutritional Analysis: One serving equals 313 calories, 8 g fat (4 g saturated fat), 91 mg cholesterol, 57 mg sodium, 58 g carbohydrate, 5 g fiber, 7 g protein.

Chocolate Souffles

(Pictured above)

Baked in individual custard cups, these chocolaty delights are ideal for serving with Christmas dinner. For variety, try sprinkling fresh raspberries or chocolate curls on top.
—Jeannette Mango, Parkesburg, Pennsylvania

    7 teaspoons plus 2/3 cup sugar, *divided*
1/2 cup packed brown sugar
1/3 cup cake flour
1/2 cup baking cocoa
    2 teaspoons instant coffee granules
3/4 cup water
    4 squares (1 ounce *each*) semisweet chocolate, chopped
    3 egg yolks, beaten
    6 egg whites
1/2 teaspoon cream of tartar
    1 teaspoon confectioners' sugar

Spray seven 10-oz. souffle dishes with nonstick cooking spray. Sprinkle 1 teaspoon of sugar into each dish, tilting to coat the bottom and sides; set aside.

In a saucepan, combine 1/3 cup sugar, brown sugar, flour, cocoa and coffee granules. Stir in water until blended. Bring to a boil; cook and stir for 1 minute (mixture will be

🍎 Tasty Dessert Toppings

● I add a little extra flavor to reduced-fat frozen whipped topping with different extracts, such as coconut, cherry, lemon, etc. My family thinks they're getting a real treat!
—*Dorothy Funderburg, Renton, Washington*

● Here's a simple way to frost an angel food cake—or any other cake. Simply thaw a large container of frozen light whipped topping and fold in one package of any flavor sugar-free gelatin powder. This flavorful frosting mixes up in seconds and tastes great!
—*Sandy Sinclair*
London, Ontario

Fine Dining Pared Down

A special occasion calls for candles,
fine china and a marvelous meal. But there's
no need to add to your guests' waistlines
at the same time. Pamper friends and family
with these elegant but light menus.

Cranberry-Pear Tossed Salad, Lemon Pecan Pilaf and Tangy Pork Loin Roast (page 240)

Take Stock in Steak

Flank Steak with Horseradish Sauce

An overnight marinade from our Test Kitchen gently flavors and tenderizes this lean cut of beef. It can be grilled to perfection in only minutes.

1 beef flank steak (1 pound)
3 tablespoons lemon juice
2 tablespoons Dijon mustard
2 tablespoons Worcestershire sauce
2 garlic cloves, minced
1/8 teaspoon hot pepper sauce
HORSERADISH SAUCE:
1/4 cup fat-free mayonnaise
1/4 cup reduced-fat sour cream
1 tablespoon Dijon mustard
2 green onions, finely chopped
2 teaspoons prepared horseradish

Using a sharp knife, score the surface of the steak with shallow diagonal cuts at 1-in. intervals, making diamond shapes. Repeat on other side. In a large resealable plastic bag, combine the next five ingredients. Add steak. Seal bag and turn to coat; refrigerate for 8 hours or overnight. Combine the sauce ingredients in a small bowl; cover and refrigerate.

Drain and discard the marinade. Grill the steak, covered, over medium-hot heat for 7-9 minutes on each side or until meat reaches desired doneness (for rare, a meat thermometer should read 140°; medium, 160°; well-done, 170°). Thinly slice steak across the grain; serve with the sauce. **Yield:** 4 servings.

Nutritional Analysis: One serving (1/4 of steak with 2 tablespoons sauce) equals 225 calories, 10 g fat (5 g saturated fat), 51 mg cholesterol, 353 mg sodium, 5 g carbohydrate, trace fiber, 26 g protein.
Diabetic Exchange: 4 lean meat.

Vegetable Couscous

Our Test Kitchen came up with this different way to serve vegetables. These tiny pasta granules pull together the flavors of the chicken broth and vitamin-rich veggies. Carrots, celery, peppers and zucchini add crunch and color.

2 medium carrots, diced
1/2 cup diced celery
1 medium onion, diced
1/4 cup julienned sweet yellow pepper
1/4 cup julienned sweet red pepper
2 tablespoons olive *or* canola oil
1 medium zucchini, diced
1/4 cup minced fresh basil *or* 4 teaspoons dried basil
1/4 teaspoon garlic salt
1/8 teaspoon pepper

Dash hot pepper sauce
1 cup uncooked couscous
1-1/2 cups chicken broth

In a large skillet, saute the carrots, celery, onion and peppers in oil for 5-6 minutes or until crisp-tender. Add the next five ingredients; mix well. Stir in the couscous. Add broth; bring to a boil. Cover and remove from the heat; let stand for 5-8 minutes. Fluff with a fork and serve immediately. **Yield:** 4 servings.

Nutritional Analysis: One serving (1-1/4 cups) equals 272 calories, 8 g fat (1 g saturated fat), 0 cholesterol, 513 mg sodium, 43 g carbohydrate, 4 g fiber, 8 g protein.
Diabetic Exchanges: 2 starch, 1 lean meat, 1 fat.

Raspberry Cream Cake

Guests will say this stunning dessert from our Test Kitchen looks too pretty to eat. But the combination of golden cake, vanilla cream, fresh raspberries and chocolate glaze will prove too tempting to resist.

1 package (18-1/4 ounces) reduced-fat yellow cake mix
1/4 teaspoon baking soda
1-1/3 cups water
2 tablespoons baking fat replacement*
4 egg whites
1-1/3 cups cold fat-free milk
1 package (1 ounce) sugar-free instant vanilla pudding mix
3/4 teaspoon vanilla extract
1-1/2 cups unsweetened raspberries, *divided*
1/2 cup fat-free hot fudge ice cream topping
1 tablespoon light corn syrup

In a mixing bowl, combine cake mix and baking soda. Add water, fat replacement and egg whites; beat on low speed for 2 minutes. Pour into two 9-in. round baking pans coated with nonstick cooking spray. Bake at 350° for 28-32 minutes or until a toothpick comes out clean. Cool for 10 minutes before removing from pans to wire racks to cool completely.

For filling, beat milk, pudding mix and vanilla in a mixing bowl on low speed for 2 minutes. Let stand for 5 minutes. Place one cake layer on a serving plate. Spread with pudding mixture; sprinkle with 3/4 cup raspberries. Top with second cake layer. Combine ice cream topping and corn syrup to achieve a glaze consistency; spread over top of cake, letting glaze drip over sides. Arrange remaining berries on top. **Yield:** 14 slices.

***Editor's Note:** This recipe was tested with Smucker's Baking Healthy. Look for it in the baking aisle of your grocery store.

Nutritional Analysis: One slice equals 248 calories, 2 g fat (1 g saturated fat), trace cholesterol, 371 mg sodium, 53 g carbohydrate, 1 g fiber, 4 g protein.
Diabetic Exchanges: 2 starch, 1 fruit, 1/2 fat.

Roast Receives Raves

Tangy Pork Loin Roast

(Also pictured on page 237 and the cover)

I often rely on the recipe for this moist and tender herb-rubbed roast. Flavored with grapefruit, the gravy is surprisingly light and tangy—a lovely complement to the meat.
—Pauline Curtis, Armstrong, British Columbia

1-1/2 teaspoons garlic powder
1-1/2 teaspoons ground mustard
1-1/2 teaspoons dried marjoram
   1 teaspoon salt
   1 bone-in pork loin roast (5 pounds)
1/2 cup unsweetened grapefruit juice
   2 tablespoons brown sugar
   1 tablespoon grated grapefruit peel
1/8 teaspoon ground mace
GRAVY (not shown):
   3 tablespoons all-purpose flour
1/2 teaspoon salt
Dash pepper
   1 medium grapefruit, peeled, sectioned and chopped

Combine garlic powder, mustard, marjoram and salt; rub over roast. Place on a rack in a shallow roasting pan. Bake, uncovered, at 325° for 1-1/2 hours. Remove from the oven; drain. Combine grapefruit juice, brown sugar, grapefruit peel and mace; pour half over roast. Bake 30 minutes longer or until a meat thermometer reads 160°, basting occasionally with remaining juice mixture. Remove roast to a serving platter and keep warm.

Stir drippings in pan to loosen brown bits; pour into a measuring cup. Skim off fat; reserve 2 tablespoons drippings. Add enough water to remaining drippings to measure 2 cups; set aside. Place reserved drippings in a saucepan; stir in flour until smooth. Gradually stir in reserved liquid until smooth. Add salt and pepper. Bring to a boil; cook and stir for 2 minutes or until thickened. Reduce heat; add grapefruit. Serve with the roast. **Yield:** 12 servings.

Nutritional Analysis: One serving (with 2-1/2 tablespoons gravy) equals 304 calories, 11 g fat (4 g saturated fat), 112 mg cholesterol, 393 mg sodium, 8 g carbohydrate, 1 g fiber, 41 g protein.
Diabetic Exchanges: 3-1/2 lean meat, 1 fruit, 1 fat.

Lemon Pecan Pilaf

(Also pictured on page 237)

Grated lemon peel brings delicate flavor to this rice side dish, while pecans add a satisfying crunch. This crowd-pleaser can be quickly prepared. My sister gave me the recipe. It's easy to make and very tasty.
—Cindie Ekstrand, Duarte, California

   5 cups chicken broth
2-1/2 cups uncooked long grain rice
   2 tablespoons butter *or* stick margarine

1/2 cup pecan halves
   3 tablespoons lemon juice
   1 teaspoon grated lemon peel
1/4 cup minced fresh parsley

In a saucepan, bring broth to a boil. Stir in rice; return to a boil. Reduce heat; cover and simmer for 20-25 minutes or until the rice is tender. Meanwhile, melt butter in a nonstick skillet. Add the pecans; saute until golden. Stir in the lemon juice and peel. Pour over rice and stir to coat. Sprinkle with parsley. **Yield:** 10 servings.

Nutritional Analysis: One serving (3/4 cup) equals 247 calories, 8 g fat (2 g saturated fat), 6 mg cholesterol, 527 mg sodium, 39 g carbohydrate, 1 g fiber, 5 g protein.
Diabetic Exchanges: 2-1/2 starch, 1 fat.

Cranberry-Pear Tossed Salad

(Also pictured on page 237)

I like to treat dinner guests to this colorful, fruity salad. Pears, dried cranberries and mixed greens are combined with sugarcoated walnuts and blue cheese, then drizzled with a sweet apricot-flavored dressing that's sure to tantalize taste buds.
—Kris Hernandez, Oneida, Wisconsin

1/3 cup apricot nectar
1/3 cup red wine vinegar *or* cider vinegar
1/3 cup canola oil
   2 teaspoons Dijon mustard
1/4 teaspoon salt
1/8 teaspoon pepper
   2 tablespoons sugar
1/2 cup chopped walnuts
 12 cups torn mixed salad greens
   3 medium ripe pears, sliced
1/2 cup dried cranberries
3/4 cup crumbled blue cheese

For dressing, in a bowl, whisk together the first six ingredients; set aside. In a heavy skillet, melt sugar over medium heat, stirring constantly. Add walnuts; stir to coat. Remove from the heat. In a large salad bowl, combine greens, pears and cranberries. Drizzle with dressing. Add nuts and blue cheese; toss. **Yield:** 12 servings.

Nutritional Analysis: One serving (1 cup) equals 161 calories, 12 g fat (2 g saturated fat), 5 mg cholesterol, 184 mg sodium, 13 g carbohydrate, 3 g fiber, 3 g protein.
Diabetic Exchanges: 2 fat, 1 vegetable, 1/2 starch.

Meat-and-Potatoes Meal

Brisket with Chunky Tomato Sauce

Guests agree this is the best beef they've ever tasted.
—Linda Blaska, Atlanta, Georgia

1 fresh beef brisket* (4-1/2 pounds)
1 teaspoon salt
1/4 to 1/2 teaspoon pepper
1 tablespoon olive *or* canola oil
3 large onions, chopped
2 garlic cloves, minced
1 cup dry red wine *or* beef broth
1 can (14-1/2 ounces) diced tomatoes, undrained
2 celery ribs with leaves, chopped
1/2 teaspoon dried thyme
1/2 teaspoon dried rosemary, crushed
1 bay leaf
1 pound carrots, cut into 1/2-inch slices

Season brisket with salt and pepper; brown on both sides in oil in a Dutch oven. Remove. In the same pan, saute onions and garlic until tender. Place brisket over onions. Add next six ingredients. Cover and bake at 325° for 2 hours, basting occasionally. Add carrots; bake 1 hour longer or until meat is tender. Discard bay leaf. Cool 1 hour; cover and refrigerate overnight. Trim visible fat from brisket; skim fat from tomato mixture. Thinly slice beef across the grain. In a saucepan, warm tomato mixture; transfer to a shallow roasting pan. Top with sliced beef. Cover and bake at 325° for 30 minutes or until heated through. Serve sauce over beef. **Yield:** 12 servings.
*Editor's Note: This is a fresh brisket, not corned beef.

Nutritional Analysis: One serving equals 316 calories, 12 g fat (4 g saturated fat), 100 mg cholesterol, 394 mg sodium, 10 g carbohydrate, 2 g fiber, 38 g protein.
Diabetic Exchanges: 4 lean meat, 2 fat.

Three-Cheese Potato Souffle

Everyday mashed potatoes become appealingly elegant in this extra-cheesy souffle.
—Kathy Kittell, Lenexa, Kansas

4 cups mashed potatoes (without added milk or butter)
1 cup fat-free milk
1 cup (4 ounces) shredded reduced-fat cheddar cheese
2/3 cup shredded reduced-fat Swiss cheese
1/3 cup shredded Parmesan cheese
1/3 cup chopped green onions
1 small onion, chopped
1-1/4 teaspoons salt
1/4 teaspoon pepper
4 eggs, *separated*

In a large bowl, combine the first nine ingredients. Beat egg yolks; stir into potato mixture. In a small mixing bowl, beat egg whites until stiff peaks form; gently fold into potato mixture. Transfer to a 2-qt. souffle dish coated with nonstick cooking spray. Bake, uncovered, at 375° for 40-45 minutes or until golden. Serve immediately. **Yield:** 12 servings.

Nutritional Analysis: One serving (1/2 cup) equals 153 calories, 5 g fat (3 g saturated fat), 83 mg cholesterol, 442 mg sodium, 16 g carbohydrate, trace fiber, 11 g protein.
Diabetic Exchanges: 1 starch, 1 lean meat, 1/2 fat.

Strawberry Rhubarb Tart

(Also pictured on the cover)

This tantalizing tart tastes just like spring!
—Kristy Martin, Circle Pine, Minnesota

1/2 cup old-fashioned oats, toasted
2/3 cup all-purpose flour
1/4 cup sugar
1 teaspoon grated lemon peel
3/4 teaspoon baking powder
1/4 teaspoon salt
2 tablespoons canola oil
3 tablespoons 1% milk
1/2 teaspoon vanilla extract
FILLING:
3-1/2 cups sliced fresh strawberries, *divided*
2 cups sliced fresh *or* frozen rhubarb
1/4 cup sugar
1/2 teaspoon grated lemon peel
5 teaspoons cornstarch
1 tablespoon cold water
4 teaspoons currant jelly, melted

Process oats in a blender or food processor until finely ground. Place in a bowl; add next five ingredients. Slowly add oil, stirring until the mixture resembles coarse crumbs. Combine milk and vanilla; stir into flour mixture, a tablespoon at a time, until mixture forms a ball. Turn onto a floured surface; knead 7-8 times. Coat a 9-in. tart pan with nonstick cooking spray. Between sheets of waxed paper, roll out pastry to fit pan; place in the pan. Line pastry shell with a double thickness of heavy-duty foil. Bake at 350° for 12 minutes. Remove foil; bake 8-12 minutes longer or until lightly browned. Cool on a wire rack.

For filling, combine 1 cup strawberries, rhubarb, sugar and lemon peel in a saucepan. Let stand for 30 minutes. Cook and stir over medium-low heat for 8-10 minutes or until rhubarb is tender but still retains shape. Combine cornstarch and water until smooth; stir into fruit mixture. Bring to a boil; cook and stir for 2 minutes or until thickened. Pour into a bowl; cover surface with plastic wrap. Refrigerate for 1-2 hours. Just before serving, spread filling in pastry shell. Top with remaining strawberries. Brush with jelly. **Yield:** 12 servings.

Nutritional Analysis: One piece equals 119 calories, 3 g fat (trace saturated fat), trace cholesterol, 67 mg sodium, 23 g carbohydrate, 2 g fiber, 2 g protein.
Diabetic Exchanges: 1 fruit, 1/2 starch, 1/2 fat.

Pair Up Pork and Pasta

Breaded Pork Chops

A bread crumb coating gives a nice golden look to these tender chops developed in our Test Kitchen. Parmesan and hot pepper sauce add just the right spark of flavor to tempt taste buds.

    2 tablespoons all-purpose flour
    4 egg whites
1/2 teaspoon Worcestershire sauce
1/2 teaspoon balsamic vinegar
1/8 teaspoon hot pepper sauce
3/4 cup dry bread crumbs
    3 tablespoons grated Parmesan cheese
1/2 teaspoon dried thyme
1/4 teaspoon salt
1/4 teaspoon paprika
    6 boneless pork loin chops (1/2 inch thick and
       4 ounces *each*)
Refrigerated butter-flavored spray*

Place flour in a shallow dish. In another shallow dish, beat the egg whites, Worcestershire sauce, vinegar and hot pepper sauce. In a third dish, combine the bread crumbs, Parmesan cheese, thyme, salt and paprika. Coat pork chops with flour. Dip into egg mixture, then coat with crumb mixture. Place on a plate; cover and refrigerate for 1 hour.

Place chops in a 13-in. x 9-in. x 2-in. baking dish coated with nonstick cooking spray; spritz chops with butter-flavored spray. Bake, uncovered, at 350° for 25-28 minutes or until juices run clear. **Yield:** 6 servings.

*Editor's Note: This recipe was tested with I Can't Believe It's Not Butter Spray.

Nutritional Analysis: One serving equals 250 calories, 8 g fat (3 g saturated fat), 74 mg cholesterol, 372 mg sodium, 12 g carbohydrate, trace fiber, 29 g protein.
Diabetic Exchanges: *3 lean meat, 1 starch.*

Pasta and Peppers

This colorful pasta toss from our Test Kitchen is sure to brighten your dinner table. Garlic, basil and a splash of white wine accent the sweet peppers and spiral pasta. For a fun and different look, you can substitute bow tie or medium shell pasta instead.

12 ounces uncooked spiral pasta
    2 medium sweet red peppers, cut into 1/2-inch
       pieces
    2 medium sweet yellow peppers, cut into 1/2-inch
       pieces
    1 tablespoon butter *or* stick margarine
    3 garlic cloves, minced

    1 tablespoon cornstarch
1-1/2 cups vegetable broth
    2 tablespoons dry white wine *or* additional
       vegetable broth
    2 tablespoons minced fresh basil
    1 teaspoon salt
1/4 teaspoon pepper
    1 tablespoon minced fresh parsley

Cook pasta according to package directions. Meanwhile, in a large nonstick skillet, saute peppers in butter until crisp-tender. Add garlic; saute 1 minute longer. Combine the cornstarch, broth and wine or additional broth until smooth; stir into pepper mixture. Bring to a boil; cook and stir for 1-2 minutes or until thickened.

Remove from the heat; stir in the basil, salt and pepper. Drain pasta; toss with pepper mixture. Sprinkle with parsley. **Yield:** 6 servings.

Nutritional Analysis: One serving (1-1/4 cups) equals 249 calories, 3 g fat (1 g saturated fat), 5 mg cholesterol, 665 mg sodium, 47 g carbohydrate, 4 g fiber, 8 g protein.
Diabetic Exchanges: *2-1/2 starch, 2 vegetable.*

Melon with Raspberry Sauce

Refreshing melon slices fanned out in a pretty pool of raspberry sauce create a light but elegant ending to any special-occasion meal. Our Test Kitchen created the recipe.

2-2/3 cups unsweetened raspberries
    3 tablespoons honey
    1 teaspoon lemon juice
1/8 teaspoon ground ginger *or* 1/2 teaspoon
       minced fresh gingerroot
1/2 large cantaloupe
1/2 medium honeydew

Set aside a few raspberries for garnish. Place the remaining berries in a blender or food processor; cover and process until pureed. Add the honey, lemon juice and ginger; mix well. Strain and discard seeds; set sauce aside.

Cut the cantaloupe and honeydew into three wedges; cut each wedge widthwise in half. Remove seeds and rind. With a knife, slice each piece of melon lengthwise toward narrow end without cutting completely to the end. Open into a fan shape.

On each dessert plate, place 2 tablespoons of raspberry sauce and a cantaloupe fan and honeydew fan. Garnish with reserved raspberries. **Yield:** 6 servings.

Nutritional Analysis: One serving equals 130 calories, 1 g fat (trace saturated fat), 0 cholesterol, 19 mg sodium, 33 g carbohydrate, 5 g fiber, 2 g protein.
Diabetic Exchange: *2 fruit.*

Down-Home Ham Dinner

Baked Ham with Orange Glaze

*Our Test Kitchen baked ham in
apple cider and orange juice, then
brushed it with a sweet-tangy glaze.*

1/2 bone-in fully cooked lean ham (6 to 7 pounds)
2 cups apple cider *or* apple juice
2 cups orange juice
1/3 cup orange marmalade
1/4 cup packed brown sugar
1/4 cup Dijon mustard
1/4 teaspoon ground ginger

Place ham on a rack in a shallow roasting pan. Trim fat; score surface of ham, making diamond shapes 1/4 in. deep. Add cider and orange juice to pan. Loosely cover ham with foil; bake at 325° for 1 hour. Combine remaining ingredients; brush some over ham. Bake, uncovered, 50-60 minutes longer or until a meat thermometer reads 140° and ham is heated through, brushing occasionally with glaze. Let stand for 15 minutes before slicing. Serve with remaining glaze. **Yield:** 10 servings.

*Nutritional Analysis: One serving (3 ounces cooked ham) equals 177 calories, 5 g fat (2 g saturated fat), 49 mg cholesterol, 1,300 mg sodium, 9 g carbohydrate, trace fiber, 23 g protein.
Diabetic Exchanges: 3 lean meat, 1/2 fruit.*

Sweet Potatoes and Parsnips

*Allspice, garlic and onion season sweet potatoes and
parsnips in this side dish from the Test Kitchen.*

4 medium sweet potatoes (about 2 pounds), peeled
4 medium parsnips (about 2 pounds), peeled
1 large Vidalia *or* other sweet onion, cut into wedges
1/4 cup olive *or* canola oil
1/2 teaspoon salt
1/2 teaspoon ground allspice
1/4 teaspoon garlic powder
1/4 teaspoon pepper

Cut sweet potatoes in half lengthwise. Cut each half lengthwise into four pieces, then into 3-in. slices. Cut parsnips into quarters, then into 3-in. pieces. Place the potatoes, parsnips and onion in a 3-qt. microwave-safe baking dish. Cover and microwave on high for 3 minutes. Stir; cover and cook 2 minutes longer. Add remaining ingredients; toss to coat. Transfer to two 15-in. x 10-in. x 1-in. baking pans coated with nonstick cooking spray. Bake, uncovered, at 425° for 20-25 minutes or until vegetables are tender, stirring occasionally. **Yield:** 10 servings.

*Nutritional Analysis: One serving (3/4 cup) equals 169 calories, 6 g fat (1 g saturated fat), 0 cholesterol, 130 mg sodium, 29 g carbohydrate, 5 g fiber, 2 g protein.
Diabetic Exchanges: 2 starch, 1 fat.*

Chocolate Meringue Torte

*For a chocoholic's dream come true,
our Test Kitchen recommends this
divine dessert. It has a moist from-scratch
chocolate cake and crunchy meringue.*

4 egg whites
1/2 teaspoon cream of tartar
2/3 cup sugar
2/3 cup confectioners' sugar
3 tablespoons baking cocoa
1/2 teaspoon vanilla extract
CAKE:
1/4 cup butter *or* stick margarine, softened
1 cup sugar
1 egg
1 egg white
1 tablespoon white vinegar
1 teaspoon vanilla extract
1-1/2 cups all-purpose flour
1/2 cup baking cocoa
1 teaspoon baking soda
1/2 cup 1% buttermilk
1/2 cup water
2-1/2 cups reduced-fat whipped topping
1 tablespoon toffee bits *or* almond brickle chips
1/2 square (1/2 ounce) semisweet chocolate, shaved

Line a baking sheet with parchment paper. Trace two 8-in. circles 1 in. apart on paper; set aside. In a mixing bowl, beat egg whites and cream of tartar until soft peaks form. Add sugar, 1 tablespoon at a time, beating until stiff peaks form. Sift the confectioners' sugar and cocoa over the meringue; gently fold in. Fold in vanilla. Spread evenly over circles.

Bake at 275° for 1 hour. Turn oven off and do not open door; let meringues dry for 1 hour. Remove from oven; cool on baking sheet. When completely cool, remove meringues from paper; store in an airtight container.

In a mixing bowl, cream butter and sugar for 2 minutes. Add egg, then egg white, one at a time, beating well after each addition. Beat on high speed until light and fluffy. Stir in vinegar and vanilla. Combine flour, cocoa and baking soda; add to batter alternately with buttermilk and water.

Pour into two 9-in. round baking pans coated with nonstick cooking spray and floured. Bake at 350° for 20-25 minutes or until a toothpick comes out clean. Cool for 10 minutes before removing from pans to wire racks.

To assemble, spread 1/2 cup whipped topping over one cake layer; top with a meringue and another 1/2 cup topping. Top with second cake layer, 1/2 cup topping, second meringue and remaining topping. Sprinkle with toffee bits and shaved chocolate. **Yield:** 10 servings.

Nutritional Analysis: One piece equals 362 calories, 9 g fat (6 g saturated fat), 37 mg cholesterol, 225 mg sodium, 65 g carbohydrate, 3 g fiber, 6 g protein.

Healthy Holiday Fare

Shrimp with Creole Sauce

Dip into this zippy Creole-style sauce from our Test Kitchen and you'll never crave store-bought seafood sauce again. Chunky but not too spicy, the tantalizing tomato blend complements cold shrimp or cooked seafood.

    1 large onion, chopped
1/2 cup finely chopped green pepper
    1 celery rib with leaves, finely chopped
    1 tablespoon canola oil
    3 garlic cloves, minced
    1 can (28 ounces) whole tomatoes
1/4 cup minced fresh parsley
1/4 cup water
1/4 cup tomato paste
    2 tablespoons lime juice
    1 teaspoon dried thyme
3/4 teaspoon salt
1/2 teaspoon dried oregano
1/4 to 1/2 teaspoon hot pepper sauce
1/4 teaspoon ground allspice
   36 cooked large shrimp, peeled and deveined

In a large nonstick skillet, saute the onion, green pepper and celery in oil for 3-4 minutes. Add garlic; cook 1 minute longer. Drain tomatoes, reserving juice; add juice to skillet. Mash tomatoes; add to skillet. Stir in the parsley, water, tomato paste, lime juice and seasonings. Bring to a boil. Reduce heat; simmer, uncovered, for 15 minutes or until thickened. Serve warm with shrimp. **Yield:** 12 servings.

Nutritional Analysis: One serving (3 shrimp with 1/3 cup sauce) equals 56 calories, 1 g fat (trace saturated fat), 32 mg cholesterol, 292 mg sodium, 7 g carbohydrate, 1 g fiber, 5 g protein.
Diabetic Exchanges: 1 very lean meat, 1 vegetable.

Spinach-Stuffed Beef Tenderloin

Make this elegant but easy entree the centerpiece of Christmas dinner...and you're sure to be serving up seconds. The recipe comes from our Test Kitchen.

1/2 pound fresh mushrooms, chopped
    4 green onions, sliced
    2 tablespoons olive *or* canola oil, *divided*
    2 garlic cloves, minced, *divided*
    2 packages (10 ounces *each*) fresh spinach leaves
    1 teaspoon salt, *divided*
1/8 to 1/4 teaspoon cayenne pepper
    1 whole beef tenderloin (about 3-1/2 pounds), trimmed
1/4 teaspoon onion powder
1/4 teaspoon coarsely ground pepper

In a large nonstick skillet, saute mushrooms and onions in 1 tablespoon oil for 2 minutes. Add half of the garlic; cook until mushrooms are tender. Add spinach, 1/2 teaspoon salt and cayenne. Cook until the spinach is wilted. Remove from the heat; set aside.

Cut a lengthwise slit down the center of tenderloin to within 3/4 in. of bottom. Open so meat lies flat. Spread with spinach stuffing. Fold one side of meat over stuffing; tie several times with kitchen string. Rub remaining oil over beef. Combine the onion powder, pepper, and remaining garlic and salt; rub over beef. Place on a rack in a shallow roasting pan.

Bake, uncovered, at 425° for 40-55 minutes or until a meat thermometer reaches desired doneness (for rare, meat thermometer should read 140°; medium, 160°; well-done, 170°). Let stand for 10 minutes. Remove string before slicing. **Yield:** 12 servings.

Nutritional Analysis: One serving (4 ounces stuffed beef) equals 242 calories, 12 g fat (4 g saturated fat), 82 mg cholesterol, 293 mg sodium, 3 g carbohydrate, 1 g fiber, 29 g protein.
Diabetic Exchanges: 3 lean meat, 1 fat, 1 vegetable.

Mashed Potato Timbales

These pretty individual servings of mashed potatoes from our Test Kitchen will dress up any occasion.

2-1/2 pounds potatoes, peeled and cubed
    1 tablespoon butter *or* stick margarine
    1 tablespoon grated onion
    1 carton (8 ounces) reduced-fat ricotta cheese
    1 cup (8 ounces) reduced-fat sour cream
    1 teaspoon salt
    1 teaspoon garlic powder
1/2 teaspoon dried rosemary, crushed
1/4 teaspoon pepper
    2 egg whites
    2 tablespoons dry bread crumbs

Place potatoes in a saucepan and cover with water; bring to a boil. Reduce heat; cover and cook for 20-25 minutes or until tender. Drain. Mash potatoes with butter and onion until small lumps of potato remain; set aside. In a mixing bowl, beat ricotta cheese, sour cream, salt, garlic powder, rosemary and pepper until smooth. In a small bowl, beat egg whites until frothy; fold into cheese mixture. Fold into potato mixture.

Generously coat muffin cups with nonstick spray; evenly sprinkle muffin cups with bread crumbs. Fill with potato mixture; smooth tops. Bake, uncovered, at 425° for 27-30 minutes or until edges of potatoes are lightly browned. Cool for 15 minutes. Loosen timbales from sides of muffin cups; invert onto a baking sheet to remove. **Yield:** 12 servings.

Nutritional Analysis: One serving equals 153 calories, 6 g fat (5 g saturated fat), 23 mg cholesterol, 319 mg sodium, 20 g carbohydrate, 2 g fiber, 5 g protein.
Diabetic Exchanges: 1 starch, 1/2 reduced-fat milk, 1/2 fat.

Family-Style Suppers

In this chapter, you'll "meet" cooks who share how they prepare good-for-you fare for their families' tables. You'll also find a special dinner for Mom and meals that don't break your household budget.

Turkey Meat Loaf, Tangy Green Beans and
Cheesy Scalloped Potatoes (pages 254 and 255)

A Meal for Just $1.95 a Plate!

Tuna Patties with Dill Sauce

Our Test Kitchen shares these tender golden tuna patties, draped with a creamy dill sauce.

- **2 large parsnips, peeled and cut into 1/2-inch slices**
- **2 egg whites, lightly beaten**
- **1/2 cup soft bread crumbs (about 1 slice)**
- **1/4 cup finely chopped green onions**
- **1 tablespoon dried parsley flakes**
- **2 teaspoons lemon juice**
- **1/2 teaspoon grated lemon peel**
- **1/2 teaspoon dill weed**
- **1/4 teaspoon pepper**
- **2 cans (6 ounces *each*) light water-packed tuna, drained and flaked**
- **2 teaspoons olive *or* canola oil**
- **DILL SAUCE:**
- **1/2 cup fat-free mayonnaise**
- **1 teaspoon lemon juice**
- **1 teaspoon grated lemon peel**
- **1/2 teaspoon dill weed**

Place parsnips in a saucepan and cover with water; bring to a boil. Reduce heat; cover and simmer for 30-35 minutes or until tender. Drain well. Place parsnips in a food processor or blender; cover and process until smooth. In a bowl, combine 1 cup pureed parsnips, egg whites, bread crumbs, onions, parsley, lemon juice and peel, dill and pepper. Add tuna and mix well.

Shape into eight 1/2-in.-thick patties (patties will be soft). In a large nonstick skillet, heat oil over medium heat. Cook patties for 5-6 minutes on each side or until lightly browned. Combine the sauce ingredients in a small bowl; serve with tuna patties. **Yield:** 4 servings.

Nutritional Analysis: One serving (2 patties with 2 tablespoons sauce) equals 211 calories, 3 g fat (trace saturated fat), 53 mg cholesterol, 635 mg sodium, 16 g carbohydrate, 2 g fiber, 26 g protein.
Diabetic Exchanges: 2 lean meat, 1 starch, 1/2 fat.

Mixed Vegetables

Colorful carrot coins, broccoli and zucchini star in this appealing side dish from our Test Kitchen. Simmered in Italian salad dressing, the veggies take on that zesty flavor.

- **1 medium carrot, cut into 1/4-inch slices**
- **1/2 cup water**
- **1 cup broccoli florets**
- **1 medium onion, cut into 16 wedges**
- **1 medium zucchini, cut into 1/4-inch slices**
- **1/4 cup fat-free Italian salad dressing**
- **1/4 teaspoon dried oregano**

In a nonstick skillet, bring carrot and water to a boil. Reduce heat; cover and simmer for 5 minutes. Add the broccoli, onion and zucchini; return to a boil. Reduce heat; cover and simmer for 2 minutes. Add salad dressing and oregano. Cook and stir over medium heat for 4 minutes or until vegetables are tender and liquid is reduced. **Yield:** 4 servings.

Nutritional Analysis: One serving (3/4 cup) equals 41 calories, trace fat (0 saturated fat), 0 cholesterol, 161 mg sodium, 9 g carbohydrate, 2 g fiber, 2 g protein.
Diabetic Exchange: 1-1/2 vegetable.

Apricot Sundaes

Apricots make a lovely, lightly sweet topping that's spooned over frozen yogurt in this fruity and refreshing dessert developed in our Test Kitchen.

- **1 can (15 ounces) reduced-sugar apricot halves**
- **1/3 cup plus 2 tablespoons orange juice, *divided***
- **1 teaspoon brown sugar**
- **1-1/2 teaspoons cornstarch**
- **1 teaspoon vanilla extract**
- **2 cups fat-free sugar-free frozen vanilla yogurt**

Drain apricots, reserving juice. Slice apricots; set aside. In a saucepan, combine 1/3 cup orange juice, brown sugar and reserved apricot juice; bring to a boil. Reduce heat; simmer, uncovered, for 10 minutes. Combine cornstarch and remaining orange juice until smooth; stir into apricot juice mixture. Bring to a boil; cook and stir for 2 minutes or until thickened. Stir in vanilla and reserved apricots. Serve over frozen yogurt. **Yield:** 4 servings.

Nutritional Analysis: One serving (1/2 cup frozen yogurt with 1/2 cup sauce) equals 151 calories, trace fat (trace saturated fat), 0 cholesterol, 84 mg sodium, 33 g carbohydrate, 2 g fiber, 5 g protein.
Diabetic Exchanges: 1 starch, 1 fruit.

A Meal for Just $1.36 a Plate!

Sausage Lentil Stew

This hearty stew is chock-full of protein-packed lentils, vegetables and tasty turkey kielbasa.
—Patti St. Antoine, Broomfield, Colorado

1 pound fully cooked turkey kielbasa, thinly sliced
2 medium carrots, sliced
2 celery ribs, sliced
1 medium onion, chopped
2 garlic cloves, minced
2 teaspoons canola oil
3 cups water
2 medium potatoes, diced
1 can (14-1/2 ounces) chicken broth
1 cup dry lentils
3/4 teaspoon salt
1/2 teaspoon ground cumin
1/8 teaspoon cayenne pepper
1 can (28 ounces) diced tomatoes, undrained
1 can (4 ounces) chopped green chilies

In a Dutch oven, cook the kielbasa, carrots, celery, onion and garlic in oil until vegetables are almost tender, about 5 minutes. Stir in the next seven ingredients; bring to a boil. Reduce heat; cover and simmer for 40 minutes or until potatoes are tender, stirring occasionally. Add tomatoes and chilies; heat through. **Yield:** 8 servings.

Nutritional Analysis: One serving (1-1/3 cups) equals 268 calories, 7 g fat (3 g saturated fat), 30 mg cholesterol, 1,236 mg sodium, 34 g carbohydrate, 12 g fiber, 20 g protein.
***Diabetic Exchanges:** 2 lean meat, 1 starch, 1 vegetable, 1 fat.*

Jalapeno Corn Bread

I enjoy this corn bread with a steaming bowl of soup. It's moist and cuts nicely. Jalapeno pepper adds a little zip.
—Deanna Dillard, Advance, North Carolina

1/2 cup cornmeal
1/2 cup all-purpose flour
1 teaspoon sugar
1/2 teaspoon salt
1/4 teaspoon baking soda
1/4 teaspoon baking powder
1/4 teaspoon garlic powder
1 egg
1/2 cup cream-style corn
1/4 cup shredded reduced-fat cheddar cheese
1/4 cup 1% buttermilk
2 tablespoons minced green onion
1 tablespoon butter *or* stick margarine, melted
2 teaspoons minced jalapeno pepper*

In a bowl, combine the cornmeal, flour, sugar, salt, baking soda, baking powder and garlic powder. In a small bowl, combine the remaining ingredients. Stir into dry ingredients just until moistened. Pour into a 1-qt. square baking dish coated with nonstick cooking spray. Bake at 425° for 13-15 minutes or until a toothpick inserted near the center comes out clean. Cut into squares; serve warm. **Yield:** 9 servings.

***Editor's Note:** When cutting or seeding hot peppers, use rubber or plastic gloves to protect your hands. Avoid touching your face.*

Nutritional Analysis: One serving (1 piece) equals 112 calories, 3 g fat (2 g saturated fat), 33 mg cholesterol, 291 mg sodium, 17 g carbohydrate, 1 g fiber, 4 g protein.
***Diabetic Exchanges:** 1 starch, 1/2 lean meat.*

Chocolate Snack Cake

This rich-tasting delicious chocolate dessert is much lighter than a traditional cake or brownie.
—Carolyn Wolbers, Loveland, Ohio

2 eggs plus 2 egg whites
2/3 cup unsweetened applesauce
1/3 cup canola oil
2 squares (1 ounce *each*) semisweet chocolate, melted
2 teaspoons vanilla extract
1 cup all-purpose flour
1 cup sugar
1/3 cup baking cocoa
1 teaspoon baking powder
1/2 teaspoon salt
6 cups frozen reduced-fat vanilla yogurt

In a mixing bowl, beat eggs and egg whites. Add applesauce, oil, chocolate and vanilla; mix well. Combine dry ingredients; gradually add to egg mixture just until combined. Pour into a 9-in. springform pan coated with nonstick cooking spray. Bake at 350° for 30-35 minutes or until a toothpick comes out clean. Cool on a wire rack. Carefully run a knife around edge of pan; remove sides of pan. Cut into wedges; serve with frozen yogurt. **Yield:** 12 servings.

Nutritional Analysis: One serving (1 wedge with 1/2 cup frozen yogurt) equals 290 calories, 9 g fat (2 g saturated fat), 36 mg cholesterol, 177 mg sodium, 48 g carbohydrate, 1 g fiber, 6 g protein.
***Diabetic Exchanges:** 2-1/2 starch, 2 fat.*

A Meal for Just $1.10 a Plate!

Bran Griddle Cakes

You'd never guess there's bran in these moist, tasty pancakes that are drizzled with a sweet orange sauce. My children are grown, but they still request this for breakfast when they come home. Your family will surely flip over these flapjacks, too!
—Marie Cockerham, Rock Hill, South Carolina

1-1/2 cups all-purpose flour
  2 tablespoons sugar
  3 teaspoons baking powder
  3/4 teaspoon salt
  1 egg
  2 cups fat-free milk
  1 teaspoon grated orange peel
  1 cup All-Bran
ORANGE SYRUP:
  1/2 cup sugar
  1 tablespoon cornstarch
  1 cup orange juice
  1 tablespoon butter *or* stick margarine
  2 teaspoons grated orange peel
  1 medium navel orange, peeled, sectioned and chopped

In a bowl, combine the flour, sugar, baking powder and salt. In another bowl, beat egg; stir in milk, orange peel and bran. Let stand for 1-2 minutes or until bran is softened. Add to dry ingredients; mix well. Pour by 1/4 cupfuls onto a hot nonstick griddle; turn when bubbles form on top of pancakes. Cook until second side is golden brown.

For syrup, combine sugar and cornstarch in a saucepan. Gradually stir in orange juice, butter and orange peel. Bring to a boil; cook and stir for 2 minutes or until thickened. Remove from the heat; stir in chopped orange. Serve with pancakes. **Yield:** 7 servings.

Nutritional Analysis: One serving (2 pancakes with 2-1/2 tablespoons syrup) equals 272 calories, 3 g fat (1 g saturated fat), 36 mg cholesterol, 432 mg sodium, 56 g carbohydrate, 4 g fiber, 8 g protein.
Diabetic Exchanges: 2-1/2 starch, 1 fruit.

Lightly Scrambled Eggs

Wake up your taste buds with this fluffy entree, enhanced with sour cream, green onions and cheese. To keep it light, I simply use reduced-fat and fat-free ingredients.
—Patricia Kaliska, Phillips, Wisconsin

  9 egg whites
  3 eggs
  1/2 cup reduced-fat sour cream
  1/4 cup fat-free milk
  2 green onions, thinly sliced
  1/4 teaspoon salt
  1/8 teaspoon pepper
  6 drops yellow food coloring, optional
  3/4 cup shredded reduced-fat cheddar cheese

In a bowl, beat egg whites and eggs. Add the sour cream, milk, onions, salt, pepper and food coloring if desired. Pour into a large nonstick skillet coated with nonstick cooking spray; cook and gently stir over medium heat until eggs are completely set. Sprinkle with cheese; cover and let stand for 5 minutes. **Yield:** 6 servings.

Nutritional Analysis: One serving (1/3 cup) equals 135 calories, 7 g fat (4 g saturated fat), 122 mg cholesterol, 331 mg sodium, 4 g carbohydrate, trace fiber, 15 g protein.
Diabetic Exchanges: 2 lean meat, 1/2 fat.

Yogurt Breakfast Drink

Sleepyheads will savor this dreamy smoothie. Just blend yogurt, milk and orange juice concentrate for a fresh start to your day.
—Renee Gastineau, Seattle, Washington

  2 cups (16 ounces) reduced-fat vanilla yogurt
  2 cups (16 ounces) reduced-fat peach yogurt
  1/2 cup frozen orange juice concentrate
  1/2 cup fat-free milk
  2 cups ice cubes

In a blender or food processor, combine the first four ingredients; cover and process until smooth. Add ice cubes; cover and process until smooth. Pour into glasses; serve immediately. **Yield:** 6 servings.

Nutritional Analysis: One serving (1 cup) equals 166 calories, 2 g fat (1 g saturated fat), 10 mg cholesterol, 100 mg sodium, 30 g carbohydrate, 0 fiber, 8 g protein.
Diabetic Exchanges: 1 fat-free milk, 1 fruit.

This Cook Re-Creates Classics

GOOD EATING is all in the family, as far as Diane Werner is concerned. "I've always loved to cook," reports Diane, a registered dietitian and Associate Food Editor of *Light & Tasty*. "When I was growing up, I spent hours in the kitchen watching my mom whip up big batches of Italian spaghetti sauce.

"My husband, David, and I share a common interest in food," she says. "We met at Kansas State University years ago when we were both working on nutrition-related degrees.

"Over the years, I've always tried to introduce our four kids to a variety of foods prepared in different ways," Diane explains. "I try to put nutritious foods on the table, so they'll learn to enjoy eating healthy.

"For instance, I buy lots of grains, fruits and vegetables …and fewer sweets and desserts. I keep a basket of fresh fruit on the kitchen counter for the kids to snack on…and I don't keep sacks of candy bars around.

"But we still eat sweets—we all like ice cream. And my girls love baking cookies and other desserts. We just try not to overdo. My motto is 'everything in moderation'.

"I try to encourage my kids to drink healthier alternatives to soda, such as orange or other fruit juices, water or low-fat milk," Diane says.

"If people are trying to change their eating habits, I'd suggest they start with little things, rather than making drastic changes," Diane advises. "In many cases, family members won't even notice the difference.

"For example, I prefer cooking techniques that use low-fat or nonfat methods, such as grilling, broiling and steaming. And I rely on nonstick cooking spray or low-sodium broth instead of using fats or oils when sauteing or stir-frying.

"There are other easy ways to cut fat in your family's diet—such as using low-fat or fat-free dairy products in cooking. Try substituting light sour cream in a recipe that calls for regular—my guess is your family won't even notice the difference.

"I pay special attention to food preparation, too. I'll often make soup a day ahead, so the fat can be easily skimmed off the top the next day. Sometimes I'll cut back on the amount of meat in a recipe, or choose a leaner cut than the one called for."

Diane was happy to share her family's favorite light menu. Her Turkey Meat Loaf is a tasty alternative adapted from a standard ground beef recipe.

"Ground turkey lowers the fat while spinach gives the meat loaf even more nutritional value," Diane details. "The spinach also helps keep the texture moist…and the green flecks add such pretty color to the slices.

"My Cheesy Scalloped Potatoes still have the creamy texture and cheesy flavor my family expects, but this slimmed-down version has less fat and fewer calories."

Diane's Tangy Green Beans are delicately dressed with white wine vinegar and subtle mustard and garlic seasonings, rather than swimming in butter and salt.

"Flavor is so important," Diane confirms. "There's no point in cooking a meal that people won't eat. Gathering around the table, sharing good food and good conversation, is what eating is all about."

Turkey Meat Loaf

(Also pictured on page 250)

- 1 medium onion, finely chopped
- 1 tablespoon canola oil
- 2 eggs
- 1/2 cup 2% milk
- 2 teaspoons lemon juice
- 1 teaspoon salt
- 1 teaspoon dried basil
- 1/2 teaspoon dried oregano
- 1/2 teaspoon pepper
- 2 cups soft whole wheat bread crumbs (about 5 slices)
- 1 package (10 ounces) frozen chopped spinach, thawed and squeezed dry
- 2-1/2 pounds lean ground turkey
- 1/2 cup salsa
- 1 tablespoon butter *or* stick margarine, melted

In a skillet, saute onion in oil until tender; set aside. In a bowl, combine the eggs, milk, lemon juice, salt, basil, oregano and pepper. Add the bread crumbs, spinach and reserved onion; stir to combine. Crumble turkey over mixture and mix until blended. Shape into a 12-in. x 5-in. loaf; place in a 13-in. x 9-in. x 2-in. baking dish coated with nonstick cooking spray. Spoon salsa over top. Bake, uncovered, at 350° for 30 minutes. Drizzle with butter; bake 30-35 minutes longer or until a meat thermometer reads 165°. **Yield:** 10 slices.

Nutritional Analysis: One slice equals 263 calories, 14 g fat (4 g saturated fat), 136 mg cholesterol, 595 mg sodium, 10 g carbohydrate, 2 g fiber, 24 g protein.
Diabetic Exchanges: 3 lean meat, 1 vegetable, 1 fat, 1/2 starch.

Cheesy Scalloped Potatoes

(Also pictured on page 250)

- 5 large potatoes, peeled and thinly sliced
- 3 tablespoons all-purpose flour
- 1-1/2 teaspoons salt
- 1/4 teaspoon pepper
- 1-1/4 cups shredded reduced-fat cheddar cheese, *divided*
- 3 ounces reduced-fat Swiss cheese slices, finely chopped (3/4 cup), *divided*
- 2 medium onions, finely chopped
- 1-1/2 cups 2% milk
- 2 tablespoons minced fresh parsley

Place a third of the potatoes in a shallow 3-qt. baking dish coated with nonstick cooking spray. In a small bowl, combine the flour, salt and pepper; sprinkle half over potatoes.

Sprinkle with 1/4 cup of each cheese and half of the onions. Repeat layers. Top with remaining potatoes. Pour milk over all. Cover and bake at 350° for 50-60 minutes or until potatoes are nearly tender. Sprinkle with remaining cheeses. Bake, uncovered, 10 minutes longer or until cheese is melted and potatoes are tender. Sprinkle with parsley. **Yield:** 8 servings.

Nutritional Analysis: One serving (about 3/4 cup) equals 235 calories, 7 g fat (4 g saturated fat), 22 mg cholesterol, 556 mg sodium, 30 g carbohydrate, 3 g fiber, 15 g protein.
Diabetic Exchanges: 2 starch, 1 lean meat, 1/2 fat.

Tangy Green Beans

(Also pictured on page 250)

1-1/2 pounds fresh green beans, trimmed
1/3 cup diced sweet red pepper
4-1/2 teaspoons olive *or* canola oil
4-1/2 teaspoons water
1-1/2 teaspoons white wine vinegar *or* cider vinegar
1-1/2 teaspoons spicy brown mustard
3/4 teaspoon salt
1/4 teaspoon pepper
1/8 teaspoon garlic powder

Place beans and red pepper in a basket over 1 in. of boiling water in a saucepan. Cover and steam for 7-8 minutes or until crisp-tender. Meanwhile, in a bowl, whisk together the remaining ingredients. Transfer bean mixture to a serving bowl; add vinaigrette and stir to coat. **Yield:** 9 servings.

Nutritional Analysis: One serving (1/2 cup) equals 43 calories, 2 g fat (trace saturated fat), 0 cholesterol, 207 mg sodium, 5 g carbohydrate, 3 g fiber, 1 g protein.
Diabetic Exchanges: 1 vegetable, 1/2 fat.

🍎 The Heart of the Matter

"WE'VE tried to introduce our kids to a variety of foods," Diane says. "They learned to eat steamed artichokes at an early age.

"I'm not sure if it was the flavor that appealed to them...or the act of dipping the leaves in a little herb butter...or the novel way of 'skinning' an artichoke leaf with their teeth that kept them coming back for more.

"To this day, artichokes are highly prized at our house. The child who displays the best manners while eating one is rewarded with the much sought-after artichoke heart."

Good Food from the Grill

FOR Deb Anderson and her family, eating light comes naturally. "My main focus is to use less processed foods," Deb shares. "When we want soup, I make it. That way I know exactly what's in the recipe. Once you get into the habit of cooking from scratch, dishes come together quickly."

Deb and her husband, Bruce, live in Joplin, Missouri with their two sons—Jay and Roger. Their daughter, Angela, goes to a university in Kansas.

Deb says she started cooking lighter to help some family members lose weight, but it was also a way to improve everyone's health.

"Now it's a way of life," Deb notes. "We've been eating healthier for so long that I don't even think about it anymore."

The key to their success is making sensible yet realistic eating choices, she asserts.

"We still have foods like pizza and cinnamon rolls, but we're smart about it. We eat a little, not the whole thing. I like the idea of moderation, rather than strict rules. If you tell me I can't have something, then I want it."

With a house full of busy teens and adults, Deb makes sure to keep plenty of good-for-you snacks on hand.

"Apples, pears, carrots, popcorn, low-fat cottage cheese and yogurt are some of our staples," Deb details. "But there's usually a frozen pizza or two around as well. I don't want to keep the kids from eating what they want, but we do talk about making nutritious choices.

"For meals, one of my mainstays is chicken," Deb adds. "I make sure to keep some in the freezer. Its versatility allows me to come up with dishes everyone likes.

"Our other family favorite is Mexican cuisine. I use a lot of spicy seasonings, onions, garlic and habanero peppers."

Deb's biggest challenge is cooking on a tight schedule. Both she and Bruce work (she's a building contractor and he manages a mining company) and their boys are active in sports. So she often turns to her gas grill.

"Even in winter, I'll grill some chicken or potatoes for dinner. The weather doesn't stop me."

It's no surprise Deb decided to share recipes for her barbecue specialties. Her Grilled Burgers with Horseradish Sauce are a twist on the traditional backyard favorite. A dollop of dill and horseradish dressing gives extra bite to this standard.

The burgers are made with lean ground beef to keep the fat content low, and Deb includes grated carrots and chopped fresh mushrooms to sneak in some veggies.

Add Vegetable Kabobs and you have the perfect pairing for a relaxed evening at home on the patio.

"They're so easy to make," Deb remarks. "The grill helps the vegetables retain their fresh flavor, and the savory marinade shines through because it's brushed on while grilling."

To finish off the meal, there's Tangy Fruit Topping, which Deb spoons over reduced-fat frozen vanilla yogurt.

"Eating healthy is important, but the food has to taste good and fill you up," Deb reflects. "My husband is a real meat-and-potatoes guy, so if a dish doesn't have substance, he won't eat it."

Grilled Burgers with Horseradish Sauce

    1/2 cup reduced-fat sour cream
      1 tablespoon snipped fresh dill *or* 1 teaspoon
        dill weed
      1 tablespoon finely chopped onion
      1 tablespoon sweet pickle relish
      2 teaspoons prepared horseradish
BURGERS:
    3/4 cup chopped fresh mushrooms
    1/3 cup shredded carrot
    1/4 cup finely chopped onion
      2 tablespoons minced fresh parsley
      1 tablespoon Worcestershire sauce
    1/2 teaspoon salt
    1/4 teaspoon hot pepper sauce
    1/8 teaspoon pepper
1-1/4 pounds lean ground beef
      6 whole wheat hamburger buns, split
      6 lettuce leaves
     12 tomato slices

In a bowl, combine the sour cream, dill, onion, pickle relish and horseradish; cover and refrigerate. In another bowl, combine the first eight burger ingredients. Crumble beef over mixture and mix well. Shape into six 1/2-in.-thick patties.

Grill patties, covered, over medium-hot heat for 3-4 minutes on each side or until juices run clear and a meat thermometer reads 160°. Serve on buns with lettuce, tomato and horseradish sauce. **Yield:** 6 servings.

Nutritional Analysis: One serving (1 burger with about 4 teaspoons sauce) equals 418 calories, 15 g fat (7 g saturated fat), 41 mg cholesterol, 688 mg sodium, 42 g carbohydrate, 3 g fiber, 29 g protein.
Diabetic Exchanges: 3 lean meat, 2-1/2 starch, 1 fat.

Vegetable Kabobs

      2 tablespoons orange juice concentrate
      2 tablespoons reduced-sodium soy sauce
4-1/2 teaspoons honey
      1 teaspoon canola oil
    1/4 teaspoon salt
    1/8 teaspoon crushed red pepper flakes
      2 medium red potatoes, cut into 1-1/2-inch
        chunks
      1 teaspoon water
      1 medium zucchini, cut into 1/4-inch slices
      1 medium sweet yellow pepper, cut into 1-inch
        pieces
     14 cherry tomatoes

In a bowl, combine the orange juice concentrate, soy sauce, honey, oil, salt and red pepper; mix well and set aside. Place potatoes and water in a 1-1/2-qt. microwave-safe bowl. Cover and microwave on high for 3-4 minutes; drain. On metal or soaked bamboo skewers, alternately thread potatoes, zucchini, yellow pepper and tomatoes. Grill, uncovered, over medium heat for 8-10 minutes or until tender, turning and basting frequently with orange juice mixture. **Yield:** 7 servings.

Editor's Note: This recipe was tested in an 850-watt microwave.

Nutritional Analysis: One serving (1 kabob) equals 71 calories, 1 g fat (trace saturated fat), 0 cholesterol, 261 mg sodium, 16 g carbohydrate, 2 g fiber, 2 g protein.
Diabetic Exchanges: 2 vegetable, 1/2 fruit.

Tangy Fruit Topping

(Not pictured)

2 medium navel oranges, peeled, sectioned and cut into bite-size pieces
1 cup sliced unsweetened strawberries
2 kiwifruit, peeled, sliced and quartered
1 tablespoon lime juice
2 teaspoons sugar

Dash ground ginger *or* 1/2 teaspoon minced fresh gingerroot
3 cups reduced-fat frozen vanilla yogurt

In a bowl, combine the first six ingredients; mix gently. Serve over frozen yogurt. **Yield:** 6 servings.

Nutritional Analysis: One serving (1/3 cup fruit mixture with 1/2 cup frozen yogurt) equals 146 calories, 2 g fat (1 g saturated fat), 9 mg cholesterol, 66 mg sodium, 30 g carbohydrate, 2 g fiber, 5 g protein.
Diabetic Exchanges: 1 starch, 1 fruit.

One Habit That Fizzled

IT'S a staple in many homes, especially those with teens. But one thing you won't find in Deb Anderson's refrigerator is soft drinks.

"I don't even buy soda pop anymore," Deb says. "If we kept it in the house, we'd drink it all the time. Instead, we reach for a glass of water."

With active youths to please, Deb thought she'd have to fend off complaints about the change.

"I'll admit, at first the kids didn't like not having it around. But now they're used to it. I don't think they even notice it's gone."

Enjoy Pizza on the Patio!

FAMILY SUPPORT is the most important "ingredient" in Martha Haseman's pantry! "I'm so fortunate that my family has encouraged my attempts to change the way we eat," she says.

After beginning a weight loss program based on lean cooking, Martha took another look at the way she'd been preparing meals. At first, the Hinckley, Illinois cook kept herself motivated by focusing on her own eating habits.

"But it wasn't long before I realized that low-fat meals would also benefit my husband, Al, and our daughters Kari and Rebecca," she says. "So I began to adjust a few of the ingredients in my family's most requested recipes.

"Now I make fewer dishes that call for beef, for instance," she says. "I usually cook with chicken, turkey or fish instead. Plus, we eat lots of fresh fruits and vegetables."

Before she knew it, both she and her husband were losing weight, the whole family was eating more nutritiously and Martha's gang stood behind her efforts every step of the way.

"My husband and daughters are willing to try anything I make," she says proudly. "That means a lot to me because I practically changed our eating habits overnight."

While no one in her house is opposed to trying new foods, Martha admits that consistently finding meals that appeal to her teenagers can make menu planning a bit difficult.

"I understand that sometimes the girls want to eat teen cuisine," Martha notes. "So once in a while I'll make a low-fat dinner for Al and me…and I'll surprise the kids with a separate meal that's geared a little more toward their tastes."

Teenage appetites aren't the only culinary challenge Martha faces—she's often racing against time as well. Besides helping operate the paint store she and Al own, Martha works part-time as an accountant for a collision repair shop.

But she doesn't let a hectic lifestyle stand in the way of planning and preparing good healthy meals. Instead, she relies on her microwave and outdoor grill.

"The microwave is great for heating vegetables in a snap," Martha says. "And our family has always enjoyed grilling."

Individual Grilled Pizzas are one of Martha's favorite meals to serve. Featuring garden-fresh vegetables and a light pesto sauce, she says the pizzas are especially popular because each family member can add whatever toppings he or she prefers.

"I make an easy homemade crust that bakes right on the grill. But you could use a prebaked Italian bread shell," she says.

A perfect complement to her grilled meal is Touch-of-Mint Iced Tea. "We love the mild mint and lemon flavors in this iced tea," Martha says. "It's a wonderful alternative to soft drinks."

She admits that her family doesn't often indulge in desserts, but when they do, her Cookout Caramel S'mores are a hands-down favorite. A scrumptious substitute for that fireside standby, they contain just traces of fat and cholesterol, so the gooey goodies can be enjoyed without the guilt.

Individual Grilled Pizzas

    1-1/2 cups all-purpose flour
    1/2 cup whole wheat flour
        1 package (1/4 ounce) quick-rise yeast
    1/2 teaspoon salt
    1/2 teaspoon sugar
    3/4 cup warm water (120° to 130°)
        1 tablespoon olive *or* canola oil
PESTO:
        1 cup chopped fresh basil
    1/4 cup fat-free plain yogurt
        2 tablespoons unsalted sunflower kernels
        1 tablespoon olive *or* canola oil
        1 garlic clove, minced
    1/8 teaspoon salt
    1/8 teaspoon pepper
TOPPINGS:
        1 cup (4 ounces) shredded part-skim mozzarella
            cheese, *divided*
        2 medium tomatoes, thinly sliced
        2 green onions, finely chopped
Coarsely ground pepper
        2 tablespoons grated Parmesan cheese

Coat grill rack with nonstick cooking spray before starting grill. Prepare grill for indirect medium heat.

In a mixing bowl, combine flours, yeast, salt and sugar. Add water and oil; mix just until a soft dough forms. Turn onto a floured surface; knead until smooth and elastic, about 5-7 minutes. Cover and let stand for 10-15 minutes.

Meanwhile, combine the pesto ingredients in a blender or food processor; cover and process until smooth, scraping sides often. Set aside.

Divide dough into fourths. Roll each portion into a 6-in. circle; place on grill over directly heated area. Cover and cook for 1 minute or until puffed and golden. Turn; place over indirectly heated area of grill. Spread pesto over crusts; top with 2/3 cup mozzarella cheese, tomatoes, onions, pepper, Parmesan and remaining mozzarella. Grill for 3-5 minutes or until cheese is melted and crust is lightly browned. **Yield:** 4 servings.

Editor's Note: Individual prebaked Italian bread shells may be substituted for the homemade crust.

Nutritional Analysis: One serving (1 pizza) equals 430 calories, 16 g fat (5 g saturated fat), 19 mg cholesterol, 579 mg sodium, 55 g carbohydrate, 5 g fiber, 18 g protein.

Diabetic Exchanges: 2-1/2 starch, 2 lean meat, 2 fat, 1 vegetable.

Touch-of-Mint Iced Tea

6 cups boiling water
4 individual tea bags
1 cup packed fresh mint
3/4 cup frozen lemonade concentrate
Lemon slices and additional mint, optional

In a heatproof bowl or pitcher, pour boiling water over tea bags; cover and steep for 5 minutes. Remove tea bags. Cool for 15 minutes. Add mint; steep for 5 minutes. Strain. Add lemonade concentrate; stir well. Refrigerate. Serve over ice; garnish with lemon and mint if desired. **Yield:** 6 servings.

Nutritional Analysis: One serving (1 cup) equals 58 calories, trace fat (trace saturated fat), 0 cholesterol, 6 mg sodium, 15 g carbohydrate, 1 g fiber, 1 g protein.
Diabetic Exchange: 1 fruit.

Cookout Caramel S'mores

8 large marshmallows
2 teaspoons fat-free chocolate syrup
8 reduced-fat graham crackers (2-1/2-inch square)
2 teaspoons fat-free caramel ice cream topping

Using a long-handled fork, toast marshmallows 6 in. from medium-hot heat until golden brown, turning occasionally.

Drizzle chocolate syrup over four graham crackers; top each with two toasted marshmallows. Drizzle with caramel topping. Cover with remaining graham crackers. **Yield:** 4 servings.

Nutritional Analysis: One serving equals 87 calories, trace fat (trace saturated fat), trace cholesterol, 82 mg sodium, 20 g carbohydrate, trace fiber, 1 g protein.
Diabetic Exchange: 1 starch.

◗ A Fruitful Change...

CHANGING snacking habits is a tough job. Or, is it?

After suggesting that her family try fresh fruit in place of high-calorie munchies, Martha Haseman says she was pleasantly surprised at the response she received.

"I always thought I would be in for a battle if I decreased the amount of goodies in the house," Martha notes. "So I was shocked when my teenagers accepted fruit as a snack without complaining. They even eat apples and peaches instead of potato chips!

"I shouldn't have assumed they wouldn't take to fruit. I'm sure we could have made this switch a long time ago."

Snappy Southwestern Supper

COOKING LESS doesn't necessarily mean eating less. Just ask Carol Birkemeier, who says her eating habits took a wrong turn when her sons left for college.

"I've always promoted good nutrition," says the Nashville, Indiana cook. "Our children, Glenn, Kyle and Alan, grew up eating healthy, so I was curious to see if they would continue those habits once they entered college and began their own lives. Surprisingly, it was my husband and I who let our diets get off track."

After their sons moved out, Carol and her husband, Ken, found they had extra time on their hands. "We decided to do more volunteer work at our church, with a local family health program and with my philanthropic sorority," Carol says.

Carol also continued to hold two part-time jobs, working for a children's health care service and a local retail shop, and Ken kept long hours as a commercial loan officer.

"As our schedules became busier, our cooking habits started to change. We found ourselves eating a lot of fast food," Carol confesses. "Unfortunately, we suffered the consequences.

"Ken's cholesterol skyrocketed, my blood pressure increased and we both gained weight," she admits. "We had no choice but to revert to eating habits we'd previously practiced.

"We began by reducing the amount of red meat we ate," she says. "We started eating chicken, fish and vegetables again. I read labels for fat and fiber content, and I stocked the pantry with items like salsa, tuna, rice cakes, and reduced-fat spaghetti sauce and mayonnaise," she adds.

Carol also returned to lighter cooking, taking advantage of butter substitutes and creating her own low-calorie recipes. "Fresh fruit mixed with reduced-fat blueberry yogurt became a favorite treat," she recalls.

Their efforts quickly paid off. "In only 5 months, I lost 25 pounds…and Ken lost more than 30," Carol reports. "I was making delicious, nutritious meals and still had time to do the things I liked, such as reading, quilting and hiking in the woods.

"I guess it took an empty nest to remind me that with just a little meal planning and a commitment to yourself and your loved ones, a healthy diet can easily become second nature."

One of the meals Carol enjoys serving is Corn 'n' Bean Burritos. "This is a great summer dish," she says. "Because all of the cooking is done in the microwave oven, you won't heat up your kitchen."

While Carol and her husband enjoy this as a meatless entree, cooked chicken, pork or extra-lean beef can easily be added to suit your family's tastes.

"If you're looking for new ways to use up tomatoes in the garden, be sure to try End-of-Summer Tomato Salad," Carol advises. "This is one of our favorites."

For a refreshing ending, whip up Lime Sherbet Slush. "With only five ingredients, this beverage is quick and easy to make," Carol assures. "It's an icy cool way to end a hot day."

Corn 'n' Bean Burritos

    1 can (4 ounces) chopped green chilies, drained
1/3 cup lime juice
    2 tablespoons white vinegar
    2 tablespoons honey
    2 teaspoons Dijon mustard
    2 garlic cloves, minced
    1 teaspoon grated lime peel
1/2 teaspoon ground cumin
    1 can (15 ounces) black beans, rinsed and drained
    1 package (10 ounces) frozen corn, thawed
    1 can (16 ounces) vegetarian refried beans
    1 medium cucumber, peeled, seeded and diced
3/4 cup salsa
1/4 cup chopped green onions
    2 tablespoons minced fresh cilantro *or* parsley
    8 flour tortillas (8 inches), warmed

In a large resealable plastic bag, combine the first eight ingredients; add black beans and corn. Seal bag and turn to coat; refrigerate overnight.

Drain and discard marinade. Place beans and corn in a large microwave-safe dish. Add the refried beans, cucumber, salsa, onions and cilantro. Cover and microwave on high for 5-6 minutes or until heated through. Spoon about 3/4 cup down the center of each tortilla. Fold ends and sides over filling and roll up. **Yield:** 8 servings.

Editor's Note: This recipe was tested in an 850-watt microwave.

Nutritional Analysis: *One serving (1 burrito) equals 305 calories, 4 g fat (1 g saturated fat), 0 cholesterol, 825 mg sodium, 56 g carbohydrate, 8 g fiber, 12 g protein.*
Diabetic Exchanges: *3 starch, 1 lean meat.*

End-of-Summer Tomato Salad

    8 small tomatoes (2 pounds), sliced
1/2 cup chopped ripe olives
    2 tablespoons olive *or* canola oil
    1 tablespoon white wine vinegar
    4 teaspoons Dijon mustard
    2 teaspoons sugar
    2 garlic cloves, minced
    1 teaspoon salt
1/2 teaspoon pepper
Leaf lettuce, optional
1/4 cup minced fresh parsley
1/4 cup chopped green onions

Arrange tomatoes in a 13-in. x 9-in. x 2-in. dish; sprinkle with olives. In a jar with a tight-fitting lid, combine the oil, vine-

gar, mustard, sugar, garlic, salt and pepper; shake well. Pour over tomatoes. Cover and refrigerate overnight, turning tomatoes occasionally. Serve on lettuce if desired. Sprinkle with parsley and onions. **Yield:** 6 servings.

Nutritional Analysis: One serving (1 cup) equals 98 calories, 7 g fat (1 g saturated fat), 0 cholesterol, 589 mg sodium, 10 g carbohydrate, 2 g fiber, 2 g protein.
Diabetic Exchanges: 2 vegetable, 1 fat.

Lime Sherbet Slush

    1 pint lime sherbet
1-1/2 cups diet lemon-lime soda, chilled
    3/4 cup limeade concentrate
    1 teaspoon grated lime peel
    14 ice cubes

In a blender or food processor, combine all ingredients; cover and process until smooth. Pour into glasses; serve immediately. **Yield:** 5 servings.

Nutritional Analysis: One serving (1 cup) equals 173 calories, 2 g fat (1 g saturated fat), 5 mg cholesterol, 43 mg sodium, 41 g carbohydrate, trace fiber, 1 g protein.
Diabetic Exchange: 3 fruit.

Rounding Out Meals

LOOKING for a way to jazz up your favorite low-cal fare? Consider corn or reduced-fat flour tortillas!

"When I decided to eat healthier, I found tortillas to be a terrific alternative to bread," says Carol Birkemeier.

"They're great stuffed with chopped peppers, tomatoes, onions and low-fat cheese," she suggests.

Tuna salad, red beans and rice, turkey, salad greens and low-fat mayonnaise also make wonderful fillings for tortillas. Or try wrapping scrambled eggs and salsa in a tortilla for breakfast on-the-go when your family's in a hurry.

Some grocers now stock flavored tortillas, which make a tasty snack on their own. "I'm particularly fond of the tomato-basil variety," Carol adds.

So consider bringing a taste of the Southwest to your table today. Whether stuffed with homemade chicken salad or garden-fresh veggies, low-fat tortillas are a quick and healthy way to wrap up any meal!

Soup & Salad Always Satisfy

YOU MIGHT SAY good nutrition is just what the doctor ordered for Anne Smithson's family!

"My husband, Chip, and I are both physicians," she says from her home in Cary, North Carolina. "So we're well aware of the importance of maintaining a healthy diet for ourselves and our children, Rob and Connor.

"I work part-time as a physician at Meredith College, a women's college in Raleigh. It's a fantastic job! I get to talk to students about nutrition and health issues regularly," she says. "I'm happy to answer patients' questions about healthy eating because it can be hard to sort through all of the information out there."

And if college students can get confused about nutrition, Anne knows that her sons could easily become misinformed as well. So she talks to them regularly about eating right.

"Chip and I have always emphasized healthy eating choices with our children," Anne comments. "And because our sons are so involved in sports, we explain how good nutrition enhances performance on the playing field.

"The boys understand that while deep-fried foods and candy bars might taste great, they don't provide a lot of energy," she adds. "Now, when the kids want a snack, they ask for fat-free pretzels, light microwave popcorn or fruits and veggies."

Anne encourages both her family and her patients to eat six to nine servings of fruits and vegetables a day. "If you include two servings with every meal, this isn't hard," she assures.

"For example, you could have orange juice and a banana with breakfast. Pack a lunch that includes grapes and a sandwich topped with a few spinach leaves and tomato slices. And prepare a salad and a veggie side dish or two for supper."

By snacking on an apple or pear in the afternoon and having frozen yogurt with strawberries after dinner, you'll have consumed nine servings of fruits and vegetables by day's end.

"Or try adding chopped veggies to soups or sauces," she suggests. "I do that with pizza sauce, and the kids love it."

Updating recipes to make them healthier is something Anne truly enjoys. "In addition to exercising, going to the theater and attending my sons' after-school events, I like to cook in my free time," she remarks.

"In fact, cooking light is such a big part of our lives that no one in the family can tell when I've substituted fat-free or reduced-sugar items for their heavier counterparts," she adds.

"I like to surround my family with their favorite nutritious foods," Anne says with a smile. "I truly believe that doing so helps keep us on the road to healthy living."

One of her family's favorite mainstays is hearty Southwestern Chicken Soup. "The spices really liven up the flavor in this filling soup," she remarks. Anne often doubles the recipe, freezing leftovers for future meals or quick lunches. "Rob even prefers a bowl of it to cookies after school as a snack."

A perfect accompaniment is Anne's colorful Fruity Spinach Salad. A tangy dressing turns strawberries, kiwifruit and blueberries into a delightful change-of-pace salad. "Add more or less fruit depending on your family's tastes," she suggests.

No one would guess that her grand finale, Pumpkin Pecan Frozen Yogurt, is light. "I always keep fat-free frozen yogurt on hand," informs Anne. "By combining it with just four other ingredients, I can quickly whip up this great-tasting treat."

Southwestern Chicken Soup

- 1 can (49-1/2 ounces) reduced-sodium chicken broth
- 1 can (14-1/2 ounces) crushed tomatoes, undrained
- 1 can (14-1/2 ounces) diced tomatoes, undrained
- 1 pound boneless skinless chicken breasts, cut into 1/2-inch cubes
- 1 large onion, chopped
- 1/3 cup minced fresh cilantro *or* parsley
- 1 can (4 ounces) chopped green chilies
- 1 garlic clove, minced
- 1 teaspoon chili powder
- 1 teaspoon ground cumin
- 1/2 teaspoon dried oregano
- 1/4 teaspoon cayenne pepper
- 3 cups frozen corn, thawed
- Baked tortilla chips
- 1 cup (4 ounces) shredded reduced-fat cheddar *or* Mexican-blend cheese

In a large saucepan, combine the first 12 ingredients. Bring to a boil. Reduce heat; cover and simmer for 1 hour. Add corn; cook 10 minutes longer. Top each serving with tortilla chips; sprinkle with cheese. **Yield:** 8 servings.

Nutritional Analysis: One serving (1-1/2 cups soup with 3 tortilla chips and 2 tablespoons cheese) equals 234 calories, 4 g fat (2 g saturated fat), 41 mg cholesterol, 873 mg sodium, 29 g carbohydrate, 5 g fiber, 23 g protein.
Diabetic Exchanges: 2 lean meat, 1-1/2 starch, 1 vegetable.

Fruity Spinach Salad

- 1/3 cup sugar
- 1/4 cup cider vinegar
- 1/4 cup olive *or* canola oil
- 1 tablespoon sesame seeds
- 1 teaspoon dried minced onion
- 1 teaspoon poppy seeds
- 1/4 teaspoon paprika
- 1/4 teaspoon Worcestershire sauce
- 12 cups torn fresh spinach
- 2 cups sliced fresh strawberries
- 2 kiwifruit, peeled and sliced
- 1 cup fresh blueberries
- 2 tablespoons chopped pecans, toasted

In a blender, combine the first eight ingredients; cover and process until blended. In a salad bowl, combine the spinach, fruit and pecans. Drizzle with dressing and toss to coat. Serve immediately. **Yield:** 8 servings.

Nutritional Analysis: One serving (2 cups) equals 160 calories, 9 g fat (1 g saturated fat), 0 cholesterol, 41 mg sodium, 19 g carbohydrate, 3 g fiber, 3 g protein.
Diabetic Exchanges: 1-1/2 fat, 1 fruit, 1 vegetable.

Pumpkin Pecan Frozen Yogurt

  1 quart fat-free frozen vanilla yogurt, softened
1/2 cup canned *or* cooked pumpkin
1/3 cup packed brown sugar
3/4 teaspoon pumpkin pie spice
1/4 cup chopped pecans, toasted

In a large mixing bowl, combine the first four ingredients; mix well. Transfer to a freezer container; freeze until serving. Sprinkle each serving with pecans. **Yield:** 8 servings.

Nutritional Analysis: One serving (1/2 cup) equals 161 calories, 3 g fat (trace saturated fat), 2 mg cholesterol, 69 mg sodium, 30 g carbohydrate, 1 g fiber, 5 g protein.
Diabetic Exchange: 2 starch.

Appealing Alternatives

COOKING light is Anne Smithson's hobby. "I love experimenting with healthy easy-to-prepare recipes," she says. "And I've found a few simple substitutions that keep my family eating right.

"I try to cook with ground turkey instead of ground beef," shares Anne. "But when I have to use beef, I buy the leanest variety available."

Instead of cooking with creamy sauces, Anne finds herself opting for tomato sauces. And she uses vinegar-based salad dressings rather than those made from mayonnaise or sour cream.

"Raw spinach is a great alternative to lettuce, particularly on sandwiches and burgers," she comments. "Spinach is better for my kids, and they don't really notice the difference in taste."

In addition, Anne replaces the white rice in her recipes with brown rice. "Brown rice has become a staple in my kitchen," she adds. "My family loves the switch!"

Trimmings for the Turkey

PRACTICE what you preach—that's a phrase Beth Ask lives by. Beth is a registered dietitian and works at a health-care agency, where she facilitates a health and wellness program. "In my line of work, I'm constantly stressing the importance of healthy eating," explains the Ulster, Pennsylvania cook.

"As a dietitian, I'm on the lookout for ways to lighten up my family's favorite foods," she says. "But as a wife and mother, I want my family to enjoy the things I prepare for them…so I'm always experimenting with recipes.

"It's fun and challenging to reduce the calories and fat in a recipe, yet still create something that tastes great. My husband, Tom, and our two children—Eric and Elayna—have responded very well to my lightened-up cooking. Most of the time, they like my revised recipe better than the original!"

Beth says that by making a few simple changes, anyone can start eating healthier. "Begin by eliminating or replacing some of the fat in your favorite recipes," she suggests. "It's all right to make a pasta salad, for example, but use a reduced-calorie dressing instead of regular mayonnaise, and leave out things like pepperoni.

"For heavy desserts, cut back on the sugar by about a third," Beth recommends. "Or try substituting unsweetened applesauce for some of the fat."

Her husband and children are willing to try new foods, which makes Beth's job a little easier. "My family has adventurous appetites—they like experimenting with different things," she notes.

According to Beth, that's an important part of switching to a more nutritious diet. "By trying a few of the reduced-calorie or fat-free products your grocer offers, you'll find it's much easier to stick with a commitment to healthy eating.

"Sample whatever items you may not be familiar with," she suggests. "Experiment with foods that have a higher grain content than you're used to—flours, pastas and breads made with whole wheat, for instance."

While adjusting cooking habits might take some getting used to, Beth assures it doesn't necessarily mean you'll spend more time in the kitchen. "Even though I cook light, I still have time for needlepoint and hiking," she points out.

"I truly believe that by making a few adjustments to the way they eat, people can not only succeed on the road to healthy living, but they can enjoy themselves along the way," she adds.

Beth's refreshing Orange Romaine Salad is a healthy and colorful beginning to any meal. "The almonds are wonderful when combined with the greens, oranges and the tangy dressing," she remarks.

Beth recommends including Parmesan Potato Wedges alongside the salad for a light lunch lineup. Or, serve these tender spuds as a side dish with a chicken or beef entree.

"Because the potatoes are baked, they're more nutritious than those that are fried," says Beth. "We like the Parmesan cheese, oregano and garlic flavors, but you can adjust the seasonings to match your family's taste."

And few things satisfy the sweet tooth like a slice of luscious Black Forest Ice Cream Pie.

"Desserts shouldn't take a backseat to nutritious eating," notes Beth. "This frozen dessert is a perfect example of how light ingredients can reduce the fat and calories without cutting back on taste."

Orange Romaine Salad

6 tablespoons unsweetened pineapple juice
3 tablespoons cider vinegar
2 tablespoons water
2 tablespoons chicken broth
2 tablespoons canola oil
1 tablespoon minced fresh basil *or* 1 teaspoon dried basil
1 teaspoon sugar
1/2 teaspoon garlic powder
2 bunches romaine *or* red leaf lettuce, torn (about 12 cups)
1 can (11 ounces) mandarin oranges, drained
1/3 cup sliced almonds, toasted

In a jar with a tight-fitting lid, combine the first eight ingredients; shake well. In a large salad bowl, combine the lettuce, oranges and almonds. Add dressing and toss to coat. Serve immediately. **Yield:** 8 servings.

Nutritional Analysis: *One serving (1-1/2 cups) equals 93 calories, 6 g fat (trace saturated fat), 0 cholesterol, 23 mg sodium, 9 g carbohydrate, 2 g fiber, 3 g protein.*
Diabetic Exchanges: *1 fat, 1/2 fruit.*

Parmesan Potato Wedges

4 large baking potatoes (2 pounds)
1/4 cup grated Parmesan cheese
1 teaspoon garlic salt
1/2 teaspoon garlic powder
1/2 teaspoon dried oregano
1/2 teaspoon paprika

Line a baking sheet with heavy-duty foil. Cut each potato into eight wedges; place on foil. Coat with nonstick cooking spray. Sprinkle with Parmesan cheese and seasonings. Bake at 400° for 30 minutes or until tender. **Yield:** 8 servings.

Nutritional Analysis: *One serving (4 wedges) equals 129 calories, trace fat (trace saturated fat), 1 mg cholesterol, 249 mg sodium, 29 g carbohydrate, 3 g fiber, 3 g protein.*
Diabetic Exchange: *1-1/2 starch.*

Black Forest Ice Cream Pie

1 prepared chocolate crumb crust (9 inches)
3-1/2 cups reduced-fat vanilla ice cream
1 cup reduced-sugar cherry pie filling
2 whole chocolate graham crackers, broken into bite-size pieces
1 cup fat-free hot fudge ice cream topping, warmed

Fill crust with scoops of ice cream. Top with dollops of pie filling. Insert graham cracker pieces between scoops. Invert plastic cover from crust and place over pie. Freeze for 2 hours or until firm. Remove from freezer 15-20 minutes before serving. Drizzle with fudge topping. Cut into wedges. **Yield:** 8 servings.

Nutritional Analysis: One piece equals 306 calories, 7 g fat (2 g saturated fat), 5 mg cholesterol, 194 mg sodium, 58 g carbohydrate, 5 g fiber, 5 g protein.

🍎 Stashing Satisfying Snacks

HEALTHY SNACKING may sound like a contradiction, but not to Beth Ask. "I try to keep my home stocked with nutritious alternatives to junk food," she says. "And I like to keep those items easily accessible.

"For example, I put fresh vegetables at the front of the refrigerator and place a bowl of fruit on the kitchen counter. That way, all of us are much more likely to grab a veggie or a piece of fruit for a snack."

And when it comes to those not-so-nutritious goodies, Beth relies on an old saying—out of sight, out of mind. "When we do indulge in a sugary snack or a salty treat, we keep it on a high shelf or somewhere slightly inconvenient to reach," she confirms. "That way, we're not tempted by it every time we open the cabinet!"

A Meal for Mom Served with Love

WHAT BETTER WAY to pamper Mom than with a home-cooked meal served especially for her? She'll appreciate taking a break from the kitchen...and the fact that the fabulous-tasting foods you've prepared are lighter fare.

With these recipes, you can sit Mom down to a savory entree and luxurious dessert for a lunch or dinner she'll long remember. As a special treat, tell her you'll do the dishes, too!

Honey Orange Chicken

I couldn't get enough of the sweet-and-citrusy marinade flavoring this grilled chicken. So I saved some to drizzle on top.
—*Mary Hart Easterling, Santa Clarita, California*

    1 cup chicken broth
    1 cup orange juice
1/2 cup honey
    1 tablespoon lemon juice
    1 tablespoon cider vinegar
    1 tablespoon reduced-sodium soy sauce
    1 teaspoon grated orange peel
    1 teaspoon ground ginger
1/2 teaspoon salt
    4 bone-in chicken breast halves (10 ounces *each*)
    1 tablespoon cornstarch
    2 tablespoons water
    4 cups hot cooked rice

Chopped green onions, orange slices and parsley sprigs, optional

In a saucepan, combine the first nine ingredients. Bring to a boil. Remove from the heat; cool. Pour 1-1/3 cups marinade into a large resealable plastic bag; add chicken. Seal bag and turn to coat; refrigerate for 4-8 hours or overnight, turning occasionally. Cover and refrigerate remaining marinade.

Drain chicken, discarding marinade. Grill, covered, over medium heat for 12-15 minutes on each side or until juices run clear. Meanwhile, combine cornstarch and water in a small saucepan until smooth; stir in reserved marinade. Bring to a boil; cook and stir for 2 minutes or until thickened.

Remove and discard skin from chicken. Serve chicken over rice; drizzle with sauce. Garnish with green onions, orange slices and parsley if desired. **Yield:** 4 servings.

Nutritional Analysis: One serving (1 chicken breast half and 6 tablespoons sauce with 1 cup rice) equals 504 calories, 2 g fat (1 g saturated fat), 66 mg cholesterol, 755 mg sodium, 89 g carbohydrate, 1 g fiber, 32 g protein.
Diabetic Exchanges: 4 lean meat, 3 starch, 1/2 fruit.

Berry Phyllo Tarts

Lightly glazed fresh fruit nestled in delicate pastry creates a looks-like-you-fussed dessert. One taste of the crisp-tender shell topped with sweet berries, and I don't miss those confections with more fat and sugar.
—*TerryAnn Moore, Oaklyn, New Jersey*

    6 sheets phyllo dough (18 inches x 14 inches)
    3 tablespoons butter *or* stick margarine, melted
    3 tablespoons sugar
1/2 teaspoon grated orange peel
FILLING:
    1 cup sliced fresh strawberries
    1 cup navel orange sections
1/2 cup *each* fresh raspberries, blueberries and blackberries
1/4 cup orange marmalade, melted
    1 teaspoon lemon juice
    1 teaspoon lime juice
1/2 teaspoon grated lemon peel
1/2 teaspoon grated lime peel
Fresh mint, optional

Roll up phyllo dough and cut into 1/4-in.-wide strips. Place strips in a bowl; toss with butter, sugar and orange peel until coated. Divide strips into six portions; shape into nests on a baking sheet coated with nonstick cooking spray. Bake at 400° for 5-7 minutes or until golden.

In a bowl, gently combine fruits, marmalade, juices and lemon and lime peel; chill. Just before serving, spoon into nests. Garnish with mint if desired. **Yield:** 6 servings.

Nutritional Analysis: One serving (1 tart with about 1/2 cup fruit) equals 204 calories, 7 g fat (4 g saturated fat), 16 mg cholesterol, 159 mg sodium, 35 g carbohydrate, 3 g fiber, 2 g protein.
Diabetic Exchanges: 1-1/2 starch, 1 fruit, 1/2 fat.

Trimmed-Down Dishes for Two

Turn to this chapter if you're cooking
for just two and neither of you
cares to eat leftovers. These lighter
recipes yield smaller quantities
without sacrificing the flavor.

Beef Burgundy Over Noodles (page 271)

Nutritional Analysis: One serving (1 pork chop and 1 cup sauce with 1 cup rice) equals 508 calories, 10 g fat (2 g saturated fat), 71 mg cholesterol, 1,282 mg sodium, 74 g carbohydrate, 3 g fiber, 31 g protein.
Diabetic Exchanges: 3 lean meat, 3 starch, 1 fruit, 1 fat.

Blue Cheese Dressing

(Pictured at left)

No one will ever guess that this thick chunky salad dressing that's chock-full of blue cheese is low in fat.
—Carolyn Steele, Marathon Shores, Florida

1/2 cup fat-free mayonnaise
2 tablespoons 1% milk
1 tablespoon lemon juice
1/2 teaspoon sugar
1/4 teaspoon garlic powder
1/4 teaspoon ground mustard
1/2 cup (2 ounces) crumbled blue cheese
Salad greens

In a small bowl, combine the first six ingredients; blend until smooth. Add blue cheese; mix well. Serve over greens. Cover and refrigerate any extra dressing. **Yield:** 14 tablespoons.

Nutritional Analysis: One serving (2 tablespoons dressing) equals 46 calories, 3 g fat (2 g saturated fat), 8 mg cholesterol, 253 mg sodium, 3 g carbohydrate, trace fiber, 2 g protein.
Diabetic Exchange: 1 fat.

Apple-Leek Pork Chops

(Pictured above)

The sweet and savory combination of apples and leeks goes so well with these golden pork chops. This dish is nice served with rice.
—Elaine Williams, Sebastopol, California

2 lean boneless pork loin chops (4 ounces *each*)
2 teaspoons canola oil
1 medium tart green apple, sliced
1 medium leek (white portion only), sliced
1 cup unsweetened apple juice
1/2 teaspoon grated orange peel
1/2 teaspoon dried rosemary, crushed
1/2 teaspoon salt
1/4 teaspoon pepper
1 tablespoon cornstarch
2 tablespoons water
2 cups hot cooked long grain and wild rice mix

In a nonstick skillet, brown pork chops in oil for 3-4 minutes. Turn chops; add apple and leek. Cook for 3-4 minutes. Add the apple juice, orange peel, rosemary, salt and pepper. Bring to a boil. Reduce heat; simmer, uncovered, for 3 minutes. Combine cornstarch and water until smooth; add to skillet. Bring to a boil; cook and stir for 2 minutes or until thickened. Serve with rice. **Yield:** 2 servings.

Strawberry-Orange Phyllo Cups

(Pictured above left)

These flaky cups filled with fresh fruit and a tangy sauce are delicate in flavor and make a pretty presentation. But they're easy to do, too.
—Sally Hook, Houston, Texas

2 sheets phyllo dough (18 inches x 14 inches)
Butter-flavored nonstick cooking spray
3/4 cup sliced unsweetened strawberries, *divided*
3-1/2 teaspoons confectioners' sugar, *divided*
1/8 teaspoon grated orange peel
2 tablespoons fat-free vanilla yogurt
1 medium navel orange, peeled and sectioned

Place sheets of phyllo dough on top of each other. Cut stack in half lengthwise, then in half widthwise. Spritz top sheet of each with cooking spray. Lightly press one stack into a 6-oz. custard cup coated with nonstick cooking spray. Lightly press a second stack on top. Repeat with remaining stacks in another custard cup. Bake at 375° for 10-12 minutes or until golden brown. Cool for 5 minutes. Carefully remove phyllo cups to a wire rack to cool completely.

Meanwhile, place 1/2 cup strawberries, 3 teaspoons confectioners' sugar and orange peel in a blender; cover and process until smooth. Blend in yogurt. Place phyllo cups on serving plates. Fill with orange segments and remaining strawberries. Top with yogurt sauce; dust with remaining confectioners' sugar. **Yield:** 2 servings.

Nutritional Analysis: One serving equals 136 calories, 1 g fat (trace saturated fat), trace cholesterol, 104 mg sodium, 29 g carbohydrate, 3 g fiber, 3 g protein.
Diabetic Exchanges: 1 starch, 1 fruit.

Mushroom Cream Chicken

(Pictured below right)

This special dish stars wonderfully tender chicken smothered in a delicious mushroom cream sauce. It tastes like you fussed, but it's really simple to prepare.
—Marian Slattery, Whitewater, Wisconsin

2 boneless skinless chicken breast halves (1/2 pound)
3 tablespoons all-purpose flour, *divided*
2 teaspoons butter *or* **stick margarine**
1 teaspoon olive *or* **canola oil**
1 cup sliced fresh mushrooms
1 tablespoon sliced green onion
1 garlic clove, minced
3/4 cup chicken broth
1/2 cup Madeira wine *or* **additional chicken broth**
1 tablespoon fat-free half-and-half cream

Flatten chicken to 1/4-in. thickness. Dredge in 2 tablespoons flour. In a nonstick skillet, brown chicken in butter and oil over medium heat for 2-3 minutes on each side or until juices run clear. Remove chicken and set aside.

In the same skillet, saute the mushrooms, green onion and garlic for 2 minutes or until tender. Sprinkle with remaining flour and stir to blend. Gradually add broth and wine or additional broth. Bring to a boil; cook and stir for 2 minutes or until thickened. Reduce heat; add the cream. Return chicken to skillet. Cook for 2-3 minutes or until chicken is heated through (do not boil). **Yield:** 2 servings.

Nutritional Analysis: One serving (1 chicken breast half with 3/4 cup sauce) equals 327 calories, 9 g fat (3 g saturated fat), 78 mg cholesterol, 457 mg sodium, 18 g carbohydrate, 1 g fiber, 29 g protein.
Diabetic Exchanges: 3 lean meat, 1 starch, 1 vegetable, 1 fat.

Green Beans with Red Peppers

(Pictured at right)

Balsamic vinegar adds zing to these colorful sauteed veggies that cook in a flash. Trim the beans and julienne the pepper ahead to make this side dish in a snap at the last minute.
—Chris Kallies, Oldsmar, Florida

1/4 pound fresh green beans, trimmed
1/2 cup julienned sweet red pepper
1/2 teaspoon olive *or* **canola oil**
1 teaspoon balsamic vinegar
1/8 to 1/4 teaspoon dried basil
1/8 teaspoon pepper

In a nonstick skillet coated with nonstick cooking spray, saute beans and red pepper in oil for 4 minutes or until crisp-tender. Stir in the vinegar, basil and pepper. **Yield:** 2 servings.

Nutritional Analysis: One serving (2/3 cup) equals 79 calories, 3 g fat (trace saturated fat), 0 cholesterol, 10 mg sodium, 14 g carbohydrate, 3 g fiber, 3 g protein.
Diabetic Exchanges: 2 vegetable, 1/2 fat.

Citrus Ice

(Pictured below)

It's hard to resist the refreshing flavor of lemon and lime in this frosty treat that's served up by our Test Kitchen crew. Each delightful spoonful will melt in your mouth!

1-1/4 cups water
1/3 cup sugar
1/4 cup orange juice
2 tablespoons lemon juice
2 tablespoons lime juice

In a small saucepan, combine all of the ingredients. Bring to a boil. Reduce heat; cook and stir over medium heat until sugar is dissolved, about 2 minutes. Cool. Pour into a 13-in. x 9-in. x 2-in. dish; cover and freeze for 45 minutes or until edges begin to firm. Stir and return to the freezer. Repeat every 20 minutes or until slushy, about 1 hour. **Yield:** 2 servings.

Nutritional Analysis: One serving (about 3/4 cup) equals 151 calories, trace fat (trace saturated fat), 0 cholesterol, 1 mg sodium, 39 g carbohydrate, trace fiber, trace protein.
Diabetic Exchange: 2-1/2 fruit.

Marinated Beef Kabobs

(Pictured at right)

*A zesty marinade gives tongue-tingling flavor
to this change-of-pace beef dish.*
—Susie Freeman, Irons, Michigan

1 small navel orange
3/4 cup orange juice
2 tablespoons teriyaki sauce
1 tablespoon Dijon mustard
2 teaspoons honey
2 garlic cloves, minced
1/8 teaspoon pepper
1/2 pound boneless beef sirloin steak (1 inch thick)
8 large fresh mushrooms
8 medium green onions, cut into 2-inch pieces
1 teaspoon cornstarch
2 teaspoons cold water
2 hot cups cooked rice

Grate orange peel; remove remaining peel and pith. Separate orange into eight segments. In a bowl, combine grated peel, orange juice, teriyaki sauce, mustard, honey, garlic and pepper. Cut beef into 1-in. cubes; place in a resealable plastic bag. Add oranges, mushrooms, onions and half of marinade. Seal bag; refrigerate overnight. Refrigerate remaining marinade for sauce.

Drain and discard marinade. On four metal or soaked wooden skewers, alternately thread beef, oranges and vegetables. Broil 3 in. from the heat for 15-20 minutes or until meat reaches desired doneness and vegetables are tender, turning often.

In a saucepan, combine cornstarch and water until smooth. Stir in reserved marinade. Bring to a boil; cook and stir for 2 minutes. Serve over kabobs and rice. **Yield:** 2 servings.

Nutritional Analysis: One serving (2 kabobs with 1/4 cup sauce and 1 cup rice) equals 503 calories, 8 g fat (3 g saturated fat), 67 mg cholesterol, 631 mg sodium, 75 g carbohydrate, 5 g fiber, 34 g protein.
Diabetic Exchanges: 3 starch, 3 lean meat, 1 fruit, 1 fat.

Greens with Balsamic Vinaigrette

(Pictured above right)

*I see to it that my salads are well-dressed for dinner,
so I keep a bottle of this light dressing in the fridge.*
—Sandy Hunt, Racine, Wisconsin

1 tablespoon Dijon mustard
1/4 cup water
2 tablespoons olive *or* canola oil
1/4 cup balsamic vinegar
1 tablespoon minced fresh basil
1/2 teaspoon pepper
Salad greens and vegetables of your choice

In a jar with a tight-fitting lid, combine the first six ingredients; shake well. Serve over salad. **Yield:** 2/3 cup vinaigrette.

Nutritional Analysis: One serving (2 tablespoons vinaigrette) equals 53 calories, 6 g fat (1 g saturated fat), 0 cholesterol,

terol, 77 mg sodium, 1 g carbohydrate, trace fiber, trace protein.
Diabetic Exchange: 1 fat.

Dilly Salad Croutons

(Pictured above)

*These quick croutons make the ideal salad-topper. For a
fun snack, you can serve them with a low-fat dip, too.*
—Gerry Vail, Connersville, Indiana

4 cups cubed French bread
Garlic-flavored nonstick cooking spray
1 teaspoon dill weed
1 teaspoon butter-flavored sprinkles

Place bread in a 15-in. x 10-in. x 1-in. baking pan. Spray evenly with cooking spray; sprinkle with dill and butter-flavored sprinkles. Bake at 300° for 12-15 minutes or until golden brown, turning once. Store in an airtight container. **Yield:** 3 cups.

Nutritional Analysis: One serving (1/2 cup) equals 53 calories, 1 g fat (trace saturated fat), 0 cholesterol, 118 mg sodium, 10 g carbohydrate, 1 g fiber, 2 g protein.
Diabetic Exchange: 1/2 starch.

Cookie Lime Parfaits

(Pictured above)

*When I need a simple refreshing dessert,
I dish up these pretty parfaits.*
—Becky Gillespie, Boulder, Colorado

1-1/2 cups lime sherbet, softened
1 teaspoon grated lime peel

1/4 cup broken chocolate sandwich cookies
1 tablespoon finely chopped macadamia nuts

In a bowl, combine sherbet and lime peel. Spoon into chilled parfait glasses. Sprinkle with cookies and nuts. **Yield:** 2 servings.

Nutritional Analysis: One serving (3/4 cup) equals 305 calories, 9 g fat (3 g saturated fat), 9 mg cholesterol, 199 mg sodium, 57 g carbohydrate, 1 g fiber, 3 g protein.
***Diabetic Exchanges:** 2 starch, 2 fat, 1 fruit.*

Beef Burgundy Over Noodles

(Pictured below and on page 267)

I got this delightful recipe from my sister-in-law many years ago and have used it ever since.
—Margaret Welder, Madrid, Iowa

1/2 pound boneless beef sirloin steak, cut into
   1/4-inch strips
2 tablespoons diced onion
2 teaspoons butter *or* stick margarine
1-1/2 cups quartered fresh mushrooms
3/4 cup red wine *or* beef broth
1/4 cup plus 2 tablespoons water, *divided*
3 tablespoons minced fresh parsley, *divided*
1 bay leaf
1 whole clove
1/4 teaspoon salt
1/8 teaspoon pepper
1 tablespoon all-purpose flour
1/2 teaspoon browning sauce, optional
1-1/2 cups hot cooked egg noodles

In a Dutch oven or nonstick skillet, brown beef and onion in butter over medium heat. Add the mushrooms, wine or broth, 1/4 cup water, 2 tablespoons parsley, bay leaf, clove, salt and pepper. Bring to a boil. Reduce heat; cover

and simmer for 1 hour or until beef is tender.
   Combine flour and remaining water until smooth; stir into beef mixture. Bring to a boil; cook and stir for 2 minutes or until thickened. Discard bay leaf and clove. Stir in browning sauce if desired. Serve over noodles. Sprinkle with remaining parsley. **Yield:** 2 servings.

Nutritional Analysis: One serving equals 410 calories, 12 g fat (5 g saturated fat), 125 mg cholesterol, 403 mg sodium, 37 g carbohydrate, 2 g fiber, 33 g protein.
***Diabetic Exchanges:** 3 lean meat, 2 starch, 1 vegetable, 1/2 fat.*

Tomato Couscous Soup

I like this simple soup because the fresh tomato flavor really stands out. It's a favorite at our house.
—Joyce Woldt, Waupaca, Wisconsin

1/4 cup chopped onion
1 garlic clove, minced
2 teaspoons olive *or* canola oil
1-1/2 cups reduced-sodium chicken broth, *divided*
2 medium tomatoes, peeled, seeded and chopped
1 teaspoon fresh oregano *or* 1/4 teaspoon dried
   oregano
3 tablespoons uncooked couscous
1/8 teaspoon salt

In a saucepan, saute onion and garlic in oil until tender. Add the broth, tomatoes and oregano. Bring to a boil. Reduce heat; cover and simmer for 20-25 minutes or until tomatoes are tender. Remove from the heat; stir in couscous and salt. Let stand for 5 minutes. **Yield:** 2 servings.

Nutritional Analysis: One serving (1-1/3 cups) equals 152 calories, 5 g fat (1 g saturated fat), 0 cholesterol, 625 mg sodium, 22 g carbohydrate, 3 g fiber, 6 g protein.
***Diabetic Exchanges:** 1 starch, 1 vegetable, 1 fat.*

No-Fuss Rice Pudding

I use my microwave to prepare this creamy, lightly spiced rice pudding.
—Sheila Wilde, Welling, Alberta

1 cup cooked rice
1 egg white
1 cup fat-free milk
1/4 cup sugar
1/4 cup golden raisins
Dash *each* ground cinnamon and ground nutmeg

In small microwave-safe bowl, combine rice and egg white. Stir in the milk, sugar and raisins. Microwave, uncovered, on high for 2 minutes; stir. Microwave at 50% power for 9 minutes, stirring every 2 minutes. Sprinkle with cinnamon and nutmeg. Cover and let stand for 15 minutes. **Yield:** 2 servings.
   Editor's Note: This recipe was tested in an 850-watt microwave.

Nutritional Analysis: One serving equals 306 calories, trace fat (trace saturated fat), 3 mg cholesterol, 99 mg sodium, 68 g carbohydrate, 2 g fiber, 9 g protein.

General Recipe Index

This index lists every recipe by food category, major ingredient and/or cooking method, so you can easily locate recipes to suit your needs.

APPETIZERS & SNACKS

Cold Appetizers
Corn Salsa Tostadas, 20
Fresh Veggie Pizza, 22
Olive Pepper Pinwheels, 25
Roasted Garlic Appetizers, 25
Salmon-Stuffed Snow Peas, 32
Shrimp with Creole Sauce, 248

Dips and Spreads
Asparagus Guacamole, 21
Cheesy Bean Dip/Makeover
    Cheesy Bean Dip, 23
Ginger-Cranberry Chutney
    Spread, 20
Herbed Cheese Dip, 30
Layered Oriental Dip, 18
Lemon Fruit Dip, 18
Maple Fruit Dip, 28
Raspberry Tomato Salsa, 26
Savory Swiss Cheesecake, 30
Tomato Black Bean Salsa, 24

Hot Appetizers
Asparagus Ham Rolls, 28
Asparagus in Puff Pastry, 24
Cheesy Zucchini Bites, 19
Chicken Salad Wonton Stars, 32
Eggplant Snack Sticks, 26
Mozzarella Pepperoni Bread, 18
Spinach Cheese
    Mushrooms, 26
Vegetable Spiral Sticks, 29

Snacks
Chocolate Cereal Bars, 22
Chocolate Pudding
    Sandwiches, 32
Soy Good Snack Mix, 22

APPLES
Apple Breakfast Popover, 110
Apple Carrot Muffins, 104
Apple Cobbler, 219
Apple-Leek Pork Chops, 268
Apple Pear Salad, 67
Applesauce Cake, 234

APRICOTS
Apricot-Glazed Shrimp, 164
Apricot Noodle Kugel, 202
Apricot Oat Bars, 204
Apricot Peach Smoothies, 29
Apricot Sundaes, 251
Zesty Apricot Turkey, 128

ASPARAGUS
Asparagus Cashew Stir-Fry, 190
Asparagus Guacamole, 21
Asparagus Ham Dinner, 157
Asparagus Ham Rolls, 28
Asparagus in Puff Pastry, 24
Asparagus Mushroom
    Casserole, 88
Asparagus-Stuffed Pork
    Tenderloin, 150
Chicken and Asparagus
    Bundles, 137
Roasted Asparagus Salad, 54

BACON & CANADIAN BACON
Bacon-Mustard Salad Dressing, 53
Canadian Bacon Potato Soup, 34

BANANAS
Banana Cocoa Smoothies, 22
Banana Spice Cake, 210

BARLEY
Barley Casserole, 85
Barley Corn Salad, 74
Triple-Grain Pilaf, 83
Vegetable Barley Salad, 58

BARS & BROWNIES
Apricot Oat Bars, 204
Chocolate Cereal Bars, 22
Chocolate-Glazed Brownies, 230
Deluxe Brownies/Makeover
    Deluxe Brownies, 217
Frosted Zucchini Bars, 234
Fudgy Peanut Butter
    Brownies, 228
Granola Blondies, 230
Marbled Chocolate Cheesecake
    Bars, 202
Spice Bars, 200

BASIL
Basil-Marinated Fish, 170
Basil Shrimp Fettuccine, 163
Basil-Tomato Tuna Steaks, 163
Basil Tortellini Soup, 40
Basil Vinegar, 84

BEANS & LENTILS

Main Dishes
Baked Lentils with Cheese, 186
Bean and Sausage
    Rigatoni, 134
Bean and Veggie Pitas, 181
Black Bean Enchiladas, 176
Chickpea-Stuffed Shells, 189
Corn 'n' Bean Burritos, 260
Pinto Bean Stew, 188
Pinto Beans with Kielbasa, 144
Sausage Lentil Stew, 252
Southern Okra Bean Stew, 187
Tasty Lentil Tacos, 179
Three-Bean Cassoulet, 178
Zesty Rice 'n' Bean
    Casserole, 186

Salads
Black Bean Pasta Salad, 60
Cannellini Spinach Pasta
    Salad, 64
Confetti Bean Salad, 48
Garlic Green and Wax
    Beans, 60
Green Bean and Tomato
    Salad, 76
Kidney Bean and Chickpea
    Salad, 52
Tortellini Bean Salad, 61
Tuscan Bean Salad, 73

Side Dishes
Green Bean Casserole/
    Makeover Green Bean
    Casserole, 97

Homemade Chicken Stock, 41
Italian Chicken Soup, 41
Southwestern Chicken
    Soup, 262

CHILI
Bulgur Chili, 44
Flavorful White Chili, 45
Vegetable Beef Chili, 46
White Bean Turkey Chili, 37
Zippy Vegetable Chili, 35

CHOCOLATE
Bars and Brownies
Chocolate-Glazed
    Brownies, 230
Deluxe Brownies/Makeover
    Deluxe Brownies, 217
Fudgy Peanut Butter
    Brownies, 228
Marbled Chocolate
    Cheesecake Bars, 202
Bread and Muffins
Chocolate Chip Bread, 198
Raspberry Chocolate Chip
    Muffins, 193
Cakes and Cupcakes
Chocolate Snack Cake, 252
Dark Chocolate Layer Cake/
    Makeover Dark Chocolate
    Layer Cake, 229
Double Chocolate
    Cupcakes, 200
German Chocolate Torte, 204
Raspberry Cream Cake, 238
Ultimate Chocolate Cake, 234
Candy
Marshmallow Fudge, 206
Cookies
Chocolate Chip Cookies, 209
Cookout Caramel S'mores, 259
Crinkle-Top Chocolate
    Cookies, 216
Crispy Cereal Meringues, 206
Double Chocolate Biscotti, 235
Desserts
Chocolate Meringue Cups, 224
Chocolate Meringue Torte, 246
Chocolate Mint Eclair
    Dessert, 231
Chocolate Souffles, 236
Cookie Lime Parfaits, 270
Mock Ice Cream
    Sandwiches, 203
Pies
Black Forest Ice Cream Pie, 265
Chocolate Brownie Crust, 211

Fudgy White Chocolate Pudding
    Pie, 218
Peanut Butter Pie/Makeover
    Peanut Butter Pie, 233
Ribbon Pudding Pie, 210
Snacks and Beverages
Banana Cocoa Smoothies, 22
Chocolate Cereal Bars, 22
Chocolate Pudding
    Sandwiches, 32
Frosty Chocolate Malted
    Shakes, 21

CHOWDER
Mediterranean Seafood
    Chowder, 39
Sweet Pepper Chowder, 36

COLESLAW
Crab Coleslaw Medley, 74
Two-Cabbage Slaw, 58
Zucchini Slaw, 68

CONDIMENTS
Basil Vinegar, 84
Cherry Almond Granola, 106
Chinese Five Spice, 82
Citrus Cranberry Relish, 89
Herb Butter, 100
Horseradish Sauce for
    Veggies, 100
Raspberry Vinegar, 84
Salt Substitute, 93

COOKIES *(also see Bars & Brownies)*
Chewy Oatmeal Raisin
    Cookies, 212
Chocolate Chip Cookies, 209
Crinkle-Top Chocolate
    Cookies, 216
Crispy Cereal Meringues, 206
Double Chocolate Biscotti, 235
Ginger Thins, 226
Meringue Candy Canes, 231

CORN
Barley Corn Salad, 74
Corn 'n' Bean Burritos, 260

Corn Relish Salad, 62
Corn Salsa Tostadas, 20
Grilled Corn Pasta Salad, 58
Roasted Corn and Garlic Rice, 93
Scalloped Corn, 88
Tex-Mex Corn on the Cob, 95

CORN BREAD & CORN MEAL
Blueberry Corn Muffins, 193
Jalapeno Corn Bread, 252
Southwestern Corn Bread, 198

CRANBERRIES
Citrus Cranberry Relish, 89
Cranberry Beets, 98
Cranberry Cake with Orange
    Sauce, 222
Cranberry Gelatin Salad, 74
Cranberry-Pear Tossed Salad, 240
Ginger-Cranberry Chutney
    Spread, 20

DATES *(see Raisins & Dates)*

DESSERTS *(also see specific kinds)*
Apple Cobbler, 219
Apricot Sundaes, 251
Berry Phyllo Tarts, 266
Chocolate Meringue Cups, 224
Chocolate Meringue Torte, 246
Chocolate Mint Eclair Dessert, 231
Chocolate Souffles, 236
Citrus Ice, 269
Cookie Lime Parfaits, 270
Cool Mandarin Dessert, 213
Cream-Filled Strawberries, 214
Frozen Strawberry Torte, 216
Fruity Sherbet Dessert, 220
Melon with Raspberry Sauce, 244
Mixed Berry Pizza, 220
Mock Ice Cream Sandwiches, 203
Orange Delight, 204
Pears with Spiced Caramel
    Sauce, 224
Pumpkin Pecan Frozen Yogurt, 263
Raspberry Dessert with Vanilla
    Sauce, 218
Raspberry-Filled Meringue
    Torte, 232
Raspberry Peach Delight, 226
Strawberry Almond Pastries, 225
Strawberry-Orange Phyllo
    Cups, 268

Alphabetical Index

This handy index lists every recipe in alphabetical order
so you can easily find your favorite dish.

Reference Index

Use this index to locate the many healthy cooking hints located throughout the book.